D1643982

WARSHIP 1989

WARSHIP 1989

Edited by Robert Gardiner

FRONTISPIECE
The Royal Navy's latest SSN, the Trenchant, *commissioned in 1989.* (VSEL)

TITLE PAGE
The Soviet cruiser Slava *at anchor off Solum, Libya. Photographed by a Sea King from* HMS Illustrious, *November 1983.* (MoD)

First published in Great Britain by
Conway Maritime Press Ltd,
24 Bride Lane, Fleet Street,
London EC4Y 8DR

ISBN 0 85177 530 6

Designed by Michael Leaman
Typesetting and page make-up by
Swanston Graphics Ltd, Derby
Printed and bound in Great Britain by
Richard Clay Ltd, Bungay, Suffolk

CONTENTS

EDITORIAL

After twelve years of quarterly publication *Warship* has been transformed into an annual, and while we see this as a wholly positive development, it perhaps warrants a few words of explanation. The reason for the change is principally a response to the readership itself – previously, a hardback version incorporating four individual issues was produced in most years, and although this was intended mainly for libraries and institutional sales, it proved so popular with subscribers that many transferred their allegiance to the bound volume. Once the balance had shifted beyond a certain point, it became difficult to justify quarterly publication, and the decision was taken to adopt the once-a-year formula we are presenting here.

Now a book rather than a journal, the new format has many advantages that will be readily apparent. As a hardback, the volume will open more easily (with less lost in the spine gutter) and will better withstand the frequent handling that reference works are prone to. But more importantly, the quality of the contents can be improved – being freed from tight quarterly deadlines allows the editor more choice of material, so higher standards can be maintained; planning over 256 pages instead of 64 means better balance of subjects (and between pictures and text); the articles are more readable because they are not divided into multiple parts; and the whole is made more accessible by the inclusion of an index within each volume.

The foregoing is obviously addressed to existing subscribers, most of whom switched to the annual, but for the benefit of new readers this is the appropriate point to set out the aims and policy of *Warship*. These have not changed significantly for the annual:

1. The subject is the design, development and service history of naval vessels, including auxiliaries and the craft of other paramilitary forces, naval use of merchant ships, and shipboard aviation. The focus is on the ships themselves, their design background and technical details, with any accounts of battle providing a critique of the design in action.
2. The scope is entirely international, unlimited by country, ship type or period, but inevitably the interest centres on the major navies since the introduction of steam.
3. The common denominator in all *Warship* articles is originality. This can be expressed as new research into unusual or little known aspects of the subject or as original interpretation of more popular areas of warship history.
4. Needless to say, all material must be both accurate and detailed, but the ultimate goal of *Warship* is to encourage a deeper understanding of the whole context of the procurement, design, building and operation of fighting ships. Therefore, we favour articles which look more closely at *why* and *how* rather than just describing the *what* of warship design.

These basic aims are not altered: indeed, if anything, they have been reinforced by conversion to annual publication. However, certain subtle changes have been dictated by the new frequency. Features can no longer run almost *ad infinitum*, so series articles have been dropped, and all potential serial pieces organised as a single part. This has tended to produce shorter, tighter and more readable material. Obviously once-yearly publication is not conducive to the regular exchange of information, news and views, so there is no correspondence column or an 'Alterations & Additions' updating; but we have preserved a Notebook section to accommodate short pieces of novel or unusual information that are too slight or esoteric to make a feature article.

On the other hand, the principal innovation of this issue – The Naval Year In Review – would not have been so appropriate to a quarterly, but serves a very useful function in an annual. Most warship enthusiasts, however historical their main interests, like to keep abreast of contemporary developments, although this is becoming increasingly expensive to achieve. *Jane's* now costs £100 and although *Combat Fleets* is only half that, neither can be a regular purchase for the average enthusiast. Furthermore, because of the way in which the yearbooks are organised, new information takes a lot of unearthing, and many related aspects are not covered at all. For these the reader must turn to the defence periodicals, at further substantial cost.

We feel, therefore, that there is a real need for a brief overview of the principal developments of each year, and this is what The Naval Year In Review sets out to accomplish. Bearing in mind the themes outlined earlier, it concentrates on ships – new designs, orders, commissionings as well as refits, transfers and deletions – but also includes some reference to strategic and budgetary factors, and events of naval significance. While we do not have the space or resources to make this exhaustive, we believe that it must be of real value to our readers, so invite suggestions for improvements for the next issue.

Turning to the feature articles in *Warship 1989*, the coverage is both broad and deep. Chronologically, it ranges from the very first steam warship to missile-firing hydrofoils; warship types run the whole gamut from capital ships to coastal craft, with most major navies represented; alongside conventional ship histories, there are unusual topics like Net Defence, and Airships for AEW; while operations are not ignored, with articles on the first air attacks on ships, and the sinking of the *Yamato*. Throughout, great effort has been expended on obtaining good illustrations and ensuring that they have been reproduced as large as possible, that they have been cropped intelligently, and that where large drawings have to cross the centre gutter, they are separated into two distinct halves so that nothing is lost.

We believe that the annual format is a great improvement over the old quarterly, and are certain that this first edition will convince even our most demanding readers.

Robert Gardiner

THE US NAVY AND THE STEAM ENGINE 1815–1870

'Chaos and farce and catastrophe' was one authority's view of the introduction of steam into the US Navy. Donald L Canney, a rising young historian, revises this negative view.

Historians have not been kind to the early developmental years of the American steam navy, with one recent authority characterizing a 'big part' of that era as 'Chaos and farce and catastrophe...'. Furthermore, the sole major volume centring around the early steam era (from 1815 to the first steel vessels of the 1880s) was written by Frank M Bennett in 1896. The only vessel of the period to receive in-depth attention has been John Ericsson's *Monitor* of Civil War fame.

Unfortunately, 'chaos' and other perjorative terms *are* applicable to some facets of the era, and certainly the progress of steam technology in the US Navy was not a smooth continuum. However, given the primitive state of marine engine technology at the time, and the possibly unique policy milieu in the nineteenth century Navy, one can arrive at a reasonably coherent account of the technological history of the times.

The paddle wheel era

The side-mounted paddle wheel, which predominated until the submerged screw propeller was perfected, required exceedingly simple steam machinery. Their location – high and amidships – posed few restrictions on engine size. More importantly, the power train from the cylinder to cross-wise mounted paddle wheel shaft, could be as simple as a single rod connecting piston to shaft. In fact, all save two American side-wheel engines were direct-acting. The majority utilized an inclined cylinder with the piston rod's reciprocating motion fore and aft and the cylinder itself securely fastened on the vessel's keelson. One vessel, the *Fulton II* of 1837, was built with horizontal cylinders abaft the shaft. These uncomplicated engines made for fast vessels, with the *Fulton II* making 14kts easily, with her two-cylinder machinery. The Civil War light-draft 'double-enders' easily matched this with single-cylinder engines.

The first of the indirect-acting engined vessels was Robert Fulton's *Demologos*, built as a block ship in the War of 1812. A single vertical cylinder operated gears and levers to turn a central midships paddle wheel – located in between the vessel's catamaran-like hulls. The British invasion expected at New York never materialized and she was relegated to storeship duties until her accidental destruction in 1829. She was said to have made 5kts on one of her rare sorties under power.

The frigate *Mississippi* of 1841 had engines of the side-lever, indirect-acting type, a design imported from England and common in transatlantic steamers. A vertical cylinder operated a horizontal lever. The forward end of this lever operated another vertical rod, which operated the crankshaft. Though the vessel was not economical (few early steamers were), she accompanied Commodore Perry to Japan and circumnavigated the globe twice, testifying to the reliability of her machinery. She was one of the few pre-war built naval ships lost to enemy fire during the Civil War – in the Mississippi River campaign of 1863.

The greatest assets of paddle wheel engines were simplicity and reliability, many times leading to long service lives. The iron lakes steamer *Michigan* of 1844 operated nearly without breakdown until 1923. Her paddles revolved at 10 revolutions per minute (at a steam pressure of about 15psi), and the stroke of her piston was *eight* feet. At that rate her piston moved about 30 inches per second, driving the 160ft vessel at 10kts – for literally generations.

The deficiencies of paddle wheel warships were as obvious as their obtrusive paddle housings. On larger vessels, these structures blocked thirty feet of valuable broadside space, bisected the gun deck, and made for wonderful targets. Finally, in an era when inefficient engines necessitated the continued use of sail power, the central location of engine and boilers prevented locating the mainmast at the centre of effort of the vessel's hull. The *Mississippi*, for instance, was a particularly poor sailer: her mainmast was so far aft that efficient sailing was only possible with the wind nearly astern.

The negative aspects of paddle wheel propulsion have a direct bearing on the most common criticism of the navy in the early steam era: the reluctance to break with sailing vessels. It was over twenty years between the *Demologos* and the construction of the second naval steamship, the *Fulton II*, an interval in which critics pointed to the 'hundreds' of steam vessels in merchant service in the US as reason enough for the navy to turn to steam. However, prior to the creation of the American battle fleet in the 1890s, the peacetime role of the navy was that of cruising on foreign stations – requiring vessels with self-sufficiency incompatible with the coal-hungry engines of the age.

Unfortunately, the performance of the *Fulton II* did little to encourage the advocates of steam in the US Navy: though she was fast, even at moderate speed she could steam for less than three days at sea.

In all, the navy built only five paddle steamers for ocean-going service: *Mississippi, Missouri, Saranac, Powhatan,* and *Susquehanna.* The last of these was commissioned in 1852. It should be noted that the last American sailing frigate was added in 1854, and more sailing ships were brought into the inventory between 1850 and 1854 than steam vessels.

Transition to screw propulsion

This transition was fraught with difficulties, as evidenced by the passage of over ten years between the first screw steamer, the *Princeton*, and the second, the *San Jacinto.* Further evidence: the first was a success, the second was not.

Contributing factors in this protracted transition were the engineering problems inherent in applying steam power to screw propulsion. First was the requirement that the engine be low in the hull, creating the kinds of space restrictions not dealt with in paddle wheel machinery. Second, the screw required engine speeds higher than the slow-turning paddle wheel installations.

The space limitations, in conjunction with the longitudinal orientation of the propeller shaft resulted in the necessity for drastically reducing the stroke of an engine, compared to paddle wheel practice. Therefore, in order to maintain comparable cubic capacity of the cylinder, its diameter was increased to compensate. Whereas a few of the larger side-wheelers had strokes of up to 90in, by the end of this era a few screw propeller engines had piston diameters of this dimension or larger – and strokes of about half that of the paddle wheel powerplants.

Two other changes in engine design accompanied this re-orientation of the steam marine engine. First, cylinder diameter became so ungainly as to require more stability than a single piston rod would provide, hence the rise of the double piston rod. Second, many ingenious (and less than ingenious) attempts were made to obtain longer strokes in these engines. The most common method of gaining length was by locating the cylinders in some manner above the propeller shaft with linkage by levers or gears or combinations thereof.

Finally, the increasing engine speed created amounts of friction and heat hitherto unknown in the leisurely ambience of paddle wheel technology. The most critical areas where such stress manifested itself were in the bearing surfaces where technology and materials had yet to produce methods of machining the requisite smooth surfaces. Only the introduction of steel and precision machining techniques would alleviate such problems. Until then massive application of lubricants and long running-in periods were the norm.

It also should be pointed out that the 'shoehorning' of complicated machinery into confined spaces resulted in exacerbating the friction factor. The multiplication of journals, levers, arms, and bearing surfaces which arose in designing screw propelling engines militated against efficiency, reliability and uniformity of stress factors.

With the completion of the steam screw sloop *Princeton* in 1843, it appeared that the United States was in the forefront of warship screw propulsion technology. She was

Fulton II, *1837, the first navy-built steamer. Her two direct-action cylinders could push her to over 14kts, but at high fuel consumption. She soon became a floating test bed and training ship for the newly introduced shell guns. Not apparent in the illustration are her other two funnels to starboard. (*Naval Historical Center*)*

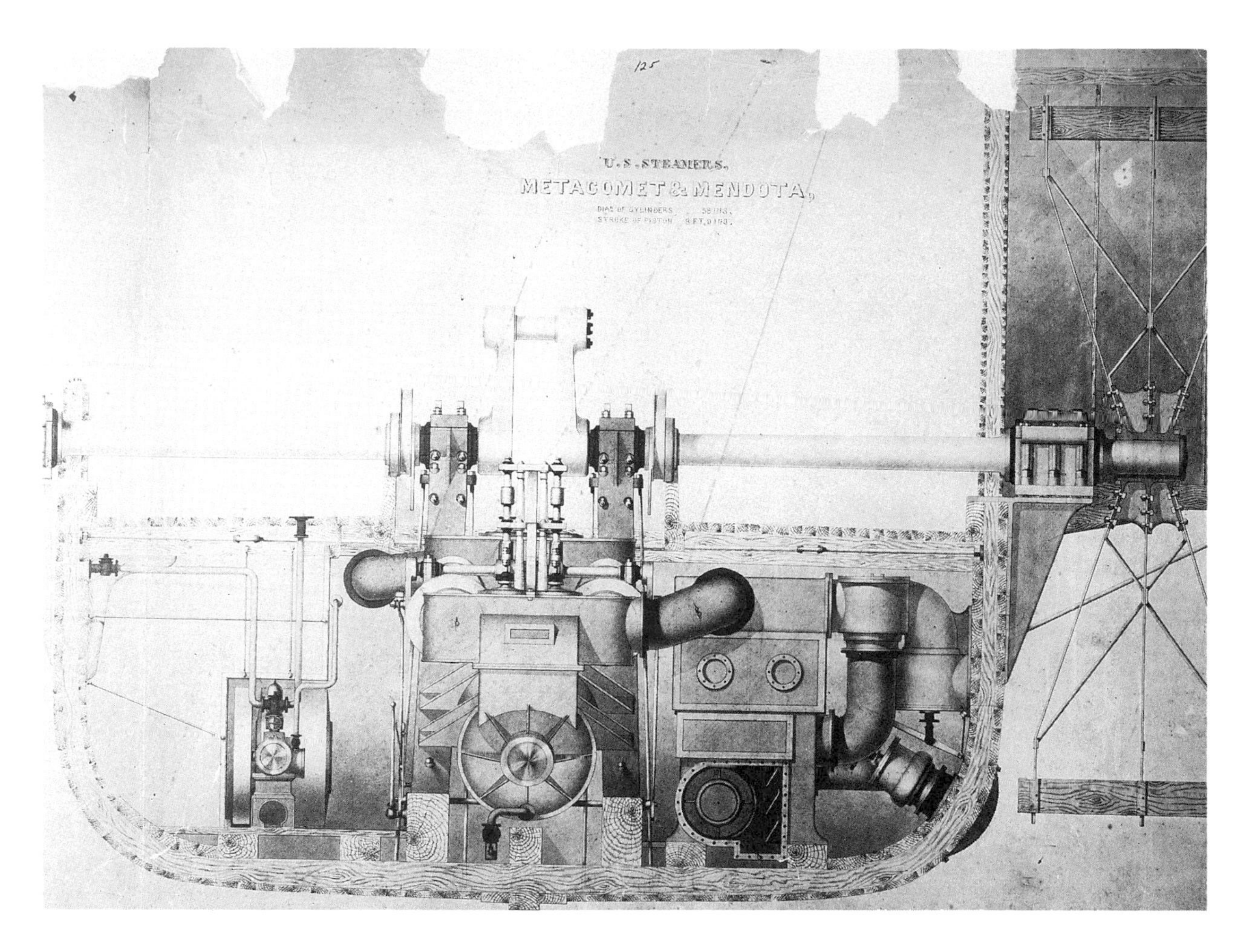

Cross section showing the direct-action paddle engine (single cylinder) of Civil War gunboats Mendota *and* Metacomet. *Head of inclined cylinder is secured to the vessel's keelsons; crank for paddle shaft was above deck. These ships were for coastal and river duties.* (National Archives)

the world's first steam warship built to use the screw propeller (the British in 1844 converted the *Amphion* to the screw). John Ericsson, who later designed the *Monitor*, approached the engine design in a unique manner. His 'vane' or pendulum engine had two 'cylinders' which were semi- or half-cylinders with the 'pistons' hanging pendulum-like and allowed to swing through their arcs as steam was admitted on alternate sides. Power was taken off by levers from an exterior extension of the 'hinge' of the vane. The installation was light, compact, and simple. It was reasonably economical, though the vessel was not particularly fast. However, there is some reason to believe that Ericsson intended from the first to make the *Princeton* an auxiliary steamer only – she was fully rigged and possessed quite sharp lines.

It remained only for the navy to follow up and build on Ericsson's pioneering, it seemed. However, a disastrous accident occurred onboard the vessel in 1844 – an experimental shell gun whose design was falsely attributed to Ericsson, exploded and killed visiting dignitaries, including the Secretary of the Navy. In the recriminations which followed, Ericsson's relationship to the Department soured and his designs (and patents) were ignored.

In any case, the navy was certain they could avoid the use of the screw propeller altogether, with Hunter's Horizontal Wheel. An American naval officer, William W Hunter, proposed mounting paddle-type wheels horizontally *within* the vessel's hold. The paddles were snugly encased except for apertures at the sides – between bilge and waterline – where several blades would be exposed to produce forward motion.

The first of these vessels, the *Union*, was authorized simultaneously with the *Princeton*, and two others were constructed according to Hunter's ideas – the *Water Witch* and the *Alleghany*. (The *Water Witch* was to be a tow boat.) From the first, they were found to be intolerably inefficient. There was no way to prevent the paddles from pumping water *into* the wheel casings, and thus forcing the engines to work against both internal and external water pressures. The navy, however, was so enamoured with the concept of submerged, protected, propulsion systems that the experiments continued, to grind to a halt in 1846 with the failure of the *Alleghany*.

Shortly afterward, the coming of the Mexican War encouraged Congress to authorize four steam vessels. In the Department, there is some evidence that the Hunter's Wheel catastrophe caused a severe technological backlash, and three of the four ships were built with the obsolete paddle wheels. The fourth, the *San Jacinto*, a 1500-ton sloop, was selected for screw propulsion.

Though John Ericsson offered his services, the Department assigned Charles Haswell to the task. Haswell, the navy's first steam engineer, had little experience with screw

◀ *The iron-hulled Great Lakes' steamer* Michigan. *Her slow turning paddle engines were paragons of reliability and she had no serious mechanical problems until a connecting rod broke in 1923, nearly 80 years after her commissioning. She was finally scrapped in the 1940s.* (Naval Historical Center)

machinery, and the upshot was a 'fearful botch' of the engine design. Though the plans were shortly afterwards destroyed, contemporaries described the engines as overly complicated, 'un-symmetrical' and 'irregular in their motions'. One cruise proved the undoing of these machines and a private firm was contracted to replace them with engines of their design.

Haswell, despite fifteen years' experience, was dismissed. It would be appropriate to note at this point that the engineering profession in the early nineteenth century was an informal one. There were no engineering schools as such and no professional standards or organizations. Many practitioners were self-taught or served apprenticeships in engine-manufacturing firms, and beyond that simply advanced by their own merits or by virtue of luck or influence in the right places. W W Hunter was an example of the baleful results of this improvised system, and Hunter was not the last to adversely effect the steam navy.

In any case, the navy's next screw steamer was in fact Hunter's vessel *Alleghany*, which was to be re-engined and fitted with a screw propeller. A young navy engineer named Benjamin F Isherwood designed a 'back-acting' installation for the vessel. In this configuration, there were two piston rods per cylinder. These 'straddled' (over and under) the propeller shaft, and a crosshead connected the two rods. The horizontal reciprocating motion of the crosshead provided a basis for the movement of a connecting rod 'back' to the propeller shaft. As will be seen, this type of engine was to become a standard in the navy for many years.

The converted *Alleghany* served for a short time in 1853, but was plagued by structural problems. However, when Congress authorized six large frigates in 1854, there was no question as to their propulsion. Except for special purpose river vessels, the paddle wheel was no longer utilized in navy-built ships.

The screw propeller and the simple expansion engine

In contrast to the transitional years, this era was one of comparative stability and, particularly in the Civil War, of expedience. In the war years, two types of engines came to predominate in US naval vessels. The few non-standard engines for the most part were distinguished by variations on the mechanical, practical aspects of the power train, rather than by divergent approaches to basic theory.

The first of the two standard types was a development of the back-acting engines of the *Alleghany*. Early in the war, Isherwood became head of the Bureau of Steam Engineering and he proceeded to install various sized versions of this engine (known also as return connecting rod engines) in many wartime vessels. By 1870, over fifty of these engines were in service, and some were later converted to compound expansion. The smallest had cylinders of 30in and powered the 700-ton '90-day' gunboats of 1861; the largest was a unique 68in cylinder installation for the 5170-ton frigate *Franklin*.

Isherwood was targeted for much criticism for these engines. They were characterized as exceedingly heavy for their power output and therefore inefficient. The Chief Engineer retorted that the extra weight was necessary to build durability into the designs. He reasoned that they would be operated by rank amateurs – men brought into the service for the war who may have had little experience as engineers, and who could not be expected to deal with sophisticated machinery or machinery with high incidence of breakdowns at sea.

The second criticism was that Isherwood ignored other types of engines for use in naval vessels. Of course, many of these critics were in fact builders of marine engines themselves – men who were competing for government contracts. In response, it was pointed out that standardization of engine types was a method of facilitating ease of manufacturing the many engines necessary for the war effort. Furthermore, standardization would assist the individual steam engineers in dealing with machinery in many types of vessels, all of which had variations of a single engine type.

The second widely used type was that designed by John Ericsson, whose *Monitor* had restored him to the good graces of the Department. His vibrating lever design (sometimes referred to as a 'grasshopper' engine) was used in the majority of the monitor-type vessels, as well as two other armoured ships (*Keokuk* and *Galena*) and two wooden

Engines of John Ericsson's pioneering screw steamer Princeton *(1843), showing the 45-degree swing of her pendulum-piston and the low placement of machinery in her hull. These engines were comparatively economical, but she was considered an auxiliary steamer only.* (From *Steam Navy of the United States* by F M Bennett)

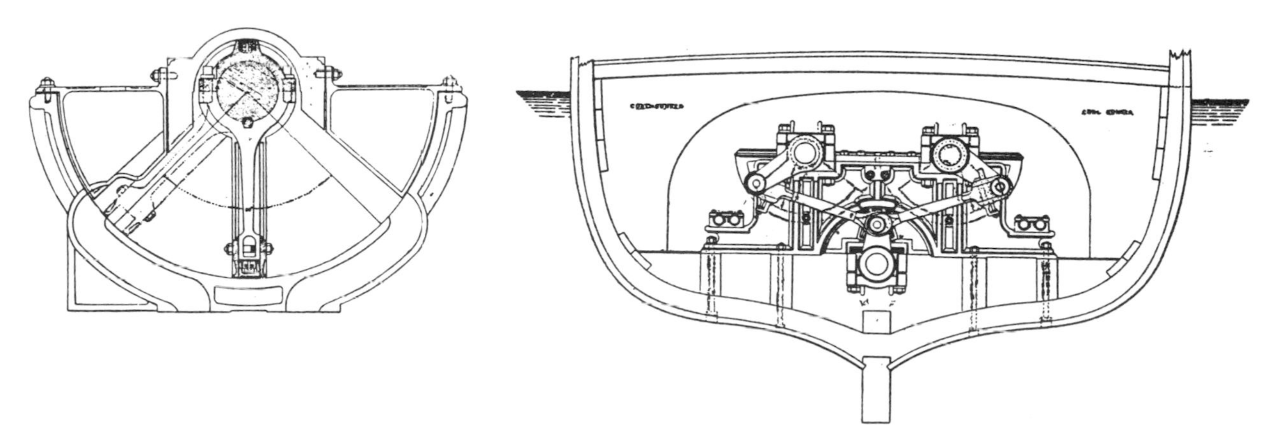

Steam frigate Colorado *(1854), one of six 40-gun vessels: the first entire class of US steamers to use the screw propeller. Another of this class became the Confederate ironclad* Merrimack *(re-named* Virginia*). The photo was taken about 1870. (*Naval Historical Center*)*

sloops (*Maumee* and *Madawasca*). In all some twenty-seven vessels used this engine, the most numerous group being the *Passaic* class monitors.

The two cylinders of the vibrating lever engine were arranged in a shallow 'vee' (17 degrees) over the propeller shaft. The pistons operated upward and outward to L-shaped levers on the outboard ends of the cylinders. The levers' fulcrum was at the intersection of the arms, and the bottom arm cranked the rod to the propeller shaft. The *Madawasca*, later renamed *Tennessee*, reached over 15kts with these engines in 1867. (The original *Monitor*'s engines operated vibrating levers, but there was no inclination of the cylinders and in fact there was only a single 'cylinder' in which two pistons operated in tandem.)

Other types of screw machinery were utilized, for the most part on a one-off basis – and in some cases for competitive consideration *vis-à-vis* navy-designed engines (somewhat mitigating the critics' contentions that Isherwood's engines monopolized the service). The largest number of non-back-acting engines were the indirect-acting inverted-vee motive power of the unsuccessful light draft monitors. Twenty such ships were begun, though only eight saw service. For the entire era until compound engines were introduced, engine types utilized (in addition to Isherwood back-acting) were: direct-acting horizontal, geared, vertical beam, 'trunk', oscillating, 'harp', inverted-vee, Ericsson and non-Ericsson vibrating lever, and segmental. Only the trunk and segmental designs departed from conventional cylinder and piston arrangements.

The trunk engine followed a British design of John Penn, which featured a washer- or doughnut-shaped piston operating in a complementary shaped cylinder. The piston rod reciprocated through the centre aperture thereby allowing the length of the rod to occupy the same athwartships space as the length of the cylinder. Three of the *Merrimack* class frigates (*Colorado*, *Roanoke*, and *Minnesota*) used this type of machinery.

The Wright segmental engine was used in a 900-ton gunboat, the *Pequot*. This unique design had a piston which swung in a 45-degree arc, somewhat akin to the idea behind the *Princeton*'s pendulum piston, but with a circular piston and a U-shaped tube serving as the cylinder. The vessel was speedy but her engineers balked at her machinery's idiosyncrasy.

A few other general characteristics of screw propeller machinery are in order at this point. With few exceptions, these were two-cylinder installations. One three-cylinder engine powered the large (5500-ton) frigate-sloop *Niagara* – the largest navy steamer built before the end of the Civil War. Two ships, the *Idaho* and *Pensacola*, had experimental and unsuccessful four-cylinder machinery (discussed later in this article).

The norm for wooden cruising vessels was a single screw, usually with hoisting apparatus or disconnecting propeller shaft for more efficient sailing. The first operational twin-screw ship was the light-draft sloop *Pawnee* of 1858. Twenty-six monitors, including the light-draft ships, incorporated twin screws, plus the ironclad *Keokuk*. (For the

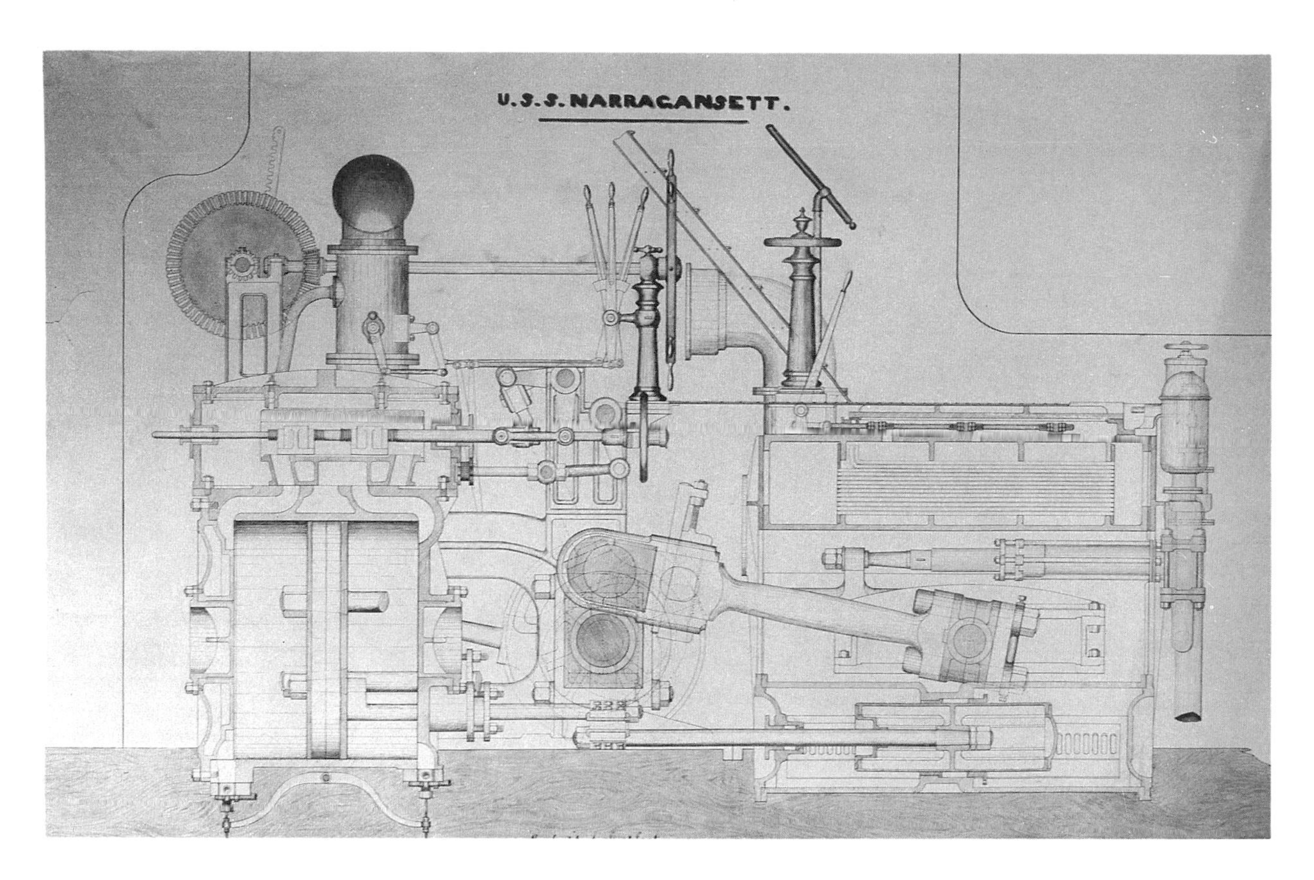

Pre-Civil War back-acting (return connecting rod) engines of steam sloop Narragansett *(1858). To the left is the cylinder, cut away to show the twin piston rods. In the centre is the propeller shaft, with connecting rod operating 'back' from crosshead which would have been to the right.* (Photo by author, of plan in National Archives)

purpose of this discussion, the many unusual river vessels of the Civil War have been ignored, including four with *quadruple* screws.)

The majority of these engines (for paddle as well as screw) were low-pressure, condensing installations. Use of condensers was appropriate for ocean-going vessels as it allowed re-use of boiler water. This obviated the need to utilize corrosive salt water in the boilers. Condensation also served to create a partial vacuum in the cylinder, thus reducing back-pressure. High-pressure, non-condensing engines were rarely seen, except in the riverine vessels of the Civil War.

Only three vessels of the era differed radically in theory and practice from the mainstream of standardization. These, the *Pensacola, Algonquin,* and *Idaho*, reflected the ideas of E N Dickerson, a lawyer-cum-engineer with potent influence in the US Congress. Dickerson favoured the 'short cut-off' theory of the expansion and usage of steam, while the navy, under Isherwood, utilized the 'long cut-off' theory. The difference in the two is quite simple: Dickerson and others maintained that steam expanded sufficiently to allow a relatively small amount of steam to accomplish a great deal of work in a cylinder. Hence, the duration of the opening of the steam intake valve could be relatively short, in contrast to the 'long cut-off' required when one had a high estimate of the amount of steam needed for the stroke. Consequently, in Dickerson's powerplants, navy practice was reversed: rather than large boilers and small cylinders, there were small boilers and large cylinders (or more numerous cylinders). This was the rationale behind the four-cylinder engines of the *Pensacola* (1861) and *Idaho* (1866). (The *Algonquin* was a paddle steamer also tested in 1866.) The strength of Dickerson's ideas – and influence – is evident, particularly in view of the total failure of the first of his ships, the *Pensacola*. His engines were found to be excessively heavy and undeniably uneconomical.

The Dickerson episode did, however, point up a growing consensus that the expansion of steam was more useful than previously thought. The key problem in attempting to harness this expansion was that of condensation: the necessarily large cylinders' inner surfaces were relatively cool and caused the steam to condense into useless water *before* finishing its task. Types of insulation, including wooden lagging, were tried in efforts to warm the cylinder walls. The quandry was not solved until the introduction of the compound or double-expansion engine, which utilized the same unit of steam twice, first in a small high-pressure cylinder, then in a larger, low-pressure cylinder. A few years later, triple-expansion engines were developed, building on the same principle. The first US Navy ship with compound engines was the frigate *Tennessee* in 1871. Unlike the transition from paddle to screw, the navy eagerly adopted the compound system, as it was considerably more economical than the simple expansion system.

By the time the compound engine was introduced, the simple expansion system had reached its limits, as illustrated by the Isherwood-designed machinery in the USS *Wampanoag*. This 335ft, 4200-ton sloop-of-war was intended as a commerce destroyer, specifically to cope with any European intervention in the Civil War, and was one of a class of seven such vessels. To obtain the requisite high

U.S.Flagship Tennessee

◀ *US frigate* Tennessee, *the first American warship to use compound engines. Originally, the 350ft vessel had Ericsson vibrating lever machinery (and was first named* Madawasca*). Compound (or double-expansion) engines allowed a given amount of steam to expand once in a high-pressure cylinder, then further in a low-pressure cylinder. (*Naval Historical Center*)*

The Wampanoag, *probably the fastest steam wooden warship ever built. Her twelve-boiler, 100-inch cylinder, geared powerplant (as well as fine hull lines) enabled her to reach over 17kts in January 1868. Built to deter foreign (specifically British) intervention in the Civil War, she was completed too late to be of use and was immediately laid up. (*From *Steam Navy of the United States)*

speed, 100in cylinders were used, with gears at a 2-to-1 ratio, and no less than twelve boilers, four of which were superheating. Fully half of the hull was devoted to machinery. On the vessel's sole high speed run, in January 1868, she reached 17.75kts, and averaged 16.6kts over a 38-hour run. She was for a short time the fastest vessel afloat, and the navy would not match her speed until some twenty years later. However, the war was long over and the *Wampanoag* was immediately laid up.

The *Wampanoag* and the *Tennessee*, representing the extent of simple expansion development, and the introduction of compound engines, respectively, form a logical end to the study of early engines in the US Navy. From 1870 to the mid-1880s, the navy suffered in its peacetime fiscal and policy doldrums, and substantive progress was not to be had. The reawakening of the navy would only occur with the steel vessels of the 'White Squadron' which became the precursors of the modern US battle fleet.

Bibliographical Note

The above summary is based on a book soon to be published by Naval Institute Press on *The Old Steam Navy*. The only previous book-length work is *The Steam Navy of the United States* (1896). Other sources may be summarized as follows: Department of the Navy, *Annual Reports of the Secretary of the Navy, Official Records of the Union and Confederate Navies in the War of the Rebellion*, articles (contemporary) from *Journal of the Franklin Institute* (1835 to 1867) and Naval Institute *Proceedings*, and *US Nautical Magazine and Naval Journal*. Primary sources are for the most part from the National Archives record groups 19, 45, 80 and 74 (Department of the Navy records, including Bureau of Construction and Repair, Bureau of Steam Engineering, and Bureau of Ordnance).

USS OLYMPIA

The design, construction and fighting career of Dewey's flagship at Manila Bay, described by William Emerson. Now preserved at Philadelphia, *Olympia* is the last surviving protected cruiser.

In 1865, at the end of the American Civil War, the US Navy ranked among the most powerful in the world, with some 600 ships of which 54 were armoured. But the nation which had built the first turreted ironclad ships and had participated in the first battle between ironclads at Hampton Roads soon allowed a steep decline in its naval strength. By the mid-1880s the navy was too weak to be capable of even a minor combat mission. With barely a dozen obsolete monitors and unarmoured craft in commission, President Grover Cleveland reported to Congress in December 1885, '...we have not a single vessel of war that could keep the seas against a first-class vessel of any important power.' As late as March 1889, apart from a few old ships long since obsolete and fast deteriorating, the navy consisted of only three modern steel vessels with a total tonnage of 7863 tons and mounting thirteen 6in and four 8in guns.

Far more than merely the ships were lacking. America's steel industry was as yet incapable of producing forgings for the large guns and these consequently had to be purchased from abroad. Likewise, before 1890 no large armour plates could be made in the US. While the navy had ships fitted for their use, not a single torpedo had ever been built or assembled domestically. The US had no rapid-fire heavy guns nor any armour-piercing shells, with only a few firms in Europe having a monopoly on these. And it was the same for smokeless powder.

Alarmed in the early 1880s by several minor international disputes and with concerns over Latin American acquisitions of modern warships, Congress acted. Between 1883 and 1900 it authorized some 17 battleships, 10 monitors, and 24 cruisers. These steel ships signalled a permanent break with the wooden hulled ships of the past; they were the start of what was soon referred to as the 'new navy'. Among these early steel ships was the cruiser *Olympia.*

Toward the end of the nineteenth century cruiser designs were of three types – unarmoured, protected and armoured. Unarmoured cruisers had no hull or deck protection and little or no armour for gun casemates. Protected cruisers mounted no side armour, but were designed with a water-tight, armoured deck over vital propulsion and ammunition storage areas. Armoured cruisers were the most heavily protected, and in addition to a protective deck and barbette or turret armour, these ships had a band of side armour for some distance along their waterlines.

Description

Classified a protected cruiser, the *Olympia* was authorized in 1888 and laid down at the Union Iron Works in San Francisco in 1891. Counting the *Olympia*, sixteen protected cruisers were built or under construction by 1893. Built as a single ship class and commissioned early in 1895, the *Olympia* was 340ft on the load waterline and 53ft broad. She had a displacement of 5870 tons and a normal coal capacity of 400 tons. With a maximum coal capacity of 1170 tons, she had good endurance at 6100 nautical miles.

Armament

With the advent of the rapid-fire gun in the late 1880s, the secondary battery of warships was considered very important. It provided defensive protection against the newly introduced torpedo-boats that were being built in increasing numbers by most navies. In addition, the secondary battery was intended to augment the large calibre guns as an offensive weapon by raining shells upon the unarmoured or lightly protected portions of ships – superstructures, unarmoured ends, and personnel. Even the light calibre machine-gun, with motor attachment for high-speed fire and mounted in the military tops, was considered an effective secondary weapon. At close range these guns could penetrate the thin sides of unarmoured ships and were effective against personnel at up to 2000yds. Whereas the secondary weapons would never themselves win a battle, it was theorized that the large number of expected hits and the resultant fires and confusion would seriously damage the enemy.

The *Olympia* was armed with a mixed battery of light and heavy guns – four 8in breech-loading rifles mounted in two armoured turrets, ten 5in rapid-fire guns, and twenty-four other guns, ranging from 6pdrs to Gatling guns. She was also armed with six 18in Whitehead above-water torpedo tubes.

The 8in guns were 35-calibre rifles (each calibre represented a barrel length of one bore diameter, so a 35cal 8in gun had a barrel length of 280in). These guns weighed 13 tons, and fired explosive shells weighing 250lbs and having a muzzle velocity of 2100 feet per second (fps). At a range of 180yds, these shells could penetrate 10.2in of ordinary steel. Elevation and loading was done by hand, with training by motor with hand power as an alternative. With this arrangement, a good gun crew could fire one round per minute from each gun. Up to this time in the steel navy all guns were fired with percussion primers, but the *Olympia* was the first to be fitted with electric firing devices on its main armament.

The secondary weapons included ten 5in 40cal rifled cannon weighing 7000lbs each which fired shells weighing 50lbs. The muzzle velocity was 2300fps, and at 156yds shells from these guns could penetrate 4.6in of steel. To round off the secondary armament there were fourteen rapid-fire guns which fired shells of 6lbs and six which fired

The USS Olympia *in peacetime white and buff paint scheme, about 1895. Note the platform just behind the forward turret and above the conning tower. Although this platform does not appear on the original plans for the* Olympia, *it can be seen in numerous photos taken before and just after the Spanish–American War and was certainly in use at Manila Bay.* (US Naval Historical Center)

shells of 1lb each. Both types were mounted on hydraulic recoil mounts. Except the small rapid-fire guns, in which black cubical powder was used, brown prismatic powder alone was issued. Not until the late 1890s was the US capable of manufacturing smokeless powder for service use.

Two developments in naval ordnance considered important at the time were made in the early 1890s and were included in the *Olympia*'s design. The first of these was the application to guns of medium calibre of an improved breech mechanism and fixed ammunition, which formed the two essential features of the so-called rapid-fire type gun. Up to that time, the rapid-fire system was applied only to secondary battery guns of which the largest was a 6pdr. By 1892 these were successfully applied to 4in and 5in guns. During trials the 4in guns had attained a rapidity of fire of five rounds in 14 seconds, while the 5in rate for five rounds was 19 seconds.

The second improvement was made by substituting manual operation for hydraulic power in the 8in gun mounts. This feature was worked out successfully in the design of the carriages for the 8in guns, which were manipulated by hand power throughout. The practical results were a significant decrease in weight which had been required by the hydraulic machinery, and the elimination of the possibility of putting the gun out of action by an injury to the complicated hydraulic mechanism. The breech mechanism, a modified Farcot design, could be opened and closed by one man in only 9 seconds.

The percentage of displacement assigned to armament and its protection – guns and mounts, ammunition, armour used to protect guns and shields, etc – was much lower for cruisers than the battleships of their day, owing to the much lighter displacements and need for higher speeds. For the *Olympia*, this percentage was 7.7; for the contemporary battleship USS *Indiana*, the figure was 25.3 per cent.

By 1898 the US was at last capable of producing its own torpedoes. The navy first experimented with the Howell torpedo, which obtained its motive force by means of a heavy flywheel brought up to speed by a steam driven engine just before firing. The navy abandoned the Howell and correctly chose the Whitehead torpedo as its service weapon.

The *Olympia* was built with an additional offensive weapon – a strongly reinforced ram bow. The ram bow was a distinctive visual and important design feature in the early steel ships of all nations. The ram, originally adopted in the age of oared men-of-war, was of no value in the age of sail when warships lacked speed and manoeuvrability. It was revitalized during the age of steam, building on a number of battle successes including the sinking of the USS *Cumberland* while at anchor by the steam ram CSS *Virginia* during the US Civil War. In the 1880s and 1890s the design of virtually all capital ships included powerfully reinforced ram bows.

Protection

As a general rule, protected cruisers of the era had exposed main armament and little or no armour other than the deck and perhaps minor amounts on the gun sponsons. In this the *Olympia* deviated substantially, being the only American ship of her type ever to have turrets, which with their cylindrical sides were reminiscent of those designed by John Ericsson for Civil War monitors.

Armour used in the US after 1893 was made by a process of hardening called Harveyizing, an early form of surface hardening. Early tests by the navy showed increases in

USS OLYMPIA
DISPLACEMENT-- 5870 TONS
SCALE OF FEET.

1.

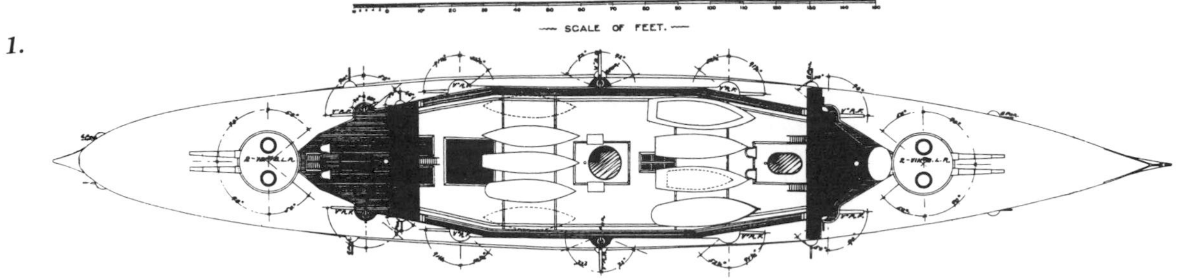

2.

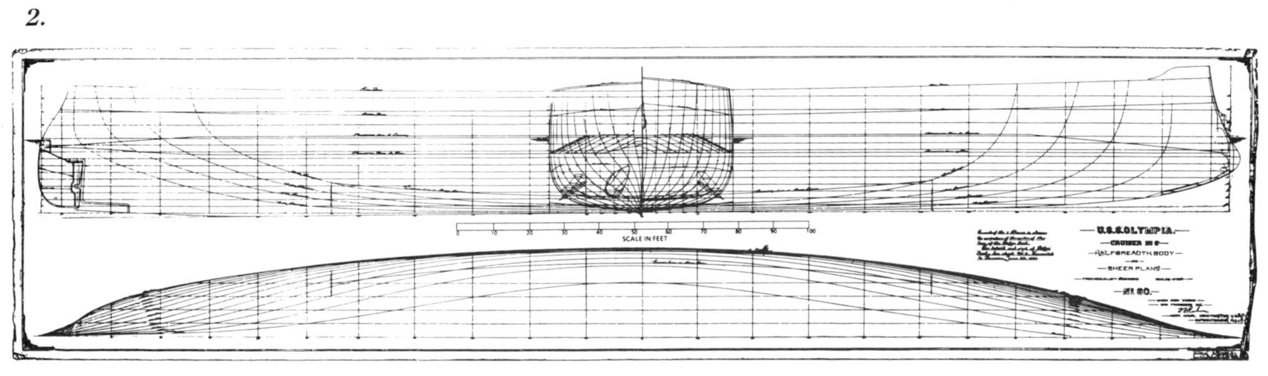
SCALE IN FEET
U.S.S.OLYMPIA.
SHEER PLANS

3.

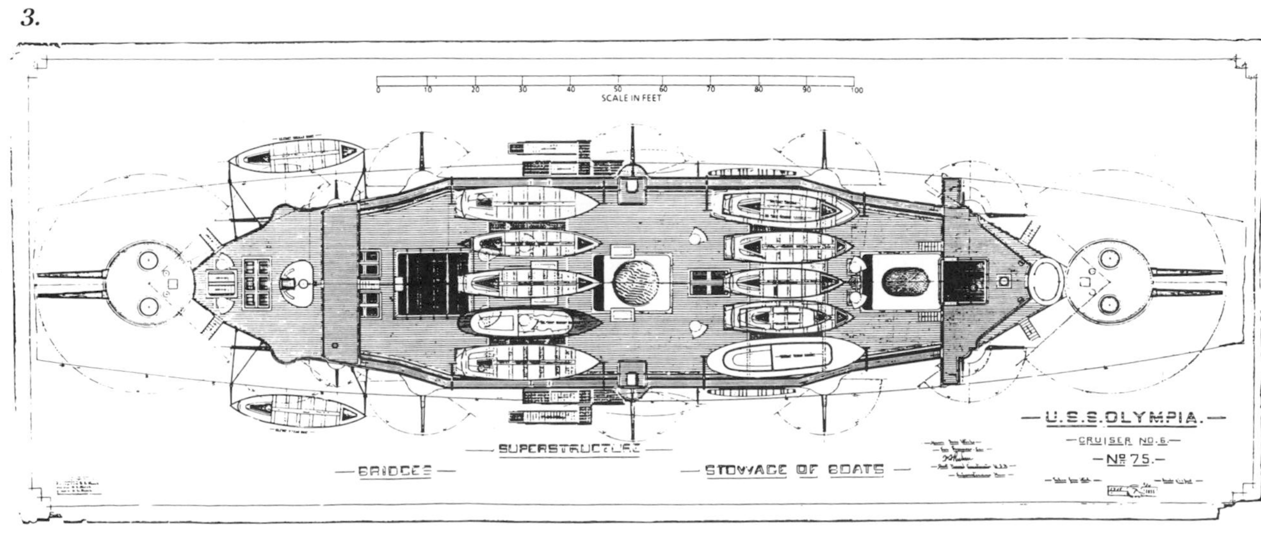
SCALE IN FEET
U.S.S.OLYMPIA.
CRUISER No. 6.
No 75.
SUPERSTRUCTURE
BRIDGES
STOWAGE OF BOATS

1. *Outboard profile and plan view of* Olympia *from official 1893 navy plan. Smokestack covers were removed soon after launch.* (US National Archives)

2. *Half-breadth, body and sheer plans of Cruiser No 6.* (US National Archives)

3. *Navy Department drawing depicting stowage of the fourteen boats carried on the* Olympia. *Note the unusual plan-shape of funnels – one oval and one circular.* (US National Archives)

4. *Mid-section view showing coffer dam and location of armoured protective deck.* (Society of Naval Architects and Marine Engineers)

5. *Lines of* Olympia *taken from original construction plans. Visible are the bow torpedo port, lines of the protective deck, and bilge keels needed for stability.* (US National Archives)

4.

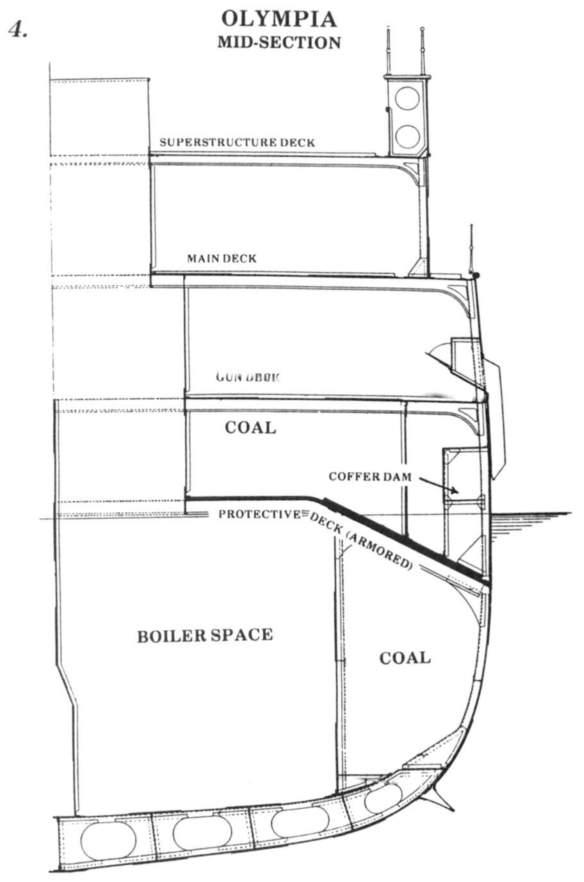

5.

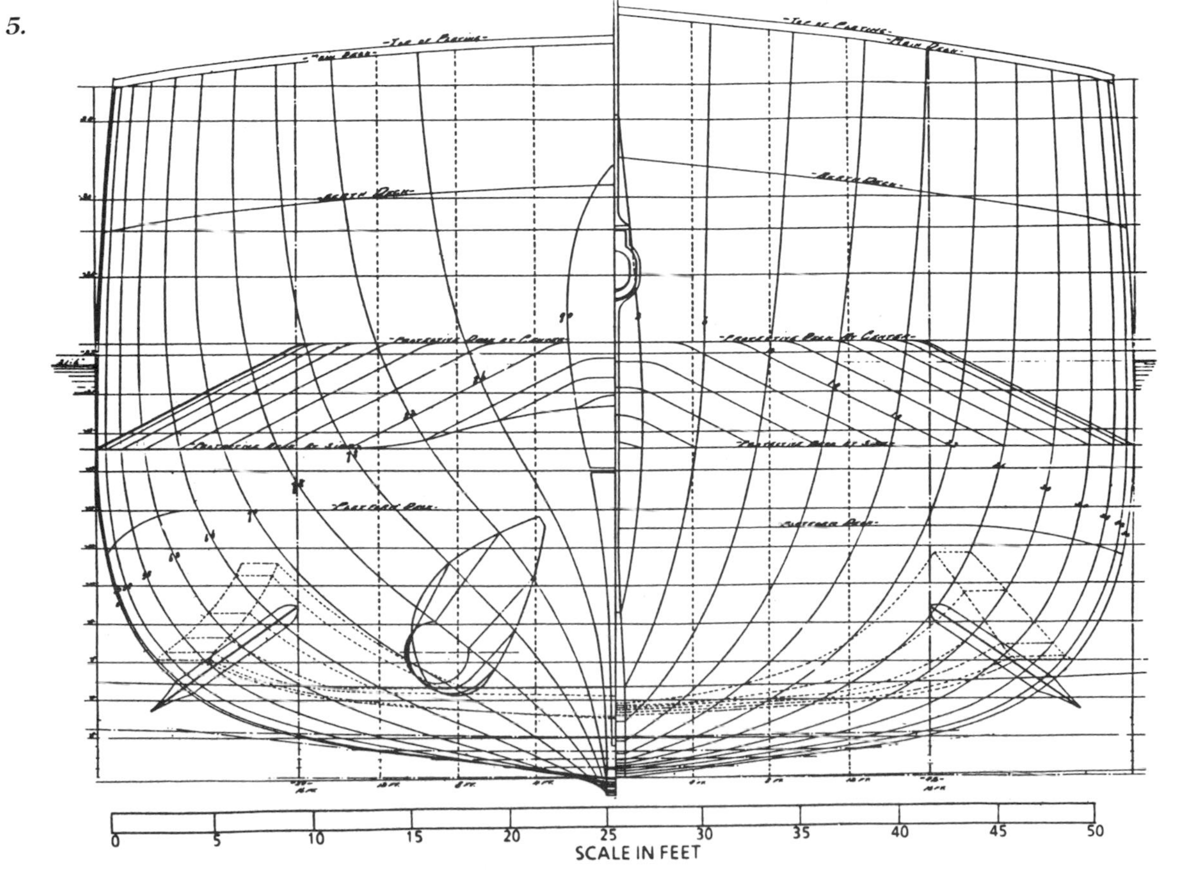

The Olympia *in drydock at the Mare Island Navy Yard, about 1897, showing the early arrangement of the anchors (altered during the 1899–1902 overhaul) and a mainmast crane, soon to be removed. (*Naval Historical Center*)*

resistance to shell penetration of nearly 50 per cent over the nickel steel then in vogue, allowing greater protection with no increase of armour weight. Because the building of the *Olympia* had already commenced when these tests were completed, a mix of nickel steel and Harveyized steel armour was used in her construction.

Turret armour was intended to offer protection against the recently developed rapid-fire guns but not large calibre weapons, and consisted of 3.5in of Harveyized steel. The barbettes had 4.5in of armour which was laid down too early to receive the Harvey process and was thus of the standard nickel steel variety.

Weight considerations also limited armoured decks on previous protected cruisers to the areas over the ammunition stowage and machinery areas, but on the *Olympia* the deck extended the entire length of the ship. Located just above the waterline at the centre and sloping downward to meet the sides just below the waterline, this deck was 4.75in thick on the slopes where with the flat trajectory shells of the day were most likely to hit, and 2in thick on the flats. This heavy deck was worked in forward such that it was the main element used to strengthen the ram.

Additional armour included the conning tower with 5in of nickel steel, and the ammunition tubes with 3in. As with many ships of the day, coffer dams were constructed along the interior at the waterline and packed, in this case, with cocoa fibre. This material was designed to slow or stop a shell entering at the waterline and swell when exposed to the incoming water as a means of plugging up the hole. Never very successful, this means of protection was abandoned early in the new century.

Machinery

Because the navy had given up its foreign coaling stations after the Civil War, endurance was a key factor in cruiser design. Thus, to increase range, the *Olympia* was equipped with a two-masted schooner auxiliary sail rig; but in practice this was seldom used. Instead, propulsion was provided by two triple-expansion engines driven by six scotch boilers, the *Olympia* being one of the first naval vessels to incorporate these lightweight, minimum height vertical reciprocating steam engines. In these engines the steam from the boilers drove pistons in a series of three cylinders, each with a larger diameter than the one before, allowing more complete use of the available steam pressure. Consequently, such engines were much more efficient than the earlier single and double expansion engines. With this arrangement more than 13,500 horsepower was generated and the *Olympia* had a very respectable trials speed of 21.7kts. Today, the engines on the *Olympia* are designated a National Historic Mechanical Engineering Landmark!

Sailors posing with the 18in Whitehead torpedoes aboard the Olympia. *The Mark I torpedo of 1898 was 16ft 5in long, weighed 1160lbs and had a 220lb warhead of wet gun-cotton. At a speed of 28kts, the range was about 850yds. (*Library of Congress*)*

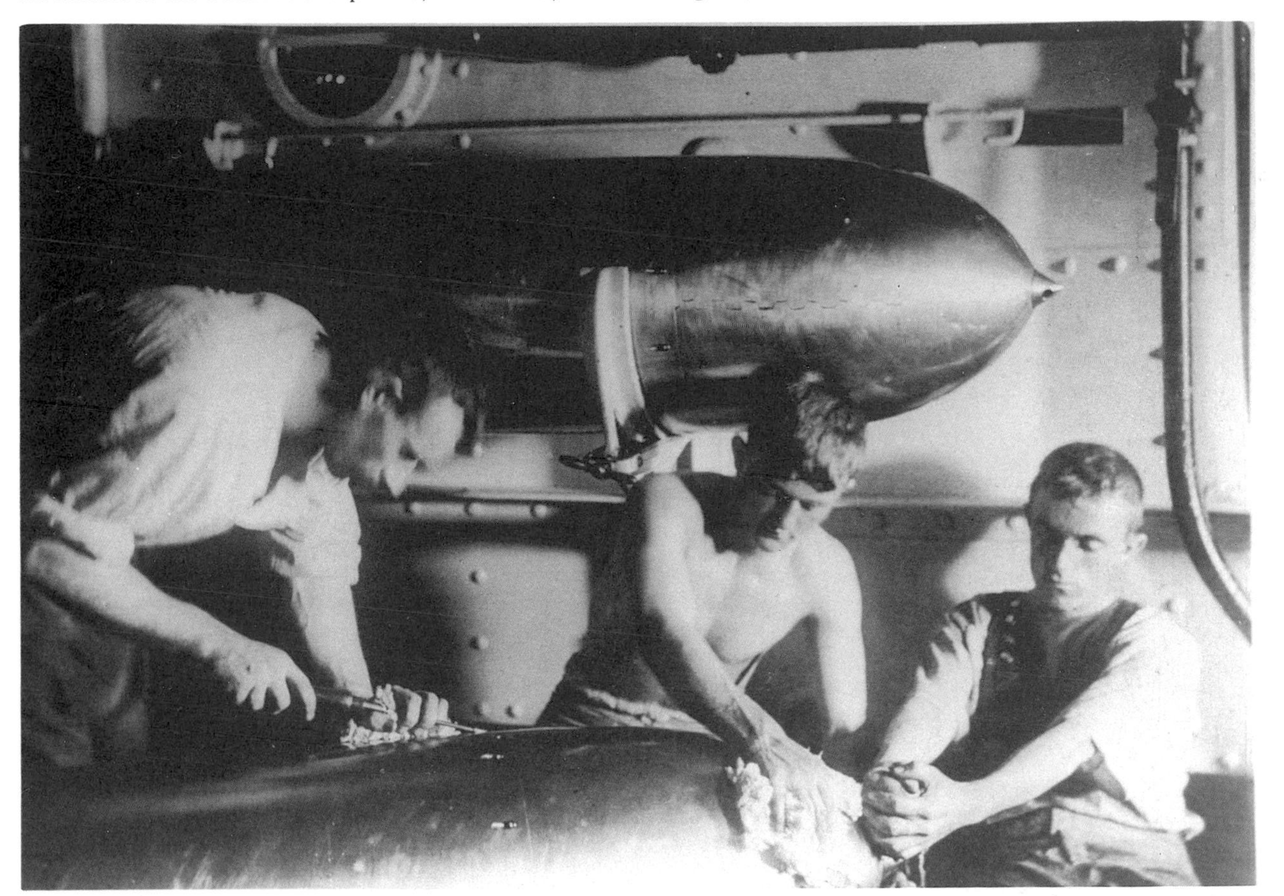

Olympia. *TECHNICAL SPECIFICATION*

Construction Data

Builder	Union Iron Works, San Francisco, California
Authorized	7 September 1888
Contract signed	10 July 1890
Laid down	June 1891
Launched	5 November 1892
Commissioned	5 February 1895
Construction costs	$1,796,000

Design Particulars

Rig	Two-masted schooner
Displacement	5870 tons
Gross tonnage	4012 tons
Net tonnage	1886 tons
Total weight of machinery	1163 tons
Tons immersion at normal draft	29.36 per inch
Design speed	20kts
Trial speed	21.7kts
Length load waterline	340ft 0in
Max breadth	53ft 0$\frac{5}{8}$in
Mean draft	21ft 6in
Max draft aft at lowest point of keel (ship ready for sea with bunkers full)	24ft 9$\frac{3}{4}$in
Coal capacity	400 tons (normal) 1170 tons (bunker capacity)
Endurance	6105nm at 10kts

Armament	4–8in/35cal Mark II 10–5in/40cal Mark II RF 14–6pdr DS trunnionless, long RF with hydraulic recoil 6–1pdr heavy Hotchkiss, Mark 1 RF 4 short Colt machine-guns 6–18in Whitehead torpedo tubes
Armour (total weight)	
8in turrets	3.5in (42.9 tons)
8in barbettes	4.5in (48.9 tons)
Conning tower	5in (21.4 tons)
Protective deck	4$\frac{3}{4}$in on slopes 2in on flats
Ammunition tubes	3in (24.1 tons)
5in sponsons	2/4in (81.9 tons)
Other protection	
Obturating material	11,333 cubic feet cocoa fibre (in waterline coffer dams)
Machinery	
Boilers	4 double-ended, 2 single-ended scotch
Engines	2 vertical triple expansion reciprocating
Indicated hp	13,500
Max indicated hp	17,313
Propellers	2
Complement	34 officers 416 men

Boats

There were fourteen boats carried on the *Olympia*. Twelve of these were stowed on skids in two lines over the superstructure deck, and two hung from davits at the stern. These boats, from port to starboard, were as follows:

1-32ft sailing launch	(located on the forward skids)
2-26ft cutters	(on forward skids, one nested in the sailing launch)
2-28ft cutters	(on forward skids)
1-20ft dinghy	(nested in a 28ft cutter)
1-33ft steam launch	(on forward skids)
2-30ft cutters	(on aft skids)
1-30ft whaleboat gig	(on aft skids)
1-30ft barge	(on aft skids)
1-30ft steam cutter	(on aft skids)
2-29ft whaleboats	(port and starboard stern quarter davits)

The stowage of boats on skids was rather inconvenient – it required two full hours of work by the ship's company, unassisted by steam winches (lacking on the *Olympia*), to launch them. Despite the known danger during battle of fire and splinters, this time factor forced Dewey to meet the Spanish fleet at Manila Bay with the boats in place. While none of the boats aboard Dewey's fleet was damaged by enemy fire that day, fire from his own guns damaged many of the boats hanging outboard on davits.

Colour scheme

As with the peacetime fleet of most nations, the US fleet was primarily painted white with buff details. The original colour scheme on the *Olympia* was somewhat different from the one in which she appears at present. Today the superstructure, turrets, masts and funnels are buff, but when launched only the masts and funnels were buff with most other areas white. Red lead was used on the underwater hull then as now. The standard wartime colour for US ships was a dark grey. However, photos of the *Olympia* immediately before the war and upon her arrival back in the US in 1899 show her in the white and buff colour scheme. This suggests that she was still in her peacetime colours at the battle of Manila Bay.

Career

The *Olympia*, designated cruiser No6, was laid down on 17 June 1891 at the Union Iron Works in San Francisco, California, and launched on 5 November 1892. She was commissioned on 5 February 1895, with Captain John J Read in command. The first three years of her career were rather uneventful, being employed as flagship of the Asiatic Fleet on cruises in the Far East, visiting Japan, China and the Philippines.

In early 1898, with Captain Charles V Gridley in command and flying Admiral George Dewey's flag, she lay at Hong Kong. Upon receiving orders from Assistant Secretary of the Navy (and later President) Theodore Roosevelt to

Olympia. *Contract Trials (Full Power, Forced Draft)*

Date of trial	15 December 1893
Duration of trial	4 hours
Place of trial	Santa Barbara Channel
Condition of sea and weather	Smooth, light breeze
Draught, mean, on trial	20.73ft
Displacement	5,586 tons
Immersed midship section	970sqft
Coefficient of fineness, prismatic	0.517
Type of engines	Vertical triple expansion
Cylinder, diameters	
High pressure	42in
Intermediate pressure	59in
Low pressure	92in
Stroke of pistons	42in
Number and type of boilers	4 double-ended, 2 single-ended
Length and diameter of boilers, in feet	21.25 by 15.25 for double-ended 10.96 by 15.25 for single-ended
Furnaces, number and diameter	40 x 41in
Grate surface used on trial	824sqft
Heating surface used on trial	28,298sqft
Condensing surface used on trial	19,900sqft

Screw propellers	
Diameter	14.75ft
Pitch, mean	19ft
Pitch, adjustable	Between 18.5ft and 19.5ft
Area developed	136sqft (both screws)
Number of blades	3

	Starboard		Port
Steam pressure (psi)			
At engines, per gauge	163.7		160.0
In first receiver, absolute	77.6		85.1
In second receiver, absolute	30.9		33.5
Vacuum in condensers, in inches of mercury	24.94		25.25
Revolutions of main engines per minute	139.98		138.53
Mean engine pressures (psi)			
High pressure	49.63		47.65
Intermediate pressure	38.51		40.05
Low pressure	16.27		17.8
Equivalent on low measure	42.45		44.18
Indicated horsepower			
High pressure	2001		1903.2
Intermediate pressure	3097.3		3185.6
Low pressure	3198.5		3463.4
Aggregate each main engine	8297.6		8552.2
Aggregate both main engines		16.849.8	
Air-pump engines	18.22		35.78
Circulating pump engines	63.50		65.20
Feed pumps		94.7	
Blowers		130.56	
Other Auxiliaries		102.32	
Aggregate of all machinery		17.363.08	
Speed per hour in knots		21.686	
Slip of propeller (mean)		16.87 per cent	
Indicated thrust (main engines only) per square foot of developed area of propeller	1514		1576.8
Indicated hp per square foot of grate, based on mean ihp		21.01	
Heating surface per ihp		1.634	
Condensing surface per ihp		1.148	
Weight of propelling machinery (including water)		1215.23 tons	
Indicated hp per ton of machinery		14.247	
Coal			
Kind of quality used		Welsh: Harris' navigation	
Total burned per hour		37.937.5lbs	
Per hour, per sqft of gate		44.7lbs	
Per hour, per ihp		2.19lbs	

prepare for the likely eventuality of war, Dewey sought both coal and munitions for his partially stocked ships. He obtained coal by the purchase of two British-owned colliers, the *Zafiro* and the *Nanshan*, that came complete with crews who volunteered to stay aboard. After a considerable struggle, he was able to add to his other supplies but went into battle with less than full loads of ammunition.

With war imminent, and at the request of the governor of neutral Hong Kong, Dewey moved his force to Mirs Bay, China. There,on 25 April, Dewey received the following order: 'War has commenced between the United States and Spain. Proceed at once to Philippine Islands. Commence operations particularly against the Spanish fleet. You must capture vessels or destroy. Use utmost endeavour.' Steaming the 600 miles to Manila Bay with his small fleet of four protected cruisers (including besides the *Olympia*, the *Boston*, *Baltimore*, and *Raleigh*), two gunboats (the *Petrel*, and the *Concord*), and the revenue cutter *McCulloch*, plus the supply ships in a second column, Dewey arrived at the entrance to Manila Bay in the early morning hours of 1 May, just six days after war with Spain was declared.

At 11.30pm, and with his ships darkened, Dewey successfully slipped past the powerful harbour defences which opened fire only after half the squadron had passed. None of the shots took effect and were answered with shells from the *Boston* and *McCulloch*. The squadron proceeded across the bay at slow speed so as not to arrive at the Spanish positions before daybreak. At 5.15 the squadron

◀ *Another view in the Mare Island drydock in 1897. The simple bow decoration shown was replaced by gilded scrollwork in the 1899–1902 overhaul. Her forward torpedo tube is located just above the waterline.* (Naval Historical Center)

The Olympia *at anchor in 1898 with Admiral Dewey's pennant at the main mast. Note the two steam launches and the cutter in operation.* (US National Archives)

was fired upon by three batteries at Manila and two at Cavite and by the Spanish fleet anchored on an approximately east and west line across the mouth of Bakor Bay, with their left on shoal water in Canacao Bay.

The eleven Spanish ships anchored there under the command of Rear-Admiral Don Patricio Montojo Y Pasaron were considerably older, less heavily armed and less well protected than the American ships they faced that day. The squadron consisted of: two small protected cruisers, *Isla de Cuba*, and *Isla de Luzon*; five unprotected cruisers, *Cristina*, *Castilla*, *Don Antonio de Ulloa*, *Don Juan de Austria*, and *Velasco*, only one of which was constructed of steel with the others being of iron or wood; two gunboats, *General Lezo*, and *Marquis de Duero*; one armed transport, *Isla de Mindano*; and one armed survey vessel, *Argos*.

Ignoring the shore batteries, which fired ineffectively throughout the battle, Dewey approached to within 5000yds of the enemy and gave the now famous order, 'You may fire when you are ready, Gridley.' The 8in guns of the *Olympia* opened the battle at 5.40am. The *Olympia*, under Dewey's personal direction, led the way with the *Baltimore*, *Raleigh*, *Petrel*, *Concord* and *Boston* following in that order at intervals of about 200yds. Shortly after the battle began two mines were exploded ahead of the flagship, too far away to be effective. The squadron maintained a continuous fire at ranges from 5000 to 2000yds, steaming back and forth in a line approximately parallel to that of the Spanish fleet. The Spanish fire was vigorous but generally ineffective.

Early in the engagement two launches put out toward the *Olympia* with the apparent intention of using torpedoes. One was sunk and the other disabled before either had an opportunity to fire. At 7am the Spanish flagship *Reina Cristina* made a desperate attempt to leave the line and come out to engage at short range but was driven back by the entire battery of the *Olympia*, including small arms fire from the decks. The fires started in her were not extinguished until she sank. In his official report of the battle, Rear-Admiral Montojo gave this account of a portion of the battle giving an idea of the pounding received by his ships and the suffering of his men:

◀ *The engine hatch and after bridge viewed from the superstructure deck, about 1899. Just visible below the bridge is the emergency steering wheel.* (US National Archives)

▲ *Underway, shortly after the 1899–1902 refit. Gone are the single-piece pole masts and fighting tops, replaced by masts with separate topmasts and topgallants. Visible is the newly installed mahogany pilot house on the after bridge.* (US National Archives)

◀ *The sailor's mess on the gun deck. With space for accommodation always scarce, tables were suspended by lines from above and were removed after meals.* (Library of Congress)

The Americans fired most rapidly. There came upon us numberless projectiles, as the three cruisers at the head of the line devoted themselves almost entirely to fight the *Cristina*, my flagship. A short time after the action commenced one shell exploded in the forecastle and put out of action all those who served the four rapid-fire cannon, splintering the forward masts, which wounded the helmsman on the bridge. Another shell exploded in the orlop, setting fire to the crews' kit-bags which they were fortunately able to control.

The enemy shortened the distance between us, and, correcting his aim, covered us with a rain of rapid-fire projectiles. At 7.30 one shell completely destroyed the steering gear. I ordered steering by hand while the rudder was out of action. In the meanwhile another shell exploded on the poop and put out of action nine men. Another destroyed the mizzen masthead, bringing down the ensign and flag, which were replaced immediately. A fresh shell exploded in the officers' cabins, covering the hospital with blood, and destroying the wounded who were being treated there. Another exploded in the after ammunition room, filling the quarters with smoke and preventing the working of the hand steering gear. As it was impossible to control the fire, I had to flood the magazine when the cartridges began to explode.

Amidships several shells of smaller calibre went through the smokestack and one of the large ones penetrated the fire room, putting out of action one master gunner and twelve men serving the guns. Another rendered useless the starboard bow gun; while the fire astern increased, fire was started forward by another shell, which went through the hull and exploded on the deck...

The ship being out of control, the hull, funnel, and mast riddled with shot or confused with the cries of the wounded; half of her crew out of action, among whom were seven officers, I gave the order to scuttle and abandon the ship before the magazines should explode...

◀ *The* Olympia *in 1905. Gilded scrollwork at the bow has replaced the original coat of arms, which is now displayed in the Navy Yard Museum in Washington DC, and the four-sided mahogany pilot house has been replaced by a more spacious six-sided structure. The colour scheme and arrangement of the anchors are much the same as today.* (US National Archives)

Boat stowage as seen from the after signal house in 1902. The two rows of boats had to be hoisted by hand, a very laborious task. Under the boats is the engine hatch covered by a tarpaulin. (US National Archives)

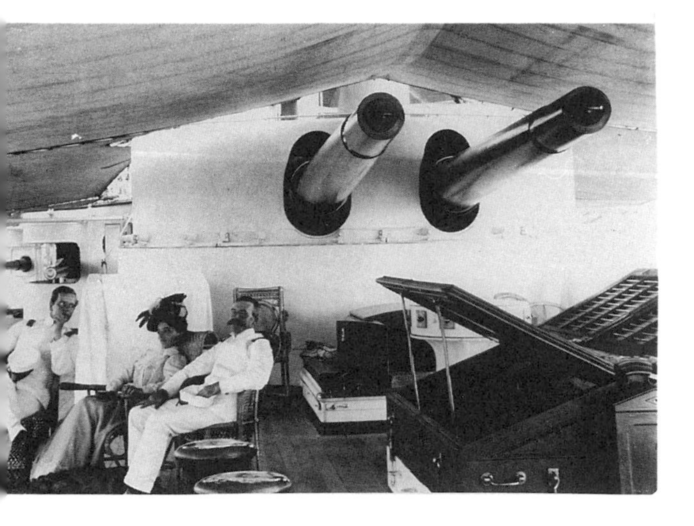

▲ *Officers and guest relaxing near the after 8in gun turret following the war.* (Library of Congress)

Starboard view in 1902, with two-masted schooner in background. (Library of Congress)

After view of 1902. Note that boxy pilot house has not as yet been replaced by roomier six-sided version. (US National Archives)

At 7.35am, when he was incorrectly informed that barely five minutes of 5in rapid-fire ammunition remained aboard the *Olympia*, Dewey withdrew the squadron for redistribution of ammunition. After his men had breakfast he returned to the battle, just before 11am, and found most of the Spanish fleet in flames with many abandoned. Only the *Ulloa* and the shore batteries opposed his advance, and by 12.30pm the *Ulloa* had been sunk and the batteries had been silenced.

The *Olympia* had fired a total of 36 shells from her 8in guns and 281 from her 5in guns. She also fired 1000 rounds from her 6pdr battery, 360 from her 1pdrs and 1000 rounds of small-arms ammunition. The poorly aimed Spanish fire did very little damage to the American ships. One of the two shots which struck the *Baltimore* injured eight men – the only casualties sustained by the Americans during the action. Others struck the masts and rigging of other American ships with one bursting near Admiral Dewey on the bridge of the *Olympia*, and another passed in front of Captain Wildes, on the bridge of the *Boston*. The *Olympia* was hit thirteen times with only minor injury.

The destruction of the Spanish fleet was complete. The *Reina Cristina*, Montojo's flagship, received a large portion of the gunfire for the first engagement, and 130 of her crew were killed. Following a shell burst in her superheater she was completely burned out and abandoned by her crew. One large shell swept the bridge and the smokestack was torn down. Examination following the battle indicated an estimated 39 total hits, ten of which had gone entirely through the vessel without exploding. Most other Spanish ships received similar damage and resulted in a total of 381 Spanish officers and men killed or wounded in the battle.

The victory gave the fleet control of the bay and by the end of the summer the city of Manila had surrendered. This single battle resulted in the fall of the Philippines and pushed Spanish naval power out of the Pacific. After supporting the US army in the suppression of insurgents the *Olympia* left the Philippines and eventually arrived at Boston in October 1899. Dewey was given parades and speeches, and congress gave him a sword and his men special medals of honour.

Badly in need of an overhaul, the *Olympia* was decommissioned the next month and underwent an extensive refit between 1899 and 1902. Commissioned and decommissioned several times, she eventually escorted convoys off Nova Scotia during the First World War. One of her last official tasks came in October 1921 when she returned the remains of the Unknown Soldier to the United States.

Over the years many modifications to her original design were made. The pilot house was enlarged, a radio cabin was added on the after bridge, and her single-piece masts were

Bow-on view of Olympia *at Washington Navy Yard, in November 1921. Less than a year before her final decommissioning, her turrets have long since disappeared.* (US National Archives)

▲ *Casket of the Unknown Soldier transported to America by the* Olympia. *(*US National Archives*)*

◀ *Tied up in Philadelphia Navy Yard, on 11 June 1926. Note bow 5in gun which replaced the 8in turret. (*US National Archives*)*

The Olympia *against a modern Philadelphia skyline. Often barely noticed in the daily life of this active city, she is nevertheless the only surviving ship of her era in the western world. (*Author*)*

▲ *A view today of the after bridge with its remembrance of the famous battle. Notice the differences in arrangements from the earlier photo.* (Author*)*

A 6pdr stands ready in a lightly armoured position on the superstructure deck. (Author*)*

▲ *The emergency steering station as it appears today.* (Author)

A restored 5in gun extends through a starboard gun deck sponson. (Author)

OLYMPIA

Aft companionway to gun deck with Admiral's cabin in background aft. (Author)

◀ *The* Olympia *is open to the public daily. Visitors may also tour the Second World War submarine* Becuna *alongside.* (Cruiser Olympia Assoc)

View of bow from bridge. Snow covers the composite material which has replaced the teak decks of earlier times. (Author)

The Author's 48in scale model of the Olympia *as in 1898.* (Author)

replaced. The arrangement of her anchors was changed and her turrets were removed with new 5in/51cal guns added. Decommissioned for the last time in 1922 the *Olympia* languished for more than 20 years in the Philadelphia Navy Yard. The need for scrap metal during the Second World War threatened many obsolete warships including the *Olympia* and the *Oregon*, an early pre-dreadnought battleship; ultimately, the *Olympia* (but not the *Oregon*) was spared. Turned over to the Cruiser Olympia Association in 1957, she is now open to the public at Penn's Landing, on the Philadelphia waterfront. Visitors can explore unhindered from the bridge where Dewey gave his famous order to the starboard engine room where the brass and steel engine components are kept carefully polished.

Although preserved her restoration has been slow – no government funds have been provided since she left the navy. Her original teak weather decks are long since gone, and to avoid leaks the decks are covered with a multi-layer waterproof composite. Sheet metal replicas of the turrets have been installed with dummy 8in guns. She retains the bow scroll and paint scheme that followed her 1899 refit. Yet her nearly 100-year-old steel hull is water-tight and she sits proudly afloat – along with the Japanese battleship *Mikasa*, the only surviving example of the world's steel pre-dreadnought battle fleets.

Sources

1. *Dictionary of American Naval Fighting Ships*, Naval History Division, Navy Department.
2. National Archives, Cartographic & Architectural Branch, Washington, DC 20408 (ship plans).
3. Naval Historical Center, Washington Navy Yard, Washington, DC 20374 (ship photos).
4. Still Pictures Branch (NNSP), National Archives, Washington, DC 20408 (ship photos).
5. *Transactions*, the Society of Naval Architects and Marine Engineers, (1893 and 1898 editions).
6. *US Cruisers: an Illustrated Design History*, by Norman Friedman, US Naval Institute Press.
7. 'USS *Olympia*, a National Shrine of Naval History,' reprinted from the US Naval Institute *Proceedings*.
8. *Report of the Secretary of the Navy*, US Navy Department, 1865-98.
9. *Admiral Dewey and the Manila Campaign*, by Commander Nathan Sargent, USN Naval Historical Foundation.
10. *Proceedings*, the US Naval Institute, Volumes 13-25.

THE FIRST FLOWERS

The famous British corvettes of 1939–45 had a First World War precursor and equivalent in the minesweeping and convoy sloops that were every bit as valuable. Keith McBride outlines their origin and development.

The naval mine first put in an appearance in the mid-nineteenth century, and proved itself a major threat during the Russo-Japanese War of 1904–5, sinking one Russian battleship, with a share in a second, and two Japanese ones, as well as many lesser vessels. The Royal Navy recognized the threat and began thinking about countermeasures at an early stage, though at the time it was thought that mines would only be laid in the territorial waters of belligerents.

Early minesweeping efforts

In 1907 the Trawler Section of the Royal Naval Reserve was formed, to take advantage of the experience of deep-sea fishermen with rope and wire work and to capitalize on the suitability of their vessels for a slightly different form of fishing; 142 trawlers and 1279 officers and men had been enrolled by 1912. In 1914, ninety-four trawlers were taken up in the first four days of war, and another hundred in the next fortnight. For keeping ports and channels open they were admirable, but their average speed of 7kts or thereabouts was quite inadequate for sweeping ahead of a fleet and their draught was deep enough to make the clearance of large minefields extremely hazardous – in the opening months of the war, one trawler was lost, with half her crew, for every five mines swept. On average a minesweeper was mined every week of the war.

Clearly, a different type was wanted for fleet sweeping and field clearance, and discussions on characteristics and design had been going on since 1908. An Admiralty committee had reported in November of that year, recommending the building of eighteen minesweepers. It was realized that with the existing state of the art, minesweeping would be very dangerous, and it was desired to keep the vessels and their crews as small as possible; a speed of 16kts, a displacement of about 600 tons, maximum draught of 10ft and good sea-keeping qualities were sought. A single screw, to lessen the risk of entanglement, and an overhanging bow and counter were specified. A radius of action of 1200 miles, triple expansion engines with water-tube boilers and mixed firing were called for, but armament was not mentioned. The crew was to be 3 officers and 17 men.

Philip Watts, the Director of Naval Construction, considered these parameters and put forward some sketch designs. These ranged from *A1* of 575 tons, 1100ihp and 14kts, costing £30,000, to *D* of 900 tons, 2000/3000ihp for 16/17kts for 8 hours, costing £55,000. The Coast Guard vessels *Safeguard* and *Watchful* of 825 and 580 tons were also considered. The DNC agreed that 600 tons was the smallest displacement for reasonable sea-keeping in all conditions; he provided for rather heavier engines than specified to withstand hard usage, and also expressed doubts about unarmed warships. He felt that something was needed 'to test the explosive character of any object found floating in the path of the ships and if necessary to destroy it, to preserve morale when an attack by a destroyer or other craft appears imminent and to prevent the vessel being put out of action by any light craft watching the mine field.' He wondered if a modern sea-going tug could not carry out the task.

It was proposed to build such minesweepers in small batches starting in 1910–11 and building up to a strength of sixteen or eighteen, but the first batch were postponed until 1911–12. In 1910 it was agreed not to build any minesweepers. The minesweeping role was being filled by six old torpedo gunboats, which were fairly fast and had been deprived of their original role by destroyers, and an Inspecting Captain of Mine Sweepers (ICMS), Captain Greatorex, had been appointed, to act as their administrative and technical parent. Trials of minesweeping gear had been held at Portland with two hired Grimsby trawlers; fishing trawls proved ineffective against mines, but a pair-sweep towed by two vessels and kept to its depth by two kites was devised and proved effective.

Exercises in the Moray Firth showed that the torpedo gunboats were too few and inadequate. They had a small fuel capacity and were almost worn out; but no action was taken. The matter came up in 1911 and 1913, by which time Sir George Callaghan, of the 1908 Committee, was C-in-C Home Fleet. During this period the fitting of destroyers for minesweeping was authorized but cancelled – no doubt other things had higher priority. In the spring of 1914 the matter was again discussed and it was agreed that something ought to be done.

A design for a fleet sweeper was considered in February 1914, but none had been authorized by the outbreak of war. It seemed to naval opinion of the day that it was a waste of resources to build minesweepers when there were all those trawlers and plenty of civilian small vessels that could be impressed. In the various proposals, it was suggested that the minesweepers could earn their keep in peacetime by towing targets, recovering torpedoes and taking libertymen to and fro.

Minesweeper designs revived

On the outbreak of war, it was found that, in fact, there were not many small fast civilian craft, while the sinking of HMS *Amphion* within 24 hours emphasized the power of the mine. The events of 22 September 1914 (the sinking of *Aboukir*, *Cressy* and *Hogue*) showed that the other underwater menace was a real threat, too. Various forms of bow protection gear had been devised, but they obviously did not inspire confidence: on one occasion 'A battleship of the *King*

▲ Primrose, *one of the 'second twelve' ordered, in wartime dazzle camouflage. Wartime improvements include gun shields, enclosed crowsnest and Carley Floats.* (IWM)

Edward VII class was placed at the head of each division of the Fleet, to indicate the presence of mines.' The 1908 designs were dug out of the archives, but, since U-boats had developed a habit of attacking merchant ships, unarmed minesweepers were clearly not viable. Vessels were needed which could deal with both mines and submarines: the pair-sweep existed for mines, but there was also a 'Modified Sweep' – alias the 'Boatswain's Nightmare' – by which a ship could tow explosive charges underwater and, with luck, destroy a submarine (it did work, occasionally). The ships also needed guns, for use not only against surfaced U-boats but also against German destroyers, especially if the plan to 'dig the High Seas Fleet out of its harbours' was attempted. It was felt that two 12pdrs would suffice, as 'the German destroyers are, as a rule, badly gunned, the best only having two 15pdrs and four machine guns.' (This incidentally, was a serious error since many had 88mm guns, and their gun-power was soon increased).

Though DNC rapidly produced a design for a combined minesweeper/anti-submarine vessel, there were serious problems in building and manning it in numbers. It was an article of faith in the Royal Navy that six years' service were needed to produce a competent man-of-war's-man – hence the twelve years enlistment – and the available reserves were soon exhausted. Furthermore, after the outbreak of war, the building of light cruisers and destroyers was rapidly increased, and the regular warship building firms were soon swamped with work.

The Controller instructed the DNC to proceed with the design on 25 September 1914, and work went ahead rapidly. The 1908 designs were borne in mind and it seems likely

◀ *The prototype,* Acacia *with original unshielded 12pdr armament, possibly on trials.* (IWM)

that some calculations were worked forward from those of the *Seagull* type torpedo-gunboats (in those days it took a very long time to calculate a design *ab initio* and it was usual to develop from an existing design if possible). The first 'New *Seagull*' was 750 tons and 220ft x 27ft x 9½ft, with 1500ihp machinery – heavier than that of the *Sharpshooter* but lighter than that of the *Safeguard*, which had been built under Lloyd's survey. The hull was of light construction and fine form to get the required speed on low power. Water-tight compartmentation was more complete than usual and the boiler and engine rooms were sub-divided, which required six more men. There was a clipper bow with rigid bowsprit to take mine-catching gear, several types of which were under development, and facilities for a trawl winch and other minesweeping gear. At some point the decisions were taken to provide triple bottom plating forward for safety against mines, to put the magazine above water aft, protected by armour, and to provide an anti-submarine ram forward. Endurance was to be 2000 miles at 10kts plus 16 hours at full power.

The 'New *Seagull*' design was considered at a meeting chaired by the Controller on 19 October 1914, where it was found to be satisfactory as a ship, but Admiral Oliver, the Chief of Staff, argued that it should be modified to permit building by firms who normally built merchant ships, that the machinery should be in line with merchant ship practice and that, to provide the necessary inspection, the ships should be built under Lloyd's survey, 'like the *Safeguard*'. It was accepted that this would mean larger ships, but the cost would not go up in proportion. Protection to the machinery spaces was abandoned, and the clipper bow eliminated. The Constructors said that they could modify the plans in four days. It was hoped to build forty ships as soon as possible, but even if the war ended soon, as was still expected, the ships would be of use in their 'Fleet Tender' role.

The change involved the fitting of cylindrical boilers and a considerable increase of weight, the ships coming out at 250ft x 33ft x 11ft 7in for 1210 tons with two-thirds coal. A towing hook and beam were provided, the towing point being well forward of the transom to avoid loss of control.

The proposal to build forty ships – a flotilla of eight to each battle squadron – was put to Winston Churchill, the First Lord, on 20 October, but was promptly turned down. He wrote that

> This is a proposal to spend £2,400,000 on forty small vessels of weak fighting power and slow speed but each costing as much as a small submarine. Any one of these vessels could easily be destroyed by a torpedo-boat. They will be valuable enough to be worth attacking and too expensive to be sufficiently numerous. None.....can be ready...for nine months from now, namely July 1915.

He recognized the need for small craft 'not 40 or 50 but 300 or 400, vessels of the lowest possible value consistent with seaworthiness for all the purposes of sweeping, picket and patrol'. Like the Admiralty in peacetime he felt that 'The British Islands teem with nondescript small vessels. Trawlers are the obvious and immediate resource, and we should go on taking them up, organising them, supplementing them by small yachts and other vessels, fitting all with wireless, which is more important to them than the guns.'

The other members of the Board returned to the charge, repeating that civilian craft convertible to fast minesweepers were in fact very scarce, that light cruisers and destroyers were fully employed in fleet work, and that seaworthy light craft capable of dealing with mines and submarines would have to be built. The *Badger* episode was reflected in doubts about the usefulness in this role of destroyers: 'TBDs cannot apparently sink submarines by ramming either with certainty or with safety to themselves and other suitable vessels are practically unobtainable.' Churchill reluctantly gave way on 26 November; 'My opinion is expressed in my minute of 21/10/14. If more fleet sweepers cannot be otherwise procured I am willing to sanction twelve being built, provided that six can be ready in four, and the remainder in six months from the order being given.'

The 'Flower' class design

The design was the work of J H Narbeth RCNC and outwardly looked very like the original *Seagull*, with two widely separated funnels – a sign of the divided boiler rooms. There were two Scotch or 'Tank' boilers and either a three- or four-cylinder triple expansion engine of mercantile type. Designs and weights varied according to engine and hull builder and varying amounts of sand ballast were carried to establish a – nearly – common trim. Generally, the Scottish-built ships has three-cylinder engines and the English-built ones four. For the first twenty-four, power was typically 1800ihp. From the 'third twelve' onwards (the *Arabis* and *Azalea* classes) power went up to 2200ihp and the later 'Convoy Sloops' could develop 2500ihp and 2700 for very short bursts. A total of 250 tons of coal, rather more than was originally wanted, was carried in side and cross bunkers. The intention was that when sweeping or in dangerous waters, the side bunker doors would be shut and the ship fired from the cross bunkers to improve water-tight integrity. The bunkers completely surrounded the two boiler rooms and in themselves gave considerable protection. The required endurance was 2000 miles at 10kts plus 16 hours at the full speed of 16kts. This equalled 3700 miles at 10kts and was usually attained. Legend has it that it was advisable to take a careful look round when descending the ladder, to see where the boilers had wandered to, but in general the powerplants gave sterling service – one ship was under steam for 121 days continuously, and the distance the average member of the class covered must have been astronomical.

Apart from their engines, they had a fore staysail and main trysail, which often came in very useful for steadying purposes. There was a 7½-ton trawl winch to handle sweeps, while the electrical system was 105-volt DC.

Structurally, the ships had a forecastle and centre island but no poop. The island was aft of amidships, over the

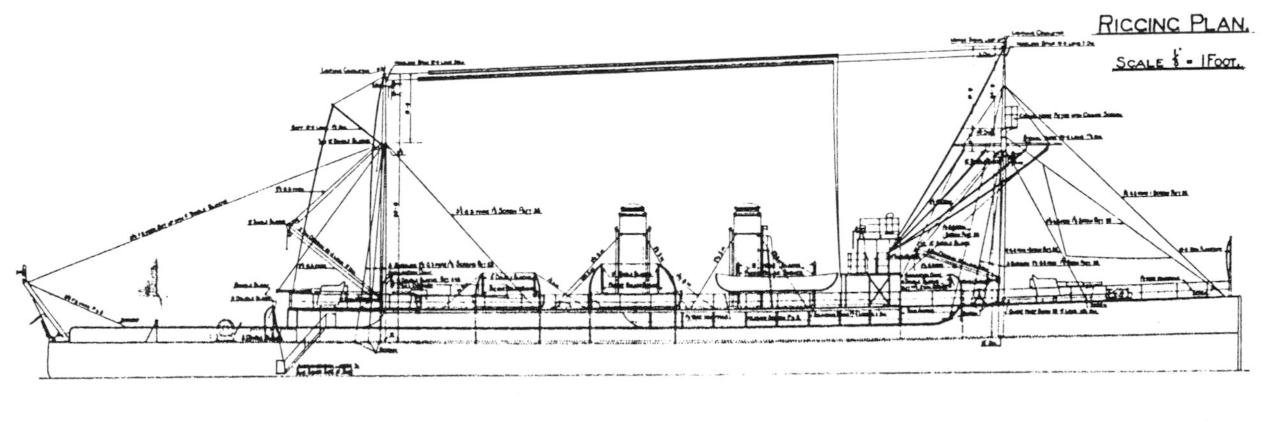

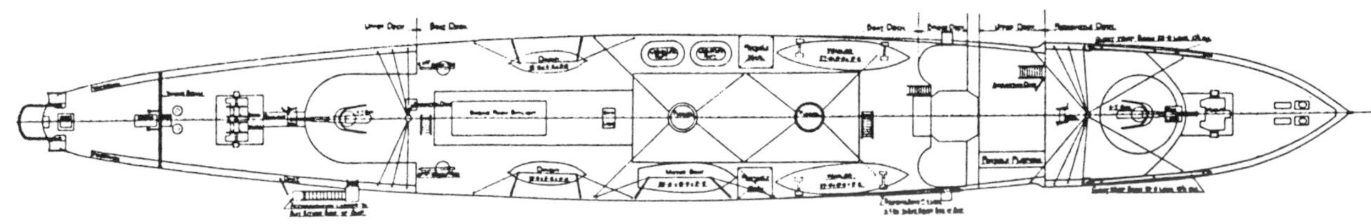

The rigging plan of Marguerite *and* Mignonette *demonstrates the basic layout of the Minesweeping Sloops.* (NMM)

Carnation, *with bow section removed after damage. The simple structure of the hull is clear.* (IWM)

machinery spaces, with the bridge structure extending part-way into the forward well deck. The superstructure included a hurricane deck, intended to protect the deck-load of libertymen, if carried. The foremast rose from the forecastle and was fitted with a crowsnest – a feature which pre-war small ship design had tended to neglect – with voice pipe. The forward gun was squeezed in between the foremast and the anchor gear, while the other gun was at the after end of the island raised to fire over the sweeping gear. The mainmast was just forward of it and carried a substantial derrick to handle the sweeping gear. The stem was straight.

The placing of the magazine aft created problems in arranging the 'course of ammunition' (= US 'Loading Train'), especially for the forward gun which was nearly 200ft away. It could run either through the tween decks or along the upper deck. The Admiralty assumed rightly that the typical action would be brief – with a surfaced submarine – and for that, ready-use ammunition would suffice. The magazine was protected by 1½in high tensile steel on the front, back and sides and ½in underneath and on top. It proved its worth: when the *Rosemary* was torpedoed on 4 July 1916, the after end was blown away, the roof curled up over the trawl winch and the contents scattered, but the plating absorbed the explosion and the ammunition did not explode. It is believed that none of these magazines ever did explode.

About one 'Flower' in six was fitted as a Senior Officer's ship; these were built by Barclay Curle, with Type II wireless and 110ft masts, while ordinary ships had Type IV wireless and 64ft masts.

Apart from equipment, these novel and numerous ships had to be provided with names; according to tradition, a senior admiralty official who was a keen gardener solved the problem by taking a seedsman's catalogue out of his desk. This official may have been the secretary, Sir William Graham Greene, but no one, not even his relatives, can now say for sure.

Armament

The original planned armament was two 3in and two 2pdr pom-poms, all on high-angle mountings, but the exigencies of war altered this drastically. For the 'first twenty-four', the *Acacia*s', 12 or 18cwt 12pdrs, firing separate ammunition, were supplied. At one time it was feared that they would have to be fitted with 6pdrs (and 100rpg) as a stopgap, but this necessity did not arise. It is not clear whether the pom-poms were ever fitted; in late 1915 Admiral Bayly at Queenstown suggested that 3pdrs should be fitted instead and this was done.

Early experience showed that because of their distinctive appearance, the 'Flowers' hardly ever got within 12pdr range of a U-boat before it dived, so from the 'Third dozen' the design was enlarged and modified. Apart from higher power, the main armament was changed to two 4.7in, and these much heavier guns did the trick, but their 50lb shell meant that supply had to be reduced from 216 to 50rpg. This was later increased to 100rpg and the magazine and its armour enlarged accordingly. The ideal gun would have been the 4in, but these were needed for 'real' warships, such as light cruisers and destroyers. Nevertheless, six 'Flowers' based at Scapa Flow somehow acquired 4in. The 4.7in was in a state of limbo at this time; it had not been fitted to any new ships since the mid-1890s and the guns themselves were old. Like the 12pdrs, they fired separate ammunition, which was a drawback, and they were not ideal for working in small, lively ships.

There was a severe shortage of guns for much of the war, and many 4.7s fitted to the 'Flowers' were removed from auxiliary cruisers on the latter being re-armed with 6in guns. Proposals were made to re-arm the 'first twenty-four' with 4in, but because of their smaller magazines, they were ordered to be given one 4.7in and one 12pdr. It is not clear whether the newly made 3in were ever fitted. Several 'Flowers' were built for the French Navy, and they were fitted with 5.5in guns! In this context it should be noted that the French *Arras* class, smaller equivalents of the Convoy Sloops, also carried two 5.5in each, and were described as rolling 'comme des vieux sabots'.

The 4.7in were fitted on PIII, PIV and GII mounts and much later on new specially designed MkIV ones. Spray shields only were fitted, these being made in the dockyards; 4in, where fitted, were on pedestals. Only once did 'Flowers' engage enemy surface ships, and on that occasion the *Arabis*' forward 4.7in jammed at the second round. (It is recorded that one captain had his guns double-shotted with shell and armour-piercing suet dumplings and fired at a passing Zeppelin, but the nature of gun and the effect on the Zeppelin are not recorded.)

In a sense, the main armament of the sloops was their minesweeping and anti-submarine equipment. At first the Modified Sweep was the only means of striking at a

Amaryllis, *of the* Azalea *group, at Malta in 1916; guns and crowsnest are still unshielded.* (IWM)

submarine below periscope depth, but very few were sunk with it and, apparently, none by a 'Flower'. Its name was deliberately deceptive, but it consisted of a loop of wire about 200ft long, kept to the correct depth by kites, fitted with a number of small explosive charges and suspended from wooden floats. An electric circuit ran through it, and if it fouled anything, a needle flicked over on a dial. A switch was then thrown, the charges went off and – the users hoped – down went the U-boat. Towing speed was 8–10kts; the explosive paravane was similar and had at least one success. (The French *Torpille Remorquée Ginocchio* was of the same ilk.)

Much more effective were depth charges, which were introduced in late 1915 and scored their first success in June 1916. A batch of 21 Type C and 11 Type E arrived at Haulbowline Dockyard, Queenstown, in early 1916 and were regarded with great suspicion by Admiral Bayly and his men. The Type Cs were issued to the small auxiliary patrol craft, but the Es were returned to Chatham, as it was feared that they would be set off on deck when the sloops were pooped, as often happened (the US 'flush-decker' *Wasmuth* was lost in this way in 1942). Their proper depth charge was the type 'D', and as soon as possible they were supplied with twelve each, which were dropped from hydraulic racks. There was virtually no means of underwater detection, so attack was a matter of charging at a periscope or along a torpedo track and letting fly, but at least they *could* sink a U-boat, while the noise and concussion shook up the U-boats and worried their crews no little. Kite balloons, seaplanes, lance bombs, depth mines, and stick bombs (fired from the guns like rifle grenades) were also carried or considered.

Against their other enemy, the 'Flowers' carried the Types 'A' or 'B' sweep, some the 'French Sweep'. Provision was made for underwater signalling apparatus, but it was apparently not generally installed. Both 12ft and 6ft kites were carried and proved tricky to handle. Much attention had been paid to getting the various pieces of 'pully-hauley' gear into the right places with proper clearance, but the handling of the sweeps involved a lot of hard, dangerous old-style seamanship.

The towing hook and beam proved very effective; though not as useful as a tug, the 'Flowers' proved capable of towing large ships for hundreds of miles at a reasonable rate.

Construction and Fitting-out

The building of these ships in numbers and in a great hurry required an industrial mobilization of a kind not foreseen; if the length of the war had been correctly predicted, no doubt designs would have been prepared, drawings issued to selected builders, and equipment earmarked. As it was, everything had to be improvised very quickly. A lot of the burden fell on C J W Hopkins RCNC, who was in effect Project Engineer and troubleshooter-in-chief. The builders involved ranged from big firms like Swan Hunter to small specialized ones like Lobnitz and simple builders of tramp steamers, and most were quite unused to the Admiralty's exacting requirements. Swan Hunter later provided drawings at £200 a set to the smaller firms. Lloyds undertook the survey task, which, again, was much more detailed than for merchant or fishing vessels. The fee proved burdensome, and eventually the Admiralty agreed to pay part of it. There was as yet no direction of labour or conscription; it was still 'business as usual' and, although they were supposed not to, firms poached labour from each other. At times, feelings ran high between the Admiralty staff and the tough men of the Clyde, the Tees and the Tyne over what seemed like Admiralty nit-picking.

Many small firms had only the basic construction facilities

Primula, *one of the later ships of the class, with gallows deployed.* (IWM)

and depended on sub-contractors for much of their material, which led to a lot of trouble. The Admiralty supplied not only the obvious items like armament and wireless, but compasses and binnacles, coaling rims, scuttles, cooking equipment, sanitary ware, generating plant and other items. As time went on, good-quality merchant ship items were substituted in many cases. Chatham became the parent and the manning depot for ships built on the East Coast, Portsmouth and Devonport sharing the task for the other yards.

The Admiralty had ordered the reduction of woodwork to the minimum, but this had to be disregarded as the small builders had plenty of joiners but virtually no sheet-metal workers. There were innumerable problems, mostly in matters of detail, but Barclay Curle completed the *Foxglove* in 17 weeks from the date of order and Swan Hunter were very close behind with the *Acacia*. At one stage the Admiralty prepared a 'working timetable' of when it expected ships to be completed. This was kept a closely-guarded secret – especially from the builders. Churchill's four- and six-month deadlines were not quite met, but the last of the 'first twelve', *Marigold* (Bow McLachlan) was delivered on 4 August. The 'second twelve' were ordered on 12 January 1915, the third on 4 May, nine on 6 July, twenty-one on 15 July and six on 27 July. Another dozen, the first of the 'Convoy Sloops', were ordered on 23 January 1916, with two more (*Cassiopée* and *Regulus*) for France on 23 September 1916. Thirty-four more (one for France) were ordered between 26 December 1916 and 21 February 1917. Thereafter, their place on the ways was taken by *Hunt* class minesweepers, '24' class sloops, and other types.

Among other initially fitted were various forms of bow protection gear. These seem to have taken the form of some type of bib suspended from the bow and held in place by various ropes and stays. In practice, they do not seem to have been effective and experience showed that mines rarely exploded at the bow: they were usually forced aside by the bow wave and sucked in again aft of it, typically exploding abreast the bridge and the machinery spaces. The ultimate solution came in the forms of the Paravane and the Oropesa Sweep, but in the meantime the 'Flowers' and other minesweepers relied on pair sweeps, good station-keeping – and Providence.

Construction and engine-building were in general done well but there were many complaints about detail work, which was hampered by many workers having joined up and by the Admiralty's requirements being so much tighter than those of merchant ship-owners. At one stage the Admiralty ordered seven sets of engines to prevent the builders running out of work. Speed troubles sometimes arose, and were in many cases due to the screws having the wrong pitch. Builders varied: Barclay Curle and Lobnitz were among the best, though the former were also rather expensive. The French Navy complained that, even allowing for wartime pressures, the *Bellatrix* (D & W Henderson) was not very stable and her engines gave trouble, whereas their Barclay Curle-built ships gave no trouble whatsoever. *Gladiolus* was found to have no less than thirty defects on delivery, mostly detail matters, and was sent to Hawthorn Leslie to be put right, while a stiff letter went to her builders (Connells) and to Lloyds. *Campanula* stuck on the ways on 25 September 1915, due, improbably enough, to a tree trunk getting under her stern. Barclay Curle freed her in 24 hours and though the launching ways subsided, she floated little the worse except for a crushed bilge keel.

In service

The *Clematis*' engineer wrote to her builders that after much experience in bad weather, 'I have that confidence that I believe she could climb a lamp-post and get down the

◀Valerian, *possibly on trials.* (IWM)

other side easily.' He added that he had seen water breaking over the cylinders and a heavy sea running in the wardroom, but had been able to maintain 140rpm.

In general the sea-keeping qualities of the 'Flowers' won great admiration; if anything they were too lively. Being long and narrow, there was a tendency for the propeller to come out of the water and race, so later ships were given a slightly shorter shaft to cure this. On 12 November 1915, twelve of them ran into gales of Force 10 to 12 and came through very well; generally their crews had great confidence in them. Vibration at full speed was reported as a nuisance, but it did not affect gun sighting and was much less than in reciprocating-engined destroyers. The big rudder made them fairly handy, despite having only a single screw.

In the last resort, however, all depended on 'the men in 'em'. These included many RNR (ex-Mercantile Marine) officers and men and actual MM men serving under T124 articles, around a Royal Navy nucleus. The standard complement was 70, made up of: 1 Lieutenant in Command; 2 Lieutenants or Sub-Lieutenants, one as Navigator; 1 Sub-Lieutenant or Gunner; 1 Chief Artificer, Artificer or Warrant Mechanician; 1 Chief Petty Officer; 1 Chief Writer; 1 Ship's Steward; 1 Shipright; 2 Petty Officers; 9 Stoker Petty Officers; 3 Engine Room Artificers; 2 Leading Seamen; 10 Able or Ordinary Seamen; 1 Leading Signalman; 1 Signalman; 1 Leading Telegraphist; 1 Telegraphist; 1 Armourer's Mate; 5 Leading Stokers; 21 Stokers; 1 Leading Cook's Mate; 1 Domestic 2nd Class (for CO); 2 Domestics 2nd Class (for Wardroom). The engine-room complement were in three watches and the upper deck in two; there were not enough for a full three-watch system. On average the ships spent four days out of five at sea, with coaling when in port.

War losses were heavy: 9 RN sloops and one French out of 72 and 9 Convoy Sloops out of 40. Of the former, one (*Arabis*) was sunk by surface craft, four mined, and four by U-boat; of the latter, eight by U-boats and one by mine. The *Begonia* was converted to a convoy sloop and was lost in ramming a U-boat, and the French sloop *Rigel* was torpedoed twice by a U-boat. Her captain at once asked for a sister ship! The loss of the *Begonia* was peculiarly tragic: on the night of 2 October 1917, *U-151*, one of the big converted merchant U-boats, was off Casablanca when she saw a 'destroyer' charging at her. She dived, but was struck while at periscope depth. Her officer of the watch saw a 'wall' passing across her stern, and then a heavy explosion was heard. That was *Begonia*. There were no survivors; probably her own depth-charges killed anyone in the water. *U-151*'s casing was badly damaged, but she was able to effect repairs at sea and continue a successful patrol to the Central Atlantic. It is assumed that *U-151* had got just deep enough to tear out the sloop's bottom as she scraped over.

On the other side of the ledger, the 'Flowers' must have accounted for a large proportion of the 40,000 or so mines swept by the Royal Navy during 1914–18; the Germans laid 43,000 and the task of clearing them went on long after the Armistice. Against U-boats, despite the lack of detection equipment and their big turning circle, they were fairly successful. *Buttercup* and *PC-56* sank *U-87* by ramming,

A fine atmospheric photo of Snapdragon *at sea in 1916, possibly in the Mediterranean.* (IWM)

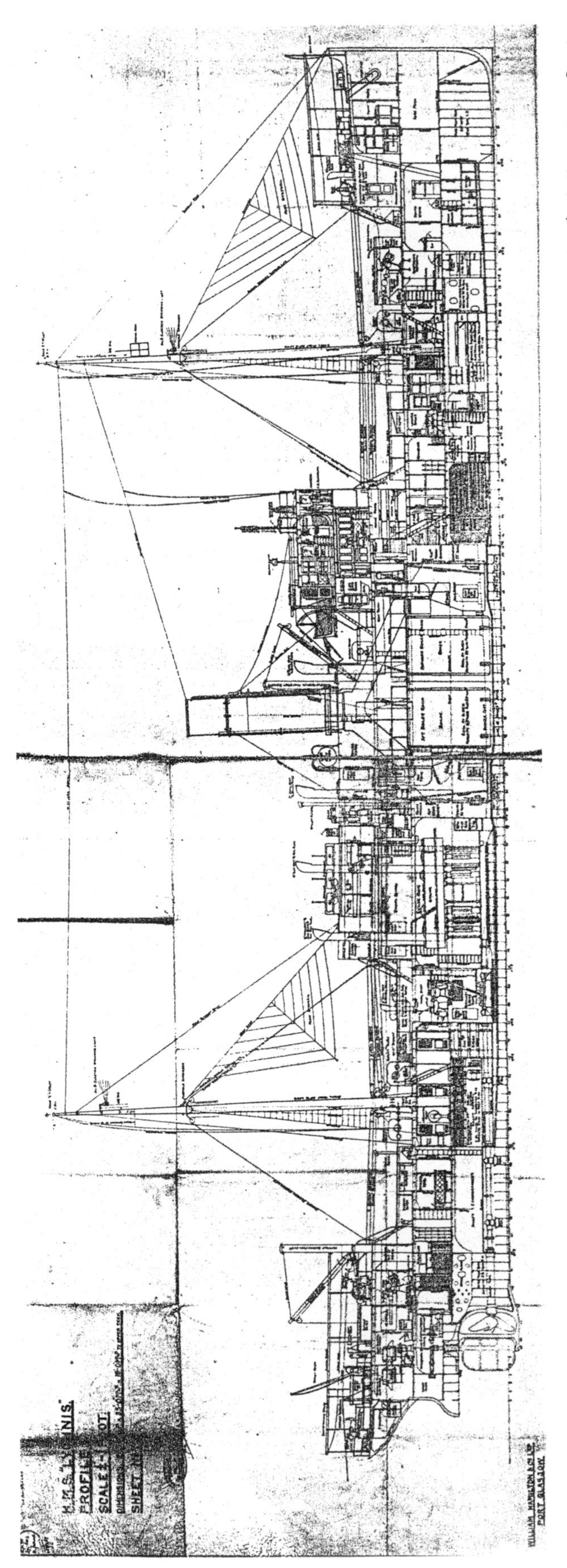

The internal profile of Lychnis, *a Convoy Sloop. Note the fake counter stern.* (NMM)

gunfire and depth-charges in the Irish Sea on 25 December 1917, *Campanula* depth charged *UB-66* off Cape Bon on 18 January 1918, *Cyclamen* sank *UB-69* in the same area on 8 January 1918 by explosive paravane and depth charge, *Jessamine* and USS *Cushing* got *U-104* on 25 April 1918, and *Lychnis* sank *U-64* by gunfire and depth charge in the Tyrrhenian Sea on 17 June 1918, taking five prisoners, including her Captain, the celebrated Mohrart. Finally, *Wallflower* accounted for *U-32* in the Sicilian Channel on 8 May 1918. Unfortunately, *Cyclamen* had also sunk the Italian *Gugliemotti* in error – a type of mishap only too easy in wartime.

It is noticeable that most of these kills occurred in the Mediterranean, perhaps due to good visibility, and that four out of six resulted from attacks on convoys: if the pitcher came to the well, it stood a good chance of being broken.

Defensively, the class showed their ability to take punishment time and again; it usually took at least one torpedo or mine to sink them, and *Candytuft* floated onto the Tunisian coast minus bows and stern after two torpedo hits. If the big engine room flooded the ship usually sank, but otherwise the subdivision into 13 water-tight compartments, the coal, cork and magazine protection, the strong construction and good damage control proved their worth. The placing of the magazine aft avoided heavy casualties such as had occurred in the *Amphion* and *Pathfinder*. To avoid casualties on the mess decks forward, the hurricane deck was plated up and used as accommodation, with roller-blind type doors at the forward end.

Due to the Admiralty's refusal to adopt convoy until April 1917, a lot of time was spent on futile patrols and offensive sweeps against U-boats – what President Wilson called 'Hunting the hornets all round the farm'. (The Queenstown 'Flowers' referred to themselves as 'The Irish Lifeboat Service'.) The Admiralty never seemed to realize that the U-boat would normally see surface ships first, and could evade, dive or attack at its choice. Hence the emphasis on the Q-ship technique, by which a U-boat could sometimes be induced to expose itself to close-range gunfire. It also, understandably, caused the Germans to resort to 'sink on sight'.

The convoy sloops

This was the justification for the building of the 73rd and later 'Flowers', from the end of 1916 onward, as 'Convoy Sloops', or purpose-built Q-ships. The smaller *PC-boats* were similarly inspired. 'Convoy Sloop' was an intentionally misleading title since convoy was not yet adopted for normal traffic. Basically they were 'Flower' hulls, with extra power and with their hulls and superstructure built up to resemble merchantmen. Broadside on, the illusion was complete, but from bow, quarter or end-on their fine lines gave them away. Great care was taken with their appearance; they were usually modelled on ships built by the same firm and of appropriate length. The uptakes fed into one funnel and there was a normal three-island silhouette. Armament was originally planned as four 4in, but was usually two 4in, two 12pdr, depth charge throwers, and howitzers (usually 7.5in, but the *Pelargonium* had a 13.5in); 14in torpedo tubes taken from old torpedo-boats were not unknown. Actually, non-standard armaments were often fitted (the *Heather*, for example, had three 12pdr and two 3pdr).

The Aubretia *class Convoy Sloop* Tulip *in full Q-ship disguise. It fooled* U-62, *but the first torpedo hit brought down the screens of the armament.* (IWM)

Problems of scale often arose – hatches, ports and fittings had to be the right size, draft marks had to be falsified, rigging, aerials, boats and everything else had to be of mercantile type. Above all, inculcated naval smartness had to be forgotten. At least two ships were given away by flags being hoisted too smartly, while at least twice, an initial torpedo hit caused the armament to be exposed. The French *Andromede* was disguised as a ship 1½ times her length and was given a crew of men of two-thirds average height! One gun, or a dummy, was usually left exposed, to simulate the normal defensive gun. By 1917, U-boats usually carried an ex-merchant service reserve officer, to look out for such niceties.

Habitability posed a problem. The crew of about 90 was two or three times that of a small freighter, and all but a few of them had to stay below during daylight, in compartments where the holds should be, so that there was little ventilation. Derricks were so slight, for 'scale' reasons, as to be almost useless. The *Lychnis* reported having a small 'real' ventilator inside a large dummy one!

The coming of convoy spelt the end of the Q-ship trick, which was almost played out anyway, despite all the courage and ingenuity put into it, and in February 1918, the Admiralty decided that the crews of the Convoy Sloops should revert to normal conditions of service, which included wearing uniform. Minimum changes were made to the ships, which were mostly dazzle-painted, though no doubt their mercantile silhouettes created doubts in the minds of U-boat captains and thereby helped some merchantmen to escape.

In the original role

All this time, the minesweeping 'Flowers' swept on; they were succeeded on the slipways by the 'Twin Screw' or 'Hunt' class minesweepers, ordered after Jellicoe became First Sea Lord. (He had always hankered after faster sweepers, and had not liked the suggestion that he convert some of his 'M' class destroyers.) The 'Hunts' though faster, had nothing like the sea-keeping qualities of the 'Flowers'. In the anti-submarine role, the 'Flowers' were succeeded by the '24' class double-ended sloops, whose design was handed over to the Controller of Auxiliary Ships (a Major-General in the Royal Engineers), after the Constructors disowned them.

For most of the war, the 'A' and 'B' pair sweeps were used, with paravanes and single sweeps coming in. Minesweeping is said to require the mind of an intelligent ploughman, and with a pair sweep, poor station-keeping caused mines to slide remorselessly towards the lagging sweeper. Superb navigation and pilotage were essential. Spotting from the air helped, hence the seaplanes and balloons, and the 'Flowers' swept on, in line-abreast of pairs, line-of bearing of pairs, chains of up to five abreast, rarely line-ahead of pairs, V formations of pairs and sometimes, with an unusually tough field, a harrow of pairs, with the pairs in the rear line covering the gaps in the front line – a difficult formation for single-screwed ships.

The task went on long after Armistice Day; *Gentian* and

The Pelagonium *in dazzle camouflage. Even from this angle the fine warship lines give away the ship's true identity.* (IWM)

Myrtle were mined in the Gulf of Finland during the Russian 'Intervention'. When that was done, some of the more worn-out were scrapped, but others remained in reserve until the early 1930s. Some served far afield and they were fairly good for showing the flag – their two funnels made an impression out of proportion to their size. Their radius of action proved short for the China Station, and coaling gradually became more difficult with the world-wide change to oil. Refinements such as director control, oil firing and extra Lewis guns were gradually introduced. *Snapdragon* became a specialist target tug and *Bryony* was converted as the C-in-C Mediterranean's yacht – without proper authority, which led to some uproar. *Marjoram* and *Elphinstone* (ex-*Ceanothus*) were wrecked and *Valerian* was lost in a hurricane off Bermuda on 22 October 1926. (The Constructors and those in her engine room thought she had been blown onto a shoal.)

'Hull lives' proved unpredictable, but no-one would guarantee them beyond 1940. *Lupin*, *Rosemary* and *Foxglove*, the first of class, were still on the active list in 1939, but saw harbour service only. Soon thereafter, there were other ships with Flower names flying the White Ensign. Of the 120 original 'Flowers' the only survivors are *Chrysanthemum* and *Saxifrage* (as *President*), until very recently RNR training ships on London's Embankment. When the London Division acquired a 'stone frigate' for its headquarters the ships were sold to a trust which is currently refitting the *Chrysanthemum*. Unfortunately, the latest information suggests that their future is once again in doubt.

Principal sources

Flower Ship Covers ADM 138/488 to /496
Convoy Sloop Covers ADM 138/539 and 540
Loss & Damage Reports in PRO, ADM/137/3093
Salvia, /3150 *Begonia*, /3211 *Rosemary*, /3284 *Myosotis*, /3292 *Arbutus*, /3445 *Anchusa*, /3737 *Gaillardia*.
ADM 137/3374 *Cyclamen* v *Guglielmotti*.
ADM 137/3488 *Cyclamen* v *UB-69*.
Conways' all the World's Fighting Ships 1906–22, London 1985
Robert M Grant, *U-boats Destroyed*.
Martin Niemoller, *From U-boat to Pulpit*.
'Taffrail' *Swept Channels*, London 1935

The author would also like to acknowledge help from the staffs of the NMM, PRO and Admiralty Library, and from Mrs Elizabeth Dennys.

The 'Flower' Class. *BUILDING DATA AND FATE*

Name	*No (if known)*	*Builder*	*Launched*	*Fate*
ACACIA CLASS				
The first twelve: ordered 1 January 1915				
Acacia	1	Swan Hunter	15.4.15	Sold 1922
Anemone	2	Swan Hunter	13.5.15	Sold 1922
Foxglove	3	Barclay Curle	30.3.15	Sold 1946
Hollyhock	4	Barclay Curle	1.5.15	Sold 1930
Dahlia	5	Barclay Curle	21.4.15	Sold 1932
Daphne	6	Barclay Curle	19.5.15	Sold 1923
Bluebell	7	Scott	24.7.15	Sold 1930
Daffodil	8	Scott	17.8.15	Sold 1935
Aster	9	Earle	1.5.15	Mined Med 4.7.17
Honeysuckle	10	Lobnitz	29.4.15	Sold 1922
Iris	11	Lobnitz	2.6.15	Sold 1920
Marigold (ex-Ivy)	12	Bow, McLachlan	16.7.15	Sold 1922
The second twelve: ordered 12 January 1915				
Lily	1	Barclay Curle	16.6.15	Sold 1930 (ex depot ship)
Mallow	2	Barclay Curle	13.7.15	RAN; expended 1935
Sunflower	3	D & W Henderson	28.5.15	Sold 1921
Lilac	4	Greenock & Grangemouth	29.4.15	Sold 1922
Magnolia	5	Scott	26.6.15	Sold 1922
Veronica	6	Dunlop Bremner	27.5.15	Sold 1935
Jonquil	7	Connell	12.5.15	Sold 1920
Laburnum	8	Connell	10.6.15	Scuttled 2.42
Lavender	9	McMillan	12.6.15	Torpedoed, *UC-75* 4.5.17
Larkspur	10	Napier & Miller	11.5.15	Sold 1922
Primrose	11	Simons	29.6.15	Sold 1923
Mimosa	12	Bow McLachlan	16.7.15	Sold 1922
AZALEA CLASS				
The Third twelve: ordered 4 May 1915				
Azalea	1	Barclay Curle	10.9.15	Sold 1.2.23
Begonia	2	Barclay Curle	26.8.15	Sunk by *U-151* 2.10.17
Zinnia	3	Swan Hunter	12.8.15	Belgian Navy 19.4.20
Jessamine	4	Swan Hunter	9.9.15	Sold 1922
Narcissus	5	Napier & Miller	22.9.15	Sold 1922
Peony	6	McMillan	25.8.15	Sold 1919
Snowdrop	7	McMillan	7.10.15	Sold 1923
Clematis	8	Greenock & Grangemouth	29.7.15	Sold 1931
Carnation	9	Greenock & Grangemouth	16.9.15	Sold 1923
Camellia	10	Bow McLachlan	25.9.15	Sold 1923
Heliotrope	11	Lobnitz	10.9.15	Sold 1935
Myrtle	12	Lobnitz	11.10.15	Mined Gulf of Finland 16.7.19
ARABIS CLASS				
The Fourth nine: ordered 6 July 1915				
Alyssum	1	Earle	5.11.15	Mined SW Ireland 18.3.17
Amaryllis	2	Earle	9.12.15	Sold 1923
Arabis	3	D & W Henderson	6.11.15	Sunk by destroyers 10.2.16
Buttercup	4	Barclay Curle	24.10.15	Sold 1920
Campanula	5	Barclay Curle	25.12.15	Sold 1922
Crocus	6	Lobnitz	24.12.15	Sold 1930
Delphinium	7	Napier & Miller	23.12.15	Sold 1933
Gentian	8	Greenock & Grangemouth	23.12.15	Mined Gulf of Finland 16.7.19
Gladiolus	9	Connell	25.10.15	To Portugal 1920
The fifth twenty-one: ordered 15 July 1915				
Celandine	1	Barclay Curle	19.2.16	Sold 1923
Cornflower	2	Barclay Curle	10.3.16	Scuttled 19.12.41
Godetia	3	Connell	8.1.16	Scrapped 1937

Name	*No (if known)*	*Builder*	*Launched*	*Fate*
Hydrangea	4	Connell	2.3.16	Sold 1920
Asphodel	5	D & W Henderson	21.12.15	Sold 1920
Berberis	6	D & W Henderson	3.2.16	Sold 1923
Lobelia	7	Simons	7.3.16	Sold 1920; hulk 1924
Lupin	8	Simons	31.5.16	Sold 1946; sunk, BU 1947
Marguerite	9	Dunlop Bremner	23.11.15	RAN; expended 1935
Mignonette	10	Dunlop Bremner	26.1.16	Mined Galley Head 17.3.17
Myosotis	11	Bow McLachlan	4.4.16	Sold 1923
Geranium	12	Greenock & Grangemouth	8.11.15	RAN; expended 1935
Nasturtium	13	McMillan	21.12.15	Mined Malta 27.4.16
Genista	14	Napier & Miller	26.12.16	Sunk by *U-57* 23.10.16
Nigella	15	Hamilton	10.12.15	Sold 1922
Pansy	16	Hamilton	1.2.16	Sold 1920; requisitioned WWII
Pentstemon	17	Workman Clark	5.2.16	Sold 1920
Petunia	18	Workman Clark	3.4.16	Sold 1922
Poppy	19	Swan Hunter	9.11.15	Sold 1923
Primula	20	Swan Hunter	6.12.15	Sunk by *U-35* 1.3.16
Cyclamen	21	Lobnitz	22.2.16	Sold 1932
The sixth six: ordered 27 July 1915				
Rosemary	1	Richardson Duck	22.11.15	Sold 1947
Snapdragon	2	Ropner	21.12.15	Sold 1934
Valerian	3	Rennoldson	21.2.16	Lost 22.10.26
Verbena	4	Blyth SB	9.11.15	Sold 1933
Wallflower	5	Irvine	8.11.15	Sold 1931
Wisteria	6	Irvine	7.12.15	Sold 1931

The French 'Flowers'	Builder	*Launched*	*Commissioned*
Aldebaran	Barclay Curle	15.2.16	3.2.16
Algol	Barclay Curle	23.2.16	28.7.16
Altair	P G Hamilton	28.2.16	14.9.16
Antares	P G Hamilton	8.3.16	30.10.16
Bellatrix	D & W Henderson	22.2.16	17.7.16
Rigel	D & W Henderson	23.2.16	22.8.16
Cassiopée	Barclay Curle	11.16	12.4.17
Regulus	Barclay Curle	11.16	2.5.17

All similar to *Acacia/Azalea/Arabis* classes except: armament 2–14cm, 2–4.7cm and various changes to sweeping gear, accommodation, sanitation, water supply, etc to meet French requirements. Also *Andromede*, Convoy Sloop, altered to French requirements and armed with 2–14cm and 3–7.5cm.

Aubretia Class Convoy Sloops

As previously, except: 268ft oa, 255ft pp x 33½ft x 11½ft; 2500/2700ihp = 17½kts. Designed for 3–12pdr and 2–3pdr, in service (officially) 2–4in and 1–3pdr.

Name	Builder	Launched	Fate
Ordered January 1916			
Aubretia	Blyth	17.6.16	Sold 1922
Heather	Greenock & Grangemouth	16.6.16	Sold 1932
Salvia	Irvine	16.6.16	Sunk by *U-94* SW Ireland 20.6.17
Tamarisk	Lobnitz	2.6.16	Sold 1922
Tulip	Richardson Duck	15.7.16	Sunk by *U-62* 30.4.17
Viola	Ropner	14.7.16	Sold 1922
Ordered December 1916			
Andromeda	Swan Hunter	6.17	Became French *Andromede* later *Ville d'Ys*; scrapped 1945/46
Gaillardia	Blyth	19.5.17	Mined 22.3.18
Hibiscus	Greenock & Grangemouth	17.11.17	Sold 1923
Lychnis	Hamilton	21.8.17	RIM *Cornwallis*; sold 1946
Montbretia	Irvine	3.9.17	Sold 1921
Polyanthus	Lobnitz	24.9.17	Sold 1921

Name	No (if known)	Builder	Launched	Fate
ANCHUSA CLASS CONVOY SLOOPS				
As above, except: 262½ft 250ft x 35ft x 11½ft, 1290 tons; 2500(/2700?)ihp = 16½kts. Intended armament 2–4in, 2–12pdr.				
Ordered January 1917				
Anchusa		Armstrong	21.4.17	Sunk by *U-54*, off Ireland 16.7.18
Bergamot		Armstrong	5.5.17	Sunk by *U-84*, Atlantic, 13.8.17
Candytuft		Armstrong	19.5.17	Torpedoed, *U-39*, nr Bougie, CTL 18.11.17
Ceanothus		Armstrong	2.6.17	RIM *Elphinstone*; wrecked 29.1.25
Convolvulus		Barclay Curle	19.5.17	Sold 1921
Eglantine		Barclay Curle	22.6.17	Sold 1921
Spiraea		Simons	1.11.17	Sold 1922
Syringa		Workman Clark	29.9.17	Sold 1920
Ordered February 1917				
Arbutus		Armstrong	8.9.17	Sunk by *UB-65* St George's Channel 16.12.17
Auricula		Armstrong	4.10.17	Sold 1923
Bryony		Armstrong	27.10.17	Sold 1938
Chrysanthemum		Armstrong	10.11.17	RNVR 1938. Extant
Coreopsis		Barclay Curle	15.9.17	Sold 1922; BU 1924
Cowslip		Barclay Curle	19.10.17	Sunk by *UB-105*, Cape Spartel 24.4.18
Dianthus		Barclay Curle	1.12.17	Sold 1921
Gardenia		Barclay Curle	27.12.17	Sold 1923
Gilia		Barclay Curle	15.3.18	Sold 1923
Harebell		Barclay Curle	10.5.18	BU 12.39
Ivy		Blyth SB	31.10.17	Sold 1920/21
Marjoram		Greenock & Grangemouth	26.12.17	Wrecked under tow 1921
Mistletoe		Greenock & Grangemouth	17.11.17	Sold 1921
Pelargonium		Hamilton	18.3.18	Sold 1921
Rhododendron		Irvine	15.10.17	Sunk by *U-70*, North Sea 5.5.18
Saxifrage		Swan Hunter	5.10.17	RNVR *President* 1921. Extant
Silene		Simons	12.3.18	Sold 1921
Sweetbriar		Swan Hunter	5.10.17	Sold 1927
Tuberose		Swan Hunter	16.11.17	Sold 1923
Windflower		Workman Clark	12.4.18	Sold 1927

NAVAL WARFARE IN A NEW DIMENSION 1914–1918

The well-known naval aviation expert R D Layman details the surprisingly numerous aerial successes against the ships of all the belligerent powers during the First World War.

The concept of waging war from the air captured human imagination millennia before the existence of powered flight or even the balloon, as attested in the myths and folklore of many cultures. With the global rise of European seafaring and the foundation of modern sea power after the thirteenth century, the concept was increasingly projected into the realm of naval warfare, spawning hundreds of visionary proposals. Most of these centred around the balloon after its introduction in the late eighteenth century. All were pure fancy until technology caught up with imagination, an intersection that occurred during the years immediately before the First World War, the first conflict in which naval war could be waged in a new dimension.[1]

By the time that war ended, aircraft had become an integral instrument of sea power and had attacked ships hundreds or perhaps thousands of times, from the North Sea to the Pacific. The results of aerial offence in pursuit of maritime objectives during 1914–18 have almost universally been underrated, denigrated or ignored as picayune in comparison with the enormous success that aircraft had against ships in the Second World War and in comparison with the tonnage sunk by other agencies during the earlier conflict.

It cannot be denied that aircraft rate low in such comparisons, but their action was nowhere near as ineffective as often asserted. This study will discuss instances in which aircraft – a term encompassing aeroplanes, seaplanes, airships and balloons – either directly or indirectly in combination with surface craft were responsible for sinking, permanently disabling, capturing or otherwise neutralizing warships and merchant vessels.

The number of such instances is surprisingly large, considering the infancy of the air weapon. It would be even more surprising if the successes of aircraft in sinking non-mechanically powered seacraft could be included. These probably numbered hundreds – dhows and zebecs throughout the Levant, coal schooners in the Black Sea, barges on the Danube, lighters in ports from Ostend to Trebizond. Such a compilation is impossible, but could one be made and added to the successes achieved against powered vessels it is not inconceivable that, if the losses inflicted at Jutland are excepted, the conclusion would be that aircraft sent more tonnage to the bottom during 1914–18 than all the capital ships of the world combined.

Even if that is an exaggeration, the record of aircraft is remarkable for a weapon barely a decade old in 1914 and compares favourably with that of the submarine, a craft which, depending on how one defines 'submarine', had existed for at least a century but did not achieve its first true success until 5 September 1914, when *U-21* sank HMS *Pathfinder*.

That the aircraft was not even more successful was due to the limits of its still-evolving technology. Aero engines were unreliable, radius was short, navigation at sea more difficult than over land, bomb-loads light, bomb-sights inefficient. The state of naval aero weaponry was, despite some promising prewar experiments, primitive at the start. Typical attacks on ships in 1914 and early 1915 were carried out with carbines, anti-personnel darts or small hand-dropped bombs. The situation had improved radically by the end of the war; naval aircraft had been equipped with nearly every weapon they would employ in the next world conflict – machine-guns, small-calibre cannon, torpedoes, depth charges, mines, rockets, and bombs of more than 500lb weight.

There were still many handicaps to the use of these weapons. The continuing lack of a truly efficient bomb-sight made hitting a moving ship a matter of great difficulty, and the concept of achieving greater accuracy by dive bombing was only beginning to be explored. For this reason, the greatest successes were against stationary vessels, and a number of these were not intended targets but were struck accidentally by bombs aimed at harbour installations or other ships. Armoured ships remained highly resistant to aerial attack; although many armoured vessels were struck by bombs during 1914–18, none was sunk or sustained more than superficial damage. Nevertheless, remarkable progress had been made, and aerial offence at sea might well have become an important factor had hostilities continued into 1919.

While such action has been in general slighted by historians of the First World War, one aspect of it has been strangely exaggerated – its anti-submarine role. The myth

The first production torpedo plane of the Short Admiralty Type 184 series, No 184 itself, with its torpedo in place, being hoisted from Ben-my-Chree *in 1915.* (Cross & Cockade)

that aircraft sank anywhere up to a dozen German submarines continues to be published, although post-Second World War research has long demolished most of those claims.[2] Aircraft were indeed highly important in ASW, but that importance resided in deterrence rather than destruction.

On the other hand, the value of ASW aircraft acting in cooperation with surface vessels, which became such a major factor in the Second World War, has been underrated or ignored. This study will describe several examples of such cooperation. In each case, as in cases of indirect action by aircraft, the question arises as to whether the aircraft actually contributed to the result. The criterion has to be whether the same outcome could have been expected in the absence of the aircraft.

British ship losses

It has long been believed that the first British ship, and in fact the first ship of any nationality, to be sunk by aerial attack in the First World War was the 970-ton *Franz Fischer*, an ex-German war prize in use as a coastal collier. She sailed south from Hartlepool on 31 January 1916 and the next night was at anchor off the Kentish Knock when at 10.30pm, according to a contemporary account, 'a Zeppelin appeared right over the vessel ... and dropped a highly explosive bomb, which struck them [sic] amidships.'[3] The ship sank in two minutes and her master and twelve crewmen were drowned. There were three survivors, and apparently the testimony of one or more of them was responsible for attributing the attack to an airship.

Postwar research, however, established that there were no German airships over Britain on the night of 2/3 February. There had been a nine-ship raid the previous night, but the last of these Zeppelins to clear the British coast had departed at 6.25am on the 2nd and none of them on their return flights had gone farther south than extreme north-east Suffolk.

If *Franz Fischer* was indeed the victim of aerial attack, there is a slim possibility her assailant was a seaplane from *Seeflugstation Flanders I* at Zeebrugge. Aircraft from this base carried out a number of pinprick raids on the Kentish coast during early 1916, and in describing them the British official air history [4] notes that on 1 February a coastal collier at anchor off the Kentish Knock was sunk by a bomb.

A Gotha WD11, minus its torpedo, suspended from an aircraft-handling crane, probably at Zeebrugge or Nordeney. (Peter M Grosz)

Against this possibility, however, is the reported 10.30pm time of sinking, for at that stage of the war the only German aircraft operating over Britain at night were Zeppelins.

All this negative evidence points to the probable conclusion that *Franz Fischer* was not sunk from the air, but more likely by a drifting mine. Numbers of mines laid by both sides slipped their moorings during the early war years, the British devices being especially notorious for this defect. The survivors' belief that their ship had been bombed by a Zeppelin is understandable, for the airship raids were at their height, and reports and rumours about them were widespread. A trick of light and cloud seen overhead just before a devastating explosion could easily have led to the wrong conclusion.

If *Franz Fischer* is eliminated, the first British surface ship lost to aerial attack was the 84-ton drifter *Rosies*, hired by the Admiralty in May 1915 as a net vessel. [5] The morning of 26 August 1916 found her among a group of drifters working nets approximately 12 miles east-north-east of Cape Santa Maria di Leuca, Italy, near the western end of the Otranto Barrage. The group was commanded by Lieutenant Knight, RNR, in the drifter *Craigbo*, apparently the only armed vessel in the group, carrying either a 3pdr or 6pdr gun on a high-angle mount – probably one of 37 guns obtained from the Italian navy to eke out the meagre ordnance available for the drifters. [6]

Sometime between 6am and 7am the drifters were approached by three Austro-Hungarian *k u k Kriegsmarine* Lohner type T flying-boats, L132, L133 and L134, operating either from *Seeflugstation* Kumbor, the air base for Cattaro, or its sub-station at Durazzo. Upon sighting them, Knight ordered the drifters to disperse, but *Craigo* apparently stayed in company with *Rosies*. While its companions circled in support, L132, piloted by *Fliegerunteroffizier* Hasche with *Linienschiffsleutnant* Alois Poljanec as observer, picked out *Rosies* as a target. Her crewmen were firing at the aircraft with rifles when its bomb struck the forecastle. The drifter sank rapidly, but not before her crew was able to launch a boat and escape without casualty. The airmen claimed a second hit aft on the port side and reported seeing a boiler explosion as the vessel went down.

L132 then went after *Craigbo*, but was driven off by her extremely accurate gunfire. A British account states that the other two aircraft joined in this attack with ineffectual machine-gun fire before all three made off. Upon its return to base, L132 was found to have been punctured twenty-two times, probably by *Craigbo*'s gun but perhaps also by *Rosie*'s rifle fire.

The Lohner Type T was a two-seat biplane flying-boat with a single pusher-mounted engined ranging from 145 to 160hp and a bomb-load of up to 330lb. More than 90 of them were built during 1915–16 and were a mainstay of the Austro-Hungarian naval air arm during those years.

About two weeks before *Rosies* was sunk, the Royal Navy lost its first submarine to air attack. It was the obsolescent *B-10* (280/314 tons), which had arrived at Venice in December 1915, the last of six 'B' class sisters to compose a squadron formally established on 1 January 1916.

On the night of 9/10 August *B-10* was moored alongside the Italian armoured cruiser *Marco Polo*, administrative flagship for the submarine squadron, when the sixth Austro-Hungarian air raid since the previous September hit Venice. There was apparently advance warning of the raid, for *B-10*'s crew had closed her hatches and taken shelter

A torpedo ready for placement in the fuselage casing of a Gotha WD11. The propellers of the aircraft's pusher engines have been removed. (Peter M Grosz)

below decks in the cruiser before the bombs began to fall.

The attack was mounted by 21 aircraft, all flying-boats, from *Seeflugstation* Trieste (L99, L98, L114, L136, L126, L125, L137 and K301), its sub-stations at Puntisella and Cosada (L65, L95, L94, L90, L74, L123, L76, L117, L62 and L69) and *Seeflugstation* Parenzo (L116, L115 and L119). Their general target was the Italian navy yard (*Regio Arsenale di Venezia*), so it is impossible to ascertain which particular aircraft dropped a bomb that exploded about 5ft below the surface close to *B-10*. The explosion blew a large hole in the submarine's lower port side, started several leaks elsewhere and sank the boat instantly. The concussion caused battery leaks in *B-8*, moored 40ft away. *B-10* was raised on 23 August and placed in drydock, where damage survey concluded that repair would be uneconomical. She was sold locally for scrapping in October.

Several months were to elapse before the next British vessels fell victim to aircraft. All were merchantmen and all were sunk by torpedo or combined torpedo and bomb attack.

The torpedo plane came relatively late to the German navy. Patents for aerial carriage and discharge of torpedoes had been issued before the war in Britain, the United States and Italy; experiments in torpedo dropping had been carried out in Britain and Italy, and the first British torpedo planes became operational in 1915. Early British torpedo plane design centred on single-engine floatplanes that although moderately successful were never really satisfactory, for reasons to be explored later.

The German navy, after unsuccessful early-war experiments with single-engine aeroplanes, concentrated on large twin-engine floatplanes sturdy enough to carry 450mm (17.7in) torpedoes. Nearly 150 aircraft designed along these lines were produced, in at least nine separate types, including one intended purely for torpedo attack training. Although differing in horsepower and configuration (including even some variants within types), all were basically two- or three-seat, twin-engine, twin-float biplanes. Only three types, however, saw operational use in their intended role – the Gotha WD11 (13 produced), Gotha WD14 (69 produced) and Hansa-Brandenburg GW (26 produced).

During late 1916 and early 1917 torpedo plane squadrons were established on the Baltic coast, the North Frisian island of Nordeney, and at Zeebrugge in occupied Belgium, where the first WD14 to be assigned was first test-flown on 25 March 1917. Eventually, two torpedo plane squadrons were based at Zeebrugge.

From mid-April to early September 1917 the British official air history records 15 torpedo plane attacks on shipping in the general area of the southern North Sea north of the Dover Straits. Only three, however, were successful. The first success came on 1 May when the 2478-ton collier *Gena* was sunk north-east of Southwold by a torpedo from Hansa-Brandenburg GW No701 (*Oberleutnant zur See* Wedel, pilot; *Leutnant der Reserve* Kruger, observer) from Zeebrugge's *Torpedostaffel* II. The torpedo, dropped at a range of about 3950yds, struck abreast a forward cargo hold, sending the vessel down by the bow. No701 was accompanied by Hansa-Brandenburg GW No703, which was forced down on the water either by the second of two shots *Gena*'s crew managed to get off from their single light gun or by mechanical failure. Its pilot, *Leutnant zur See* Freude, and observer, *Flugmaat* Berghoff, were captured by nearby patrol vessels that rescued *Gena*'s crew without casualty.

The next victim was the 3718-ton merchantman *Kankatee*, torpedoed off Harwich on 14 June by Gotha WDII No 991 of *Torpedostaffel* II with the loss of three crewmen.

The last of the unfortunate trio was the 440-ton *Storm*, caught with her cargo of coke off the Sunk light vessel on 19 September by seven aircraft from the Zeebrugge *Torpedostaffel* I. After one torpedo had passed beneath her, she was hit aft by one from Gotha WDII No 1213, then by a bomb that destroyed the steering gear and the captain's cabin. Going down, *Storm* was hit by at least one more bomb and her decks were raked by machine-gun fire. Three crew members were killed.

This example of overkill was the swan-song of the German torpedo plane in the North Sea. The long campaign had not achieved results commensurate with cost in material, personnel and time. Only three successes had been attained and at least three torpedo planes lost. The aircraft, even with two engines, were still dangerously underpowered: they were tricky to fly, requiring highly skilled pilots who had to undergo lengthy training in torpedo tactics, and the low, straight runs they need for accurate aiming left them vulnerable to gunfire. Consequently, aerial torpedo attack was abandoned after 1917 and the remaining aircraft were used for long-range patrolling, many of them fitted with extra fuel tanks in place of torpedoes.

Elsewhere during 1917, far from the North Sea, a single aircraft was directly or indirectly instrumental in the loss of more British mercantile shipping than could be credited to the entire German navy and army air services combined throughout the war. It was a Friedrichshafen FF33e (No 841) embarked on the commerce raider *Wolf*. A twin-float, two-seat, single-engine 150hp biplane, it was one of more than 400 craft of similar configuration produced during the war by *Flugzeugbau* Friedrichshafen GmbH, a subsidiary of *Luftschiffbau* Zeppelin, builder of the giant airships. The pilot was *Leutnant zur See der Reserve* M A Stein and the observer *Oberflugmeister der See* Paul Fabeck, with *Flugzeug-Obermaschinen-Maat Remy* attached as mechanic.

The role of the seaplane, quickly nicknamed *Wölfchen* ('Little Wolf' or 'Wolf Cub'), was to scout out pray for the raider, but it was also given a supply of hand-held bombs that proved their value on several occasions. The first came on 1 March 1917 in the Indian Ocean, when the combined threat of bombing by the aircraft and gunfire from *Wolf* forced the 4152-ton British *Jumma* to surrender. She was sunk three days later. On 11 March, still in the Indian Ocean, a reconaissance flight enabled *Wolf* to chase down and capture the 3509-ton British *Wordsworth* after she was identified from the air as a merchantman and not a warship that *Wolf* would not dared to have approached. She was sunk on 18 March.

Soon after this the raider steamed into the Pacific and on 2 June was sheltering in an uninhabited anchorage off Raoul (Sunday) Island, with two boilers shut down for cleaning, when a merchant vessel came into view, close enough to establish that she was wireless-equipped. *Wolf* being in no condition to give chase, her commander, *Fregattenkapitän* Karl Nerger, ordered the seaplane to intercept. A message bag was dropped on the merchantman's deck with a note in English ordering her to maintain wireless silence and steer for *Wolf* under threat of bombing, and this was followed by a warning bomb off the bow. The ship complied and soon the 3947-ton *Wairuna*, of New Zealand registry, was in *Wolf*'s hands. After 1200 tons of much-needed coal was taken from

*A Hansa-Brandenburg GW, the second type of torpedo plane active against British shipping in 1917. The GW's engines, unlike those of the WD11, were in the tractor position. (*Peter M Grosz*)*

Wolf's *Friedrichshafen FF33e on deck after the raider's return to Germany. The insignia, serial number and nickname have been painted on for display; the aircraft carried no markings during its operational career. It is typical of the Friedrichshafen series, which were the principal aircraft of the German carriers. (*Peter M Grosz*)*

her, she was sunk on 17 June.

On 28 July *Wolf* began stalking the 1618-ton Australian freighter *Matunga*, having learned through intercepted wireless messages that she was en route from Sydney to Rabaul with a valuable cargo. Daily flights by the seaplane failed to find her. Finally, on 5 August, a wireless signal from *Matunga* was heard announcing her arrival time at Rabaul the next day. A night flight, highly dangerous because the aircraft could easily be lost in the darkness, located the freighter and her course was signalled to *Wolf* by flares.

Skilful piloting by Fabeck returned the seaplane safely, and *Wolf*'s lookouts sighted *Matunga*'s lights at 11pm. She was captured at 7am the next day, *Wolfchen* again aiding with the threat of bombing. She was sunk on 26 August.

In these captures, and two others to be described later, the seaplane proved of inestimable value to *Wolf*, for in each case the prize would almost certainly have evaded or escaped the raider except for aerial reconnaissance and/or the threat of aerial bombing. Its work was accomplished under considerable handicaps, for it was constantly being damaged by wind, wave, climate, blast from *Wolf* 's guns and, on one occasion, by funnel sparks, and its maintenance was an epic of improvisation. Despite these problems, it made between 54 and 56 flights (records disagree), the greatest number by far of any shipboard aircraft of 1914-18, and with *Wolf* pioneered the techniques that would be used by aircraft-equipped German surface raiders of the Second World War.[7]

The first two British naval casualties of air attack in 1918 were submarines, one sunk mistakenly by an ally, one disabled by enemy action.

The first was *D-3* (550/620 tons), attached to the 6th Submarine Flotilla at Portsmouth. Under command of Lieutenant William McK Maitland-Dougall, RCN, she sailed on 7 March 1918 for anti-submarine patrolling in the English Channel with a return rendezvous scheduled for 14 March off the Brighton light ship. At 11.37am on 12 March the French airship *ATO*, commanded by *Enseigne de vaisseau 1ère classe* Saint-Remy, lifted off from the Le Havre airship base, also for anti-submarine patrol in the Channel. This non-rigid was the former British *C-1*, first of the 'C' (Coastal) class. It had first flown in June 1915 and was transferred to France when a French naval airship service was established in 1916. The 'C' class ships were lofted by 170,000cuft of hydrogen, powered by two 150hp engines, carried a crew of three to five and were armed with one or two Lewis guns and a bomb-load of varying weight.

At 2.20pm one of *ATO*'s crewmen sighted a vessel which when approached could be recognized as a surfaced submarine heading west. No identification markings could be seen on it, and as the airship neared it began firing rockets. These, it was realized later, were obviously an attempt of establishing identity, but they conformed to no signal or code known to the Frenchmen and seemed to be aimed at *ATO*. Believing the vessel to be hostile, Saint-

HMS/M D-3, *sunk by accident by the French airship* ATO. *(*CPL*)*

Remy ordered his Lewis gunner to fire at it, and tracers could be seen striking the hull just before the boat started to dive. *ATO* dropped two 52kg (115lb) bombs, but they missed by more than 60ft and their release caused the airship to rise and lose sight momentarily of the submarine.

When control was regained the vessel had vanished underwater but was leaving a distinct wake. *ATO* aimed four more 52kg bombs at this track, two falling directly on its projected path. The airship again jinked skyward, and upon descending once more its crewmen saw a patch of frothing water from which the submarine's conning tower emerged briefly. Four men were seen clambering from it before the vessel went down.

Saint-Remy brought the airship down to about 60ft from the surface, where when its motors were stopped he could hear the survivors shouting in English. Unable to force *ATO* low enough to pick them up, he dropped his crew's lifejackets and ordered the wireless operator to call for assistance. The signals, however, were too weak to be heard through heavy wireless traffic in the Channel, and the wireless set itself appeared to have a defect. Consequently, after making a landfall to establish as nearly as possible the survivors' position – about 30 miles north-west of Fécamp on the French coast – Saint-Remy tried to find a surface ship to assist. The first two he found, a trawler and a motorboat, refused to leave their assigned stations. The next, the French destroyer *Typhon*, was more cooperative, casting off the disabled fishing vessel she was towing and following *ATO* to the site of the submarine sinking. Their combined search, however, found no sign of the survivors and *ATO* returned to Le Havre at 7.25pm.

D-3 was reported missing on 15 March after failing to keep her rendezvous the previous day, which accounts for the fact that her loss is often incorrectly listed as having occurred on the 15th. A French court of inquiry, at which a British liaison officer testified favourably for *ATO*'s crew, concluded that Saint-Remy had acted correctly under the circumstances and absolved him of blame for the tragic accident – although it was kept secret for some time.

The ordeal of the next British submarine casualty, *C-25*, began at 12.45pm on 6 July 1918, when she was sighted on the surface off Harwich by five German seaplanes from Zeebrugge's fighter *Staffel* I. These aircraft were not, as many accounts have stated, returning from a raid on Lowestoft but had taken off an hour and 45 minutes earlier for a North Sea patrol. They were Hansa-Brandenburg W29s, single-engine, two-seat, twin-float, low-wing monoplane fighters designed by the famous Ernst Heinkel. The W29 has been called Heinkel's outstanding First World War design, and beneath its tangle of float struts and forest of jutting exhaust pipes of its 150hp engine could be seen in embryo the sleek lines of his Second World War aircraft. It was armed with one flexible and one or two fixed forward-firing machine-guns.

After manoeuvring to dive with the sun behind them, the seaplanes attacked *C-25* with a torrent of fire from these guns. The four men on the submarine's conning tower had at first assumed the aircraft were friendly, and were cut down as they tried to man the Lewis gun that was *C-25*'s sole aerial defence. Three, including the commanding officer, Lieutenant Bell, were killed instantly and the fourth, a leading seaman, died after being pulled into the vessel. *C-25* tried to rig for diving but was delayed when the leg of one of the dead men became wedged in the conning tower hatch. Two more men were killed in attempts to dislodge it until in a final grisly expedient it was amputated. By the time this had been accomplished *C-25* was incapable of diving, for the pressure hull had been holed numerous times and the electric motors destroyed. The aircraft continued to attack for 35 minutes, firing more than 5000 rounds. Near the end of this action, the submarine *E-51*, returning from patrol, approached and fired a few shots at the seaplanes from her 12pdr gun. Some accounts say this drove the aircraft away, but the log of *Seeflugstation Flanders I* makes it clear that they broke off because ammunition had been exhausted.[8]

Meanwhile, four more seaplanes had taken off at Zeebrugge to join the action, possibly summoned by a wireless report from the attacking flight.[9] One of them tried to bomb *C-25* with missiles that fell close but failed to hit. (This aircraft probably was not a W29 but an earlier Heinkel biplane design, the Hansa-Brandenburg W12.) A final attack by three monoplanes occurred sometime before 4pm. At some point, machine-gun fire was directed at *E-51* but she apparently was not damaged and she towed *C-25*, now completely broken down, into port. It is unclear whether repair of *C-25* was undertaken, but she never returned to wartime service and was sold for breaking-up in 1921.

Hansa-Brandenburg W29s figured prominently in the Royal Navy's final air-inflicted losses of the First World War – six motor torpedo-boats sunk, scuttled or forced into internment on 11 August 1918 during a running battle off the Dutch coast. This action resulted from the fifth attempt since the previous June to attack German minesweepers and their supporting units with coastal motor boats (CMBs), as the torpedo craft were originally called, carried by

Two Hansa-Brandenburg W29s of the Nordeney air station on patrol in 1918. W29s were the principal types involved in action against a British CMB squadron and submarine C-25. (Cross & Cockade)

cruisers of the Harwich Force and supported by flying-boats towed on special lighters by Harwich Force destroyers.

None of the earlier attempts had been successful. The fifth and what was to prove the final such operation began with the sailing of the Harwich Force at 9pm on 10 August – light cruisers *Curacoa*, *Coventry*, *Concord* and *Danae* and thirteen destroyers. Three of the cruisers carried two CMBs each in their davits. They were 5-ton, 40ft sisters built in 1918, Nos *39*, *40*, *41*, *42*, *44* and *47*, under command of Lieutenant-Commander A L Coke. Destroyers *Retriever*, *Thisbe* and *Teaser* each towed a flying-boat on a lighter and another destroyer (probably *Starfish*) towed a kite balloon, for it had been found during the earlier operations that a balloon was an excellent homing mark for returning aircraft. Finally, because the Harwich Force had been attacked by a Zeppelin during the previous foray, an innovation was added – a Sopwith 2F1 Camel (No N6812, now on display at the Imperial War Museum), the shipboard version of the famous fighting plane, was towed by the destroyer *Redoubt* on a lighter from which it could take off at high speed. Further aerial support was to be supplied by flying-boats from Yarmouth that were to rendevous with the surface force after the CMBs were launched.

Curacoa wore the flag of Acting Rear-Admiral Sir Reginald Tyrwhitt, redoubtable commander of the Harwich Force throughout the war and an able and ardent advocate of shipboard aviation and combined air–sea tactics. Since April, his supporting aircraft were no longer components of the navy but under the jurisdiction of the newly formed Royal Air Force. This had little effect upon joint operations, however, mainly because many of the RAF aviators were from the now-defunct Royal Navy Air Service. At 6am (7am local time) the Harwich Force reached the CMB launching point, about 25 miles north-west of the Dutch island of Vieland, from whence they were to enter German waters in the Heligoland Bight after skirting the Dutch islands of Terschelling and Ameland. All the CMBs were in the water within 10 minutes, but the destroyer-towed flying-boats were unable to take off because of a combination of ground swell and absence of wind.

About the time the CMBs were being lowered the British force was spotted by one or more of four patrolling German seaplanes. They were probably from *Kampfstaffel* V based on Borkum island, for four of its aircraft had taken off earlier for patrol. They were three W29s and a Friedrichshafen FF49c biplane. In response to reports of the British presence, five aircraft from Borkum's *Kampfstaffel* I took off – probably W29s but possibly including a biplane or two. They were followed by two W29s, two W12s and an FF49c from the Nordeney air base.

These 14 aircraft mounted among them a minimum of 32 machine-guns, and this massive firepower was soon directed at the CMBs. Their first attack came as the boats were abreast Terschelling. The CMBs, which had been cruising in quarter-line pairs to avoid each other's wakes, closed up to concentrate fire from the one or two Lewis guns each carried. For the first 30 minutes or so the boats sustained little damage, but as increasing numbers of seaplanes appeared they began to suffer badly. Some bombs were dropped, probably from the Friedrichshafens, but none hit; the real damage was from the machine-guns, whose bullets sliced easily through the CMB's mahogany and plywood hulls.

The situation worsened about 8am when Coke, realizing he must retire, turned the boats westward and placed the sun behind the aircraft, blinding the British gunners. At this point, as the British air history puts it, 'The action developed into one of target practice for the enemy pilots.'[10] A contemporary British report describes the seaplanes' tactics: 'They flew low and from dead astern, the pilot keeping up a sustained and accurate fire, then turned in a steep bank while the observer fired.'[11]

Although the CMS manoeuvred at 30kts or more, the aircraft retained a speed advantage that made their fire nearly impossible to avoid. At the same time, high-speed manoeuvring began to exhaust the boats' 100-gallon fuel tanks while sustained firing depleted their Lewis gun ammunition. While their bullets remained, however, the gunners fought back bravely. W29 No 2297 was shot down, probably by some of the last rounds from Nos *40* and *44*, and its two-man crew killed. W29 No 2051 was forced down, but its occupants were rescued.

Shortly after 8am *CMB 40* and *42* were wallowing helplessly. Out of fuel and ammunition, riddled by gunfire, they were scuttled. *CMB 47*, set afire, was blown up by her crew after drifting to within a half mile of Terschelling. No *41* beached on the island and was ultimately interned, as were Nos *39* and *44*, taken in tow by a Dutch torpedo-boat after drifting into Dutch waters. British casualties were surprisingly light – four officers and two ratings wounded by bullets or burned. Two burn victims from *CMB 47* were rescued from the sea by Dutch sailors swimming from Terschelling who were subsequently awarded the Board of Trade Silver Medal for life-saving.

Earlier, at 7.10, three flying-boats from Yarmouth had rendezvoused with the Harwich Force as prearranged, but because visibility in the air was strangely less clear than on the surface had failed to see Tyrwhitt's signal directing them toward the CMBs. How successful they might have been in protecting the boats is questionable, for the flying-boats, although heavily armed, usually did not fare well when tangling with the nimble German seaplane fighters. They might, however, have diverted the Germans from their surface prey.

Although the flying-boats could not discern the CMBs or the German aircraft, they did spot a Zeppelin that they reported to Tyrwhitt by visual signal. He had already been appraised of its presence by wireless from the Admiralty. The airship was *L-53* and a quite accurate reading of its position had been gained from a wireless message intercepted and decoded by the famous (and then highly secret) Room 40. The Harwich Force turned seaward in an attempt to lure the airship farther out to sea, and at 8.41 the Camel took off from its lighter. Exactly one hour later the fighter's Canadian pilot, Lieutenant S D Culley, brought *L-53* down in an inferno of flaming hydrogen that killed its entire crew. It was the final German airship loss of the war.

Because of the odd conditions of aerial visibility that morning, it took Culley two hours to locate the Harwich Force, alight at sea and be picked up. By then the CMBs had been long overdue, and Tyrwhitt had turned to search for them, assisted in the afternoon by three flying-boats summoned from Yarmouth by wireless. They found nothing and were ordered to return. After more futile searches, the Harwich Force retired, harassed unsuccessfully until nightfall by a few German aircraft.

So ended an action unique at the time in the annals of naval warfare, 'historic', as a British aero historian noted later, 'in that during it, aircraft inflicted a greater loss on sea-going craft than at any other time during the war'.[12] In

fact, not until a quarter of a century later, during the Battle of the Bismarck Sea in 1943, was such total destruction of a surface force achieved solely by aerial action.

German losses

The first German vessel that may have been lost to air attack in the First World War was the submarine *UB-7* (127/142 tons), which with her sister *UB-8* was sent in sections by rail in early 1915 to Pola for erection at that Austro-Hungarian Adriatic port. After delays caused by leakage and engine trouble, *UB-7* arrived at Constantinople on 21 June 1915 to become the first German submarine to operate in the Black Sea.

On 27 September 1916 *UB-7* left the Bulgarian port of Varna for patrol off the Crimea and was never seen again. A captured Russian aviator later testified that a submarine had been bombed by a flying-boat off the Kheronese peninsula on 1 October, and on this basis it was generally accepted that the target was *UB-7*. One German source[13] pin-points her loss as occurring at 44°30′N/33°15′E, which roughly coincides with the area mentioned by the aviator. Other sources, German and Russian, are less definite, suggesting the loss may have been due to a mine, mechanical defect, or other unknown cause. A Soviet history of the Russian navy in the First World War[14] notes *UB-7*'s loss but does not describe the circumstances or attribute a cause. If the submarine was indeed sunk by a flying-boat, the aircraft undoubtedly was a Gregorovich M5 or M9, the principal types operated by the Black Sea Fleet. Both were two-seat biplanes, differing mainly in the type and horsepower of their single pusher engines.

The first German surface vessels to fall victim to aircraft were the 187-ton tug *Zuiderzee* (a former Dutch vessel acquired in 1916), and *Hafenwache II*, which meagre data indicate was a small harbour craft. They were hit and sunk by some of the 59 bombs dropped on Bruges harbour on 16 February 1917 in a raid by eight Sopwith 1½-Strutters (officially Sopwith Type 9700) of No 5 Wing, Royal Naval Air Service, based near Dunkirk. The attack was directed at the harbour in general, and the two ships undoubtedly were struck by chance. One crewman was wounded on *Zuiderzee*, which was soon raised, repaired and returned to service. She was scuttled in October 1918 during the German withdrawal from Belgium but her fate is untraceable. The smaller craft was apparently a total loss.

Similar random bombing accounted for torpedo boat *A-13*, the only German surface warship known to have been sunk by air attack during the war. A war-built unit of 137 tons, she was hit at Ostend during a night raid on 16 August 1917 by twin-engine Handley-Page 0/100s of No 7 Squadron, RNAS, which dropped seventy-two 112lb, seven 65lb and four 250lb bombs. One crew member was killed. *A-13* was raised but found beyond economical repair. The wreckage was towed to Bruges and scrapped later in 1917.

A German loss that is difficult to place chronologically was submarine *UC-70*, a minelaying craft of 427/508 tons, for she was sunk twice with aircraft as the indirect or contributary cause. The first occurred on 5 July 1917 when she was lying alongside an oil lighter that was hit during a bombardment of Ostend dockyard by British monitors *Erebus* and *Terror*, whose fire was directed by two De Haviland DH4 land-based observation planes. Casualties, if any, seem to have been unrecorded. *UC-70* was raised and repaired, only to meet her final fate after sailing from Zeebrugge on 21 August 1918 to operate in the North Sea off Whitby. Seven days later she was trailing an oil wake from bunker leakage or mine damage that was sighted by the crew of a land-based Blackburn Kangaroo patrol bomber from Seaton Carew. The aircraft followed the slick to its apparent source, where it dropped a 520lb bomb that produced a gush of oil and bubbles. The aviators summoned the destroyer *Ouse* to the site with flare signals, and ten depth charges from the ship and another bomb from the aircraft destroyed *UC-70*, her entire 31-man crew dying. The loss and the submarine's identity were established by British divers on 14 September.

◀ *A Sopwith 1½-Strutter (Sopwith Admiralty Type 9700) of the single-seat bomber version responsible for the first German losses of surface ships to aerial attack.* (Author's collection)

The aircraft involved in this action, the Blackburn Kangaroo, represents a significant evolutionary step in use of aircraft in ASW, helping to establish the superiority of land-based aeroplanes over seaplanes and airships in that role, although it was produced in only a small quantity (11 to 14 machines) and had some unpleasant flight characteristics. Stemming from an original seaplane design, it was a three-seat twin-engine biplane. With a one-ton bomb capacity and an endurance of eight hours, it was superior in those respects to the Avro Anson, Coastal Command's principal anti-submarine aeroplane in 1939, and nearly comparable to the Anson's successor, the American Lockheed Hudson.

Returning to 1917, a German submarine lost in July of that year may have been an indirect victim of aerial observation, but the facts are muddled. Shortly before, Admiral Sir David Beatty had ordered the formation of a special anti-submarine division of six of the Grand Fleet's destroyers at Scapa Flow to carry out independent hunting sweeps of known North Sea U-boat routes, some of the vessels towing kite balloons whose observers would be able to spot a surfaced submarine's low silhouette before it was visible from shipboard.

The second of these sweeps began on 11 July 1917 by five destroyers, three lofting balloons. The next morning the balloonist of the destroyer *Patriot* sighted a surfaced U-boat at 28 miles distance. It dived as *Patriot* headed for it, then surfaced and resubmerged as the destroyer opened fire. A depth charge attack resulted in a violent underwater explosion and a large gush of oil. It was believed this marked the death of *U-69* (791/933 tons), which had sailed from Emden on 9 July for Irish waters. Much later research, however, indicated that wireless signals had been received from *UC-69* as late as 23 July. Some sources state she was lost in the Irish Sea on 24 July, while others accept the 12 July date in the North Sea, and still others list the date and cause of loss as unknown. The puzzle remains unsolved.

A case of mixed identity long clouded the fate of the only German submarine of the First World War almost certainly sunk by direct, unassisted aerial action. The mix-up involved *UB-32* (247/308 tons), believed to have been sunk on 18 August 1917 in the English Channel off Cap Barfleur by an RNAS seaplane from Cherbourg, and *UC-72*, whose destruction was credited to a British flying-boat on 22 September 1917 in the West Hinder area. Not until after the Second World War was it established that *UC-72* had in fact been sunk by the Q-ship *Acton* on 20 August 1917 in the Bay of Biscay, while *UB-32* had not sailed from Zeebrugge for the western Channel until 10 September, more than a month after the date of her supposed loss. With the facts sorted out, it appears virtually beyond doubt that *UB-32* and her 23 crewmen were the victims of the attack made at 50°08′N/01°13′W on 22 September by Curtiss H12 flying boat No 8695, flying from Dunkirk with a Sopwith Camel fighter escort.

UB-32's sister, *UB-31*, was lost in the same general area the next year, partially as the result of aerial observation. On the morning of 2 May 1918 this Zeebrugge-based minelayer encountered the British drifters *Lord Leitrim*, *Loyal Friend* and *Ocean Roamer*, accompanied by the airship *SSZ-29*, in the Dover Straits. Guided by signals from *SSZ-29*, which may have been assisted by the French airship *VZ-22*, the drifters forced *UB-31* to submerge in the vicinity of a mine field, where she and her crew of 26 were destroyed at 51°06′N/01°28′W either by depth charges from the ships or by striking a mine.

The non-rigid *SSZ-29* was one of the 'Submarine Scout Zero' class constructed during the war. Powered by a single 75hp engine, they were armed with a Lewis gun and could carry two 65lb bombs as well as wireless.[15] Although these ships, together with the earlier 'Submarine Scout' (SS) class, flew countless ASW patrols, *SSZ-29* was the first to be active in a U-boat kill.

Another of the minelaying boats, *UB-59* (516/646 tons), was put permanently out of action on 16 May 1918 when she was hit by a random bomb while in the floating drydock at Bruges undergoing repair of mine damage. The attack was probably by Handley-Page 0/100 or 0/400 bombers of No 24 Squadron, Royal Air Force. The additional damage resulted in an estimate that complete repair would require six months, and consequently *UB-59* never returned to sea. She was blown up in early October during the German evacuation of Belgium.

Two days after *UB-59* was struck, a combination of wireless intelligence and aerial attack ended the career of the second most successful submarine of both world wars in terms of tonnage sunk. She was the notorious *U-39* (685/878 tons), credited with sinking 154 ships totalling 404,478 tons. Most of her successes were gained while she was commanded by one of the greatest U-boat skippers, *Kapitänleutant* Walter Forstmann. She was no longer under his command, however, when on 15 May 1918 French wireless monitors intercepted a signal from her that located the boat west of Cartagena, Spain, at 37°15′N/01°40′W and indicated she was headed westward. On the basis of this information *U-39* was intercepted on the afternoon of 18 May by between two and six French seaplanes. She immediately dived, but was damaged by two bombs when she was 12m underwater. Upon surfacing, it was found that damage to the pressure hull made resubmergence impossible.

Consequently, *U-39* made for Cartagena as the nearest port of refuge. Later in the afternoon she was again attacked by two seaplanes that she beat off with machine-gun and rifle fire, sustaining no damage but losing two crewmen overboard. She reached Cartagena without further incident and was interned. Surrendered to France postwar, she was broken up at Toulon in 1923. The author has been unable to identify the French aircraft involved, but they were probably Tellier flying-boats from an Algerian or Moroccan base. The site of either the first or second attack has been given as 36°36′N/00°02′W.

Observation from the air brought destruction to three more of the UB-boats in September 1918. On the 10th, the kite balloon observer of the destroyer *Ophelia*, which was patrolling the Fair Isle passage between the Orkney and Shetland islands, spotted a patch of oil from which presently emerged the conning tower of a submarine. It had dived by the time that *Ophelia* reached the site, but three depth charges were followed by a large underwater explosion and more oil. Nothing more transpired then, but later in the day an oil track, obviously from a damaged submarine, was sighted from *Ophelia*. She dropped four charges at its source and thus perished *UB-83* (516/647 tons) and her crew of 35 at 58°28′/01°50′W.

Leaking oil also led to the detection of *UB-103* (519/649 tons) by the crew of the British non-rigid airship *SSZ-1*, flying from Capel, in the Channel about seven miles west of Cape Griz-Nez on 16 September. Returning from an operational cruise, she was the last U-boat to attempt passage of the Dover Straits. The airship called the trawler *Young Crow* to the site and depth charges from that vessel and probably from one or more other trawlers or drifters

U-35 *at Cartagena in 1916. Her sister* U-39 *was later interned at the same port.* (CPL)

The British seaplane carrier Ben-my-Chree *in 1916. Her aircraft were very active against Turkish shipping during the Gallipoli campaign.* (By courtesy of Roger Chesneau)

destroyed *UB-103*, killing her 37 crewmen. British divers found the wreckage at 50°52′N/01°27′E.

Two days after *UB-103*'s demise, her sister *UB-115* left Zeebrugge for her first operational cruise, the last submarine of the war to set out from that port. She, too, was betrayed by an oil track, spotted on 29 September in the North Sea by the British rigid airship *R-29* flying from East Fortune and escorting a Scandinavian convoy. The airship dropped one of its 230lb bombs at the source and signalled the destroyer *Ouse* (*UC-70*'s nemesis) to the hunt, dropping another bomb and then a flare to mark the site. *Ouse*, joined by the destroyer *Star* and three or more trawlers, carried out a prolonged depth charge attack until the trawlers' hydrophones could no longer hear the submarine's sounds. *UB-115* became a tomb for her 39 crewmen at 55°14′N/01°22′W.

The incident is unique as the sole instance in which a rigid airship played a role in a submarine's destruction. *R-29* was one of two ships of the so-called '23X' class, completed earlier in 1918 a part of the belated and largely unsuccessful British effort to match the High Seas Fleet's Zeppelins. With a gas capacity of 990,000cu ft, it was powered by four 250hp engines and carried a crew of 17. Like most of the British rigids, it saw little operational service and was broken up in 1919–20.

Turkish losses

Turkey had the dubious distinction of being the first nation to have ships attacked by aerial torpedo. Much has been written about these attacks, carried out in August 1915 by aircraft from the British seaplane carrier *Ben-my-Chree*, but although there is considerable detail available from the British side, the effectiveness of the torpedo planes has been greatly exaggerated and the exact identity of their targets remains a mystery to this day.

Ben-my-Chree arrived at the Aegean island of Mitylene on 12 June 1915 to replace *Ark Royal* as the aviation vessel for the fleet supporting operations on the Gallipoli peninsula. A converted former Isle of Man passenger vessel, she carried three Short Admiralty Type 184 floatplanes, Nos 184, 185 and 842 (two-seat, twin-float, single-engine biplanes), and two Sopwith Schneider single-seat, twin-float, single-engine biplane 'scouts'.

The Short Type 184, produced in large numbers with many modifications and differing engines, was the workhorse of the RNAS and later the RAF from its introduction in 1915 until the end of the war. But although it was specifically designed as a torpedo carrier, it could not perform that role adequately. The British air history notes,

> Unhappily, the torpedo-loaded Short seaplane could only be made to get off the water and fly under ideal conditions. A calm sea with a slight breeze was essential and the engine had to be running perfectly. Further, the weight of the torpedo so restricted the amount of petrol which could be carried that a flight of much more than three-quarters of an hour was not possible. So it came about that while a number of torpedo attacks from the air were attempted, only three were successfully concluded.[16]

The attacks of *Ben-my-Chree*'s Shorts were directed at shipping in the Sea of Marmara supplying the Turkish forces on Gallipoli, thus joining the British submarine campaign against these sea lanes. The first to achieve success of a sort came on 12 August. At 4.39am that day, the carrier, deep in the Gulf of Xeros near Bulair (the narrow isthmus of the peninsula), hoisted out Shorts 184 and 842 and

The Short 184 was the main weapon of British seaplane carriers during the First World War, and carried out the first airborne torpedo attack in history, against Turkish shipping in the Sea of Marmara. (By courtesy of Owne Thetford)

Schneider No 1560. In addition to their other handicaps, the Shorts had to be flown without an observer, further to help compensate for the weight of their 14in, 810lb torpedoes. Even at that, No 184 was unable to take off. No 842, piloted by Flight Commander C H K Edmonds, RNAS, a veteran of the Cuxhaven Raid, got off the water at 4.55am, crossing the isthmus and turning north-east up the coast at 1500ft. At Injeh Burnu, a small promontory on the European side of the Marmara, Edmonds sighted a merchant steamer, which he estimated at 5000 tons lying stationary close to shore. Dropping to 14ft, he released the torpedo at 300yds and saw it strike the starboard side abreast the mainmast. Edmonds returned to *Ben-my-Chree* to report his success at 5.37am. What the Schneider had been doing is unrecorded, but the carrier's log notes that it returned at 5.43.

The identity of Edmonds' target, which he described as having a single funnel and four masts, has never been definitely determined, but it may have been the 3662-ton *Scham*. It was, at any rate, a ship that had been beached on 8 August to avoid torpedoing by British submarine *E-14* and then had been shelled and set afire by that boat and *E-11*. The aerial attack therefore cannot be considered decisive to the ship's destruction, but it may have ensured the merchantman's total loss.

On 17 August two of the carrier's Shorts got aloft, one flown again by Edmonds, the other by Flight Lieutenant G G Dacre, RNAS. Their targets were vessels taking supplies and reinforcements from the Asian side of the straits to Ak Bashi Liman on the European side just above the Chanak Narrows. Edmonds sighted three merchantmen steaming in line ahead and attacked the middle one, hitting it with his torpedo at 800yds. Again, it cannot be positively identified, but may have been the 3304-ton ex-German *Chios*. Nor can it be positively stated that the ship sank; the British air history notes only that it 'was set on fire, gutted, and eventually taken to Constantinople'.[17]

Dacre, meanwhile, had been forced to alight in the straits by the engine trouble that so often plagued the Shorts. He coaxed the engine back to life but then was unable to take off under the weight of the torpedo. Spotting what he later reported was a large steam tug in False Bay, an inlet on the Asian side north of Ak Bashi Liman, he taxied near it, dropped his torpedo and saw it strike and sink the vessel. Freed of the torpedo's weight, Dacre was able to take off, returning to *Ben-my-Chree* at 6.11am, three minutes after Edmonds returned. The identity of the craft sunk by Dacre remains unknown. It has often been called a tug, on the basis of Dacre's description, but a Turkish source terms it a 'personnel raft' indicating it may have been a powered lighter.[18]

The first Turkish ship to be lost to aerial bombing was the 4211-ton ex-German collier *Irmingard*, sunk on 6 February 1916 in an air–sea attack on the important coal-shipping port of Zonguldak, on the Anatolian coast of the Black Sea, by a Russian force consisting of the battleship *Imperatritsa Maria*, cruiser *Kagul*, seaplane carriers *Imperator Nikolai I* and *Imperator Alexandr I*, and four destroyers. The carriers were the Black Sea Fleet's largest – handsome British-built cargo liners delivered just before the war for the Black Sea–Egypt trade, and converted to carry six to eight seaplanes. After a bombardment by the warships, the carrier's planes (probably Grigorvich flying-boats), attacked the harbour area, dropping a total of 38 bombs with a

A typical Grigorvich M9 flying-boat, a mainstay type of Russian naval aviation. M9s or earlier but similar M5s probably were the aircraft that sunk the Turkish collier Irmingard *and one of them may have accounted for the German* UB-7. *(*Boris V Drashpil*)*

collective weight of 368kg. One or more of these struck *Irmingard* and sent her to the bottom, the largest merchant vessel sunk by air attack during the war. She was raised on 25 February, repaired and returned to service. On 2 October 1916 she struck a mine near the Bosporus and ran aground. The Russian submarine *Narval* completed her destruction on 17 October.

Several months later, a Turkish vessel became the largest warship to be sunk by unassisted aerial attack during the war. The incident stemmed from a decision in early 1917 to transfer a Handley-Page 0/100 bomber to Mudros on the Aegean island of Lemnos, a major RNAS base, for attacks on Constantinople and, if possible, the German (nominally Turkish) battlecruiser *Goeben*, the strongest unit of the Turko-German fleet.

The 0/100, the primogenitor of all British heavy bombers, had entered RNAS service in late 1916. Powered by two 250hp engines, it could carry up to sixteen 112lb bombs. The one destined for Mudros, No 3124, reached there on 8 June 1917 after a 55-hour, nearly 2000-mile flight with ten intermediate stops, something of an aviation epic of its time. Its pilot was Flight Commander Kenneth Savory, RNAS.

After two attempts had been frustrated by adverse winds, the bomber reached the Constantinople area on the night of 9/10 July and first tried to attack *Goeben* at Stenia Bay, a sheltered anchorage on the European side of the Bosporus above Constantinople proper. *Goeben* and *Olga*, a Russian prize in use as a hospital and depot ship, were tied up at the dockside; the light cruiser *Breslau*, the battlecruiser's near-constant companion, was in a floating drydock, and a number of Turkish destroyers and torpedo-boats were moored in the harbour.

Savory reported aiming eight bombs at *Goeben*, but only four can be accounted for – two falling on land, one dropping in the water between the destroyers *Yadighiar-i-Milet* and *Noumoune-i-Hamiyet*, which were moored abreast of

Turkish destroyer Yadighiar-i-Milet *ex-German* S66 *possibly on delivery voyage to Turkey. She was sunk by a British aircraft in 1917. (*Marius Bar*)*

Goeben, and one striking *Yadighair-i-Milet* and starting a fire. The destroyers were the former German *S-166* and *S-168*, respectively, acquired by Turkey in 1910.

Yadighiar-i-Milet flooded slowly and sank in 45 minutes. A midshipman and 25 ratings were killed and 9 ratings injured, probably the greatest number of casualties inflicted on a surface warship by aerial attack during the war. *Noumonue-i-Hamyiet* was slightly damaged, either from bomb fragments or debris thrown from her sister ship, and four of her ratings were killed. A few bomb fragments may have struck *Goeben*, but otherwise she was unscathed.

Savory proceeded to the Golden Horn and aimed two bombs at the German liner *General* – which had assisted *Goeben* and *Breslau* in their escape into Turkish waters in 1914 and was now in use as a depot ship – and two more on Constantinople itself. The bomber returned to Mudros at 3.40am on the 10th after a flight of nearly seven hours, holed in 26 places by enemy fire and with one engine partly disabled. Its crewmen believed they had damaged *Goeben*, which was untrue, and also hit *General*, which was unlikely.[19]

Yadighiar-i-Milet was raised in October, found to be beyond repair, and subsequently scrapped. Her aerial assailant had been lost in September, forced down in the Gulf of Xeros by engine failure. Its pilot on that occasion was Flight Lieutenant John Alcock, later of transatlantic flight fame.

Austro-Hungarian losses

The only Austro-Hungarian vessel of any consequence to be sunk by air attack during 1914–18 was the 168-ton *Elöre*, a merchantman acquired by the *k u k Kreigsmarine* in 1915 as an auxiliary minesweeper. She was the victim of a random bomb or bombs during an Italian air raid on Fiume (now Yugoslavian Rijeka) on 1 August 1916. The main target was the Whitehead torpedo works; unknown to the Italians, most of the plant's machinery had been removed to St Polen, near Vienna, as the result of an earlier raid.

The attack was made by 24 Caproni bombers from seven squadrons of the IV *Gruppo Aeroplani*. The aircraft were undoubtedly Caproni Ca2s, tri-motor, twin-boom biplanes, the principal type of Italian heavy bomber in 1915–16. *Elöre* was raised on 16 August, repaired and returned to service. Her ultimate fate is not known.

Russian losses

German aircraft were partially or indirectly responsible for the loss of two Russian surface warships in the Baltic during the First World War, and in both instances the planes were from the *Torpedostaffel* at *Seeflugstation* Windau (now Ventspils) on the Courland (Latvian) coast. The squadron was equipped with the Friedrichshafen FF41, which like other German torpedo planes was a twin-float, twin-engine biplane. Their use in the torpedo role, however, had been abandoned after 1916, and the Windau aircraft were employed for bombing and reconnaisance.

On 22 August 1917 one of them spotted what its observer identified as two Russian destroyers anchored near Zerel on the south-eastern coast of Ösel Island's Sworbe peninsula. One of them was in fact the 350-ton torpedo-boat *Stroini*, which had run aground during a minelaying operation, with another torpedo-boat or destroyer whose identity is unclear standing by to assist.

The grounded vessel was attacked that evening by three FF41s, each carrying eight 60kg (132lb) bombs. The bombing run was made in line astern. All missiles from the first and third attacker missed, but the fifth from the central plane – the one that had sighted the ships earlier – struck *Stroini* amidships, killing at least 13 crewmen and causing the ship to settle in the water.[20]

A reconnaisance flight the next day found *Stroini* still deeper in the water and beginning to take a starboard list. The German fliers believed, with apparent justification, that the bomb had sunk the ship. Actually, the vessel was still salvageable, but the additional damage from the bomb lengthened efforts to refloat her until the approach of

A Friedrichshafen FF41 of the type partially responsible for the loss of the Russian torpedo-boat Stroini *and indirectly for the loss of the destroyer* Okhotnik. *(*Peter M Grosz*)*

The wreckage of the torpedo-boat Stroini, *probably in late 1917 or early 1918. Storms completed her destruction after aerial bombing defeated salvage efforts.* (Boris V Drashpil)

autumnal storms, when the work had to be broken off. Succeeding storms during the winter of 1917–18 completely wrecked *Stroini*.

As part of the intense aeronaval activity in and around the Gulf of Riga in the last summer of 1917 in preparation for the German Operation 'Albion' – the capture of Dago, Ösel and Moon Islands – the Windau-based seaplanes pioneered aerial minelaying. Between late June and mid-September, flying singly at night and each carrying a 750kg (1654lb) mine, they planted 70 of the devices at three or four locations in and around the gulf.

The 615-ton destroyer *Okhotnik* struck one of these, believed to have been planted on 7 September, on 28 September and was quickly reduced to a sinking condition. Her crew, disaffected by the revolutionary propaganda that would soon sweep the entire Baltic Fleet, abandoned ship in a panicky rush. Four officers remained aboard, reportedly because the rebellious ratings would not allow them in the boats, and presumably went down with the ship. Other casualties, if any, are not known.

Okhotnik's loss was the first and only success in the First World War of a tactic that although long predicted and advocated would not gain maturity until the next world conflict.

French losses

The First World War saw several instances in which the crews of disabled seaplanes were captured by enemy submarines. In the case of the only French warship definitely confirmed as a victim of aerial attack the circumstances were uniquely reversed.

The vessel was the submarine *Foucault* (397/551 tons), which was sighted on 15 September 1916 in the Adriatic 10 miles south-west of Ponta d'Ostro, the tip of the promontory enclosing the entrance to the Bay of Topola, by the Austro-Hungarian Lohner flying-boat L132 returning to Cattaro from patrol. This was the aircraft that had sunk the British drifter *Rosies* the previous month.

After reporting the sighting at Cattaro, L132 was ordered back into the air, together with Lohner L135, to seek out the submarine. Each plane carried two 50kg depth charges, timed to explode at 10m depth, and four 20kg bombs. After a 30-minute search, L135's observer sighted *Foucault* running submerged. The aircraft dropped its depth charges, one exploding 7m off the bow, the other the same distance off the stern.

The concussion shook *Foucault* violently and breached the pressure hull. She began taking water rapidly; some reached the batteries, producing a cloud of chlorine gas. During the next 30 minutes she descended below 80m, the highest reading on her depth gauge, before pumping lightened her enough to enable her to break surface. The aircraft spotted her a few minutes later, with the crew assembled on the deck casing to abandon ship. One of the *Foucault*'s crew opened fire at the planes with a machine-gun, to which L135 replied with a bomb striking close enough to knock some crewmen overboard. The submarine sank immediately, either from the bomb's concussion, scuttling, or a combination of the two. Two officers and 27 ratings, the entire crew, were left in the water.

In a gallant action, the aircraft alighted and took aboard the Frenchmen, who clung to fuselages and wings for 30 minutes until a torpedo-boat, summoned by a shore station that had seen the action, arrived. The ship took the ratings aboard but the two officers were given aerial rides to captivity.[21]

It is possible that a 60-ton American-built French submarine chaser, either *C-2* or *C-43*, was sunk by aerial bombing at Dunkirk in 1918, but evidence is fragmentary and contradictory. If there was such a loss, it was probably inflicted by German twin-engine Gotha GV or GIV heavy bombers of *Kampfgeschwadern* I or III, both of which were active against Dunkirk in 1918.

Other aircraft-related losses

One Italian warship came within a hair of falling victim to air attack during the war – the 395-ton destroyer *Bersagliere*, struck by a bomb from one of two Austro-Hungarian seaplanes at the Albanian port of Valona (Vlore) on the night of 19/20 March 1916. The blast blew a 10ft by 7ft hole in the starboard hull abreast the engine room. The engine room being unmanned at the time, there were no casualties, but the ship took a considerable amount of water. She settled or was beached in shallow water, where temporary repair enabled her to return to Italy. Had she been in deeper water, loss would appear certain.[22]

Italian destroyer Bersagliere, *bombed by an Austro-Hungarian seaplane at Valona in 1916.* (Marius Bar)

An Austro-Hungarian Lohner T type flying-boat. Identical aircraft sank the British drifer Rosies *and the French submarine* Foucault. (Peter M Grosz) ▶

Permanently repaired and returned to service, *Bersagliere* remained in commission, rerated as a torpedo-boat in 1921, until sold for breaking up in 1923. Her aerial attackers cannot be positively identified, but were among five Lohner T type flying-boats known to have operated against Valona in March 1916 – L60, L61, L82, L87 and L88 – from either the Kumbor or Durazzo air stations.

The United States and Japan each lost a merchant vessel to aerial or aerial-assisted action in 1917, both victims of the German raider *Wolf* and her Friedrichshafen FF33e seaplane. The four-masted 567-ton US schooner *Winslow* sailed into *Wolf*'s view on 16 June 1917 while the raider was completing coaling at Raoul Island from the New Zealand *Wairua*, whose capture has been described earlier. Unwilling to expend fuel in chase of such an easy prey, *Wolf*'s commander dispatched the seaplane to force the schooner's surrender. Message bags with orders in English for the vessel to steer for *Wolf* were dropped, but all missed the deck or glanced off sails. Finally, the seaplane dropped a warning bomb and landed alongside *Winslow*, where the surrender demand was issued by voice at pistol-point. The American complied and was soon *Wolf*'s prize. After being stripped of her cargo of coal, firebrick and petrol, *Winslow* was burned on 22 June.

The bloodless seizure of the schooner was not duplicated in the case of the Japanese loss, the Nippon Yusen Kaisha line's 6557-ton cargo-mail liner *Hitachi Maru*, bound from Yokohama to London and captured by *Wolf* on 26 September 1917 off the Maldive Islands in the Indian Ocean. The raider had retraced her course to those waters after laying mines off Singapore. *Hitachi Maru* first appeared to her as smoke on the horizon. *Wolf*'s captain, ever wary of enemy warships, dispatched the seaplane to establish identity. Upon learning from the aviators that the vessel was a large merchantman, *Wolf* headed in pursuit, placing the aircraft on the water for take-off at a prearranged time in the usual procedure.[23]

When *Wolf* and her seaplane intercepted the Japanese vessel, her captain, disregarding the safety of his passengers and crew, unwisely chose to fight back with his single stern-mounted 4.7in gun. *Wolf*'s broadsides quickly reduced *Hitachi Maru* to a shambles. The exact number of casualties does not appear to have recorded, but is estimated at 30 dead (including the Japanese captain, who killed himself aboard *Wolf*) and probably an equal number of wounded. The prize was sunk on 7 November.

The seaplane aimed three bombs at *Hitachi Maru* during the engagement, but they were ineffective. However, the aircraft deserved much credit for the capture, for without its reconnaissance flight it is doubtful that *Wolf* would have closed with the merchantnman.

A number of minor vessels were captured by seaplanes in various waters during the First World War, most often by crews of disabled aircraft who commandeered passing small craft.[24] But there were at least two instances in which larger vessels were involved.

The first occurred on 23 June 1916 when German seaplanes from Zeebrugge intercepted the 1877-ton Dutch merchantman *Gelderland*, en route to the Tyne from Rotterdam, and forced her to put into Zeebrugge, where she was seized as a prize.

The second episode was unique. On 23 April 1917 the German Zeppelin *L-23*, cruising off Hanstholm on the Danish coast, sighted a schooner whose crew inexplicably took to their boats when the airship hove into sight. *L-23*'s commander put his ship down on the water and learned from the men in the boats that the vessel was the 688-ton Norwegian *Royal*, bound for West Hartlepool with a cargo of pit props for British mines. This material was legally contraband, so *L-23* put a three-man prize crew aboard the schooner with orders to steer her for Horns Reef, then wirelessed a report of the capture to its base. *Royal* was met the next morning by destroyers that escorted her into the Elbe.[25] One wonders if the airshipmen received prize money.

Footnotes

1. Strangely, in view of all that had been written on the subject, no navy in the world had carried out realistic tests of aerial bombing of ships, in the sense of dropping explosives upon mobile floating targets, before the First World War. The only verified use of aircraft against surface ships before that conflict occurred in 1913–14 during the Mexican Civil War with three unsuccessful and ill-documented attempts by Constitutionist aeroplanes to bomb Federal gunboats at Guaymas on the Gulf of California.
2. The major revisionist sources are Vols 4 (1965) and 5 (1966) of *Konteradmiral a d* Arno Spindler's official First World War submarine history *Der Handelskreig mit U-Booten* and Robert M Grant's *U-Boats Destroyed* (1964) and *U-Boat Intelligence* (1969). For an analysis based primarily on these sources, see R D Layman with Peter K Simpson and E J L Halpern, 'Allied Aircraft vs German Submarines 1916-18' in *Cross & Cockade Journal* 11 No 4 (winter 1970).
3. *Army and Navy Gazette* (12 February 1916).
4. H A Jones, *The War in the Air, Vol 2.*
5. The name is given as *Rosie* in Vol 2 of J J Colledge's *Ships of the Royal Navy* (1970).
6. Colledge, *op cit*, gives the name of this vessel as *Craigbo* and here gun as 6pdr; the name is given as *Craig-bo* and the gun as 3pdr in F J Dittmar and J J Colledge, *British Warships 1914-1919* (1972).
7. *Wolf* captured many more ships than noted in this study, which is restricted to incidents in which the seaplane played a dominant or decisive role.
8. 'The Hornets of Zeebrugge: Annotated Excerpts from the War Diary of Seeflugstation Flanders I, 1914-18,' *Cross & Cockade Journal* 11 No 1 (spring 1970).
9. Some W29s carried a wireless set in lieu of a second forward machine-gun. One wireless-equipped aircraft usually accompanied each seaplane formation.
10. H A Jones, *The War in the Air*, Vol 6.
11. 'Enemy Aircraft in the North and Baltic Seas, August 1918', issued 6 September 1918.
12. C F Snowden Gamble, *The Story of a North Sea Air Station* (1928).
13. Erich Gröner, *Die deutschen Kriegsschiffe 1815-1945*, Vol 1 (1966).
14. *Flot v pervoi mirovoi voine*, Vol 1 (1964).
15. The design was developed by Flight Lieutenant A D Cunningham, who is credited with coining the word 'blimp' to describe a non-rigid airship.
16. H A Jones, *The War in the Air*, Vol 2, p.65.
17. *Ibid.*
18. Mazlum Keyusk, *Turk havacılık turihı* (1951).
19. The attack is described in detail in E Keble Chatterton, *Seas of Adventures* (1936), and H A Jones, *The War in the Air*, Vol 5.
20. For a first-person account by one of the German aviators involved, see '*Marineflieger*: The Reminiscences of Wolfram Eisenloh', *Cross & Cockade Journal* 25 No 1 (spring 1984).
21. An account by the pilot of L135, Walther Zelezny, is given in 'The Sinking of the French Submarine *Foucault* by the Austrian–Hungarian Seaplane L135 September 15, 1916', *Cross & Cockade Journal* 4 No 1 (spring 1963).
22. E Keble Chatterton, *Seas of Adventures* (1936).
23. For a detailed account of the operations of *Wolf* 's aircraft, see Peter M Grosz, 'The Cruise of the Wölfchen', *Cross & Cockade Journal* 14 No 1 (spring 1973).
24. In a celebrated incident, two Russian aviators forced down near the Bosphorus seized a Turkish fishing vessel and sailed to safety across the entire Black Sea.
25. This incident is described in Douglas H Robinson, *The Zeppelin in Combat* (1962).

SHIPS WITH STEEL SKIRTS

L Norbury-Williams, a man closely involved with the project, investigates the fascinating and little-known Allied attempt to give anti-torpedo defences to merchant ships – defences that were deployed while the ships were underway.

For some years it has been apparent that few on land were aware that merchant ships carried Net Defence during the Second World War. In 1980, a wartime production manager of British Ropes, who had worked on the boom defences of Scapa Flow after Günther Prien had sunk HMS *Royal Oak*, argued that no such equipment had been manufactured, otherwise he would have known about it. The incident illustrates the effectiveness of wartime secrecy. He was absolutely flabbergasted to be informed that it was not a figment of my imagination, as I had served in a ship fitted with the gear.

Even today many of the older seafaring fraternity remain ignorant of the meaning of the term Admiralty Net Defence (AND) and confuse it with Boom Defence – the protection of harbours. This misconception was brought to my attention as a result of slide lectures given to members of the World Ship Society and prompted the writing of this monograph. My personal interest in the equipment arose as a result of a voyage as 3rd Officer in the military transport *Coombe Hill*, one of the many Doxford 'standard' vessels equipped with AND in their Sunderland yard. Although, at the end of the day it has to be admitted this countermeasure was only a qualified success, I have endeavoured to be objective even though my overall view is coloured by my own experience. With a cargo of war material, including Churchill tanks, petrol in No 3 deep tank and ammunition in No 1 hold, the crew of *Coombe Hill* were without exception profoundly grateful that the ship was fitted with AND, particularly during the running battle along the North African coast between Oran and Bone when *Empire Banner* and *Empire Webster* were torpedoed immediately astern of us.

The discovery that HMS *Queen of Bermuda* had been used for net trails, and wartime visits to 'Liberty' ships in Galveston, Texas and then Bone, stimulated my interest. Having sailed as 2nd Officer in *Monarch of Bermuda* towards the end of the war and spent some eighteen months in her, I was puzzled as to why such an unsuitable vessel had been chosen for net trials. According to my 'sight' book, the height of eye above the waterline from the bridge was 58ft, which means the sun deck was about 42ft above LWL. One can well sympathise with Captain C N E Currey in his efforts to coordinate the activities of the ship's company in brailing the massive nets.

Protection of capital ships – the early days

As one of the antidotes to the threat posed by the development of the torpedo-boat, a cumbersome crinoline of steel wire was devised to protect capital ships whilst at anchor, and later, to protect them when steaming at slow speed. These torpedo nets were hung from 30ft booms slung out horizontally from the ship's side and the early ones were made of 6½in diameter steel wire rings linked by smaller rings and weighing only 1lb per sq ft. Extended trials proved them capable of stopping the slow 14in torpedo which had a speed of 27kts.

The adoption of the heavy grommet net of closer mesh and weighing 5lb per sq ft, together with the introduction of the torpedo net 'shelf', proved far more satisfactory. In due course the handling technique was perfected with the booms just above the surface of the water and the nets hanging down some 25ft. In 1906, the Channel Fleet, with nets down, steamed at 6kts.

The introduction of the net cutter fixed to the nose of the torpedo, together with the development of the 'bulge' as protection against underwater attack, led to net defence crinolines being discarded. The French abandoned it, the Russians fitted it in some ships and not in others and the Americans ignored it. However, whilst the British decided to stop using them, German battleships did not lose their nets until 1916. What finally discredited them in the Royal Navy was the sinking of the battleships *Triumph* (11,985 tons) and *Majestic* (14,900 tons) off the Gallipoli peninsula on 25 and 27 May 1915 by *U-21* (Kapitänleutnant Hersing). Both had their nets out but the torpedoes fitted with net cutters went through them. Some observers maintained that the British were reluctant to discard nets only because 'Out Nets!' was a valued drill.

The Actaeon Experiments

Despite the setback, experiments with nets continued. Nose cutters were found effective against close-mesh nets such as the Boom Defence grommet nets and ship nets of similar design, but they failed against open-mesh Net Defence because, when the nose of a torpedo touched a strand of the mesh, it brushed it aside and no real pressure was exerted by the torpedo until the mesh tightened on the parallel body and was clear of the cutter.

The idea of net protection for merchant vessels under way, originated in 1915 or 1916 with Captain Edward C Villiers of the Torpedo School ship *Actaeon* at Sheerness. Experiments were carried out by a battleship at Rosyth and later at Scapa Flow, but were not a success. After many vicissitudes, including a further series of unsuccessful trials, the *Actaeon* net was finally evolved. It consisted of a 3ft x 3ft diamond mesh net and Lieutenant C N E Currey (later Captain Currey, CBE,RN) fired a torpedo at it from a submarine attached to *Actaeon*. Successful trials were carried out on 10/11 December 1917 with a net towed by the 3000-ton cruiser *Diamond*.

In March 1918 sea trials were carried out with an 'Actaeon' net fitted to the 30ft cargo derricks of T & J Harrison's 3846-ton steamship *Navigator (II)* under the command of Captain I Mowat. Whilst engaged on these trials in Lyme Bay, the vessel was actually attacked by the German U-boat *UC-75* (Oberleutnant zur See Walter Schmitz). Shortly after midnight on the morning of 18 March, *UC-75* made an unsuccessful surface attack. Schmitz considered the torpedo had missed, and fired a second torpedo at 02.00 (German time), which struck the target correctly indentified by Schmitz from her distress call as the *Navigator*. Evidently the second torpedo exploded in the starboard net at 01.00 and *Navigator* returned to Portland, anchoring in Weymouth Roads at 07.30. The vessel was surveyed by a diver, no damage being found beyond a slight indentation of the plating extending from the foremast to the after end of the bridge and from the waterline to 15ft below it, completely vindicating Captain Villiers' great confidence in his nets.

The second ship to be fitted with nets was the Brocklebank Line's *Stockwell* (5642gt), the foot of her nets being kept down by a paravane which cut an enemy moored mine whilst on passage from the Tyne to Sheerness. The third ship to be fitted was Houlder Bros twin-screw, refrigerated vessel *Duquesa* (8651gt), completed in May 1918. She was attacked by an enemy submarine but the torpedo detonated in the net and the ship was saved.

An immediate result of these successes was that the manufacture of nets was accordingly undertaken, instructions being given by the Admiralty to fit the defence to 200 ships. However the war ended before anything more could be done, and 'Actaeon' net defence (AND) was put on one side.

The inter-war years

Between 1935 and 1936, DTM directed HMS *Vernon* to explore the possibilities of 'Actaeon' Net Defence and Commander C N E Currey (then Electrical Commander of *Vernon*), reopened the dormant files. In 1936, Captain Currey made a net of 3ft x 3ft mesh on the football ground of *Vernon*. It is believed this net was fired at by a tender, but the Admiralty archives are silent on the subject.

Second World War Developments

On 21 September 1939 Winston Churchill, First Lord of the Admiralty wrote to the First Sea Lord:

> DCNS and I were much impressed with the so called 'Actaeon' net against torpedoes on which the *Vernon* are keen .... I suggest that this is a matter of

HMS Hotspur *demonstrating the deployment of the early 'crinoline' form of net defence for capital ships.* (CPL)

▲ Arandora Star, *showing the 50ft steel lattice-work booms. Note the topping lift connected to short samson posts.* (Currey collection)

Close-up of Arandora Star*'s port forward boom in lowered position. Note topping lift shackled to lead of boom.* (Currey collection)

> the highest urgency and significance. It should be fitted on merchant ships, liners, and also indeed, above all upon ships of war having solitary missions without destroyer protection. Could not a committee be formed before the week is out which would grip the idea, already so far advanced by the Naval authorities, and see whether it cannot be brought into the forefront of our immediate war preparation? If it is right, it would require a very large scale application.

In October 1939 Net Defence was reactivated, Captain Currey starting net manufacture at the Lennox Motors Garage, Southsea whilst approval was given to fit the AMC *Laconia* with nets, but this was not proceeded with. However trials in fast vessels had been carried out by the end of the year. The 23,000-ton *Queen of Bermuda*, which had been requisitioned for war service on 29 August in New York, five days before war was declared, sailed two days later for Belfast, where she was converted to an armed merchant cruiser (AMC) with seven 6in guns. Commissioned on 4 November, she sailed after 72 hours under the White Ensign for an AND trial in Belfast Lough. By 10 November she was alongside at Portsmouth for three days with dockyard parties and crew hard at work on 3ft x 3ft mesh nets, prior to four days of sea trials between 13 and 21 November with the destroyer *Vansittart* firing torpedoes at the nets in Sandown Bay.

The general principles of this defence were much as the system discarded from HM ships during the 1914–18 War. However the four booms on each side, which were swung fore and aft, when not in use, were longer, being 50ft. In addition the nets were brailed up on the Venetian blind system instead of being parbuckled. The nets used by *Queen of Bermuda* were 280ft long and had a depth of 31ft 6in which was longer and deeper than those used in 1918. Their drag proved greater than anticipated, reducing the speed of the ship between 35 and 40 per cent, but the trials gave promising results, producing a 72 per cent success rate against 35kt torpedoes and 15 per cent against 40 torpedoes. *Queen of Bermuda* was subsequently withdrawn from trials and her net defence removed, prior to working-up before her departure from Portland for the South Atlantic Station in February 1940.

◀ Queen of Bermuda *as an armed merchant cruiser. The high freeboard which made her such an odd choice as AND trials ship is evident in this view.* (A Duncan)

Four 10,000-ton Glen Line ships, *Glenearn, Glengyle, Glenroy* and *Breconshire*, which had been requisitioned initially as fleet supply ships, were approved for fitting with nets, but this was not proceeded with and the proposed use of the 14,000-ton Polish liner *Pilsudski* was overtaken by events. At 05.36 on 26 November 1939, after passing Flamborough Head, she hit two mines and sank 4½ hours later. The 7290-gt, 16kt sisters *Khedive Ismail* and *Mohamed Ali el Kebir* together with the Blue Star cruise liner *Arandora Star* (gross tonnage 15,501, 16kts) had all been suggested as replacements for the net trials. In the event the latter was selected.

Arandora Star was fitted with 3ft x 6ft nets at Avonmouth. At first she used three 50ft swinging lattice-work booms on each side, but later booms were made to top back to short posts, the heel fittings being on the ship's side, 20ft above the load waterline. The leading lower corner of the net was kept down and out by an angled otter board, which was towed from the bow paravane chain clump. The footrope was kept down by small water kites called 'planing shoes'.

Nets were brailed up on the venetian blind system. Using these nets the speed was reduced by between 18 and 20 per cent. *Arandora Star* left Avonmouth on Easter Sunday 23 March 1940. During sea trials, carried out at 12kts between Avonmouth and Plymouth, the foremost boom broke in the centre and the ship was stopped for four hours whilst the wreckage was cleared and secured. Torpedo trials were carried out in Sandown Bay and it was discovered that the net would protect the ship against 30kt torpedoes, even if the torpedo had a Fiume tail, but a 40kt torpedo would break through the net. After extended endurance trials in the Bay of Biscay in April, AND was abandoned on the grounds that the gear would be useless in a moderate sea or slight swell and the towing life of the net was limited to a maximum of 90 hours.

In March 1941 in view of the gravity of the submarine

The 'Scandinavia Type' steamer Struan, *with masts very far forward and aft, demonstrates why this sort of ship was ideal for AND.* (Tom Rayner)

menace, AND re-appeared in the form of a proposal to tow a length of 'Actaeon' nets astern of a vessel stationed on the flank of a convoy. This never went beyond the proposal stage owing to practical problems in ship handling. However it was appreciated that the difficulties met with in previous trials were due to attempting to tow a very large net at too great a speed with big passenger vessels.

In May 1941 approval was given for fitting net defence to a standard cargo ship and a tanker, Captain Currey being re-appointed for experimental work and trials. Experiments with model nets were carried out in the tanks at Haslar and subsequently at the National Physical Laboratory, Teddington under Dr Baker and his staff. These experiments led to the simplification and improvement in efficiency of the net, including the use of a new design of depressor kite to keep the forefoot down. The 50ft spread from the ship's side was achieved by using 72ft booms stepped 22ft inboard.

In June and July 1941 authority was given for the equipping of the freighter *Empire Rhodes* with net defence at Caledon Yard, Dundee, and the tanker *Empire Celt* at Furness Yard, Stockton-on-Tees. A month later, Captain Currey sailed for the USA with full power to place orders for the manufacture of fifty sets of AND gear in either the USA and/or Canada, for the standard freighters building in the United States for the British Government. The losses of merchant ships through U-boat action had become so serious that the results of the trials in the standard freighter or tanker could not be awaited.

The ideal freighter model for net defence was the specialist trades with masts near the bow and stern, such as the 'Scandinavian Type' or Baltic Timber ship. However, when merchant ships were literally being built against time, it was a matter of adaptation and compromise, resulting in reduced protection compared with that of a tanker.

Details of admiralty net defence

In freighters the defence was carried each side of the ship on two 72ft to 74ft tubular steel booms, the heels of which were some 20ft above the load waterline. The ends of these booms were connected by the 3½in circumference 'blondin' wire (named after the tightrope walker) along which the roller hangers attached to the headrope of the net ran. The nets operated on the curtain principle, being hauled along the 'blondin' wire by the towing wire using a winch whilst the brail wire was slacked away.

The footrope of the net was designed for a depth of 26ft 3in when the nets were in the water, being held down by the 400lb water kite at the forward end and the 600lb cylindrical steel drogue attached to the lower after corner. These attachments kept the net taut and the meshes extended.

When the nets were streamed, topping lifts lowered the booms to the horizontal. The booms then held the nets spread at a distance of 50ft from the ship's side at the nearest point, which was considered to be a safe distance for the detonation of a torpedo. When the equipment was not in use, the booms were topped to within 5 degrees of the vertical and latched at the mast crosstrees, the nets being brailed and then secured round the after boom in snare frames.

At the outboard end of each boom, slipping gear was fitted. This was operated from a position near the heel of the boom to allow the complete net and 'blondin' wire to be jettisoned in an emergency. Additionally, in British-built ships, a guillotine, through which the tow rope passed, was fitted on the forecastle to enable the towing wire, which ran from the forecastle head and was attached to the forward upper corner of the net (the throat) to be severed quickly in an emergency.

In British-built cargo ships, hull protection was increased by about 40ft to about 60 per cent of the hull length by splaying the forward booms 20 degrees forward and the

Proportions of hull length protected by Net Defence. (Currey collection) ▶

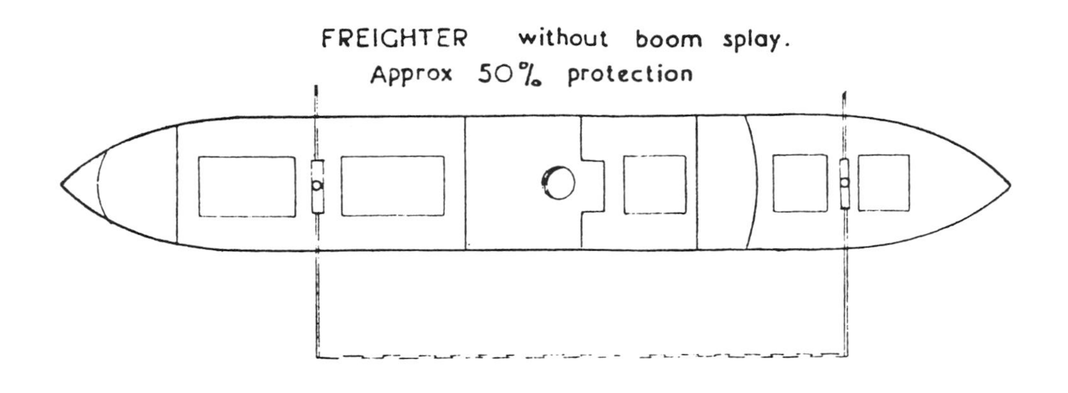
FREIGHTER without boom splay.
Approx 50% protection

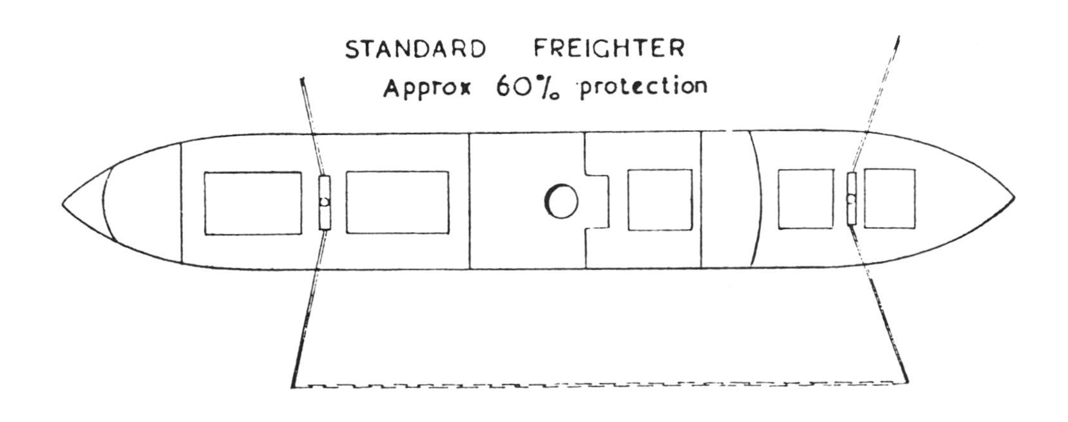
STANDARD FREIGHTER
Approx 60% protection

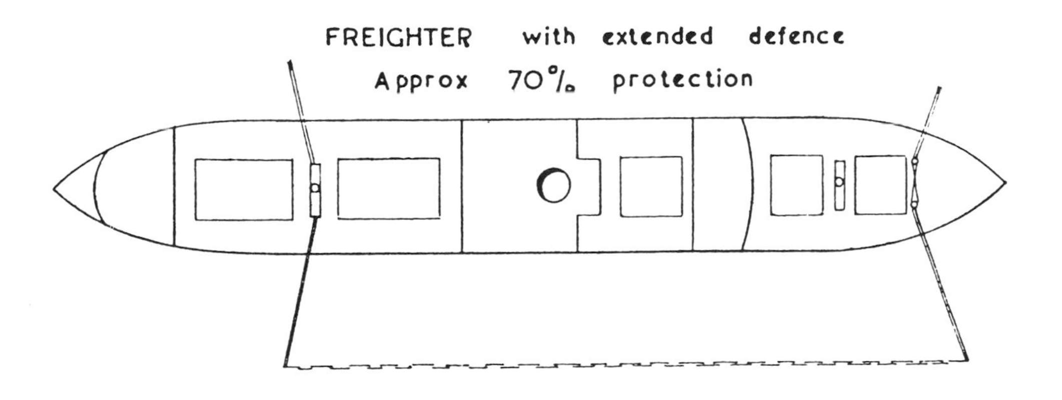
FREIGHTER with extended defence
Approx 70% protection

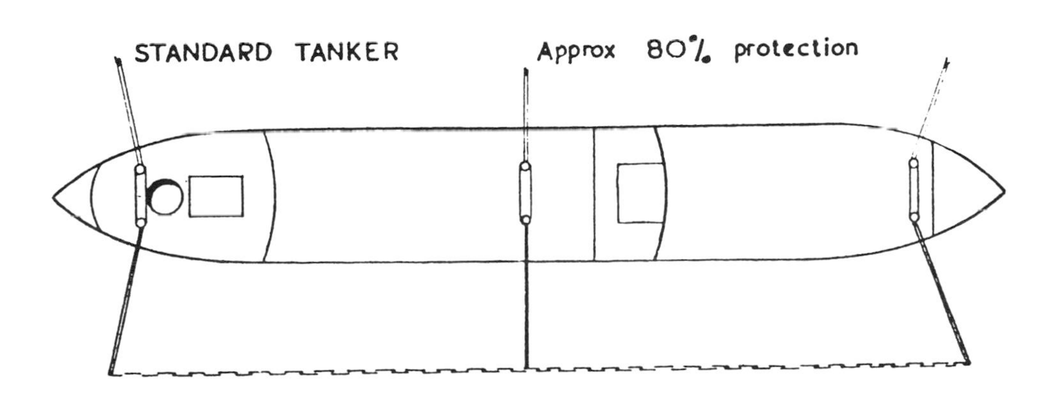
STANDARD TANKER
Approx 80% protection

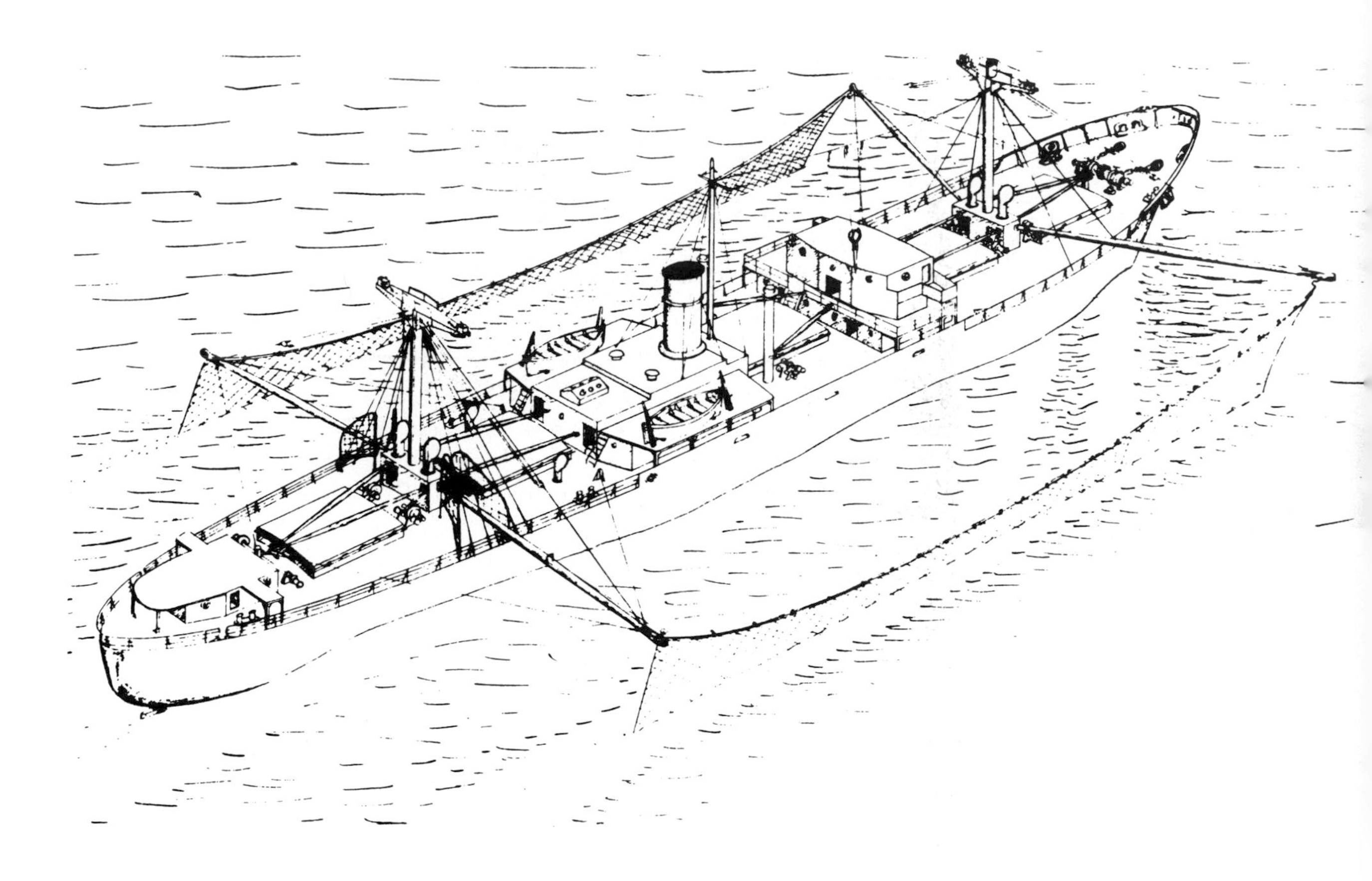

▲ *Diagram of use of splayed booms to give 60 per cent protection to a freighter.* (Currey collection)

▼ *Diagram of AND on a tanker covering about 80 per cent of the underwater hull length.* (Currey collection)

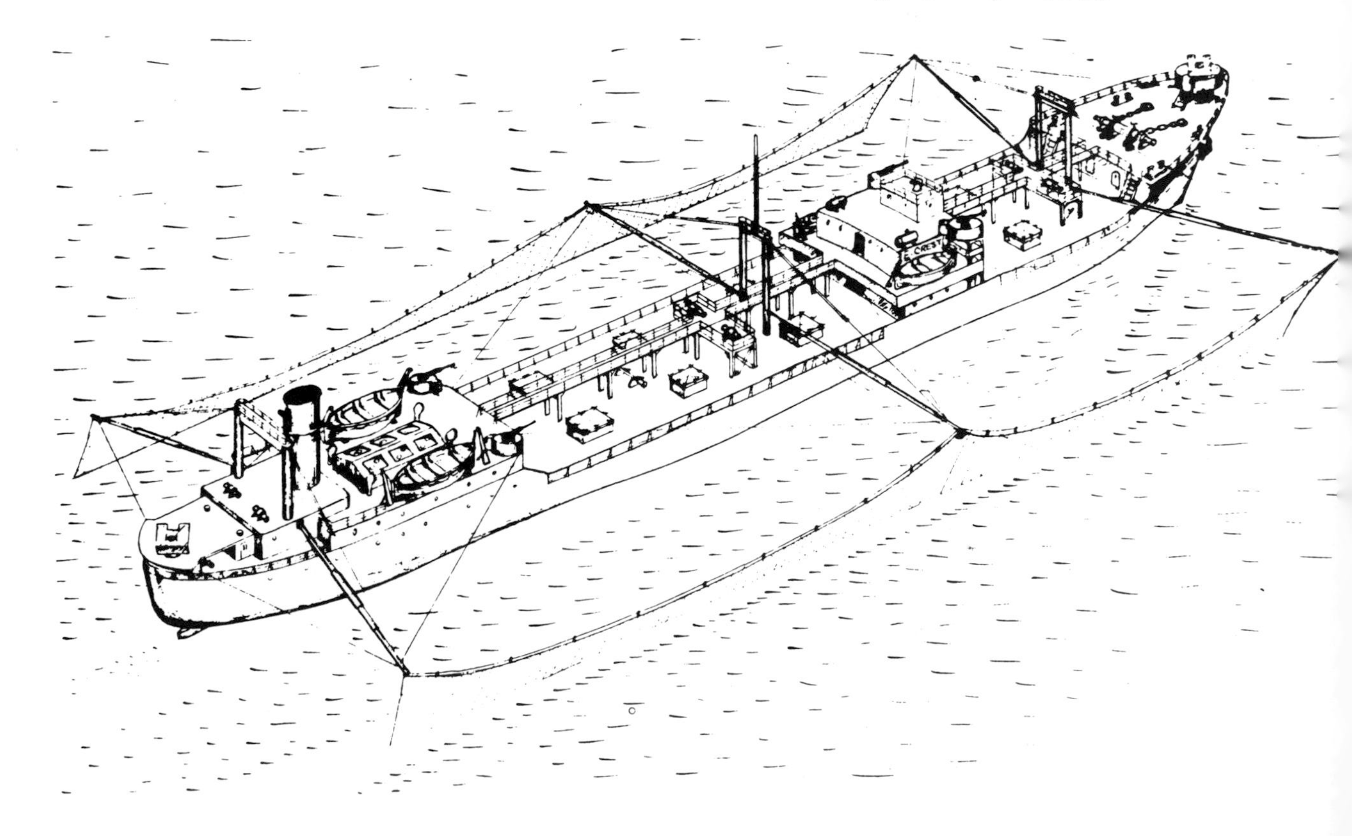

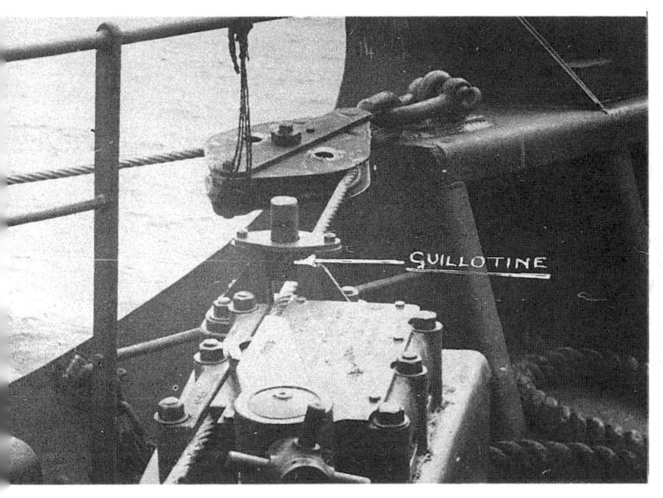

The Bullivant Nipper (centre foreground) relieved the strain on the towing-wire winch. The guillotine (indicated) consisted of a sharp blade working in a slide. It was struck with a sledge hammer, in case of emergency, to cut the towing wire. (Currey collection)

after booms 12 degrees aft using standing guys; the heels of the booms and the deck connections of the guys were so arranged on a common axis that the booms automatically splayed out as they were lowered. In American- and Canadian-built ships the splay was 15 degrees for the forward and after booms.

Tankers possessed the great advantage of being able to place AND samson posts practically anywhere where adequate support could be obtained from the ship's existing structure, since they had no general cargo holds with their associated permanent masts and derricks. With their many internal bulkheads however, it was much easier to provide tankers with a considerable amount of longitudinal protection, about 80 per cent of the underwater section of the hull being covered by the nets. Tankers carried nets up to 380ft in length on three booms each side, the nets being secured abreast the midship samson post when brailed.

Net defence committee

In October 1941 the Admiralty Net Defence Committee was formed under Rear-Admiral W B Mackenzie to review the whole problem of fitting nets in existing British and allied ships. It consisted of representatives of the following departments:

Ministry of War Transport	(MOWT)
Merchant Shipbuilding and Repairs	(CMSR)
Trade Division	(DTD)
Torpedoes and Mining	(DTM)
Naval Stores	(D of S)
Naval Construction	(DNC)

Net trials

In late December 1941 and early January 1942 the first net trials of the 8000-ton tanker *Empire Celt* were held in the Clyde. She had a length of 464ft (bp), a beam of 61ft and a designed speed of 11kts. British 21in Mark IV and German 21in G7a (T1) torpedoes were fired by the destroyer *Beagle*, which had tubes modified to fire the German torpedoes. A number of these had been acquired when the

A German G7a (T1) torpedo entangled in the net of Empire Celt *during the 1941–42 trials.* (Currey collection)

German supply ships *Gedania* and *Lothringen* were captured in the Atlantic in June 1941 by the ocean boarding vessel *Marsdale* and the light cruiser *Dunedin*; others had come from beaches in Norway and Kent after malfunctioning, and from *U-570* (captured on 27 August 1941).

The G7a (T1) was of conventional design with compressed air and steam driving the multicylinder radial engine, and had a weight of 1528kg when operational. It was fitted with a Fiume tail, two triple bladed contra-rotating propellers and had three alternative settings: 30kts at 15,300yds; 40kts at 8700yds; 44kts at 6500yds.

Initially 6ft x 3ft diamond mesh nets were used, but these were changed to 5ft x 2½ft mesh, after the first day, which brought an improvement in torpedo interception. The trials showed considerable success: when the tanker was steaming at 9kts there were five catches and two penetrations; at 6½ to 7¼kts, two catches and three penetrations. The ratio of catches and penetrations with the German G7a (T1) was much the same as for British torpedoes, although the shrouded propellers of the G7a certainly appeared to make catches less probable.

The net trials with the 5ft x 2½ft mesh nets of the freighter *Empire Rhodes* were carried out in the Clyde in February and March 1942 using the submarine *Otway* firing mainly 21in Mk II torpedoes. With 29kt torpedoes (the approximate speed of the German G7e (T2) electric torpedo, which had no Fiume tail) there was a one hundred per cent success at various track angles, but the 40kt Mk IV torpedo penetrated the net, as did the 18in aerial torpedo. This time the Fleet Air Arm Swordfish participating in the trials had the satisfaction of hitting their target, whereas in the previous trials, out of eight torpedoes dropped, not one hit *Empire Celt*'s nets.

It was subsequently arranged that all standard freighters and tankers building and to be built for Britain in the UK, Canada and USA were to be fitted with net defence.

In June 1942 the Americans fitted the first set of net defence to *Ocean Might* which they had built at Portland, Maine for the British. They adopted Net Defence the same month, having carried out trials on the British-built *Empire Rhodes* off New London, Connecticut, followed by Canada two months later.

AND equipment

The booms. British booms were manufactured by Stewart and Lloyds and the South Durham Steel & Iron Co. They

▲*Boom latching arrangement, showing boom partly lowered,* ◄*and fully stowed.* (Currey collection)

were made of different diameters of steel tube swaged together, weighed about 4¼ tons and varied in length between 72ft and 74ft according to the beam and type of ship. In freighters, the after booms were lighter than the forward booms having a maximum diameter of 17in compared with 20in for the forward booms. The booms gave more trouble than any other part of the equipment. On account of their length and weight, careful handling was essential. The fact that the crosstrees and crutch only supported the middle of the boom and that some 30ft of the boom was unsupported above the latch, resulted in the boom being easily bent if topped up too hard.

American booms were 18in in diameter at their midsection, being made from two tapered tubes, each tube consisting of two thicknesses of ¼in steel plating. The tubes were welded together in the middle with a strengthening band round the join. These booms proved themselves in every way superior to the British booms, weighing only 2½ tons and being able to bend within limits without buckling.

In view of the small crews carried by merchant ships compared with naval vessels, net defence had been designed to be operated by a minimum of four men in cargo ships and six in tankers, so that everything had to be done to make the operating of the booms as simple as possible. A latch resembling the ordinary garden gate latch (from which the idea originated) engaged on the boom latching bar in order to catch the boom as soon as it came up against the rope fender or 'pudding' secured to the curved part of the crosstrees at their extremity. This was especially necessary with the vessel rolling, when the boom, as it approached the crutching position, was liable to slam back against it. In the

◄ *AND fittings – boom heels.* (Currey collection)

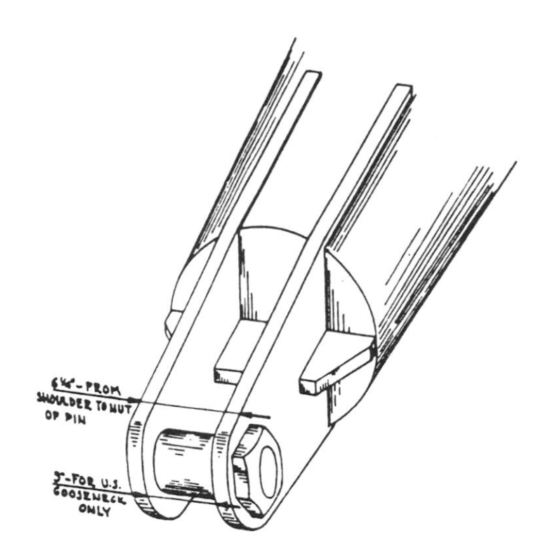

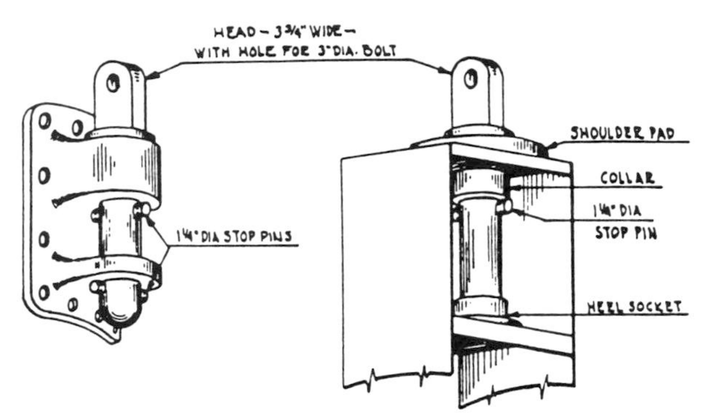

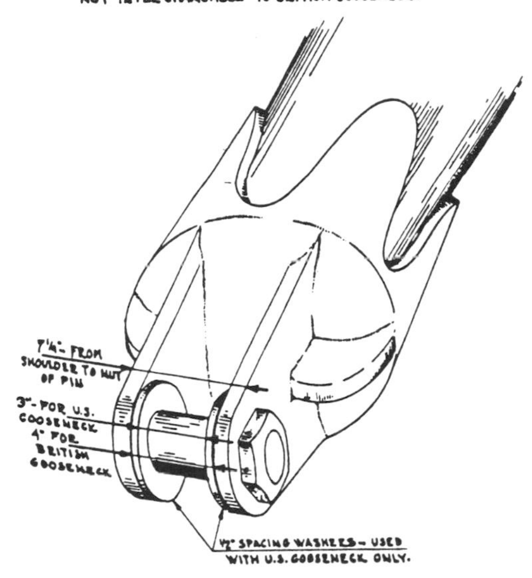

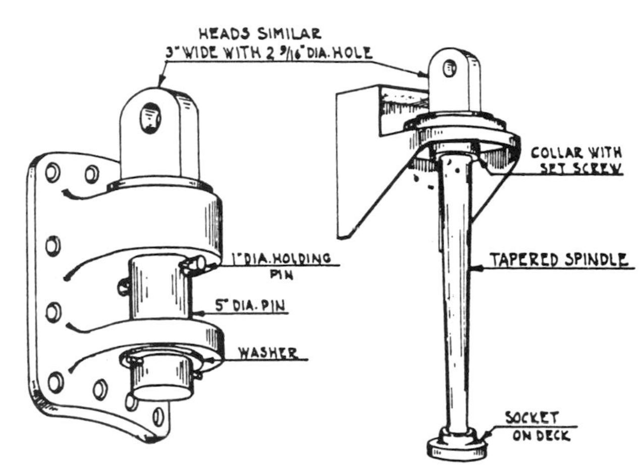

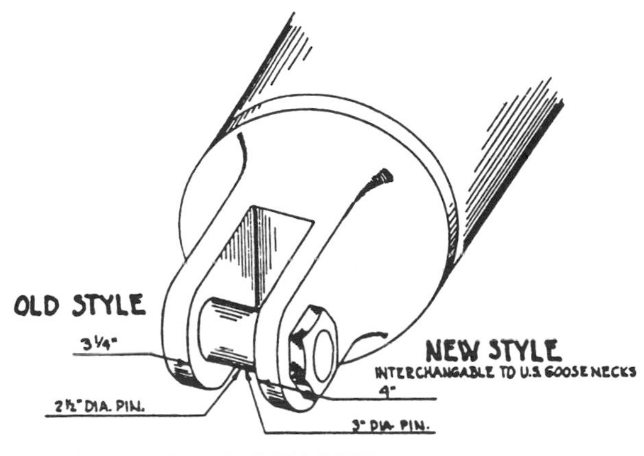

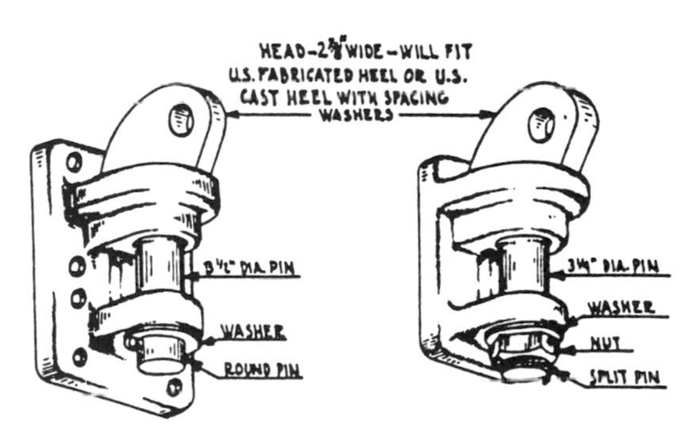

▲ *AND fittings – goose necks.* (Currey collection)

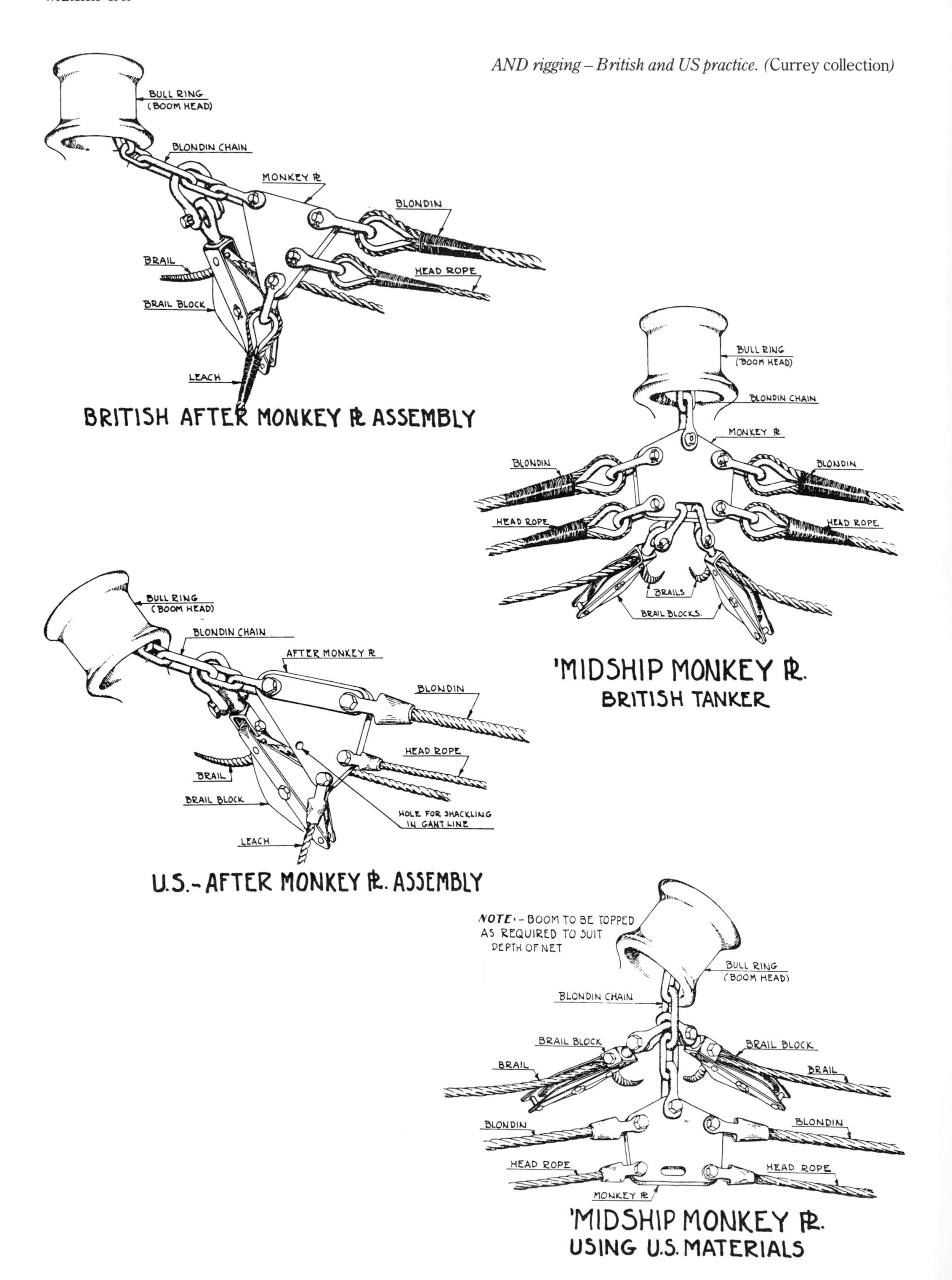

AND rigging – British and US practice. (Currey collection)

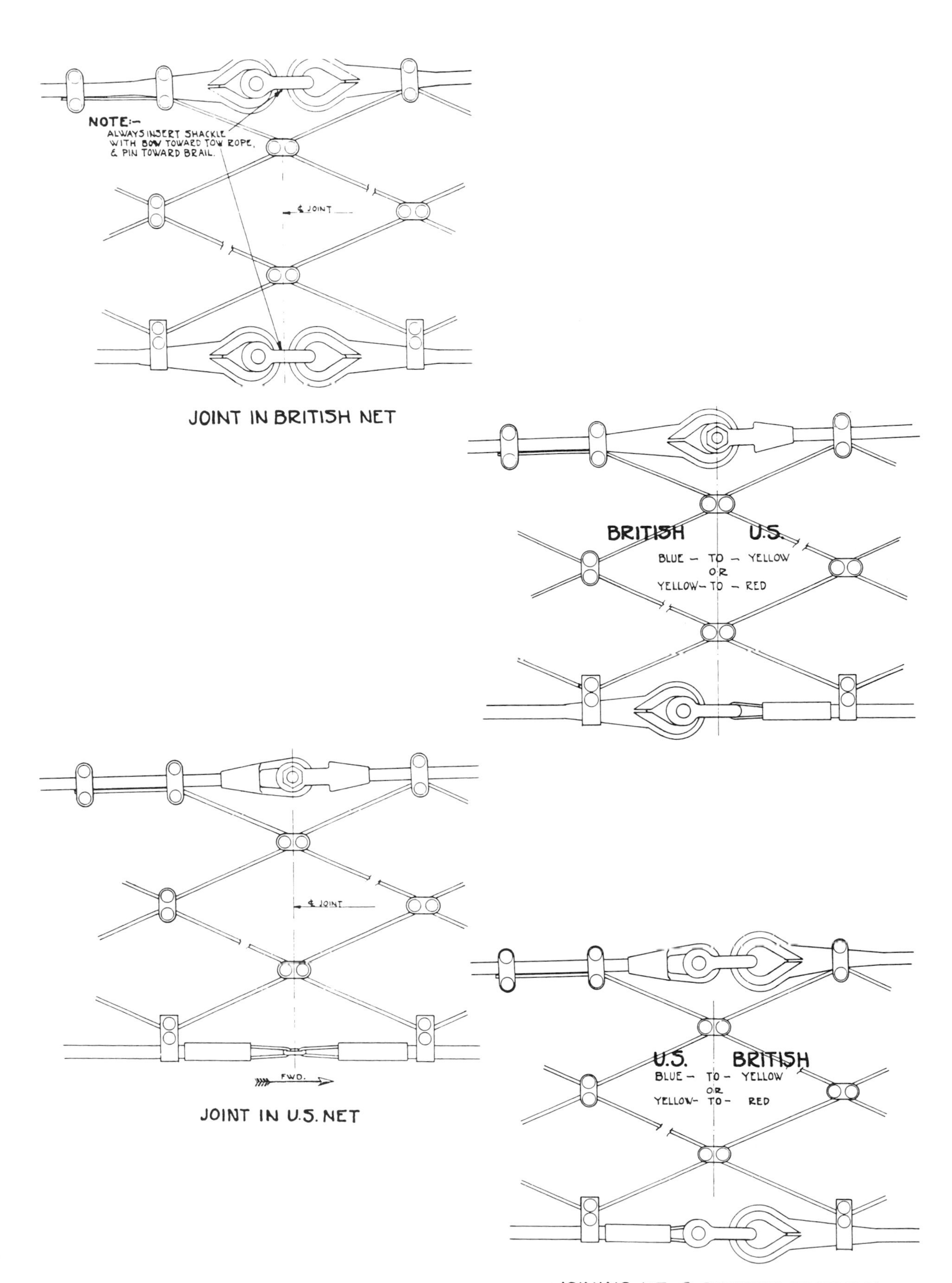

AND net details – British freighter type. (Currey collection)

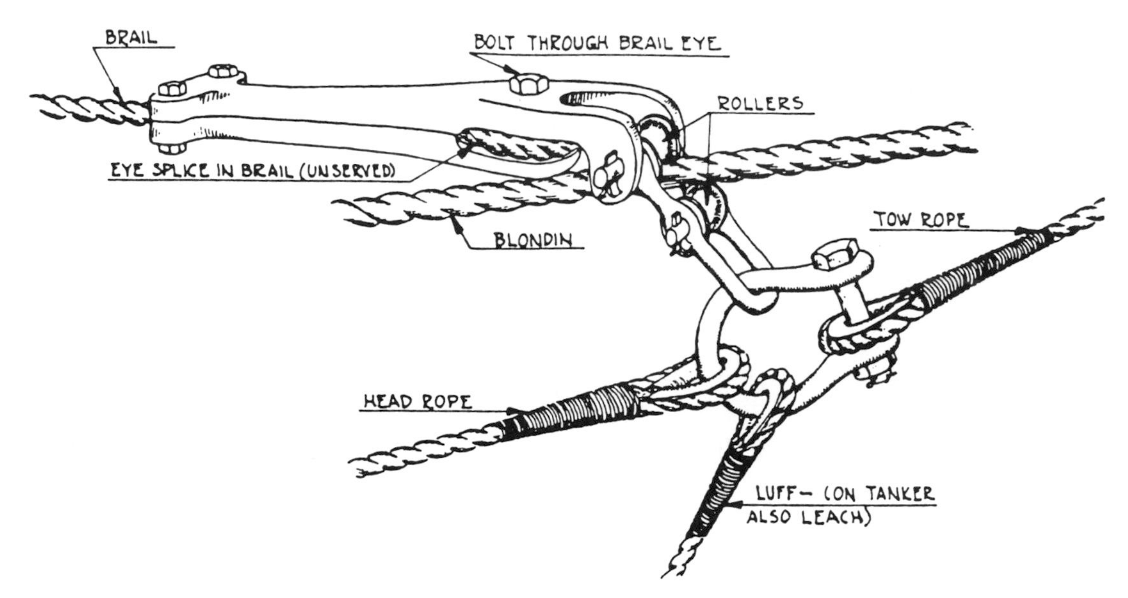

*AND net details – US and British practice. (*Currey collection*)*

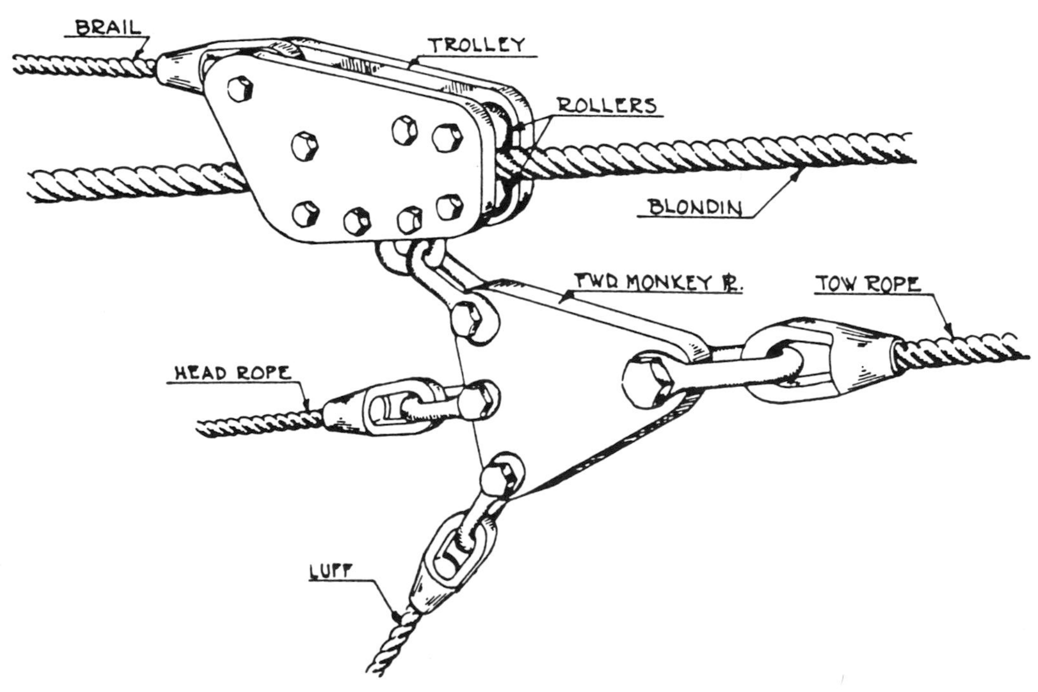

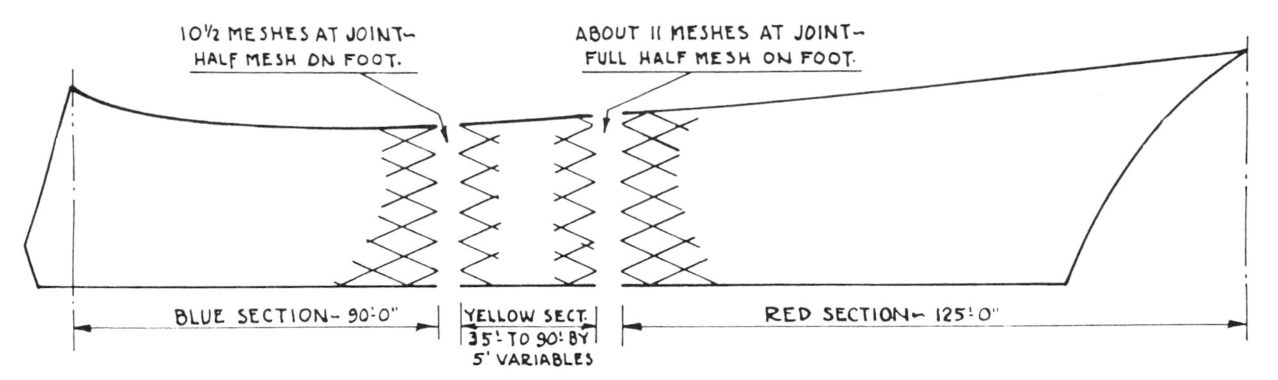

AND net details – British freighter type. (Currey Collection)

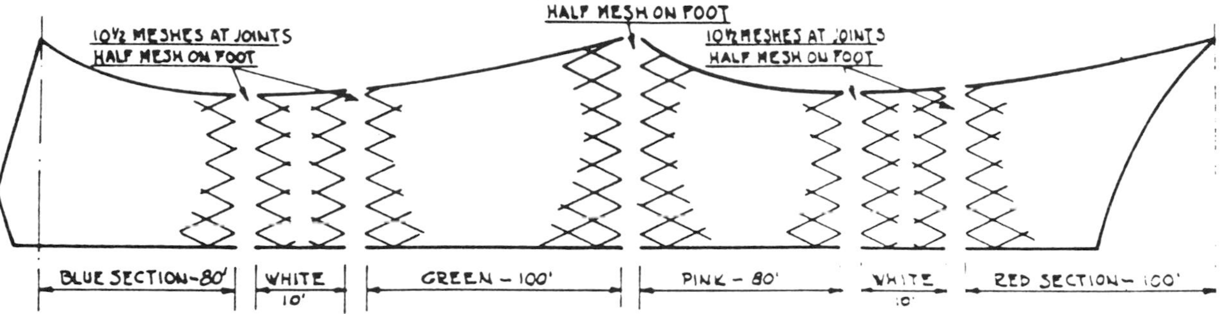

AND net details – British tanker type. (Currey collection)

original American ships this system was adopted initially but it was changed later when the boom was fitted with a wedge-shaped steel structure which fitted into a reverse wedge on the crosstrees, thus doing away with the rope fender.

The nets. The nets consisted of a continuous 5⁄16in diameter steel wire having a breaking strain of about 6 tons force, woven into a series of very open diamond meshes measuring 5ft across by 2½ft high. Grips secured the adjacent corners of each mesh and attached the mesh strands to the boundary ropes. The net weighed about 1 ton per 100ft including the head and footrope. The weight of a 260ft freighter net with kite and drogue was 3¼ tons.

To take the impact of a torpedo (about 120 foot-tons force) without breaking, and to either bring the torpedo to rest, or deflect it under the ship, the net had to be made elastic by allowing the mesh strands to slip through the mesh grips at a certain tension. (In the 1917 'Actaeon' net and those used in *Queen of Bermuda* and *Arandora Star*, rendering was designed to occur in the running lacing between the horizontal headrope and the blondin, the mesh grips being bolted up as hard as possible to prevent any slip in the body of the net.)

For convenience in manufacture, transport and repairs, freighter nets were divided into sections labelled red, yellow and blue on the diagrams and carrying identification tags showing manufacturer of net, type of design, type of vessel, colour of net, length along footrope, etc. Tanker nets were divided into red, white, pink, green and blue sections. It was possible to repair American nets with British sections and vice-versa and the British Type II and American Type II freighter nets were completely interchangeable, as were the Type II tanker nets.

Nets suffered from metal fatigue, rusting and the corrosive action of exhaust gases from the ship's funnel. Nothing is known of the endurance of the 1917 'Actaeon' net but the life of *Arandora Star*'s was determined at approximately 100 hours towing time. When reviving net defence in 1941, a target was set for a net life of 400 hours, this being the average time for an Atlantic crossing in convoy. By 1943, when nets were being turned out in sufficient numbers, it was laid down that nets should be changed if they had been fitted for more than six months or had been towed for more than 300 hours.

Loss of speed. The drag of a 360ft tanker net was 4 to 4½ tons force at 9kts. The resistance due to the length of the net did not vary greatly with its increase in length, as the after half of the net was travelling through water already disturbed by the passage of the leading half. While maintaining a constant horsepower, the towing of two standard nets made up of 1in circumference mesh strand and 26ft deep caused a reduction in the ship's speed of 17

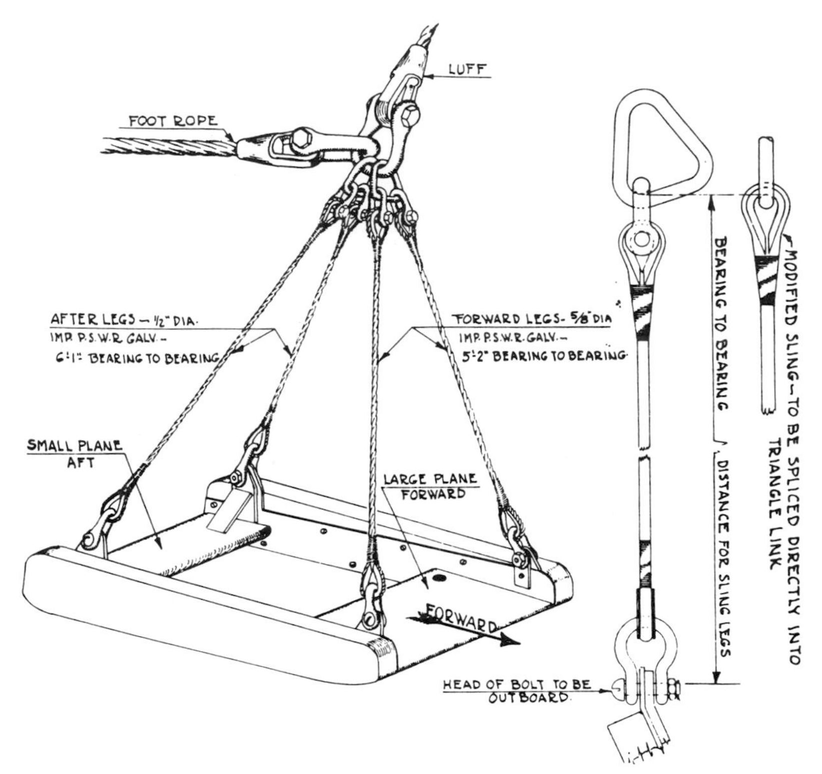

AND kite arrangement. The MkI kite for use with a standard net was so successful that, apart from being strengthened, it remained unaltered throughout the war. (Currey collection)

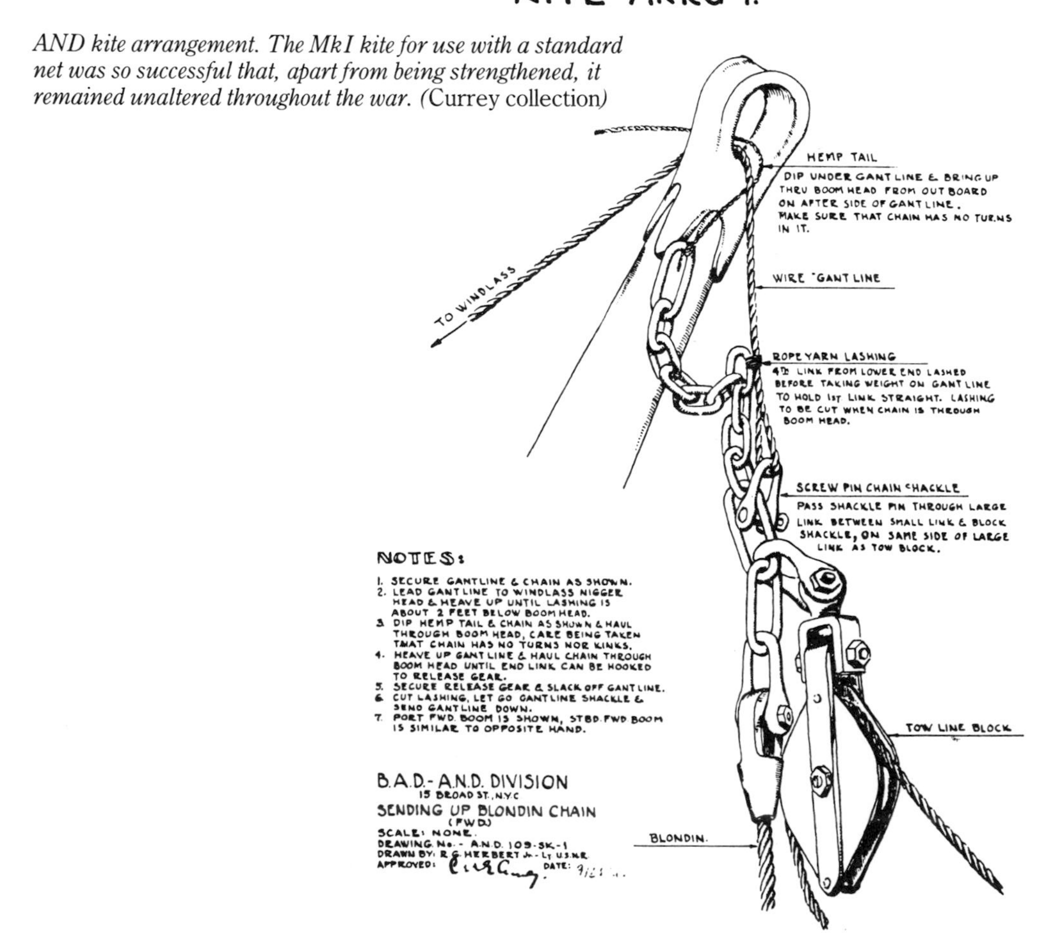

per cent. Steaming at 10kts one would expect to achieve 8.3kts with net defence streamed. When towing a net on one side only, the speed loss was 9 per cent: the steering was not affected. Between 8 and 14kts the percentage loss of speed when towing nets remained practically constant. They were reasonably effective at catching torpedoes down to a minimum speed of 7kts, although for a hundred per cent success rate against 21in 40kt torpedoes a towing speed of 9½kts was necessary, and 10½kts for 45kt torpedoes. (The slower a ship is going, the smaller should be the size of the mesh.) Thus it was necessary to strike a compromise at 5ft x 2½ft mesh and accept a less than one hundred per cent interception rate, otherwise the majority of ships towing nets could not have kept up with their convoys.

Principle of the rendering net. A torpedo travelling through water possesses kinetic energy (energy of motion) depending on its mass and the square of its velocity ($KE = \frac{1}{2}mv^2$). When the foot-tons force of the torpedo's initial KE (taking into account its velocity relative to the moving net) is equal to the foot-tons of work done against the rendering net and the water, the torpedo will be brought to rest.

If the distance available had been large, the retarding force could have been much smaller and a lighter net used. However it was not practicable to carry Net Defence more than 50ft from the ship's side and in any case this full distance was not available because a torpedo was between 20 and 22ft in length. At the moment of its closest approach to the hull of a ship, when it was entangled in the net by its tail and propellers, it was observed during trials that the nose of the torpedo was only 5ft to 6ft from the ship's side. This confirmed that the allowable 25ft of movement of the net at the point of entry was just about reached by a torpedo with a kinetic energy of 150 foot-tons force, the maximum for which the net had been designed.

Cost of Net Defence equipment. The approximate cost of supplying and fitting AND gear to a ship (ex-nets) was as follows:

	Cargo Ship	*Tanker*
1) Cost of permanent fittings	£800	£3200
2) Cost of DNC's fittings	£2300	£3100
3) Cost of winches	—	£2600
4) Cost of fitting items 2 and 3	£1500	£1800
TOTAL	£4600	£10,700
Cost of suit of nets	£950	£1250

Net Defence administration. In December 1942 Net Defence became a separate department of the Admiralty. Depots and servicing stations were established in the UK, the Mediterranean, North America, the West Indies, West Africa and South Africa. In the UK the complement employed at the depots eventually reached a total of 37 officers, 260 ratings and 75 WRNS, the total British manpower commitment being about 500 naval personnel and some 50 civilians. American and Canadian figures are not available but are thought to have been of the same order.

US Maritime Commission

In the United States the defence was called Torpedo Net Defence and was dealt with by the US Maritime Commission, Lt-Cdr (later Captain) E W Sundstrom, USNR who had long and varied experience as a Master in American merchant ships, being assigned by the US Navy to the British Admiralty Delegation under Captain Currey, RN. In November 1942 The South Portland Shipbuilding Corporation completed the hull of the SS *John Carver*, the first 'Liberty' ship to be fitted with Net Defence. The SS *William Bradford* followed a month later, and like her predecessor, after crossing the Atlantic to the UK, sailed to North Africa (convoys KMS9 and KMS10).

Net Defence depots were established at Boston, Massachusetts; Greenpoint, Brooklyn and Clifton, Staten Island in New York harbour; and at Philadelphia, Norfolk, Virginia, Savannah, Georgia, New Orleans, Galveston and San Francisco. Later the Americans assisted the Dutch with a depot at Curacao. The Canadians had depots at Victoria, BC, Montreal, Halifax, St John and Sydney, CB.

Wartime developments in Net Defence

Net Defence design was subject to continuous research

SS John Carver *the first 'Liberty' ship to be equipped with Net Defence. (US Coast Guard)*

▲ *The* Empire Tourist *fitted with 'extended defence'.* (World Ship Society)

▼ *The US 'zipper-ship'* Sarah J Hale *in 1943 fitted with 'extended defence'.* (US Navy)

throughout the war. During 1942, efforts were made to produce a better mesh grip to replace Type I and after more than a dozen types had been tested, Type XXI was introduced and adopted. Besides the 1 x 19 Filler strand generally used for net-making in the UK, three other constructions were tried at different times.

In order to give increased protection against 18in airborne torpedoes, 5ft x 2ft mesh nets were made and these were tried in the ss *Empire Heywood* where they proved highly effective, but had to be rejected because they would not clear the ship's side for brailing inboard. 50in x 25in nets ensured one hundred per cent interception of 21in 45kt torpedoes and 70 per cent probability of interception of 18in 45kt torpedoes when towed at 9kts. They resulted in a speed loss of 22 per cent, but such nets were fitted in the fast operational 5000-ton tankers in 1944 after trials in *Empire Crest*.

'Extended defence'. In addition to obtaining extra defence by using splay of booms, fifteen freighters built in Britain were fitted with what was known as 'extended defence'.

◄ *The US 'Liberty' ship* James A Farrell, *with a full cargo, during net trials off Melville, Rhode Island during August 1943. Using US Mk 14-3A 31kt torpedoes at 500–600yds range, there were four 'catches' and three penetrations.* (Currey collection)

This extension of defence was obtained by fitting a goalpost mast, similar to those in tankers, about 40ft forward of the foremast, just abaft the forecastle head. The forward ND booms were stepped on these posts instead of near the foremast. The length of defence was thus increased to 325ft as compared with 270ft, the bulkhead between No1 and No2 holds thus being protected from torpedoes fired from any track angle which was not less than 60 degrees. The MV *Empire Tourist* had 'extended defence' and was used for trials with this type of equipment in November 1943. When steaming at 9¼kts there were 10 catches and 7 penetrations using 40kt Mk IX torpedoes. In the USA, six 'zipper ships' (a re-design of the basic 'Liberty' ship) were built with 'extended defence'.

German countermeasures to Net Defence. In the case of Net Defence ships, it was to the British advantage that the Germans used the G7e (T2) torpedo much more frequently than the 44kt G7a (T1). The slower electric torpedo was easier to catch with its exposed contra-rotating propellers. The British had taken every precaution ashore and afloat in enforcing the secrecy of the development of AND, but U-boat commanders lost no time in reporting its use. Admiral Doenitz's War Diary for 22 February 1942 bears testimony to the efficiency of his officers in detecting the device, in details of the attack on convoy No12 (ON67) in which *Empire Celt* together with other ships were torpedoed.

> *U-558* reported in convoy No12 two tankers with anti-submarine nets were observed. [author's note: only *Empire Celt* had AND in this convoy.] Reports from *U-558* and *U-587* (see convoy No12) and the oral report from the commander of *U-654* have strengthened the suspicion that the English are using torpedo nets to deflect torpedo attacks. U-boats have been instructed to look out for this and report immediately. The Torpedo Experimental Establishment (TVA) have been informed of the necessity of developing a countermeasure against anti-torpedo nets.

However, despite this, one gains the impression that the Germans were never completely successful. B d U, Naval High Command, Note No4 dated 26 March 1943 stated: 'At present, the only way to deal with torpedo nets is to fire under them. Percussion firing hits on the nets have practically no effect on the vessel. The possibility of achieving hits with non-contact action can be expected only if the magnetic fields begin to decrease at depths to which nets do not reach. In this case the 'Mz-action' [ie magnetic action] of the pistol must be utilised to the lower boundary of their firing area.' The note detailed increased depth settings of the torpedoes, if rigged nets were observed.

Nose cutters were reported from time to time on German as well as Japanese torpedoes, but were ineffective against AND. The German tail cutter was only produced late in the war, which was fortunate for the allies. It would have met the mesh strand with heavy pressure, and if it had not cut through, might have weakened the strand enough for it to break, or possibly guided the strand over the tail frame without entanglement. It is not known if a cutter of this type was actually used against a ship with AND.

Allied nets were designed with the German torpedo pistol types Pi1 and Pi2 in mind and attempts were made accordingly by the enemy to adapt these two types so they would not fire in coming in contact with the net. A temporary solution of the problem was the alteration of the 'whiskers' on the Pi1 and Pi2 and the substitution of a special grey iron cap for the standard cap. The conclusions drawn from all the German tests was that only by a combination of an impact pistol with an inertia pistol was it possible to penetrate the net without firing.

A net cutter fitted to tail of a German G7e (T2) torpedo. (MoD)

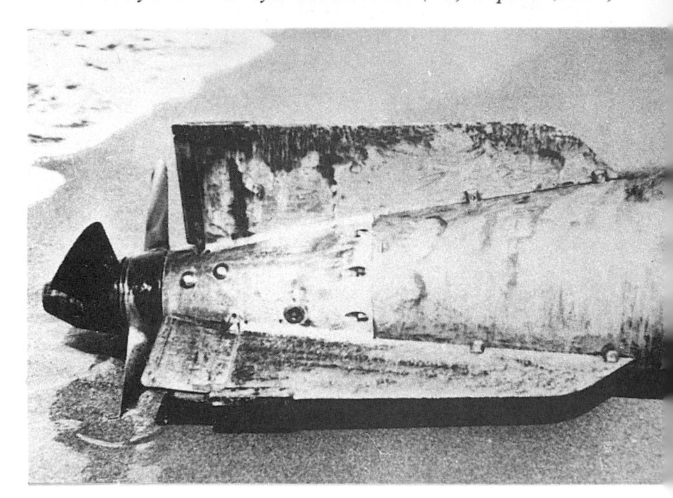

The tail of a G7e (T2) torpedo stranded at Anzio. (Currey collection)

In torpedoes fitted with inertia pistols, the sudden retardation of the torpedo due to meeting an obstruction displaces a small delicately suspended mass, which actuates the pistol. The spring suspension of the mass can be varied to fire at various decelerations, usually between 6g and 16g. The British were aware of this. The maximum deceleration of a torpedo on being caught in the net was probably about 6g, so there was not much likelihood of an inertia pistol firing the warhead. (It would have done so within about 10ft of the ship's side – a dangerous proximity compared with the 50ft distance when a torpedo exploded as a result of the whiskers catching on the mesh strand.)

Effectiveness of Net Defence

An analysis of known torpedo attacks on ships with their nets streamed shows that 62 per cent were saved by their nets, 19 per cent were sunk by torpedoes which struck the hull fore or abaft the net and 9½ per cent were sunk by torpedoes which penetrated the net; 9½ per cent were so badly damaged that they were declared a constructive total loss.

However a study of AND and its fitting in 768 ships (about 10 per cent of tonnage available) reveals that the defence might have been used advantageously on a great many more occasions than it in fact was. In many instances ships were lost because their nets had not been streamed: because ships had sailed before their equipment had been repaired; or because deck cargo precluded the streaming of nets. AND reduced the deck cargo capacity by an average of 20 per cent, if the nets were kept clear for use.

The contention between the Admiralty and Ministry of War Transport (MOWT) is highlighted in the communication of the Superintendent, Net Defence Department (Rear-Admiral W B Mackenzie) to the Assistant Chief of Naval Staff (UT) dated 27 March 1943. It is not known whether this was prompted by the sinking of *Empire Banner* and *Empire Webster* in the attack on the 'Torch' Supply convoy KMS8 off the North African coast on 7 February 1943, but this appears highly probable.

> As regards repairs and servicing of AND ships and the training of their crews.
> 1) MOWT view is that ships must not be allowed to miss a convoy.
> 2) Admiralty view is that ships should sail with their nets efficient and their crews trained, so as to afford the fullest protection practicable.

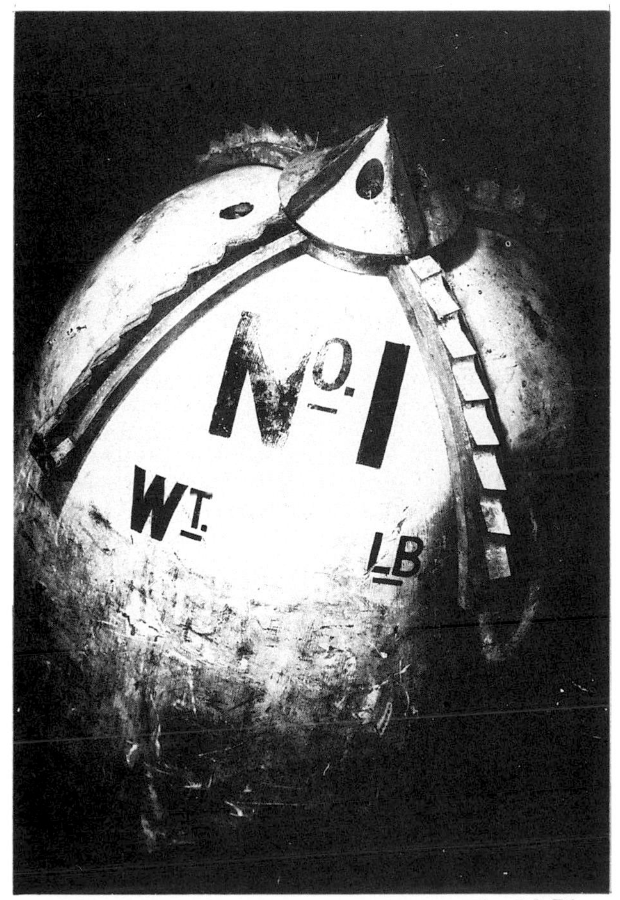

A net cutter fitted to the nose of a Japanese torpedo. (MoD)

> 3) A definite general ruling is considered essential regarding the future policy to be followed....

Deck cargoes produced heated arguments between ships' masters and Sea Transport Officers representing the MOWT and the unsatisfactory position is illustrated in the 'Report of Proceedings of Convoy KMS3'.

> *Ocean Wayfarer*, *Thistledale* and *Empire Webster* reported that they were unable to get their nets out owing to the stowage of deck cargo and shifting of cargo. Quite apart from the undoubted value that AND has proved, it would appear poor policy to spend so much time, thought and expense on an experiment and then to deliberately negative it by lack of proper supervision.
>
> B W L Nicholson, Capt, RN (Retd), Commodore
> *City of Venice*

> Although nine ships were listed as fitted with AND, only six were able to stream them; one of the masters informed the Commodore that the leading authorities insisted that carrying deck cargo was more important than the ability to work his nets.
>
> Commanding Officer, HMS *Black Swan*,
> Senior Officer Escort

However, in some instances, serious attempts were made to counteract the constraints imposed by deck cargoes. Lt-Cmdr R G Herbert, USNR (Retd), who worked with Captain C N E Currey, RN in New York recalls the case of part of a locomotive cab being removed with oxy-acetylene torches to enable the Net Defence to be used. The cab was welded back in position on arrival at its destination.

Speed was an important safety factor, so it is perhaps not surprising that there appears initially to have been a lack of appreciation of the working of Net Defence by some convoy commodores. Captain John Lennie of SS *Fort Paskoyac*, in position 13 in convoy KMS10, when his ship was torpedoed 'just under the port quarter' at 14.25 on 6 March 1943, later reported:

> On 5 March, we were ordered by the Commodore to stream our AND nets. The convoy speed at the time was 9kts, but in order to stream nets it is necessary to reduce speed to 6kts. As the maximum speed of *Fort Paskoyac* was only 10kts, I knew that it would not be possible to regain position in the convoy if I reduced speed. Accordingly I signalled this information to the Commodore: the reply came back for us to stream nets and maintain convoy speed. The port net was successfully streamed, but whilst lowering the starboard net the speed of the ship put too much strain on the winch which carried away. Consequently the net was not streamed.

As *Fort Paskoyac* was hit on the port side by *U-410*'s (Fenski) first torpedo, a G7e(T2), fired at a range of 1200m, the outcome was not materially effected by this mistake. It is not clear whether the torpedo was deflected by the net or just missed it. It is perhaps ironic that three hours after the signal to stream AND had been given, the convoy reversed course through 180 degrees for three and half hours so as not to arrive at the rendezvous before time.

The 'Official Policy as Regards the Use of Nets' is detailed in *Admiralty War Diary* on 2 March 1943:

Fort La Have, *one of many Canadian 'Victory' type ships equipped with Net Defence.* (Tom Rayner)

> In ocean convoys, ships fitted with AND should normally only stream their nets if the convoy is threatened with attack, and occasionally for drill purposes, when circumstances permit. If threatened with attack, the commodore should if necessary reduce the speed of the convoy to enable ships with AND gear to maintain their station in convoy with their nets streamed.
>
> Director Trade Division, 18.14A/2

It is significant that by 1944 in the Mediterranean, Convoy Form A1 included an additional heading 'Net Defence ships which failed to maintain convoy speed'. By 1945 the Official Policy had also been amended to '...the Commodore will order the nets to be streamed provided the towing of the nets does not reduce the speed of the convoy more than half an knot.'

According to Rear-Admiral Mackenzie, for Operation 'Overlord' (Normandy landings) vessels had their AND gear temporarily removed in compliance with special Admiralty instructions. 'Nine AND vessels were torpedoed, or presumed torpedoed, whilst at sea, as against two mined and two bombed. Statistics based on the practical results of attacks show that had these nine vessels been using their nets, four or five of them would have been undamaged.'

But statistics do not tell the whole story. The actual number of ships saved by torpedoes being deflected on striking the net will never be known, as the only evidence of this event could have been the rattling of the 'blondin rollers', which could have well passed unnoticed, particularly at night. This function of the net was definitely observed during the trials of ss *Empire Rhodes* off New London, Connecticut on 3 April 1942.

The opponents of net defence can list the cost of materials, manpower and delays whilst the protagonists produce figures to show the value of vessels and their war cargoes saved, but no price can be placed on human life. The American 'Liberty' ship *James W Fannin*, carrying some 650 troops, arrived in Malta undamaged with an 18in aircraft torpedo caught in her net after an attack on convoy UGS40. She had steamed for 36 hours unaware of the lethal 'cargo' she was carrying. The effect upon the morale of the crews of merchant ships, particularly engine-room personnel, was also an extremely important factor. By 1941 the proportion of crews lost in ships which were sunk had increased to 53.9 per cent.

Attitude of crews to Net Defence

The story of AND is not complete without a mention of the attitude of the men who had to handle the equipment under the guidance of the Chief Officer. Proficient seamen, if they had been adequately trained, took all this in their stride, despite the fact there was much standing and running gear and many moving parts requiring maintenance. Efficient ships' crews, versed in practical seamanship, kept the gear in excellent working order. Others neglected it and created problems for themselves. Those who had already survived three years of being bombed, mined and torpedoed, accepted their extra duties with equanimity and a stream of profanities when things went wrong, which was not infrequent. So much depended on the vagaries of the weather, which explains why the device's greatest potential lay in its use in the Mediterranean convoys. An increase in the height of the sea or swell required constant vigilance to avoid the ship rolling her boom ends under water. Bad weather necessitated brailing the nets and housing the booms. The only safe method of avoiding damage, when working cargo, was to lower the forward boomhead assembly complete on to the deck by means of a gantline.

But even the most circumspect masters could not foresee

The disguised motor tanker Empire Spenser. *Note the false funnel amidships and the engine exhausts on the poop.* (Currey collection)

all contingencies. On 7 November 1943 MV *Houston City* reported that her port net was put out of action by fouling a giant ray during the voyage from Kilindini to Diego Suarez.

Captain J L Fitzpatrick, MV *Empire Commerce* (3722gt), was a staunch advocate of AND. In view of this it is perhaps ironic that his ship was sunk as a result of being supplied with the wrong fuel so that it could not keep up with convoy MKS26 without housing the nets. He reported 'I have sailed in some twenty Mediterranean convoys and always kept my nets streamed unless ordered not to do so by Commodores. My gear always worked perfectly. We had six booms, as is usual for tankers, and I consider ND is a magnificent protection.'

The report of Captain W S Keay of SS *Ocean Rider* (7178gt), which was bound for Bone with some 4000 tons of military stores and damaged by aerial torpedo at 05.25 BST on 21 January 1943 near Algiers, reveals an all too frequent blunder with Net Defence ships. Convoy KMS7 had been subjected to submarine and air attack from 15.30 on 20 January.

> With regard to AND, we had orders at the Convoy Conference not to stream nets without instructions from the Commodore, and as he gave no orders to do so, the nets were kept furled during the whole outward voyage. No ships in the entire convoy had their nets streamed in consequence of this order. I have a lot of faith in these AND nets. I think they are excellent and we have no trouble at all in either streaming or housing them. The Chief Officer has taken considerable interest in them, and has taken a lot of trouble in perfecting net drill, so that we can lower or hoist the nets in a few minutes. We have been fitted with nets for the past year.

Second Officer N S Needham of SS *Empire Camp* in 1944 paints a different picture.

> After AND had been fitted, we were given a very minimal amount of training in very calm seas in the North of Scotland. Streaming of nets was achieved safely when sailing in a convoy bound for the USA, but winter North Atlantic weather gradually worsened and the dipping of the booms into the sea caused a considerable strain on the masts. Rehousing the booms in a heavily rolling tramp with a limited number of seamen proved impossible, although we managed to partially brail the heavy nets and returned alone to the UK for repairs.
>
> We sailed in another convoy on 20 January 1944. Bad weather again necessitated an attempt to house the booms, but the heavy seas flung the net over the brailing wire. In spite of extremely arduous attempts, the net could not be disengaged, and with the booms at 45 degrees from the vertical and a swinging net, we had to again return to the UK on our own.
>
> On our third attempt to reach the States, the use of nets hindered our progress. The Master said that he would not return so ignominiously for the third time, and as we had no hope of catching the convoy, we followed the stragglers route and arrived safely in Canada. The fitting of these nets certainly did not improve the morale of the crew of *Empire Camp*.

It is not known whether Captain Currey's slogan 'Two men, two minutes at two knots' was ever achieved by a highly efficient merchant crew, but he proved the point about the speed of operation by taking 2 minutes 24 seconds with Lt-Cmdr R G Herbert, USNR aboard a 'Liberty' ship. However, 20 minutes to stream both nets was considered reasonable.

To ensure quick and efficient operation, standardized

Despite her Net Defence ss Ocean Seaman *was torpedoed by* U-380 *in convoy ET14 on 15 March 1943 some 60 miles off Algier. The torpedo was fired from 500m, with a depth setting of 4m and activated by magnetic influence pistols. The ship was towed into Algiers but declared a constructive total loss.* (Author)

procedures were adopted and these were laid down in the secret 14-page *Admiralty Net Defence Handbook* supplied to the ship's master. After a brief description of the gear and its maintenance, paragraph II gave instructions for streaming nets in a cargo ship. Paragraph 25 was very important:

> To slip the net with the torpedo in it the operations should be carried out in the following order:
> a) Proceed at slow speed.
> b) Run the brail wire off the winch (there will be a few turns on the drum) and cast it overboard. (It will tow out clear from the boom head.)
> c) Slip the net from the after boom.
> d) Cut the towing rope in the guillotine.
> e) Slip the net from the forward boom *immediately the towing rope is cut.* If at all possible, it is important throughout the whole of this operation to keep the ship turning *towards* the side on which the nets are to be slipped so as to keep the stern of the ship well clear of nets and torpedo.

The success of Net Defence ships

Up to VE day there had been 51 known attacks on ND ships by torpedo: 45 by U-boats and 6 by aircraft. Of these attacks 21 were made when nets were streamed and 30 when nets were not in use. In 16 out of the 21 attacks on British and American ships with nets streamed, the records show that 23 torpedoes contacted the net.

The casualties to ships attacked were:

	Nets streamed	Nets not streamed
Sunk or total loss	8	23
Damaged	3	7
Undamaged or damage negligible	10	–
Number attacked	21	30

Lack of documentation and conflicting reports make it impossible to confirm the analysis of the attacks on ships with nets streamed, which was produced at the end of the war. However it is included because of its historic interest and by way of summary:

> An analysis of the attacks on ships with nets streamed shows that 10 were definitely saved by this protection, the torpedo being stopped by the net in 6 cases, deflected by the net in 1 case, and exploded in the net in 3 cases. Of the remaining 11 cases, 8 were sunk, being hit either forward, abaft, under or through the net, and 3 were damaged by the torpedo hitting forward, exploding in, or penetrating the net respectively.

Acknowledgements

The author wishes to record his grateful appreciation to the undermentioned:

Lt-Cmdr Charles Currey, VRD, RNR for kindly lending me all his father's files and granting permission to use the photographs.

Lt-Cmdr R G Herbert, USNR (Retd) for supplying the technical details and drawings of American Net Defence and other material.

Mr David Brown, Head of Naval Historical Branch, Ministry of Defence for granting facilities for research, and the assistance of his staff.

Mr R M Coppock, Foreign Documents Section, Miniistry of Defence (N) for his encouragement and assistance.

Mr A J Francis, Naval Historical Library, Ministry of Defence for Information on Net Defences of capital ships and the 'Actaeon' experiments.

The staff of the Public Record Office.

Mr Tom Rayner for supplying photographs as indicated.

Mr N S Needham for his recollections of Net Defence.

Mr Michael Gillen, Editor *Liberty Log.*

Lt-Cmdr A Hague, VRD, RNR, Naval Sub Committee, World Ship Society.

ROYAL NAVY ANTI-AIRCRAFT SHIPS: NAVAL AND MERCANTILE CONVERSIONS 1934–1943

Despite much written to the contrary, the Royal Navy was very alert to the threat of air power and was among the first to produce specialist AA vessels. Initially obsolescent cruisers were reconstructed but later small merchant ships were converted, producing some of the most capable auxiliary warships of the war. John English looks at the design background.

The rapid development of bomber aircraft during the 1920s and early 1930s posed a serious threat to surface fleets and their ability to operate in areas dominated by enemy aircraft. In Britain, the leaders of the Royal Navy, especially Admiral Ernle Chatfield (First Sea Lord 1932–38), attempted to overcome this threat in several ways:

1 The re-acquisition of an air component, which had been lost when the Royal Naval Air Service was combined with the Royal Flying Corps to form the Royal Air Force in April 1918. This was achieved in April 1937 when the Royal Navy acquired complete operational and technical control of the Fleet Air Arm from the RAF.
2 The provision of better anti-aircraft weapons for Fleet use. The current (1934) naval weapons – the 4.7in, 4in and 3in guns were totally unsuitable for modern requirements; however, development of the Mk XVI 4in gun with the MkXIX mounting, the 5.25in gun and the multiple machine-gun was slow and time was to show that the 5.25in weapon was over-complex and the pom poms not wholly successful in service. This problem of point-defence was not to be fully solved until the adoption of the Bofors 40mm in 1940, and even then it was several years before this weapon was in general operation.
3 The provision, by new construction of vessels which were better able to withstand aerial bombardment and armed with better weapons and director equipment. Budget constraints meant that the number of vessels constructed would always be less than requirements.
4 The conversion of obsolete naval vessels to anti-aircraft (AA) duties.
5 The conversion of suitable merchant ships to AA vessels in time of emergency.

It is with the vessels in categories 4 and 5, that this article is concerned, especially the later 'C' group cruisers and mercantile vessels converted between September 1939 and July 1943.

The cruiser squadrons contained in the 'C', 'D' and 'E' classes a legacy of the particular requirements of the First World War, which had been fought in the restricted waters of the North Sea. These cruisers, excellent when constructed, suffered from poor endurance and, like most of the fleet in 1934, had poor anti-aircraft armament and, because of their limited endurance, could not be used on the normal deployment for such vessels – that of trade protection on overseas stations. However, if modified, these vessels could provide the fleet with the handy AA vessels that were desperately needed, and at a reasonable price.

The reconstructions were to be limited in their extent and expense. The original 1934 proposals envisaged that the whole of the 'C' group would be modified between June 1936 and March 1940, after the results of the prototype conversions of *Coventry* and *Curlew* had been assessed. The re-arming of the 'D's and 'E's were to follow as soon as

One of the first group of conversions, Curlew *carried the single 4in Mk V gun on Mk III HA mounts. All later conversions were to carry the twin Mk XIX 4in mount.* Curlew *was an early war loss being sunk by aircraft off Ofotfjord, Norway on 26 May 1940.* (Wright & Logan)

finance, dockyard capacity and modern weapons became available. The programme was to suffer long delays, with the conversions of the third and fourth vessels (*Cairo* and *Calcutta*) not being completed until May and July 1939 respectively. *Curacoa* and *Carlisle* then entered dockyard hands for conversion and were still in dockyard hands when the war started. The conversion of *Capetown*, planned to start in November 1939, was cancelled on the outbreak of war and she was never subsequently re-armed. Details of the two later conversions, that of *Colombo* between June 1942 and March 1943 and *Caledon* between September 1942 and December 1943, will be given later.

The prototypes

Coventry was converted at Portsmouth during 1935–36, whilst Chatham Dockyard reconstructed *Curlew*. The conversions consisted of the removal of the vessels' original armament and torpedoes and its replacement by:

1 Ten single 4in Mk V guns on Mk III HA (high-angle) mountings (these weapons had previously been landed from other vessels).
2 Two Mk VI eight-barrel pom-pom mountings (these had to be retro-fitted to the vessels as they were not available on completion.
3 The removal of the original fire control equipment and spotting top and its replacement by two HACS Mk III – one erected on the foremast and one on the shelter deck, abaft the mainmast.

Topweight had to be reduced to accommodate these changes and this was achieved by the removal of the fore topmast, the removal of the original mainmast and its replacement by a new mast fitted further forward. Other weight-saving measures were the removal of the after

The other of the first group of conversions was Coventry. *She was to survive damage from bombs on 17 March 1940 off Crete and participate in many actions in the Mediterranean, before being lost in the disastrous combined operation raid on Tobruk on 14 September 1942.* (IWM)

Cairo *pictured at Malta on completion of the contested 'Harpoon' operation to Malta betwen 7 and 16 June 1942. She was damaged by two 8in shells during this action, but survived. She was not to be so lucky two months later, when she was torpedoed by the Italian submarine* Axum *during the 'Pedestal' convoy operation, with the loss of 23 lives; she had to be sunk by the destroyer* Pathfinder. *(IWM)*

control position and its replacement by a smaller structure carrying a 36in searchlight and its controls, and the emergency engine room controls.

The 6in magazines were converted to accommodate 4in ammunition and the existing 4in ammunition magazine amidships was expanded by providing additional stowage space on the platform deck. Pom-pom ammunition was stowed here and in the main magazines. Supplementary ammunition was stowed in ready-use lockers. Even with these weight-reduction measures, the heavier gun mountings and associated fittings, together with the HA directors being placed high in the vessels, meant that both vessels shipped permanent ballast – 100 tons in *Coventry* and 92 tons in *Curlew*.

Later modifications to both vessels were limited – both vessels had one pom-pom removed and two quadruple 0.5 mountings were substituted with consequent changes in magazine stowage during 1938–39. *Curlew* also lost her searchlight platform and mainmast. The only other modifications to the vessels were the suppression of their waist 4in mounts in late 1939, because of the effect of blast on other gun crews. Later, *Coventry* also received Oerlikons, having five single 20mm in May 1942.

The second group of conversions (1938–39)

The reconstructions of *Cairo* and *Calcutta* differed from the original conversions in the following ways:

1 The twin 4in HA/LA and mounting (Mk XIX) was now available in larger quantities and this weapon was substituted for the original Mk V guns on Mk III HA mountings. The four new mountings utilized the existing 6in gun positions and as a result the structural alterations required in these vessels were less extensive than in the prototypes.
2 No 2 6in mounting was replaced by a quadruple 2pdr on a Mk VIII mounting.
3 The obsolete 3in AA gun abreast the funnel was removed and replaced by two 0.5in quadruple machine-guns on raised platforms.
4 The torpedo tubes were removed.
5 The after control position was removed and 36in searchlights were fitted each side of the aft superstructure.
6 Original pole mast was replaced by a large tripod mast with direction-finding equipment.
7 The existing fire control equipment was removed and replaced by two HACS Mk III directors on the foremast and after superstructure. A pom-pom director platform was fitted on the compass platform.
8 The magazines were modified as in *Coventry* and *Curlew* except that there was no ammunition provided on the platform deck forward.

Again, permanent ballast was carried in both vessels – 111 tons in *Cairo*, but the figure for *Calcutta* is unknown. The later conversions of *Curacoa* and *Carlisle* were very similar (mid-1939 to April 1940 and early 1940 respectively). *Curacoa* and *Carlisle* were completed with one quadruple 2pdr, two quadruple 0.5in MGs and two single 2pdr. By September *Curacoa* had five single 20mm added. *Carlisle* had seven 20mm by April 1942 but by November they were replaced by five single 40mm.

Later cruiser conversions (1942–43)

The need to have vessels in service and urgent repair and conversion work occupied the dockyards until mid-1942,

D41

◀ *Under conversion at the start of the war,* Carlisle *first saw action off Norway. She became a victim of the disastrous Aegean campaign, being declared a constructive total loss after bomb damage in the Scarpanto Strait on 9 October 1943. She was then used as a base ship at Alexandria.* (IWM)

Curacoa *is chiefly remembered by the manner of her loss – by collision with the liner* Queen Mary *off Bloody Foreland on 2 October 1942 with the loss of 338 of her crew. She had earlier survived bomb damage off Andalsnes on 29 April 1940.* (IWM)

when the decision was made to convert two further vessels of the 'C' group – *Colombo* of the *Carlisle* class was converted between June 1942 and March 1943 and *Caledon*, the lead ship of her class and the oldest to be converted, between September 1942 and December 1943.

The whole of *Caledon*'s forward superstructure was rebuilt to resemble the converted *Ceres* and *Carlisle* class vessels and on conversion she was almost identical to *Colombo*. The basic conversions consisted of:

1 The removal of the original armament and replacement by:
- (i) Three twin 4in at No 1, 2 and 5 mountings.
- (ii) Two twin 40mm Bofors Mk IV (Hazemayer) was fitted abaft the second funnel.
- (iii) Six twin 20mm fitted.

2 The fore and main masts were replaced by light tripod masts, as a weight-reduction measure.
3 Modern radars were fitted.
4 A HACS Mk III fitted with a director above the compass platform.

The unconverted vessels

The five unconverted vessels were to see varied amounts of service. *Calypso*, a recent reinforcement to the Mediterranean Fleet, succumbed to torpedo attack by the Italian submarine *Bagnolini* off the coast of Cyrenaica on 13 June 1940 with the loss of 39 lives. *Cardiff* served as a gunnery training ship in home waters for the whole of the war and survived to be broken up post-war. *Caradoc* and *Ceres*, after service on trade-protection duties, had been relegated to subsidiary duties by 1944. *Capetown*, which had been projected to start a conversion in November 1939 was never converted and again survived to be scrapped post-war.

G C Connel in his book *Valiant Quartet* quotes the following criticism of the 4in weapons deployed aboard *Coventry* and *Calcutta*.

The gun systems:
1 were hand-operated, without power assistance;
2 suffered from inaccuracies of elevation and the firing mechanism had a margin of error of ±2° and that of the mounting of ¾°;
3 used powder-activated time fuses with an accuracy of ±100ft.

Furthermore, as far as fire control was concerned:
4 the internal communications by telephones and dials could be overwhelmed by the noise and smoke of action;
5 all elevation, training and fuse settings were obtained from a primitive hand-operated computer, termed a high-angle fire control system (HACS), which based its calculations on the HA control officer's visual findings from the rangefinders and elevation and training information from the director.

Thus, there was a large margin of error implicit in the system and the likelihood of hitting, let alone destroying, an aircraft was limited. That *Coventry* and *Calcutta* were

The oldest and last to be converted, Caledon *was rebuilt at Chatham between September 1942 and December 1943. She survived to be scrapped postwar. Her diminutive size is apparent when compared to the Greek destroyer* Navarinon *(ex-*Echo*).* (IWM)

Springbank *was one of a large group of sisters ordered in 1924 by the Bank Line. Requisitioned in October 1939, she finally emerged as a Fighter Catapult Ship in April 1941. Her career with Western Approaches Command was to be brief. Whilst escorting HG73 from Gibraltar to UK, she was torpedoed by* U-201 *in position (49°10′N, 20°05′W) on 27 September 1941, but finally sunk by the corvette* Jasmine *the next day.* (IWM)

regarded as first rate AA vessels is a tribute to the training of their crews and not the equipment they had to use and probably the lack of any suitable comparison.

The converted vessels were to have active but short lives, with five out of the six vessels, converted or under conversion on the outbreak of the war, becoming war losses and the survivor *Carlisle* being declared a constructive total loss, after being damaged by four bombs in the Aegean on 9 October 1943. All six vessels were heavily involved in the severe fighting off Norway in April and May 1940. *Curacoa* was badly damaged by bombs off the Andalsnes on 29 April 1940 and returned to the UK with her bridge destroyed and 30 of her crew killed. She was to be lost some 30 months later on 2 October 1942 in collision with RMS *Queen Mary* off the Bloody Foreland with the loss of 338 of her crew. *Curlew* did not survive the Norwegian Campaign being sunk by air attack in Oft Fiord on 26 May 1940.

Calcutta saw arduous service in the Mediterranean waters before she was sunk by some forty Ju87s, 60 miles north of Alexandria on 1 June 1941. Some 255 of *Calcutta*'s crew were rescued by her sister ship *Coventry*, which spent the first ten months of 1941 fitted with a temporary bow after being torpedoed by the Italian submarine *Naiade* on 13 December 1940. After a refit at Bombay between October 1941 and April 1942, *Coventry* saw further service on operation 'Vigorous' an abortive supply convoy to Malta in June 1942, and in the Gulf of Suez. Her end came when she was hit by four bombs from 15 Ju87s, which blew off her bow and damaged her engine and boiler room off Tobruk on 15 September 1942, when escorting a disastrous commando operation. *Coventry*'s hulk was torpedoed by the destroyer *Zulu*, which was also sunk the same day.

Cairo, which was dogged by propelling machinery defects for the whole of her war service, had seen action in North Russian waters, then escorted the USS *Wasp* on two fighter flying-off operations to Malta and was torpedoed by the Italian submarine *Axum* on 12 August 1942 during the 'Pedestal' operation. The 'Y' mounting was destroyed, as were the vessel's propellers and rudders and *Cairo* settled by the stern, her crew being taken off by the destroyer *Wilton*; 23 men were killed.

These 'C' class conversions were highly regarded in service, with *Coventry* being rated as an excellent AA vessel by the C-in-C Mediterranean Admiral A B Cunningham – a good judge. She was kept on station and in service, although damaged, by his specific request.

The mercantile conversions

On the outbreak of war, the plans for auxiliary AA vessels to supplement the cruiser conversion programme were implemented. These vessels were not intended for fleet duties, but to provide AA escorts for convoys, where their limited speed did not handicap them. The vessels had the following characteristics:

1 The vessels were to be armed with the MkXVI 4in gun on MkXIX mountings, with a director for each mounting (usually three or four per ship).
2 Initially, point-defence consisted of quadruple 2pdrs, 0.5in machine-guns and later 20mm oerlikons; all under local control.
3 The vessels were to be diesel-engined to provide the necessary range. The vessels were to have all the attributes of a warship except sub-division, protection and speed.

On 13 September 1939, *Foylebank* was requisitioned and her conversion was undertaken by Harland & Wolff and she was commissioned on 6 June 1940. The reconstruction involved removing all her superstructure except the funnel. The holds were converted into magazines and shell rooms, with attendant hoists, and survivability was improved by the provision of empty 50-gallon drums in all unused spaces and all bulkheads were shored-up. A new enclosed bridge was constructed, with a raised bandstand to mount a twin 4in gun mounting. Another 4in mounting was fitted close to the bow, with two other 4in mounts fitted aft.

Alynbank, *a sister of* Springbank, *was converted between October 1939 and August 1940 and served mainly in Irish Sea waters until May 1942. In that month she started to operate on the Arctic convoys and covered PQ16, QP13, PQ18 and QP14 before taking part in Operation 'Torch' until January 1943. Further service in the Mediterranean followed until November 1943, when she began a re-conversion to a merchant ship. However she was scuttled as part of the Mulberry Harbour on 6 August 1944.* (IWM) ▶

SECRET

Pozarica: *the completeness of her conversion by Fairfields can be seen. After operating in the Western Approaches until May 1942, she participated in the PQ17 convoy before her loss at Bougie on 13 February 1943. She had been torpedoed on 29 January 1943, but capsized during salvage operations.* (IWM)

Tripod masts were stepped abaft the bridge and forward of 'X' gun. Fire control was provided by two directors, one on the bridge and the other abaft the funnel.

Tragically, *Foylebank*'s career was to last barely a month. Even though the war situation in France was critical and air raids were to be expected, she was sent to work-up at Portland, where she was sunk at 1000 hours on 4 July 1940 after being hit by 22 bombs dropped in a coordinated attack by 20 Ju87s of *Stukageswader 51* and other bombers; 176 of her crew of 333 were lost, including Jack Mantle who won a posthumus Victoria Cross in defending the vessel to the end.

Foylebank's sister *Alynbank* underwent a similar conversion between October 1939 and August 1940. She operated as part of the Irish Sea escort Force for the next sixteen months. Following a refit at Belfast, where her radars were up-dated, Asdic installed and 20mm Oerlikons mounted, she returned to her duties with the Irish Sea Escort Force but was detached to act as an AA escort for Convoys PQ16, OP13, PQ17, PQ18 and QP14 to North Russia during the summer and autumn of 1942. Refitted once again, *Alynbank* operated in the Mediterranean until paid off during October 1943. She was, however, gutted by fire, when being re-converted to a merchant ship and was used as a block ship to form part of the Mulberry Harbour.

The third Bank Line vessel to be requisitioned was *Springbank* in November 1939. She was, however, to see no service as an AA vessel, because when nearing completion, it was decided to complete her as a Fighter Catapult Ship, utilizing the catapult from the heavy cruiser *Kent*, then under lengthy repair after torpedo damage received in the Mediterranean. She was completed on 23 April 1941 and after working-up, operated between the UK and Gibraltar, but did not survive long, being sunk by the corvette *Jasmine* on 28 September 1941 after being torpedoed by *U-201* in the Bay of Biscay.

The sisters *Pozarica* and *Polomares*, refrigerated fruit ships owned by MacAndrews of London, were requisitioned during June 1940 and August 1940 respectively. *Pozarica* was under conversion at Fairfields until March 1941. Her armament, on completion consisted of six 4in HA guns, 8 2pdr in quadruple mountings, two single 20mm Oerlikons, and eight 0.5in machine-guns. She also carried a complete radar suite, Asdic, echo-sounder and depth charges. Following a year's service with Western Aproaches Command and a refit following collision damage she escorted the ill-fated convoy PQ17 and after a period as AA guardship in North Russian waters she returned with QP14. After participating in the 'Torch' operation she remained in the Mediterranean on escort duties until 29 January 1943 when she was torpedoed by aircraft from *KG26*. Towed into Bougie; fifteen days later she capsized when salvage operations were being undertaken and became a total loss.

Her sister *Palomares* completed her conversion during September 1941, but a month later she was severely damaged in a collision and was under repair for six months. One of the escorts for the disastrous convoy PQ17, *Palmomare*, like her sister remained in Russian waters during the summer of 1942, returning with QP14 in September 1942. When on escort duty for the 'Torch' operation, she was attacked by German aircraft in Algiers Bay on 9 November 1942 and severely damaged. She was patched up and returned to the UK for permanent repairs and conversion to a Fighter Direction Ship, after less than six months active service as an Auxiliary Anti-Aircraft vessel.

Ulster Queen was converted by Harland & Wolff between August 1940 and November 1941. She was fitted with a cruiser bridge, two gun platforms forward and another aft, which supported a twin 4in gun mounting and director control tower. Two tripod masts were fitted, as were bandstands for 0.5in mountings alongside the bridge. Her conversion was the most thorough of all the Auxiliary AA vessels. Apart from detached duty escorting PQ15 and QP12, she spent a year as a member of the Irish Sea Escort Force, until joining the escort for PQ18 and acting as AA guardship at Kola until 7 November 1942. After returning to the UK with convoy QP15 on 23 November 1942, *Ulster Queen* was then re-converted to a Fighter Direction Ship in 1943.

Tynwald, completed in 1937 for the Isle of Man Steam Packet Company, was requisitioned in July 1940, after transporting over 10,000 troops from Dunkirk in the previous month. Her conversion, which was delayed by air-raid damage during January 1941 at Portsmouth, was finally completed on 30 September 1941. She was to see scarcely a year's service before being mined and sunk off Bougie Harbour on 12 November 1942. *Tynwald*'s career had been confined to service with the Irish Sea Escort Force and as an escort for the 'Torch' operation.

The only other vessel to be converted to an Auxiliary AA vessel was the Canadian-manned *Prince Robert*, which had originally commissioned as an Armed Merchant Cruiser on 31 July 1940 after a thorough conversion. After two years of patrol duties in the Caribbean, when she captured the German blockade runner *Weser* off the Mexican coast on 26 September 1940, her conversion to an AA vessel was undertaken by Burrard Dry Dock between January 1943 and July 1943. Again, the conversion was extensive, involving the following alterations:

1 A new bridge was constructed with an operations room.
2 A Type 285 radar was fitted.
3 The vessel was re-armed with five twin 4in in lieu of her obsolete 6in and 3in guns. Her point-defence weapons consisted of two quadruple 2pdr and six 20mm Oerlikons. Later the number of Oerlikons was doubled.

Prince Robert was based at Plymouth between October 1943 and September 1944 and escorted UK and Gibraltar convoys. Refitted between September 1944 and May 1945, her suitability as an AA vessel was shown by her selection as a unit of the British Pacific Fleet. She paid off in December 1945 and was reconverted to a passenger vessel.

Conclusions

Both groups of vessels were essentially stop-gaps and although these vessels performed strenuous service, they demonstrated their considerable shortcomings. The prototype cruiser conversions were armed with obsolete weapons and it was not until 1942–43 that adequate radar and director equipment was provided for the surviving vessels and later conversions. The endurance of all the cruisers was limited. The auxiliary AA conversions having adequate range did provide reasonably effective protection for convoys. However, the massive technological advances, with faster aircraft and different tactics, ensured that guns without adequate director control, could not cope effectively. By 1943 more regular warships were available with radar controlled weapons and most large convoys had aerial cover provided by an escort carrier. However, these carriers did not have enough space for comprehensive fighter-direction systems. It was in such a role, that the surviving auxiliary AA vessels – *Ulster Queen* and *Palomares* served until the end of the war.

Acknowledgements

Roger Nailor, Chapter in *Conversions for War* (World Ship Society)
J J Connell, *Valiant Quartet.*
A Raven & J Roberts, *British Cruisers of World War II.*

The most complete mercantile conversion undertaken, Ulster Queen *was reconstructed between August 1940 and November 1941. She operated in the Irish Sea between November 1941 and April 1942 before joining the escort forces for the Russian convoys between May and November 1942, operating as AA guardship at Kola for the last two months. On her return to the UK she was converted to a Fighter Direction Ship and operated as such until returned to trade during April 1946.* (IWM)

KATYUSHA – SOVIET SUBMARINE CRUISERS

Using recently released Russian sources Marek Twardowski outlines the most ambitious prewar Soviet submarine design, and casts a critical eye over their claimed successes, including the supposed attack on the *Tirpitz*.

When in 1921 the Tenth General Assembly of the Russian Communist Party decided to rebuild the Soviet Navy, the value of the submarine was already well recognized. The Russians had considerable experience with them during the First World War, when the exploits of a British submarine detachment in the Baltic against the Germans showed that even a small submarine force, properly trained and decisively led, could be a serious threat even to a large navy.

The first Soviet naval programme, authorized in 1926, provided for 12 submarines besides torpedo-boats and MTBs. The design work on submarines started in 1923 and in 1930–31 the first Soviet submarines (of the 'D' class) entered service. From then on Soviet leaders consistently developed the submarine branch of the navy, while Soviet designers and builders steadily gained knowledge and experience in this field. Up to the outbreak of the Soviet–German war in 1941, fourteen classes (or series) of submarines were built in the Soviet Union, with a total of 206 submarines commissioned into service.

The first Soviet submarines were not an outstanding success and the following classes showed little improvement. However, in the late 1930s the Soviets began to produce better designed and more modern boats. This can be attributed chiefly to knowledge gained during contacts with German submarine design bureaus (then undoubtedly leading the world) and to accumulated experience from submarine operations in the four Soviet Fleets under almost every conceivable condition.

The Soviet Navy built various kinds of submersible vessels ranging from the tiny 160-ton boats of the 'M' class, up to the 1400-ton submarine cruisers. In this article we shall deal with the latter – the powerful 'K' class (nicknamed *Katyushas* by Soviet sailors), certainly one of the best submarines produced before the Second World War by the Soviets.

Genesis of 'K' class submarines

The first Soviet attempt to produce a large submarine was the 'D' class, designed by B Malynin. However, another design team, headed by A Asafov, decided to create a true submarine cruiser – the future 'P' class – with high surface speed and powerful artillery, able to chase and destroy enemy merchant ships on the surface. Though authorized in 1929, the 'P' class were not completed until 1936. Only three boats of this class were built and none was ever fully operational. During the first stages of the 1941 Baltic campaign they were occasionally used as transports; later the two surviving boats were decommissioned and scrapped in the mid-1950s.

The Asafov team was not the only one in the USSR to be tempted by the idea of a submarine cruiser. Though the boats of the 'P' class were still on the stocks, and none had even been launched, a new design was begun. At least two design teams competed on this: the first was led by B Malinin, while the second was created in the Submarine Department of the Soviet Navy's Scientific and Research Institute of Armament and Shipbuilding. The latter prepared several preliminary designs of underwater cruisers and in 1934 won the contest with the 'KE-9' design (KE standing for *Krejserkaja, Eskadrennaja* = Squadron, Cruising). This design was approved on 15 April 1935 by the Soviet (Council) of Work and Defence and the chief of the design team was appointed – Mihail Alekseevich Rudnickij – who, being an experienced submarine officer and shipbuilder, was at that time head of the above Department. His enthusiasm for the design was great and indeed at times the design was called 'KR' = *Krejser Rudnickogo* (Rudnickij's Cruiser).

At that time Soviet designers had some opportunity to broaden their experience. The first large Soviet submariness of the 'D' and 'L' classes had been in service for about three years and in 1928 the British *L-55* was raised from the Baltic. Her refit enabled the Soviets to learn more about another submarine design. However the most important boost in this field came in about 1933, when the Soviets were allowed to inspect the Spanish submarine *E-1* (later the Turkish *Gür*) which was built to German plans. Later the Russians were given the drawings of that boat together with technical assistance and thus, finally, were able to acquaint themselves with the best and most modern in the submarine field. The medium sized 'S' class boats (IX series, 840 tons), resulting from this cooperation, were almost identical with German Type IA. Both classes were directly derived from the *E-1* and both were further developed into much bigger submarines.

Arctic based boat, probably K-1. (Lemachko collection)

The design and construction

Rudnickij's team undertook an ambitious and difficult task. Nobody in the Soviet Union had any experience in designing large submarines, the lightweight diesel engines were not yet in production and much of the necessary equipment (*ie* diesel engine superchargers) were not available in Russia. To gain some experience large scale experiments were conducted with the hull of the uncompleted submarine *Forel* of the Tsarist *Bars* class.

The 'K' class submarines were of double hull type. The pressure hull, built of 18–22mm steel plates, was riveted and divided into seven compartments. The internal arrangement rather closely followed the Spanish–German Soviet prototype. The light hull was welded and housed ballast tanks, some of which could be used for carrying fuel. Welding was also employed on the bulkheads, engine seats, fuel and ballast tanks and was one means of saving weight. Of the other means, the most important was careful design of the hull. Much attention was also paid to the improvement of the hull form to achieve great speeds and over twenty models were tested to choose the best and welding of the casing helped to streamline the boats. As well as low hydrodynamic resistance, the hull had to provide good seaworthiness, as a good deal of patrol time was on the surface. This was achieved by the very size of the boat and a large reserve of buoyancy – about 40 per cent. The raised bow made the class less vulnerable to heavy seas.

Much attention was devoted to the living conditions of the crew. Everyone on board had his own berth, while each of the officers had a separate cabin. This was a very welcome novelty, as at that time the smaller Soviet submarines had only as many berths as there were crew off duty. Other facilities included shower rooms for the crew, two provision storerooms (one of them refrigerated) and an electric galley. The ventilation and air regeneration systems are praised by Soviet literature.

The new submarines were equipped with the newly designed special lightweight, two-stroke diesel engines of the 9DKR-51/55 type, made by the Russkij Dizel Works in Leningrad. These reversible nine-cylinder engines developed 4200hp each and were completed only at the end of the 1930s. They were about 10m long and weighed approximately 69 tons each, and two per boat gave a surface speed of 22kts, though the design called at first for 22.5kts, similar to English 'River' class submarines. However, it is reported that *K-1* reached 23kts during trials. There was also an additional diesel engine of the 38K-8 type (800hp) in the electric motors compartment, for surface cruising and battery charging. The main diesel engines were hydraulically coupled to the two reversible electric motors of 1200hp each that gave a submerged speed of up to 10kts. The power for these motors was supplied from two batteries (60 cells each) housed in the second and fourth compartments, below the crew quarters.

The armament mounted on Soviet submarine cruisers was impressive. Their main weapons, the 533.4mm (21in) torpedoes of the 53-38 or 53-39 type, were fired from six internal torpedo tubes mounted in the bows, plus two internal and two external tubes in the stern. Fourteen spare torpedoes were carried. The torpedoes were augmented by

▲ *The 'K' class submarines can be easily divided into two groups, each with different bow: the first group (including* K-21*), had no flare nor hump on the bow, while the second group seen here during the war (represented here by* K-51*, or* K-52 *at Leningrad in 1941) had both.* (Lemachko collection) ▶

20 EP type mines, specially designed for these ships. By contrast to previous practice the mine shafts were situated not in the stern (as in *Krab* or the 'L' class), but under the control room, in a tank that could also be used for carrying either ballast or about 100 tons of fuel. This enabled the designers to put four torpedo tubes in the stern and to use freely the space available in the after part of the ship. The mines had a 300kg charge and were of the moored type with electric contact fuses and were carried in two rows, 10 mines in each, on the rails in the tank. All were embarked through the hatch forward, while discharging was done through two chutes in the rear of the tanks. The mines were carried to the chutes on trolleys, by means of a cable winch with electric drive. This device was complicated enough to make minelaying at least difficult; one instance is known when the defective device entirely prevented a minelaying operation (*K-3*, 27 July 1941). Later, during the war, the crews became more practised, some faults in the winch were repaired and minelaying became easier. However, in 1944 it was decided to remove the mines from the 'K' boats entirely.

The main artillery consisted of two 100mm (3.9in) guns of B-24 type. These guns were modernized versions of an old gun and were capable of anti-aircraft fire, as their elevation was 45 degrees. They were augmented by two semi-automatic 45mm AA guns of 21K type. The boats were also equipped with two or three 7.62mm machine-guns (M-1 type) which could be brought up to the conning tower deck. This gun outfit made the submarines at least equal, and sometimes superior, to the small or medium German escort vessels, which were placed in service during the war.

Other equipment consisted of 'Mars-16' hydrophones, two periscopes and short-wave radio sets of the following types: transmitters of *Skat* and *Okun* types and radio receivers of *Metel* and *Dozer* types. There was also a *Telefunken* radio direction-finder.

At one stage the designers prepared a variant of the design with a small SPL type reconnaisance floatplane carried dismantled in a hangar, instead of the 100mm guns. This concept shared the fate of most submarine aircraft carrier designs and was shelved, though three aircraft of this type were built and tested.

Comparing the 'K' class design with earlier Soviet construction – apart from its larger size, large reserve of buoyancy and much more diesel power, which were clearly the result of the submarine cruiser concept – the other qualities seem rather average for Soviet submarine building, though the hull design and shape can be considered an improvement over previous types. The same remarks are valid comparing the 'K' and 'S' classes, though the smaller endurance of the 'K' class is evident.

The 'K' class had also more reserve displacement and more horsepower than contemporary foreign submarines, but the most striking aspect of the design was an exceptionally heavy armament, exceeded only (relatively) by the German Type IXC U-boats. If we add the comparatively good endurance, the priority of offensive qualities is obvious.

The experiments and the technical design were finished in 1936, the workshop drawings followed and the first three boats of the new 'K' class (also known as series XIV) were laid down on 27 December 1936 in the Marti Yard in

Leningrad. They were followed in 1937 and 1938 by a further six, at the Ordzhonikidze and Sudomeh Yards in Leningrad. All nine belonged to the second Five Year economic programme which, among other things, called for an enormous expansion of Soviet naval shipbuilding. Three more were laid down following a repeat order to the Marti Yard in 1938. The building dates of the 'K' class are given in the table.

The first two boats, *K-1* and *K-2*, were launched on 29 April 1938. The *K-1*'s trials began in autumn 1938 and were completed next year. Their results were quite satisfactory, though some faults were found – not surprising in a prototype. The submarine proved difficult to keep at a given depth when in shallow waters, and also ascended too quickly; these faults were not rectified during war service. The stern torpedo loading arrangement was unsatisfactory and had to be redesigned, as loading of the stern torpedo tubes took 6 to 8 hours. The minelaying arrangement was found not to be properly worked out. It was also necessary to improve diesel exhaust valves, the bow hydroplane drive and some details of air systems. The new submarines were also found to be very noisy. The diving time, from surfaced to periscope depth, was 60 seconds (50 seconds, as designed). However, it was stated during trials that a well trained crew would be able to meet the specified time; this assumption later proved correct, as by the end of the war the Russians claimed to be able to crash dive in 45 seconds.

Later, in service, the boats' hull plating proved too thin. This was a serious defect, especially where fuel tanks were concerned; it could also seriously hamper a submarine's operations in ice conditions. In general, however, the acceptance committee was satisfied with the trials' results and after a work-up period the *K-1* entered service on 26 May 1940.

At this point it may be interesting to note that in 1944 the US Naval Attaché had an opportunity to visit two boats of this class, the *K-21* and *K-52*. The remarks made about these ships are interesting, as they offer comparison with foreign boats.

In both cases the Americans praised the excellent condition of the boats and noted favourably the lack of curtains, glass picture frames, ornate furniture, etc that could become a potential hazard in action. Apart from describing the interior and noting that the officers' quarters were rather cramped, the Americans reported that the main diesel engines were less accessible for inspection and repairs than on American contemporaries. Also, the access to the casing would be difficult in an emergency due to the arrangement of auxiliaries and fittings. The conning tower was described as roomy and containing much less gear than the control room. The general conclusion was that though the submarines were well designed generally, technical developments in the Soviet submarine service were behind the US Navy by a 'considerable margin'.

Returning to the 1930s, the rest of the class were gradually completed and commissioned. The first six (*K-1*, *-2*, *-3*, *-21*, *-22*, *-23*) entered service before Germany invaded the USSR, but the other six (*K-51* to *-56*) were not ready when the war began. Their construction was delayed when the siege of Leningrad produced the inevitable shortage of manpower, materials, electrical energy and due to shifting of priorities from warship building to production of army equipment and construction of small and uncomplicated vessels like submarine chasers, small minesweepers or transport barges. Despite those shortcomings, the shipyards managed to complete five of the submarines during the war.

Wartime operations

The details of their fighting careers are summarized in Table 4, but the high spot was undoubtedly *K-21*'s attack on the *Tirpitz*, which deserves closer scrutiny. On 18 June 1942 the *K-21* was sent to the area off Syltefjord, Harbaken and Makkour as part of a five-submarine force screening the PQ17 and QP13 convoys. They were located by German reconnaissance planes on 30 June and 1 July respectively and a force of U-boats was dispatched and began to harass the convoy. On 2 and 3 July two forces of German heavy surface units headed for Altafjord in preparation to attack the PQ17 convoy; the German squadron included the battleship *Tirpitz*. These movements were known to the British and the Admiralty, fearing a total destruction of the convoy, ordered it to disperse on 4 July. On the next day the breaking up of the convoy and withdrawal of cruiser cover was reported by German air reconnaissance and *Tirpitz*, *Admiral Scheer* and *Prinz Eugen* put to sea, escorted by seven destroyers and two torpedo-boats. This force was sighted by *K-21* off Ingöy and attacked with torpedoes.

The latest version of this action was published in Moscow in 1981 by L A Emeljanov in a book *Sovetskie Podvodnye lodki v Velikoj Otechestvennoj Vojne* [*Soviet Submarines in the Great Patriotic War*]:

> At that time [4 July] the *K-21* (under Kapitan 2 ranga N A Lunin) was at the exit from the Altafjord. After receiving on 5 July the news about the departure of the German squadron, the boat submerged and began the search for the enemy. At 16.33 hours, while the boat was going south, the hydrophone operator reported that he could hear the noises of ships' propellers...
>
> Lunin decided to attack the big warship steaming on the left. At 17.25 hours the submarine began to close the target. After a few minutes the commander of *K-21* clearly recognized the large ships as the battleship *Tirpitz* and heavy cruiser *Admiral Scheer*. At 17.36, when the submarine was on the torpedo attack course, the squadron unexpectedly turned 90° to the left with the large warships steaming in line ahead. The distance between them was 20–30 cables. Being in a new position the commander of the boat found the enemy warships under large relative bearings. This made him turn to the new course of attack – almost opposite. At 17.50 hours the squadron once more executed a turn 'all together', this time to the right. Now the *K-21* found herself between the course of the large warships. *Tirpitz* was on an acute relative bearing (5–7° to port) and it was easier to attack her with stern torpedoes. At 18.01, from the distance of 17–18 cables, the submarine fired four torpedoes with an interval of 4 seconds. The torpedoes ran at 2 metres depth. Just before firing the commander noticed that the leading destroyer had begun to turn. Fearing that the enemy had sighted the submarine and was beginning to counterattack, Lunin lowered the periscope just after the torpedoes were fired. When firing was completed the submarine rapidly increased depth and speed. After 2 minutes and 15 seconds the hydrophone operator reported two explosions. At 19.09 *K-21* surfaced and the commander reported on the radio that he had met and attacked the *Tirpitz*. This report was intercepted by German radio intelligence.

A wartime Party meeting on K-21, *possibly in officers' wardroom.* (Author's collection)

> Thinking that their intentions were prematurely discovered and being afraid for the battleship's fate, the Nazi command ordered the squadron to return to base.

From other Soviet sources we discover that the German squadron sailed at 23kts, that the periscope was raised fifteen times during the attack and no enemy activity was observed by the submarine crew after the attack, although a destroyer was heard passing overhead. Sixteen minutes after the attack a third explosion was heard, lasting 20 seconds, with two other explosions following.

We should note that the first reports (published in the Soviet daily newspaper *Pravda* on 10 July 1942 and in the professional naval monthly *Morskoj Sbornik* No6 of 1943) claimed that the *K-21* had hit *Tirpitz* with two torpedoes. This version was perpetuated well into the 1960s and still can be found occasionally in the more popular works.

Among those who maintain that the *Tirpitz* was hit is the Commander of the Northern Fleet at the time, Admiral A G Golovko. In his memoirs, published in Moscow in 1979 he writes about Lunin's attack and enumerates two explosions, followed by another one (not adding that 16 minutes lapsed between them) and later by two more. According to Golovko, the third of the explosions was thought by Lunin to come from the exploding depth charges of a destroyer, which might also have been sunk by Lunin's torpedoes. A few pages later Admiral Golovko even quotes as evidence a passage in Alistair MacLean's novel *HMS Ulysses* in which he says, 'The *Tirpitz* did make a brief, abortive sortie in the afternoon of the 5th, but turned back the same evening; rumour had it that she had been damaged by torpedoes from a Russian submarine.'

Other Soviet sources contrast sharply with such propaganda. The Commissar of the Navy during the Second World War, Admiral of the Fleet N Kuznecov, writes simply that '... Lunin attacked the *Tirpitz* with four torpedoes. The German command, alarmed by the fact that their force was

EP type mines ready for loading. (Author's collection) ▶

Although captioned 'In search of the enemy' in a Soviet book, this photo could have been taken after the war. (Author's collection)

discovered by the British aircraft and Soviet submarine, ordered it to return.' A similar version is given in *Krasnoznamennyj Severnyj Flot* by I A Kozlov and V S Shlomin (Moscow 1977), an official history of the Russian Northern Fleet, or in *Beevoj put Sovetskogo Voenne-Morskoge Flota* (Moscow 1974), an official history of the Soviet Navy.

While Lunin's crew listened for the sounds of their victory, the Germans were unaware of the danger. According to the *Tirpitz*'s 'Kriegstagebuch' the *K-21*'s torpedoes went unnoticed. Lunin reported his sighting and attack only at 19.09 hours; his message was intercepted by the German radio monitoring service and received aboard *Tirpitz* at 19.25 hours. Only then did the crew learn that the ship had been discovered by an enemy submarine, possibly Soviet. At 21.00 another sighting report was received (now we know it came from an Arhangelsk-based Catalina) and finally at 21.55 the Germans turned back. Thus, despite Soviet claims, none of the German ships was hit and we can only guess about explosions heard by Soviet submariners. They could be attributed to the precautionary depth charging by escorting destroyers. Another explanation is that *K-21*'s crew heard the noise of tons of water hitting the rudder planes of large ships changing course at 24kts. According to an experienced submarine officer this noise can easily be mistaken for explosions.

Nevertheless, the result of this action, together with previous achievements reported by *K-21* led to a pleasant surprise, when on 23 October 1942 the Presidium of Supreme Soviet of USSR awarded the *K-21* with an Order of the Red Banner.

This leads on to the whole question of Soviet claims of successes which are not corroborated by other sources. For example, the *K-52* in the spring of 1945 claimed 7 ships sunk and a torpedo-boat damaged, none of which is confirmed by the Germans (see Table 4). The *Erika Fritzen* sank on mines off Warnemünde on 25 February 1945 and *Bacchus* evidently survived the war and no others can be identified. In other cases, no names are given, the positions are rather vague, and moreover, the submariners often tend to exaggerate the size of attacked ships, making future studies more difficult. One can assume that Kapitan Travkin attacked several enemy ships, but not necessarily sank them. The Soviets often claimed sinkings only on the basis of hearing an underwater explosion. It is no wonder they could be misled by premature explosions (which, according to the Germans, happened very often) or by preventive depth charging by escorts. Furthermore, the submarine often remained submerged after the attack, not raising the periscope for fear of being detected. When able to scan the surface, the submarine often reported 'no trace left of enemy transport and only smoke from withdrawing escort's funnel visible'.

Last but not least, one must remember one of the everyday peculiarities of Soviet life. During peacetime it was common for economic reports to be more or less exaggerated. On few occasions was this a deliberate desire to cheat, but in the majority of cases it was done just to please superiors. In theory nobody was hurt: the superior was kept happy, the report-maker was considered a good leader and an able manager, while the workers received their awards and bonuses, which made their life easier. When the war came, it is no wonder that similar exaggerations appeared in battle reports, for exactly the same

Two views of an Arctic based boat, reportedly K-3, *in 1943.* (Lemachko collection)

reasons. Thus submarine commanders often used very thin evidence to confirm sinkings and wished the attacked ship to appear larger than it really was. The striking example of this procedure was *Lofoten* (1571 tons) damaged by artillery, which was reported as a ship of about 6000 tons sunk.

In recent years there is a tendency in Soviet literature to rectify some of the reports. Thus the *Tirpitz* affair is shown in quite another light and one of Travkin's sinkings is not mentioned anymore. Nevertheless the discrepancies between Soviet and German sources are still enormous.

Wartime modernizations

The relatively modern 'K' class submarines were not much modified during the war, although some additions were made to their equipment, augmenting the capabilities of already powerful ships. In the autumn of 1941, as soon as the German magnetic mine was known, the 'K' class underwent degaussing together with other ships of the Soviet Navy. The boats were also equipped with the 'Sprut' apparatus, enabling the stationery submerged submarine to keep depth and trim.

Most of the modernizations came later, in the second half of the war. In January 1943 some submarines received Drakon-129 sonars (among the first were those installed on *K-3* and *K-22*). Also in 1943 an extendable antenna VAN-PZ type was introduced; it enabled a submarine to keep in short-wave communications from a submerged position at the distances up to 1000km.

Some improvements were made to the arrangement. Up to 1943 the submarines used the 53–38 and 53–38U type torpedoes; from 1943 the 53–39 type torpedo began to arrive in the Arctic. Later, in 1944 a very limited number of entirely new ET-80 type torpedo with electric propulsion started to appear among ships of the Northern Fleet, but it is possible that only the 'S' class submarines received them. By the end of the war non-contact exploders for torpedo warheads began to make their way to the fleet.

Closely related to the torpedo armament was a device which, controlling the angle of torpedoes fired, enabled the submarine commander to spread the torpedo salvo. It was introduced in 1943; before then a torpedo salvo required a calculated time interval between each torpedo. The submarines were at that time equipped with a device preventing air bubble escape when a torpedo was fired, so the submarine's position was not prematurely disclosed. This device, designed by F Naumov, was introduced before the war and by June 1941 all Soviet submarines were equipped with it.

◀ *A sequence of a 'K' class boat passing the photographer: the boat is possibly* K-3. *(*Lemachko collection*)*

The mines used by the 'K' class were also improved. A modernized version was worked out, to be laid on depths of 250–400m. However, the minelaying mechanism itself was not successful; often minelaying operations had to be broken off and subsequent repairs, carried out while at sea, were dangerous to the sailors employed and to the submarines. Being impractical and complicated, often failing due to the stresses found in the midship of the hull, the minelaying equipment was removed by the end of the war and the boats were not used for minelaying after 1944. The mine tanks were rebuilt to carry fuel.

The artillery – one of the main weapons – was not modernized, as the 'K' class appear postwar with their full gun outfit. However, the *K-21* may have had the 100mm guns landed at the beginning of 1944, together with one 45mm gun, the latter replaced by a multiple barrelled AA gun. She had her guns returned postwar.

A serious drawback to their fighting capabilities was lack of gun and torpedo fire control equipment, both of which began to appear only during 1944 and 1945. Several boats of this class were also equipped with British Type 291W radars.

The biggest improvement made to Soviet submarines was an effort to mount all engines and auxiliaries on anti-shock and anti-vibration absorbers. This not only reduced the noise level of the boats, but also reduced the effects of any mines and depth charges that exploded nearby.

Postwar

When the war ended only five of the class were left in service: *K-21* in the Arctic and *K-51*, *K-52*, *K-53* and *K-56* in the Baltic. Five were lost (all in the Arctic) and one – *K-55* – was commissioned after the war; *K-54* was left uncompleted. In August 1948 the five Baltic boats were transferred to the Arctic together with their depot ships via the Great Belt and round Norway. There their service continued until the 1950s. All were renumbered in September–October 1949: the *K-21* to *K-55* received numbers *B-04* to *B-08*, while *K-56* probably bore the number *B-56*, where B stands for *Bolshaya* (= Large).

Little is known of their peacetime activities, except what could be gathered by foreign intelligence. Thus it can be believed that *K-21* was the boat that made the first Soviet submarine cruise off the US east coast in October 1948. Later two of the class returned to the Baltic (via the Belomorkanal): *B-05* in the autumn of 1949 and *B-06* probably in 1956.

According to some reports, three obsolete Northern Fleet submarines were fitted during the 1950s with large cylinders for housing and launching the forerunners of 'Shaddock' cruise missiles. One ship had a cylinder installed aft of the conning tower, while the other two had two cylinders on each side of the upper deck. That cumbersome arrangement affected the sailing qualities and was probably prone to accidents, as one of those submarines sank at sea. Though it is not clear what type of submarine was used in those experiments, the 'K' class could be a good choice being already obsolete and withdrawn from service. Their rebuilding would not affect the strength of the Soviet Navy, while their large size and good peacetime quality of construction could be of value when selecting the ships available. If the 'K' class were used in the experiments, then the boats would be *K-53*, *K-55* and *K-56*.

Magomet Imadutinovich Gadzhiev. From October 1940 he commanded the First Submarine Division of the Northern Fleet, which included 'K' class submarines. Enthralled by artillery since the beginning of his service, he advocated the use of guns by submarines, especially by powerful 'K' boats. Though at first successful, this tactic turned the submarine into a vulnerable target, as a shot in the pressure hull could deprive the boat of the ability to submerge, Gadzhiev took part in 10 war patrols, supervising the commanding officers, and died with the crew of K-23 *in May 1942, when the latter tried to fight the German submarine chasers with her guns and later to escape on the surface. Gadzhiev by that time had reached the rank of kapitan 2 ranga. Posthumously he received a title of a Hero of Soviet Union. (*Author's collection*)*

After deletion from service in the second half of the fifties some boats were scrapped (*eg K-55* in 1964), but the *K-52* became a stationary training unit on the Baltic and still existed in 1981. A similar fate met the *K-21*, which was rebuilt into a stationary training unit and in 1959 received the number *UTS-5*. In her forward compartments the damage control parties were trained, while the stern parts were used as training grounds for fire-fighting parties. In the control room and one other compartment an exhibition was set up to show young recruits the history of *K-21* and the

A well known photo, possibly K-21. *(*Author's collection*)*

traditions of the Soviet Arctic Submarine Fleet. In 1980 it was proposed to convert her into a monument. After necessary repairs and restoration to her 1940s appearance, she was towed in late 1982 to Severodvinsk and placed on a concrete cradle. On 30 July 1983 she was opened for visitors as a memorial.

The 'K' class submarine cruisers passed quietly from service. Before the war their successors were to have been ships of the 'KU' design, begun in 1939 but halted when the war broke out. Later, in 1944, another design for large submarines was under preparation. It proved obsolete while still on the drawing board, when the latest generations of German submarines were acquired by the Russians in 1945. The class were finally succeeded by the 'Zulu' class, where the experience gathered from the captured German Type XXI U-boats was utilized.

Kate (*Katyusha* in Russian), as the sailors nicknamed the submarine, was a large, powerful and respectable boat. That class belonged to a generation of Soviet warships built after a burst of cooperation with foreign navies and based on experience gathered from ships operating in the harsh conditions prevailing on most seas surrounding the Soviet Union. Undoubtedly, they were proof that Soviet designers were able to create unorthodox warships that could become a threat to the enemy. This quality has not been lost in the postwar Soviet Navy.

Nikolaj Aleksandrovich Lunin. From 1938 he commanded Shch-404, Shch-421 *and* K-21 *and for his exploits was awarded the title of a Hero of Soviet Union. In December 1943 he took command of the First Submarine Division in the Arctic. Later served ashore, reaching the rank of Rear-Admiral. He died in 1970. (*Author's collection*)*

Heavily protected sailors onboard K-21 *during a war patrol in the freezing climate of the Kara Sea.* (Author's collection)

Table 1. *TECHNICAL DATA*

Displacement:	1465 tons std, *c*1500 tons normal, 1720 tons full load, 2095 tons submerged
Length:	*c*94.00m wl, 97.65m oa
Beam:	7.41m max
Draught:	4.06m normal, 4.51m full load
Machinery:	2 diesel engines of 9DKR-51/55 type, 4200hp each 2 electric motors of 1200hp each 1 diesel engine of 38K-8 type, 800hp for cruising and battery charging
Speed:	surfaced 9kts cruising, 21.1kts max (22.5kts as designed; *K-1* reportedly reached 23kts during trials) submerged 2.9kts cruising, 10.3kts max
Oil fuel:	46 tons normal, *c*240 tons max
Fuel consumption:	1.52 tons per hour at full speed, 0.144 tons per hour at economical speed, 2.59 tons for full battery charging
Endurance:	surfaced 14,040nm at 9kts,2900nm at full speed submerged 176nm at 2.9kts, 10nm at full speed
Patrol endurance:	50 days
Batteries:	MAK-760 type, 120 cells total; capacity 4590 amp-hours at 4950 amps, 10,800 amp-hours at 180 amps charging time 12 hours
Diving depth:	80m operational, 100m max
Diving time:	50 seconds
Submerged time:	72 hours max
Metacentric height:	0.4m surfaced, 0.15m submerged
Turning circle:	740m at 22kts
Armament:	2-100mm guns, 2-45mm guns, 2 or 3-7, 62mm MGs, 6 bow TT, 4 stern TT, 14 spare torpedoes (all 533.4mm, 21in), 20 mines
Crew:	10 officers + 50 men in peacetime, 11 officers + 61 men in wartime

Table 2. *BUILDING DATA AND FATES*

Name	*Builder*	*Yard No*	*Laid down*	*Launched*	*Completed*	*Commissioned*	*Hoisted ensign*	*New number*	*Fate*
K-1	Marti	451	27.12.36	29.04.38	16.12.39	26.05.40	1940	–	Lost 10.43
K-2	Marti	452	27.12.36	29.04.38	15.12.39	26.05.40	1940	–	Lost 08.42
K-3	Marti	453	27.12.36	31.08.38	27.11.40	19.12.40	?	–	Lost 03.43
K-21	Sudomeh	108	10.12.37	14.08.38[1]	?	30.11.40[2]	3.02.41	B-04	Monument, 1982
K-22	Sudomeh	109	5.01.38	5.11.38	15.07.39?	14.04.40[3]	4.08.40	–	Lost 02.43
K-23	Sudomeh	110	5.02.38	28.04.39	1939	25.09.40	–	–	Lost 28.04.42
K-51	Marti	454	26.02.38	30.07.39	1943	17.11.43	12.41[4]	B-05	Deleted 1950s
K-52	Marti	455	26.02.38	5.12.39	11.10.42	25.11.42	–	B-06	Training hulk, extant 1981
K-53	Marti	456	30.05.38	2.09.39	31.07.43	19.09.43	1943	B-07	Deleted 1950s
K-54	Ordzhonikidze	288	30.04.37	8.03.41	Never				
K-55	Ordzhonikidze	289	29.02.37	7.02.41	25.12.44	1945	–	B-08	By 1964
K-56	Ordzhonikidze	290	17.10.37	29.12.40	29.12.42	1943	1943	B-56	Deleted 1950s

Notes:
1. Some sources claim launching in 1939.
2. Possibly completion date.
3. Possibly completion date.
4. Preparing for Baltic voyage at that time.

A silhouette of 'K' boat postwar. (Gunnar Olsen collection)

Close-up of K-21*'s conning tower, probably right after the war. Note the old number.* (Author's collection)

Table 3. *ARMAMENT*

Torpedoes

Type	53-38	53-38U	53-39	ET-80
Length (m)	7.20	7.45	7.49	7.50
Weight (kg)	1615	1725	1800	1800
Charge (kg)	300	400	317	400
Speed (kts)				
for 4km	44.5	44.5	51.0	29.0
for 8km	34.5	38.0	39.0	?
for 10km	30.5	30.5	34.0	?
Depth of operation (m)			2-14	1-14

Guns

Type	B-24	21-K
Calibre (mm)	100	45
Barrel length (cal)	51	46
Number of rounds per gun	200	550
Range (m)	22,400	11,000 horizontal, 7000 vertical
Weight of round (kg)	15.6	1.7
Rounds per minute	12	30
Crew	7	5

Table 4. *SUMMARY OF WARTIME SERVICE*

K-1

26 May 1940	Commissioned into the Baltic Fleet, under command of Kapitan 3 ranga K A Chekin
July–August 1940	Transferred to the Arctic together with *K-2*; commissioned into the First Division of Submarine Brigade of Northern Fleet
April 1941	Under repair
late June 1941	In the Kola Inlet. Claimed aircraft shot down after outbreak of war
15 July 1941	Command taken over by Kapitan 3 ranga M P Avgustinovich
August 1941	First wartime patrol, off Novaya Zemlya; no successes. Returned to Polyarnoe on 13 August damaged
13 August 1941	Under repairs until 28 August
28 August 1941	Second patrol, off Vestfjord, no successes. Returned 25 September 1941
early October 1941	Underwent degaussing
21 October 1941	Third patrol, off Porsangerfjord. On 28 October 7 mines were laid there; a

	tanker of 5000 tons and a freighter *Flottbek* (1950 tons) claimed sunk on those mines. Returned 7 November. The minefield was swept by Germans on 11 December 1941
December 1941	Fourth patrol, area unknown. Laid a mine barrage, area and number of mines unknown. Claimed a transport sunk with torpedoes. On 26 December 1941 Norwegian *Kongring* (1994 tons) and *Kongdag* (1862 tons) were damaged on unknown minefield west of Lenangen; possibly laid by either *K-1* or *K-21* in December 1941
1942	Made eight patrols during 1942. At least three, probably four minelaying operations. Claimed sunk on those mines are: freighter *Kurzesee* (754 tons, 8 April 1942, Varangerfjord), *Asuncion* (4626 tons, 23 May 1942), *Sperrbrecher 14* (7019 tons, 12 September 1942, off Nordkap) and two unidentified escort ships. Heavily damaged on mines at the end of the war.
17 December 1942	Beginning of repairs
23 March 1943	Command taken over by Kapitan 2 ranga V G Starkikov
17 June 1943	13th patrol, off Norwegian Arctic coast, together with *L-22* and *S-56*. Distant screening of Soviet BA-4 and BA-7 convoys. Returned 29 June.
August 1943	Under repairs. In place of Kpt Starikov (on leave) the command taken by Kapitan 1 ranga M F Homyakov
September 1943	14th patrol, off Novaya Zemlya, results unknown. By the end of the month radio communication with the boat ceased

K-2

26 May 1940	Commissioned into the Baltic Fleet, under Kapitan-Lejtenant V P Utkin
July–August 1940	Transferred to the Arctic together with *K-1*; upon arrival at Polyarnoe commissioned into the First Division of Submarine Brigade of Northern Fleet
April 1941	Under repair

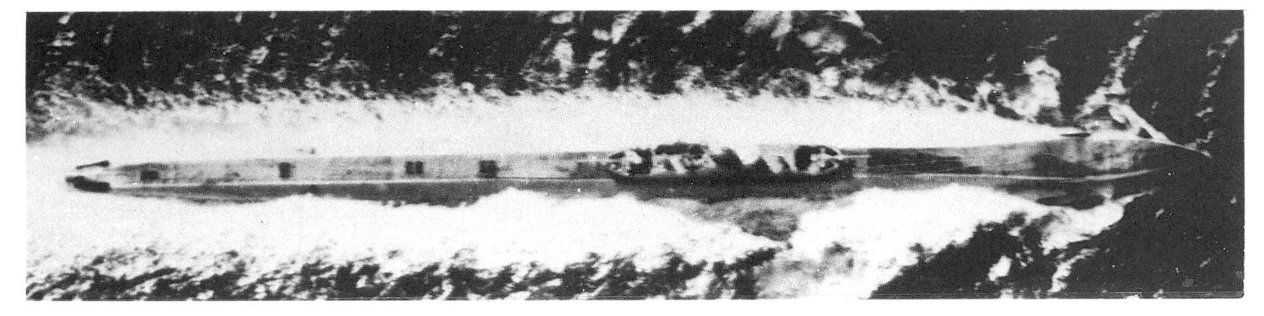

▲▼ *Two aerial views of 'K' boats.* (Gunnar Olsen collection)

7 August 1941	First patrol, in the Tanafjord and Kongsfjord. A cargo ship claimed to be damaged with artillery on 27 August in Kongsfjord. Returned 31 August
7 September 1941	Second patrol, in Persfjord, off Harbaken and Vardö Island. Laid a mine barrage off Vardö on 10 September (13 mines). Freighter *Akka* claimed damaged on them. On 12 September engaged freighter *Lofoten* with artillery and claimed damaged. Returned on 19 September. The minefield was swept on 13 December 1941.
early October 1941	Underwent degaussing
end of 1941	Under repair
9 April 1942	Sent to help the disabled *Shch-421* which was not found; *K-2* returned on the next day
April–May 1942	Third patrol. Laid a mine barrage, area and number of mines unknown. Claimed a transport sunk with torpedoes on 2 May
July 1942	Fourth patrol, Lopphavet area, screening the QP13 and PQ17 convoys
late August 1942	Fifth patrol. Lost, possibly on mines in Svaerholt-Havet area

K-3

19 December 1940	Commissioned into the Baltic Fleet in the Training Submarine Brigade.
15 May 1941	Command taken over by Kapitan-Lejtenant K I Malafeev
25 June 1941	Left Kronshtadt for Tallin; two days later left Tallin to lay mines west of Bornholm. Mission not completed due to technical difficulties
August 1941	Returned to Leningrad and later transferred to Arctic via Belomorkanal
September 1941	Arrived Molotovsk and begun the work-up period
November 1941	Commissioned into the First Division of Submarine Brigade of Northern Fleet
31 November 1941	First patrol, off Kvalen Island, Hammerfest. Laid a mine barrage off Hammerfest on 2 December. On 3 December attacked a convoy, claimed the transport *Altkirch* sunk. Depth charged, surfaced and sank with gunfire escort vessel *UJ-1708*; also claimed a submarine chaser. Returned 6 December
December 1941	Under repairs
22 January 1942	Second patrol, off Vestfjord. Screening the PQ8 convoy. Minefield laid west of Nordkap, claimed sunk on these mines: Norwegian *Ingoy* (327 tons, W of Nordkap, 30 January 1942) and *UJ-1110* (off Hammerfest, 9 July 1942)
September 1942	Third patrol, off Porsangerfjord. Damaged by depth charges and later on mines
December 1942	Fourth patrol, screening the JW51B convoy
January 1943	Fitted with sonar; exercises with similarly equipped *K-22* in joint operations of two submarines
3 February 1943	Left Polyarnoe together with *K-22*; on 5 February found, attacked with torpedoes

Soviet 533mm torpedo on exhibition in Polish Navy Museum in Gdynia. (Author)

	and sank *UJ-1108* in the Kongsfjord. On 7 February parted with *K-22*. On 12 February attacked and claimed sunk with torpedoes the freighter *Fechenheim* (8116 tons) in Bosfjord. Returned 14 February
end March 1943	Sixth patrol, took part in the first Soviet joint operation of Soviet aircraft and submarines, in the Tanafjord and Varangerfjord; later lost. According to Germans sunk on 21 March by *UJ-1102*, *UJ-1106* and *UJ-1111*, but the Soviets state that on 29 March she was still operational

K-21

3 February 1941	Commissioned into the Baltic Fleet, thoguh since 30 November 1940 temporarily commissioned, under Kapitan-Lejtenant A A Zhukov, in the Training Submarine Brigade
June 1941	Transferred to the Arctic, together with *K-23*; later in Arhangelsk for work-up period
24 October 1941	Arrived Polyarnoe and commissioned into the First Division of Submarine Brigade
7 November 1941	First patrol. Minelaying on 9 November in Bestasund (10 mines laid). Cargo ship *Rigel* (3828 tons) claimed sunk on those mines on 10 November 1941. Minelaying on 10 November off Hammerfest (10 mines). Claimed a transport sunk with torpedoes and damage to another – both on 12 November off Kvalen Island. Returned 21 November. On he same day freighter *Bessheim* (1774 tons) claimed sunk on mines off Hammerfest
December 1941	Second patrol. Minelaying, area and number of mines unknown. See also *K-1*
January 1942	Third patrol, off Kvalen. Claimed to have sunk a merchantman with torpedoes and a patrol boat with gunfire
4 March 1942	Command taken by Kapitan 3 ranga N A Lunin
12 March 1942	Despite being under repairs, she was sent NE of Nordkap to find the disabled submarine *Shch-402* and to help her. The boat was found and supplied with fuel. *K-21* returned on 14 March
21 March 1942	Fifth patrol, off Vardö. Screening the PQ9 convoy. Claimed to have been attacked by 3 German destroyers on 28 March. Claimed to have sunk the mercantile *Cordoba* (3400 tons) with torpedoes on 31 March, returned 3 April
April–May 1942	Repairs alongside tender *Krasnyj Gorn*
18 June 1942	Sixth patrol, in the area off Syltefjord, Harbaken. Screening the QP13 and PQ17 convoys. On 5 July claimed to have damaged the *Tirpitz* with torpedoes off Ingöy. Returned 9 July
14 August 1942	Seventh patrol, in Lopphavet. Minelaying (20 mines). A small escort claimed sunk on those mines. Claimed sunk with torpedoes a minelayer and an escort vessel on 19 August. Returned 23 August
31 August 1942	Eighth patrol, off Novaya Zemlya, to search for *Admiral Scheer* reported there. Later searched the area for *U-151*, reported to have shelled the Uedinenya Island. In mid-September moved further north, but left the area on 18 September due to heavy ice conditions and returned on 21 September.
23 October 1942	Awarded the Order of the Red Banner
10 February 1943	Ninth patrol, in Lopphavet. On 12 February fires broke out in diesel engine room, repairs concluded next day. Minelaying on 18 February (20 mines, off Kegsund). This field was swept on 21 March 1943, but it may be possible that steamer *Duna* (1926 tons) sank on a mine from *K-21* on 23 April 1943 in Lyngenfjord. The *K-21* landed a reconnaissance party on Arnöy on 19 February. On 20 February fired 4 torpedoes into Vogen Bay harbour and claimed five small escort ships destroyed. Returned to Polyarnoe on 21 February
22 February 1943	Sent to a shipyard for repairs
April 1943	Tenth patrol, off Harstad. Attacked with torpedoes a German destroyer on 9 April. Shelled boats in Harstad harbour on 12 April
August 1943	Minelaying (area and number of mines unknown)
September 1943	Under repair
early December 1943	Eleventh patrol, in Kara Sea, to disrupt enemy shipping
23 December 1943	Command taken over by Kapitan 3 ranga Z M Arvanov
25 December 1943	Twelfth patrol, off Ingöy, Rolvsöy, to screen the JW55B convoy against *Scharnhorst.*
April 1944	Sent to the area of Varangerfjord to disrupt enemy shipping in that area, but did not meet the enemy

K-22

4 August 1940	Commissioned into the Baltic Fleet, under Kapitan-Lejtenant I N Tuzov
November? 1940	Commissioned into the Training Submarine Brigade
end of 1940	Command temporarily taken over by Starshij Lejtenant A M Bakman
15 May 1941	Command taken over by Kapitan 3 ranga V N Kotelnikov
July 1941	Ready for patrol
August–September 1941	Transferred to the Arctic via Belomorkanal (orders received on 8 August, transfer began on 22 August)
September 1941	Arrived Arhangelsk; later work-up
27 October 1941	Arrived Polyarnoe and commissioned into the First Division
30 October 1941	First patrol, off Lofoten. Returned on 18 November

▲ *Three views of the Soviet B-24 submarine gun on exhibition in*
◀ *the Polish Navy Museum in Gdynia.* (Author)

6 December 1941	Second patrol. Laid mines off Hammerfest, in Rolvsöysund and Bestasund on 9 December. Reported sinking with gunfire a tug and a barge, off Söröysund on 11 December. Returned 25 December
13 January 1942	Third patrol, off Makkour – Nordkap. Reported attacked by a U-boat on 16 January. Reported sinking with gunfire a coaster *Vaaland* (106 tons), a transport of 3000 tons and a patrol boat of 800 tons on 19 January in Tanafjord
late January 1942	Put into dock for repairs, concluded at end of March
27 March 1942	Fourth patrol, off Nordkap. While on patrol received news about being enrolled as a 'Guard Ship' on 3 April. On the same day attacked a convoy and reported sinking with torpedoes a freighter *Stensaas* (1359 tons) and an escort vessel. On 9 April ordered to find and help disabled *Shch-421*. As the boat could not be towed due to bad weather and enemy presence, she was sunk by *K-22*'s torpedo after the crew was taken off. Returned 10 April
28 April 1942	Fifth patrol, screening the PQ15 convoy. Recalled at the end of May after stern hydroplanes were damaged
June 1942	Put into dock for repairs
early July 1942	Sixth patrol, off Fulöy, screening QP13 and PQ17 convoys. Returned after the operation was over.
sometime in 1942	A transport of 4974 tons sank on *K-22*'s mines
autumn 1942	Under repair, change of battery type
12 October 1942	Command taken over Kapitan 3 ranga V F Kulakin
late December 1942	Screening of JW51B convoy
January 1943	Equipped with Drakon-129 sonar. Later exercised together with *K-3*.
3 February 1943	Eighth patrol, together with *K-3*, off Vardö – Nordkap. On 7 February contact with *K-22* was lost and the boat did not return to the base, being possibly lost on mines

K-23

25 September 1940	Commissioned in the Baltic Fleet under Kapitan 3 ranga L S Potapov
June 1941	Transferred to the Arctic together with *K-21*. Upon arrival at Arhangelsk, the final fitting out took place, later the work-up
3 October 1941	Arrived at Polyarnoe and commissioned into the First Division of Submarine Brigade
October 1941	First patrol, off Varangerfjord. Laid mines there on 10 October
24 October 1941	Second patrol, off Kirkenes. Laid a minefield there on 25 October; recalled to base after the electrolyte poured out of batteries during heavy storm, arriving 26 October

28 October 1941	Third patrol, laid 20 mines in Varangerfjord on 29 October. Norwegian *Birk* (3664 tons) sank on 18 February 1942 on a floating mine, possibly from this minefield. Returned 30 October. Minesweeper *M-22* damaged on those mines on 11 November 1941
21? November 1941	Fourth patrol. On 26 November reported sinking with gunfire a minesweeper in Kvenangenfjord
3 January 1942	Fifth patrol. Laid 20 mines in Porsangerfjord despite difficulties with minelaying gear, on 6 and 7 January. A salvage ship reported by Soviets to be sunk on those mines on 17 January, though the Germans claim that the minefield was not found and no losses occurred. Reported sinking with gunfire a ship of 506 tons in Porsangerfjord
February–March 1942	Sixth patrol, screening of PQ12 and QP8 convoys
28 April 1942	Seventh patrol, screening the QP11 and PQ15 convoys. On 12 May went to Oksafjord to search for the missing *Shch-401*. On the same day reported attacking a convoy and sinking a transport of 6000 tons. When attacked, surfaced and reportedly sank both escorts with gunfire. Tried to escape on surface, but later was attacked by a plane and forced to dive. Found by surface ships, she was promptly sunk by depth charges of *UJ-1101*, *UJ-1109* and *UJ-1110*
K-51	
autumn 1941	Incomplete; incorporated into the fire support system for Leningrad (then under siege)
December 1941	Still incomplete, was preparing for a prelonged stay in the southern, ice-free parts of Baltic until spring 1942. Left Kronshtadt on 18 December, but on 23 December was damaged by floating ice while off Lavensaari. Returned to Kronshtadt by the end of December
1942–1943	Completion proceeded, though later delayed by lack of batteries
17 November 1943	Commissioned into the First Division of Submarines of the Baltic Fleet, under Kapitan 3 ranga V A Drozdov
November 1944	First patrol, in Gulf of Pomerania. Sank with gunfire freighter *Hansa* (493 tons) on 24 November and another in December, also with gunfire. Returned in mid-December
20 January 1945	Second patrol, in Gulf of Pomerania. Sank with torpedoes transport *Viborg* (2028 tons) off Rugenwalde on 28 January. Returned 21 February
K-52	
autumn 1941	Incomplete; incorporated into the fire support system for the Leningrad defences

1942	Completing
25 November 1942	Commissioned into the Baltic Fleet, under Kapitan 2 ranga E G Shulakov
14 March 1944	Command taken over by Kapitan 3 ranga I V Travkin
October 1944	Work-up period
29 October 1944	Left Kronshtadt for Helsinki
9 November 1944	Left Helsinki for first patrol, in Gulf of Pomerania. Found by surface ships and attacked on 16 and 21 November. Returned on 25 November, later went to Kronshtadt
2 December 1944	Under repair until 15 January 1945
7 February 1945	Left Kronshtadt, put in to Helsinki on 11 February due to heavy ice conditions
15 February 1945	Second patrol, Gulf of Pomerania. Reported sinking with torpedoes freighter *Erika Fritzen* (4169 tons) on 24 February, together with escorting vessel. On 1 March reported sinking with torpedoes freighter *Bacchus* (1716 tons), south of Öland. On 4 March reported sinking with torpedoes a transport of 6000 tons. On 7 March reported

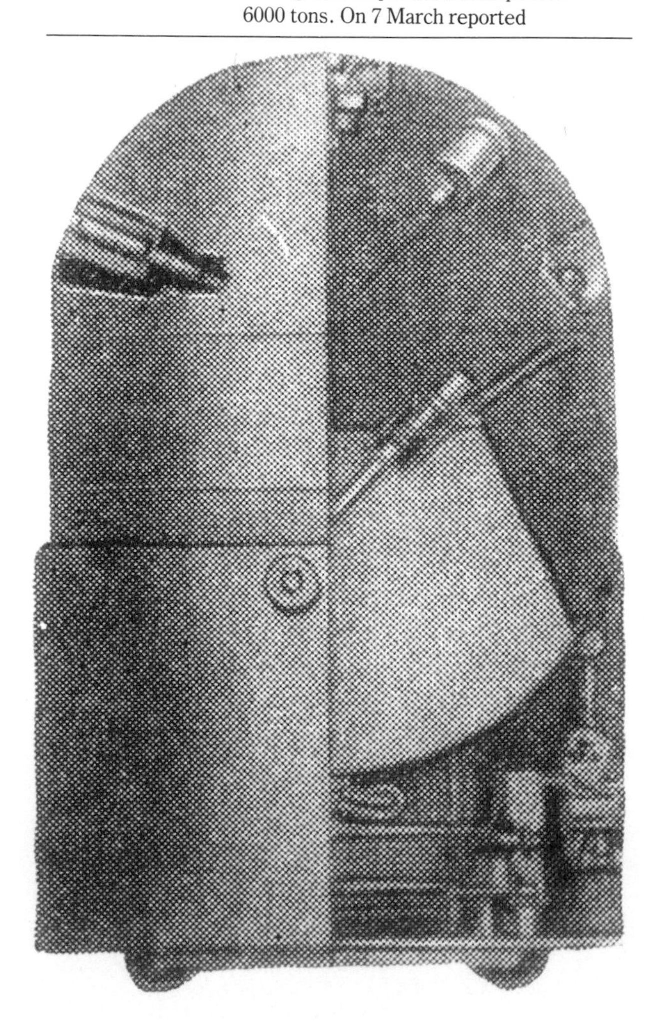

The Soviet EP type submarine mine, designed specially for the 'K' boats. Withdrawn from service in 1944 because of difficulties with minelaying installation. (Author's collection)

'K' class boat postwar. (Gunnar Olsen collection)

	damaging with torpedoes a torpedo-boat (or a small destroyer). On 8 March reported sinking with torpedoes a transport of 5000 tons. Returned on 11 March.
March 1945	Under repair
17 April 1945	Third patrol, southern Baltic. On 20 April awarded the Order of the Red Banner. On 21 April reported sinking with torpedoes a transport of 6000 tons. On 25 April reported sinking with torpedoes a transport of 10,000 tons. On 27 April reported sinking with torpedoes a transport of 7,000 tons. Returned 30 April
9 May 1945	Left Helsinki and arrived Kronshtadt on the same day
K-53	
autumn 1941	Incomplete; incorporated into the Leningrad defences
1941–1942	Completing
1943	Commissioned into the Baltic Fleet
15 March 1944	Command taken over by Kapitan 3 ranga D K Jaroshevich
November 1944	First patrol. Reported sinking with gunfire a transport on 10 December in the southern Baltic. Returned mid-December
March 1945	Second patrol, in Gulf of Pomerania. On 17 March reported sinking merchant ship *Margarette Kords* (1912 tons) with gunfire
30 April 1945	Third patrol
K-56	
autumn 1941	Incomplete; incorporated into the Leningrad defences
October 1944	Work-up in Luga Bay
about 7 December 1944	First patrol, in Pomerania. On 23 December reported sinking a freighter with torpedoes. On 25 December reported sinking with torpedoes freighter *Baltenland-2* (3042 tons). On 29 December reported sinking transport *Venersborg* (1044ft) off Karlskrona.
	Returned about 5 January 1945
March 1945	Second patrol, in Gulf of Pomerania. Reported sinking on 4 April a large two-funnelled transport. On 11 April reported sinking with gunfire sailing ship *Ramona* (500 tons)

Sources and acknowledgements
This article is based on numerous Soviet books and articles – over sixty of them – which have appeared in the USSR since 1943. Among the most important works were memoirs of commanding officers: Lunin, Kolyshkin, Travkin. Also the following works were used to the greatest extent:
V I Dmitriev, *Atakujut podvodniki*, 1964 and 1973 editions
L A Emeljanov, *Sovetkije podvodnyje lodki v Velikoj Otechestvennoj Vojne*, 1981 edition
M A Rudnickij 'Krejsery idut pod vodoj', in *Tekhnika molodezhy* 5, 1970
A I Sorokin, and V N Krasnov, *Korabli prokhodjat ispytanija*, 1982 ed
G M Trusov, *Podvodnyje lodki v russkom i sovetskom flote*, 1963 ed
E A Zholkovskij, 'Podvodnyje krejsera', in *Modelist-Konstruktor* 7, 1981

Other sources comprised, among others, reports of US Navy and German Intelligence technical data on Soviet submarines. The latter provided details for most of Table 1; both US and German documents were supplied to me by Mr Rolf Erikson, to whom I am most grateful for this help. Also, I wish to thank Mr Claude Huan for his very interesting comments on the *K-21*'s attack on *Tirpitz*.

MTB-102: FIRST OF THE MANY

This Vosper private venture boat was the prototype of the most numerous British MTB type of the war. Later she conducted highly important armament trials which established the pattern of coastal forces weapons in the first half of the war. Geoffery Hudson, honorary historian of the Coastal Forces Veterans Association, researched her history on behalf of those carrying out the recent restoration of the boat.

During the First World War Thornycroft had designed and built a series of 40ft, 55ft and eventually 70ft Coastal Motor Boats for the Royal Navy, but the CMB branch was cut back after 1918 and paid off entirely in 1926. Thornycroft continued to build similar stepped-hull CMBs but for export only. When official interest in small craft revived in the early 1930s, development was concentrated on hard chine, semi-planing boats for less aggressive duties like fast tenders, picket boats and target tugs.

The first in the field was the British Power Boat Co Ltd of Hythe, formed by Hubert Scott Paine in 1927. After commercial success with flying-boat tenders and an armoured target boat for the Air Force, the Admiralty was persuaded to order a 60ft BPB design as a motor torpedo-boat (MTB) in 1935, and six were completed by 1936. Their weakness was the torpedo launching system, whereby the 18in torpedoes were rolled stern-first from ports in the transom supported beneath guide rails, and the boat then turned away sharply after dropping the torpedo. Funds were provided for an improved 66ft boat to carry 21in torpedoes, but ironically the money was used to purchase a private venture boat built by Vosper.

Genesis of the Vosper boat

Vosper Ltd of Portsmouth had been founded in 1869 and was originally a firm of engineers and boilermakers, moving on to building small ships and launches in the 1880s. The Royal Navy's first motor boats were supplied by Vosper. After the 1914–18 war, the company built a variety of craft including small motor dinghies. In 1931, Commander Peter Du Cane, RN (Ret'd) joined the company becoming Managing Director in July of that year. In the Royal Navy he had specialized in engineering, but finding himself unable to re-enter the executive officer stream, had resigned his commission.

From 1931, Vosper began developing a range of standard basic designs, beginning with jolly boats. These were small hard chine, fast, semi-planing boats, the prototype being 16ft in length, whilst other production versions were 13ft, 15ft and 18ft long. From about 1934 Du Cane took over the responsibility for designing fast craft at Vosper; Fred Cooper, who had designed Vosper's fast craft between 1930 and 1933 having left the company. In 1935 a 25ft motor boat

Table 1. *MOTOR TORPEDO-BOATS 1935–1939*

Production series commenced at number 1

Experimental boats had numbers in the 100 series

MTB-	*Type/Builder*	*Length*	*Programme*	*Ordered*
1, 2	BPB	60ft	1935	27. 9.35
3–6	BPB	60ft	1935	19.10.35
7–9	BPB	60ft	1936	4. 3.37
10–18	BPB	60ft	1937	11. 1.38

(*-19* was the original *-1* which was used for trials and development work; *-7* became *-1* and *-13* became *-7*)

MTB-	*Type/Builder*	*Length*	*Programme*	*Ordered*
20–23	Vosper	70ft	1938	15. 8.38
24, 25	Thornycroft	70ft	1938	15. 8.38
26, 27	Thornycroft	55ft	1939 War	4. 9.39*
28	Thornycroft	70ft	1938	8. 9.39
29, 30	Vosper/Camper & Nicholsons	70ft	1938	8. 9.39
31–40	Vosper	70ft	1939 War	27. 9.39
41–48	White	70ft	1939 War	27. 9.39
49–56	Thornycroft	70ft	1939 War	27. 9.39
100	BPB	60ft	1936	4. 3.37**
101	White	67ft	1936	7.12.36
102	Vosper	68ft	1937	30.10.37***
103	Vosper	70ft	1938	10.12.38

* *MTB-26* and *-27* were CMB type boats requisitioned at Hong Kong on 4 September 1939. They had been lying there, undelivered to the Chinese Nationalist Government, following the capture of many ports by the Japanese, who had invaded China on 7 July 1937.

** *MTB-100* was originally ordered and completed, in April 1938, as an experimental high speed motor minesweeper, *MMS-51*. Trials in this role were not a success and in October 1938, she was re-designated *MTB-100* (the series of numbers used for experimental MTBs having started originally at 101). She was not actually converted into an MTB until March 1940.

*** This is the date of purchase of *MTB-102*.

February 1938: at speed during display for the press. Note that the Oerlikon has been removed although the 'dustbin' can be seen. (Wright & Logan)

was put into production, this type being used by the Royal Navy as a Captain's boat and for general duties. Shortly afterwards, 35ft versions followed which were employed as picket boats and for carrying aboard larger types of warship.

In 1935–36, with the knowledge and experience gained from these 16ft to 35ft boats, Vosper considered the possibility of developing a larger, faster and more powerful vessel, which could serve as a small warship, such as a torpedo-boat. The Company approached the Admiralty on a number of occasions, with a request to design and build such a vessel as a prototype, but without success. Although no order was forthcoming, the Admiralty did indicate that, if a contract were placed, it would be for a boat with a speed in excess of 40kts, capable of carrying two 21in torpedoes and armed with a small anti-aircraft gun in a revolving turret. Additionally, this 1936 'ghost' Staff Requirement included the ability to operate in the open sea, such as the English Channel and North Sea, in moderate sea conditions – Beaufort Scale 5 (Fresh Breeze) – and that the boat's cruising speed and range should be such that a crossing could be made during the hours of darkness from, for example, Dover to the French coast, or Felixstowe to the Hook of Holland, allowing for an engagement with an enemy during the course of the night, before returning to base.

After much thought and deliberation, the Directors of Vosper decided to design and build, at the Company's expense, a private venture boat which, provided she met the 'ghost' Staff Requirement, would be submitted for Official Admiralty Trials, in the hope that this might result in her eventual purchase for the Royal Navy.

The proposed Vosper boat would have to be larger than the 60ft BPB MTBs then under construction, if it was to meet the 'ghost' Requirement. For the project to be successful, it was necessary to choose suitable engines. Whilst Du Cane could design the hull form, its performance and ride characteristics, especially at the maximum and cruising speeds, would depend on, and have to be matched to, the weight and output of the power units. Similarly, special attention would have to be paid to the torpedo

Table 2. *CONSTRUCTION*

Hull form	Hard chine
Structure	
Bottom	Three thicknesses of mahogany planking (total thickness 1in).
Side	Two thickness of mahogany planking, worked diagonally (total thickness ¾in).
Deck	Double-diagonal mahogany planking (oiled calico was used between the layers of planking, as a waterproofing medium).
Framing	Sawn frames of mahogany, 52in spacing, with two intermediate bent timbers (following works trials, which proved the necessity for more substantial framing, the number of sawn mahogany transverse frames was doubled).
Longitudinals	Canadian Rock Elm, 1in square on the topsides and bottom panels.
Fixing	Brass and bronze screw fastening and copper nails clenched over roves.

Table 3: *DIMENSIONS*

The figures quoted below have been obtained from a number of different sources. Although in some cases figures differ, this may well be due to a different basis of measurement being used; *eg* with or without deck edge rubbers, or in a different load condition.

Length	68ft 0in	overall
	*c*69ft 6in	including trailing rudders
	72ft 2½in	including stern launching gear, 1937–38
Beam	14ft 6in	
	14ft 9in	maximum
	16ft 0in	probably when fitted with deck edge sponson for first deck tube
Depth	7ft 3in	
	7ft 6in	
Draught	3ft 2in	
	3ft 3in	
	3ft 9in	
	4ft 10in	maximum

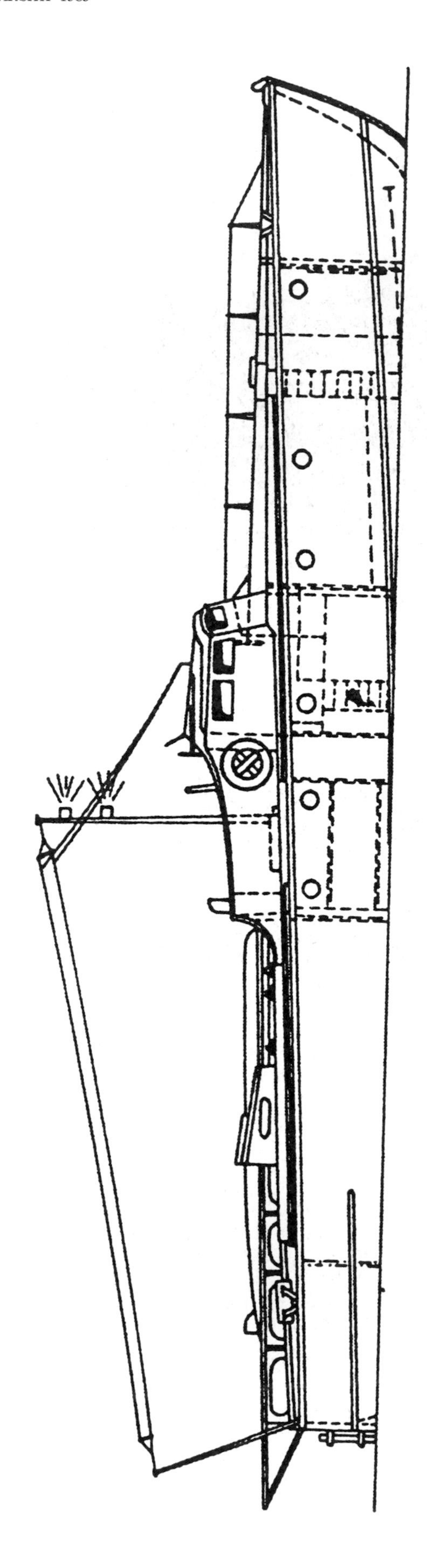

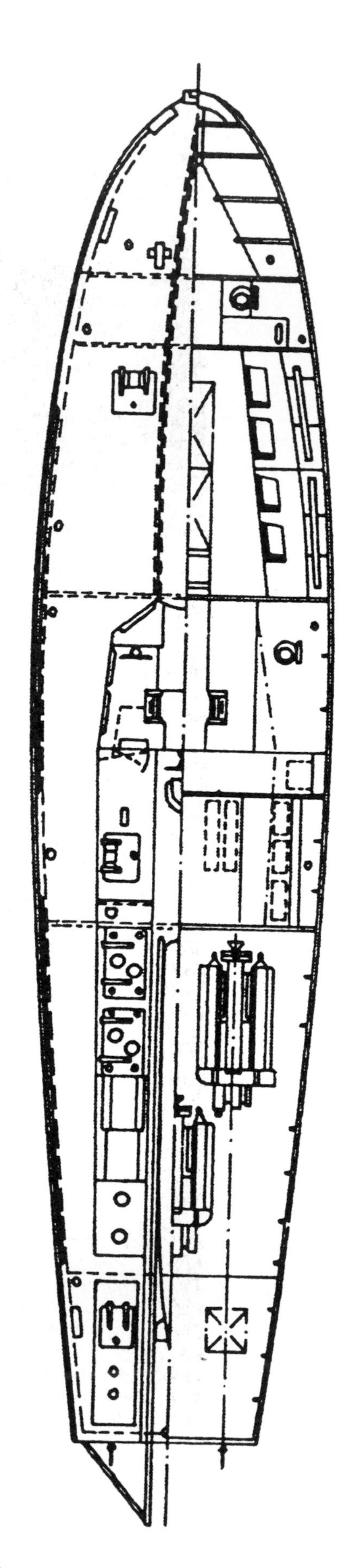

launching arrangements and gun armament.

In 1936 no suitable engine for marine use was available in Britain to power this private venture craft. Twenty years earlier, many CMBs had been powered by developments of existing aero engines and Scott-Paine had followed this course in developing a marine version of the Napier Lion aero engine, for his 60ft MTBs. As the latter motor developed only 500bhp, which was inadequate for driving a larger boat in excess of 40kts, Vosper had to look abroad. Their choice of main engine was one made by the Isotta Fraschini company of Milan, Italy. This engine was well tried and the only one currently available which had been developed specifically for marine high-speed craft. The original development contract had been given to Isotta Fraschini by the Russians, who at that time required engines for MTBs they were building. There had also been steady development of this motor through its use in the Italian Navy's MAS boats (MTBs) since 1929.

Table 4. *MACHINERY*

Main Engines

Three Isotta Fraschini Asso 1000 motors.
18 cylinders, arranged in 3 banks of 6 cylinders each at 40°.
Twin overhead cam shaft. 4 valves per cylinder.
Normal aspirated engine with 6 carburettors.
Dual ignition with two magnetos. Crankcase of electrolyte.

Capacity	57.25 litres
Bore	150mm
Stroke	180mm
Compression ratio	5.9 : 1
Petrol	87 octane rating
Lubrication	Forced. Twin oil pumps; 1 from oil tank, 1 to ready use tank. Dry sump.
Cooling	Fresh water, cooled by sea water. Two pumps; 1 for fresh water system, 1 for sea water.
Starting	Compressed air, air bottle being recharged by means of auxiliary engine.
Reverse gear	Operated by means of hand wheel.
Weight	1370kg (3020 lb).
Power : weight	1bhp : 1.3kg

The Asso 1000 motor was produced in a number of models – ASM 180 to ASM 183, with output ranging between 1000bhp and 1150bhp at 1800 rpm to 2000 rpm. The version fitted in *MTB-102* was rated at 1050bhp. Whilst no output figures for these engines have been traced, the ASM 183 model fitted in the Thornycroft 1938 class boats (*MTB-24, -25* and *-28*) completed two and a half years later, produced the following figures on trials:

1150 bhp @ 1850rpm	maximum emergency rating
950 bhp @ 1660rpm	maximum continuous rating

In *MTB-102* 1500rpm gave her normal cruising speed of 31kts.

Drive

According to Vosper plans, all three engines are shown with direct drive to their respective propellers. In the event, the centre engine was reversed and, located further aft, drove its propeller through a 'V' drive arrangement. There was no reduction gear.

Auxiliary Engines

Two Vosper V8, 75bhp each, one driving a single ½Kw generator. The Vosper V8 was based on the Ford V8 engine, which had been marinized by Vosper. These auxiliary engines could be coupled into the outer shafts and used for manoeuvring or silent approach. Speed on auxiliary engines about 9kts.

Fuel

Originally 630 gallons of 87 octane petrol aft in three tanks of 210 gallons each. Later increased to 990 gallons in tanks of 330 gallons each.

Endurance

Normal fuel load at maximum continuous speed of 35kts = 240 nautical miles.
Full fuel load at cruising speed of 17½kts = 340 nautical miles.
On auxiliary engines at 9kts = 1100 nautical miles.

Consumption

At maximum speed, the engines consumed *c*230 gallons per hour.
At maximum continuous speed the engines consumed 180 gallons per hour.

◀ *Builder's drawings showing both bow torpedo tube and stern launching gear.* (Vosper Ltd) ▶▶

The design of the new Vosper Torpedo-Boat was completed in 1936. The lines plan is dated 31 August, the construction plan 16 September and the general arragement 1 October 1936. It was for a hard chine boat, 68ft long and with a beam of 14ft 9in. Laid down later that year, she was launched in May 1937 and later in the same month carried out the first works trials. On further trials, maximum speeds of 47.8kts in light condition, and 43.7kts in loaded condition, were achieved. One of the results of these early trials, was to reveal the need to increase the strength of the boat's hull and subsequently 100 per cent additional frames were added.

Sale to the Navy

On the basis of the boat's performance, Vosper considered that she should be submitted to the Admiralty, who then arranged official trials. Part of the boat's evaluation included rough weather trials, which took place in the English Channel, south of the Isle of Wight, on a day when there was a south-west gale, officially recorded as Force 7. This trial took place in competition with one of the 60ft BPB MTBs and accompanied by a destroyer, which had been sent along by the C-in-C Portsmouth to provide assistance in case of accident. Du Cane himself drove the Vosper boat from inside the closed wheelhouse instead of from the upper steering position, but spray made this difficult as the so called clear-view screens could not cope fully with the conditions.

Following completion of the official trials and after some discussion, the Admiralty decided to acquire the boat and she was purchased on 30 October 1937 becoming *MTB-102.* There followed a short period of fitting out for naval service, which Vosper completed by December 1937 after which she was based at HMS *Vernon* for four months, for further evaluation, before being accepted and commissioned by the Royal Navy. She was crewed by RN personnel under Lieutenant Harry Glyn, but was still under the control of her builders and flew the Red Ensign.

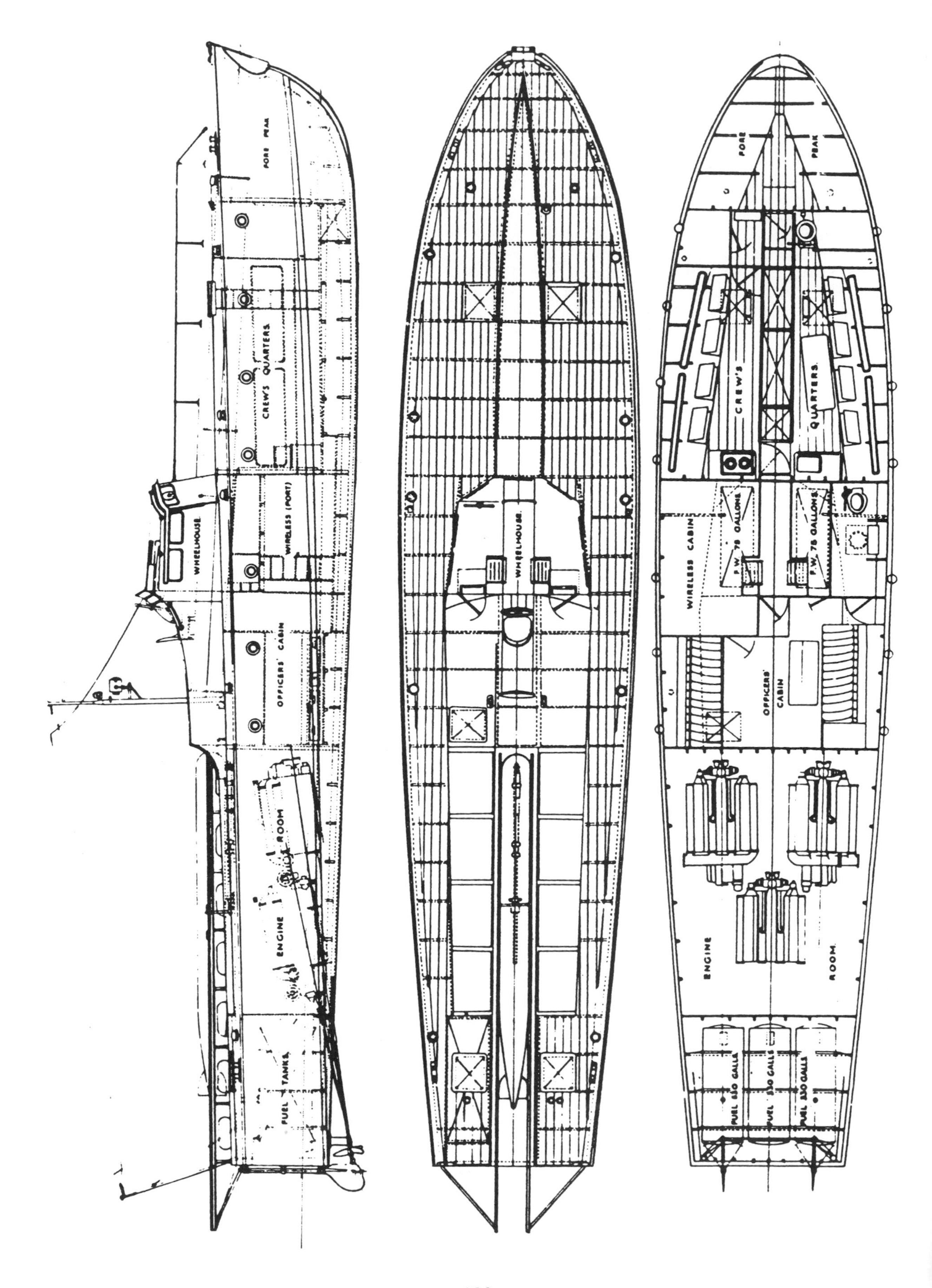
FORE PEAK
CREW'S QUARTERS
WHEELHOUSE
WIRELESS (PORT)
OFFICERS' CABIN
ENGINE ROOM
FUEL TANKS
WHEELHOUSE
FORE PEAK
CREW'S QUARTERS
WIRELESS CABIN
F.W. 78 GALLONS
F.W. 78 GALLONS
OFFICERS' CABIN
ENGINE ROOM
FUEL 830 GALLS
FUEL 830 GALLS
FUEL 830 GALLS

May 1937: Early works trials. Note Red Ensign and Vosper house flag. No bow door/flap yet fitted. (Vosper Ltd)

Torpedo trials

By late 1936, experience gained by HMS *Vernon* with the torpedo launching arrangements in *MTB-1,* the first 60ft BPB MTB, revealed certain limitations, in addition to it being considered that the 18in Mk VIII torpedo had too small a warhead – 320lb of TNT. These limitations included:

1 The lugs and rollers welded on to the torpedoes, for suspending them from the overhead rails in the engine room, caused resistance when the torpedo was running and reduced its already modest performance.
2 Opening the transon flaps and hinging over lattice frames took up valuable time at a critical period, before an attack could be carried out.
3 The boat had to be travelling at about 30kts, in order to turn away out of the track of the torpedo. Consequently low speed attacks could not be carried out.

Du Cane therefore considered alternative methods of torpedo launching, eventually deciding upon a means of bow discharge.

The original intention was to recess into the fore deck immediately above the crew's quarters, a single torpedo tube, arranged on a declivity firing through the stem of the boat. To meet the 'ghost' Staff Requirement of being able to carry two torpedoes, a second torpedo was to be carried on the deck aft, as a reload. Reloading would be through the door at the rear of the torpedo tube, which extended just aft of the small wheelhouse. An interesting feature was the provision of a seat, astride the tube, for the helmsman, when the boat was being conned from outside the wheelhouse. When the boat first appeared on works' trials, although the fore deck was 'bulged' upwards to accommodate the torpedo tube, neither the tube nor the bow door, which was to cover the exit port in the stem, had been fitted.

Concern about the boat's inability to fire more than one torpedo at a time, and the delay and difficulty of reloading the tube during action or rough weather, led to the arrangements for the reload torpedo being redesigned. Despite specific problems in the 60ft BPB MTBs, principally caused by the torpedo stowage and launching arrangements, there was support still within the Admiralty for the stern discharge method, which was proven and gave steady and straight running. This led to the Vosper boat being fitted with launching gear on the deck aft (referred to as Frame Discharge), which enabled the after torpedo to be launched astern, tail first, in a manner similar to the CMBs some twenty years earlier.

Despite these torpedo carrying and discharge arrangements existing while the boat was still the property of Vosper, up to September 1937, when Admiralty approval was given for the boat to be purchased and the system of bow discharge developed, no torpedoes had been fired from the boat. Following the purchase of the boat by the Admiralty on 30 October 1937 and with Royal Navy personnel on board from December 1937, *MTB-102* as she had become, was based at HMS *Vernon,* before being commissioned on 25 May 1938. During this period HMS *Vernon* carried out trials with the existing bow discharge tube, which was soon seen to be unsatisfactory, leading to a decision to abandon bow and stern launching.

In their place a system of torpedo discharge was evolved which officers at HMS *Vernon* had felt for some time was likely to give better results. The Whitehead department at *Vernon* had developed recently a lightweight slack-fit 21in torpedo tube, with cordite firing, for use as an upper deck

Table 5. *TORPEDOES*

Two 21in Mk VIII*E torpedoes. These were primarily a torpedo for the external torpedo tubes of submarines, but this version of the Mk VIII was also carried in *MTB-102* and the three RN 1938 class boats, retained by the Royal Navy, namely *MTB-22, -24* and *-25* only.
This weapon had an overall length of 21½ft, weighed 1½ tons, had a warhead of 750lb of TNT and a range of over 5000yds at 40kts.
In mid-1939, *MTB-102* carried out development trials with 18in torpedoes fitted with a Duplex pistol or magnetic exploder. These would be the Mk XII introduced in 1937 as an airborne torpedo. Length 16¼ft, weight 1500lbs, with a warhead of 388lb of TNT and a range of 1500yds at 40kts, or 3500yds at 27kts.

Tubes
The LC Mk I (light construction) torpedo tubes fitted in *MTB-102* had an overall length of 29ft 8in for the 21in version and 24ft 3in for the 18in.

Engine room. (Vosper Ltd)

fitting. In the early spring of 1938, prior to commissioning, *MTB-102* returned to Vosper's Camber Yard for modifications, including the fitting of the upper deck tube developed at *Vernon*. This was fitted on the starboard side, abreast the wheelhouse, and the forward end of the tube projected outboard, slightly beyond the beam of the boat, on a small sponson which was supported by two brackets, extending upwards from the boat's side. This arrangement was necessary in order to give the torpedo sufficient clearance over the deck edge when discharged, but resulted in the tube being inclined outwards from the middle line in plan by 7½ degrees. This *Vernon* tube gave the impression of being inverted, when compared with the subsequent types of MTB tube, as the orifice was extended on the bottom side, as opposed to the normal overhang in other tubes. The Vosper drawings for the seating of the *Vernon* tube and the loading and stowage chocks for the torpedoes, were dated March 1938. Within a few weeks, the *Vernon* tube was replaced by another tube, with the normal overhang. The Vosper drawing for this LC (light construction) tube, was dated May 1938. Torpedo firing trials continued with this second tube after *MTB-102* was commissioned.

During this period in 1938, *MTB-102* retained the bow door in her stem, covering the exit port for the original torpedo tube recessed into the hull forward. As a counterweight to the deck tube on the starboard side, she carried a canvas wrapped torpedo, secured to chocks on the port side deck, abreast the bridge. In addition, during discharge trials, a further torpedo was carried on the deck aft, as a reload. This avoided the need to keep returning to harbour for further torpedoes.

As a result of the experience gained from running *MTB-102* with the single upper deck tube, it was decided that the boat's trim would be improved and there would be less risk of damage to the torpedo tube when berthing the boat alongside, if certain modifications were carried out when she returned to Vospers for the fitting of the second, port side, tube. These alterations included locating the tubes further inboard and moving their position about 8ft nearer to the bow than the single tube had been, and the provision of deck edge scallops. With the new position of the upper deck tubes, scallops, about 10ft long, cut in the hull and deck at the gunwale, were necessary to ensure that the torpedoes had sufficient clearance over the deck edge when launched.

In the early summer of 1938, *MTB-102* returned to Vosper for modifications including the removal of the internal torpedo tube and bow door in her stem and the alterations involving scallops and re-positioned deck tubes, described above. When she emerged from Vospers in August 1938, after these modifications, she had dummy torpedo tubes on the upper deck, presumably while waiting for the completion of production versions of the 21in LC I tube (Light Construction, Mk I). Proper tubes replaced the dummies in the autumn of 1938, following trials with the Oerlikon gun (see Gun Arrangements section later). As in the case of first upper deck tube, these torpedo tubes were angled outwards from the centreline by 7½ degrees. The torpedo's small angling device, set to bring it back by 6½ degrees, gave a 2-degree spread between the two torpedoes and produced about a 120ft separation at a range of 1000yds. These tube arrangements were then retained for the remainder of *MTB-102s* service with the Royal Navy, although some minor changes were made. These included

Around December 1937, Vosper Camber Yard: fitting out as MTB-102. *Still flying the Red Ensign; '102' in black, outlined in white. Bow door/flap, frame discharge (stern launching gear), two mast lights, two ventilators amidships and gun position (starboard side only) now fitted.* (Charles de Cane)

fitting 18in torpedo tubes, for a short time around August/September 1939 and, later in 1939, adjusting the position and angle (to 6½ degrees) of the 21in tubes, when initial trials with the new 0.5in Mk V gun mounting were carried out.

After the initial trials with the deck tube in *MTB-102* had proved the satisfactory operation of this method of torpedo discharge, it was then adopted for all subsequent production boats. The first of these were ordered on 15 August 1938. They were six 70ft boats (*MTB-20* to *-23* from Vosper and *MTB-24* and *-25* from Thornycroft) and the first of a long line of 'short' MTBs, which served in the Royal Navy throughout the Second World War and into the early 1950s.

During the remainder of 1938 and much of 1939, *MTB-102* spent her time doing exhaustive torpedo running trials, developing techniques such as boat firing speeds, shallow water firing, horizontal rudder control settings and testing equipment such as the Duplex pistol. The latter was a magnetic exploder for 18in Mk XII torpedoes, working on a CR (coil on the rod) principle and *MTB-102* was scheduled to complete these trials by 2 September 1939. It was the prolonged torpedo running by *MTB-102,* from HMS *Vernon,* which provided the foundation on which the whole of the torpedo equipment of British MTBs was based and, as such, was an invaluable programme.

Gun arrangements

The 1936 'ghost' Staff Requirement included an anti-aircraft gun in a revolving turret, but as designed, and completed, the Vosper Torpedo-Boat had no gun armament. Soon after completion, the small bipod mast, originally stepped over the forward edge of frame 12, was moved forward 2ft 4in, to the forward edge of frame 13. As a result of this, the deck layout then permitted the fitting of two gun mountings. These positions were sided and immediately inboard of the extensions running aft from the wheelhouse. Two sided positions, rather than a single one on the centreline, were determined by the need to keep the deck on the centreline clear, in order to make possible the loading of the bow tube, through the door at its rear end.

Certain Vosper records refer to *MTB-102,* at one time, as having two quadruple 0.303in Bren machine-gun mountings. No evidence has been found of a four-barrelled version of the Bren gun going into production, or actually being fitted in *MTB-102.* However, it may be that there was an intention to fit experimental quadruple mountings in *MTB-102,* for trials, prior to the spring of 1938. (During 1937 and 1938, the 60ft BPB MTBs were still being fitted with two quadruple 0.303in Lewis guns, but by 1939, the new 70ft Vosper and Thornycroft 1938 class boats received two quadruple 0.303in Vickers 'K' guns.)

Numerous sources mention *MTB-102* being fitted with the 20mm Oerlikon. Mountings quoted vary from, a single, two singles, a twin, to even two twins! Peter Du Cane, in his book *An Engineer of Sorts* and an earlier private circulation paper, 'A History of the Principal Activities of Vosper 1931–69', refers to *MTB-102* being fitted with two Oerlikons, during the period the boat was on trial and not yet bought by the Admiralty. W J (Bill) Holt, RCNC, in his

January 1938: with 20mm Oerlikon now mounted in starboard side dustbin. Don buoy aft. (Wright & Logan)

paper 'Coastal Force Design', read before the Institution of Naval Architects in March 1947, also mentions Oerlikon guns being carried, mounted on ring supports, sided and near the middle length of the boat. Holt also stated that these Oerlikon guns were first of the type seen in Great Britain and, on trial, made an impressive showing. According to Peter Du Cane, the Oerlikons were fitted in the Vosper Torpedo-Boat, following a suggestion made to him by Commander Lord Louis Mountbatten, who had been trying without success to get the Royal Navy to give this Swiss manufactured gun a trial. Up to that time, HMS *Excellent*, the Royal Navy's Gunnery School at Whale Island, Portsmouth, had refused to consider this gun, as it was contrary to normal British practice in its functioning, with the breech not locked fully at the time of firing. Further comments by Peter Du Cane indicated that, when the boat was handed over to the Royal Navy, the Oerlikon guns were removed.

There is no indication that any gun armament was fitted in *MTB-102* prior to her purchase by the Admiralty in October 1937. The first reference appears to be a Vosper drawing dated December 1937 for a 'mounting for an automatic gun'. This shows a 'dustbin', 33in in diameter and 37in high, to be fitted port and starboard, midway between frames 12 and 13, inboard of the side extensions running aft from the wheelhouse. The drawing did not indicate the actual gun which was to be mounted, but there is no doubt that it was a single 20mm Oerlikon. Photographs of *MTB-102* taken in January and February 1938 show her fitted with a single 'dustbin' in the port side position only, as described above. In several of these photographs, a 20mm Oerlikon, on a slip ring which fitted into a channel on the top of the 'dustbin', can be seen. Further photographs, taken at the end of February 1938 indicate that the Oerlikon and ring had been removed, but the port side 'dustbin' remained. To accommodate this gun turret, it was necessary to bulge outboard slightly, the side extension from the wheelhouse, on the port side. Up to the end of February 1938, at least, no 'dustbin' was fitted on the starboard side; consequently, the side extension from the starboard side of the wheelhouse remained unbulged.

The installation of the first upper deck torpedo tube, on the starboard side, in March/April 1938, would have resulted in the removal of the gun turret on that side of the boat, if this was ever installed during March. According to a Vosper drawing of March 1938, for the seating arrangements of the first deck tube, the port side 'dustbin' was retained and photographs taken during the spring of 1938, appear to confirm the retention of this turret, but without any gun. The latter, in any event, would have been an encumbrance at a time when the upper deck tube and discharge system were being developed. Thus, whilst there was no doubt every intention to install two single Oerlikons in *MTB-102,* it would seem unlikely that the second, starboard side mounting, was ever fitted as a result of the decision to fit the upper deck tube.

When she emerged from refit at Vospers in August 1938, in addition to the alterations mentioned already in the 'Torpedo Trials' section, *MTB-102* had a single 'dustbin' on the centreline above frame 12. This turret appears to be of similar diameter to the one on the port side in January and February 1938, but somewhat higher at around 50in. In a number of photographs taken in August 1938, this new centreline turret carries no gun, but in several others taken in Portsmouth Dockyard, a 20mm Oerlikon, on a slip ring, is fitted. This turret may have been an interim fitting, installed perhaps, together with the dummy torpedo tubes carried at the same time, to provide a 'mock up' of *MTB-102's*

Around January 1938: on board during Oerlikon firing trials. Looking forward; Swiss engineers in white overalls, Cmdr Peter du Cane in trilby. (Charles du Cane)

Around January 1938: Oerlikon firing trials. Looking aft; note frame discharge (stern launching gear) between canvas covered engine room companionways. (Charles du Cane)

March-April 1938, Vosper Camber Yard: now fitted with the 'Vernon' deck tube (starboard side only). Note the unusual orifice compared with later types of tube and the deck edge sponson. Other modifications include a taller mast, '102' now in white outlined in black, taller ventilators amidships and alterations to the engine room hatches. (Charles du Cane)

modified arrangements and layout, including two upper deck tubes and a new, larger, centreline gun turret.

The Vosper drawing, dated July 1938, for this larger turret, was described as a 'mounting for 20mm Oerlikon, model FFS. This was 44in in diameter and 37in high, to be mounted 2¼in to port of the centreline and over frame 12. A slip ring which fitted on to the top of the 'dustbin', was to be supplied with the gun. This larger gun mounting does not appear to have been fitted until 1939. In the autumn of 1938, *MTB-102* was damaged due to side planking tearing away from the gunwale, when the boat was being driven at speed through sharp seas in the Needles Channel. This accident gave clear indication of the very severe stresses which come on the side, deck and gunwale structure, when hard chine type boats are driven at speed into head seas. Increased deck weight in the form of two tubes and torpedoes and a gun turret, added to these stresses. Steps taken to strengthen the structure included fitting a continuous piece of planking, about 12in deep and 1in thick over the sheer plank. This extended from frame 17 (near the front of the wheelhouse) to the stern. This additional piece of side planking can be seen in a April 1939 photograph, which also reveals the absence of any gun mounting. However, the removal of the radio aerials, rigged from stem to stern during the refit at Vospers in the early summer of 1938, probably indicates that a turret was to be fitted and that gunnery firing trials were imminent.

A photograph of *MTB-102* taken around the middle of 1939 shows a gun mounting as indicated on the Vosper drawing of July 1938, described above. A large canvas cover prevents identification of the actual weapon mounted, but *Jane's Fighting Ships* for 1940 gives the gun armament of *MTB-102* as one twin 20mm in an all-round firing position. Comparing the size and appearance of the mid-1939 turret, with a diameter of 44in, with the smaller turret of August 1938, fitted with a single Oerlikon, leads one to conclude that the 1939 turret may have mounted a twin Oerlikon. If so, this would have been an experimental mounting, as it was not until 1943 that a twin hand-operated version of the Oerlikon went into production.

Also apparent on the mid-1939 photograph of *MTB-102,* is the experimental prototype CSA smoke apparatus, fitted on the stern. In August 1939, when *MTB-102* attended the Reserve Fleet Review in Weymouth Bay, she still retained the large 'dustbin' type turret, but the actual gun(s) and the CSA gear had been removed. The radio aerials however had been re-rigged and it was not long before the large 'dustbin' turret was removed to make way for yet another experimental mounting.

This was described on a Vosper drawing dated November 1939 as 'twin 0.5in machine-gun mounting'. It was a support ring only and was fitted on the centreline above frame 12. The ring was 49½in in diameter and 10in high aft and 3½in high forward (to compensate for the angle of the boat's deck when *MTB-102* was travelling at speed). The actual gun turret fitted on to this deck ring was known as the 0.5in

May/June 1938: now refitted with the normal type of tube (starboard side). Note the canvas-wrapped torpedo, on chocks, on the port side and a reload aft. (D K Brown Collection)

Mk V mounting and contained twin Vickers machine-guns. It was hydraulically operated from a pump running off one of the boat's engines. *MTB-102* received the prototype experimental 0.5in Mk V mounting and appears to have carried out initial sea trials with this weapon early in 1940. The mounting was then removed and presumably returned to Marine Mountings Ltd of Swindon, for modification. This Company had developed this turret, which went into production in 1940, when 15 mountings were built. The first production mounting was installed in one of the new Vosper 70ft boats in July 1940 and some time after August 1940, the prototype experimental mounting was returned to *MTB-102* for permanent installation.

In addition to the various gun mountings already referred to, *MTB-102* was fitted with another turret in May 1940. Following the removal of the 0.5in turret after initial trials, *MTB-102* had no gun armament. On 26 May 1940, prior to sailing from Portsmouth to Dover en route to taken part in the evacuation from Dunkirk, *MTB-102* was fitted with a small gun turret mounting four Vickers 'K' 0.303in machine-guns on a slip ring. Apparently 'borrowed' from HMS *Vernon*, the turret was installed in *MTB-102*, above frame 12, by the base staff at HMS *Hornet*.

Following the permanent fitting of the twin 0.5in turret in *MTB-102* after August 1940, the only other change to her gun armament appears to have been the addition of light machine-guns in 1941. Mounted forward, on stanchions between the torpedo tubes and wheelhouse, in an attempt to provide fire ahead capability, these SS (shoulder shooting) guns were a standard fitting in 'short' MTBs at that time. The guns were either single 0.303in Stripped Lewis or 0.300in Savage Lewis (the American version, which was shipped over to Britain in large numbers in 1941). From 1942 onwards, the single Stripped Lewis was gradually replaced by the twin 0.303in Vickers gun, mounted on short stanchions or 'saddle' mountings on the torpedo tubes.

Table 6. *GUNS*

0.303in Lewis and 0.300in Savage Lewis

These light machine-guns weighed 27lb and had a rate of fire of 450rpm.

The 'stripped' version of this gun had the air-cooled jacket removed and the butt replaced by spade grips.

0.303in Vickers 'K' or GO (gas-operated) Mk 1

This light machine-gun weighed 20lb, with the mounting for four guns weighing 126lb. Rate of fire was up to 800rpm.

The 'K' gun originated as an aircraft gun for use by the RAF in the open cockpit aircraft of the 1930s. From 1938 quadruple mountings were fitted to some MTBs, as there main gun armament, until superseded by the new 0.5in Mk V turret. From mid-1942, single and twin 0.303in Vickers GO guns, as they were then called, were fitted in large numbers of Coastal Forces craft, to provide additional firepower. As such, they replaced the Lewis and Savage Lewis guns, which were more liable to suffer stoppages and had a lower rate of fire.

0.5in Mk V
This power-operated turret with twin Vickers machine-guns weighed 1289lb including guns and ammunition.
Each gun had a rate of fire of 650rpm.
The turret was designed in 1939 by Archie Frazer-Nash (of racing and sports car fame) and manufactured by Marine Mountings Ltd, of Swindon. It went into series production early in 1940 and was fitted to MTBs from the second half of 1940. Until replaced by the ubiquitous Oerlikon in 1944, this mounting remained the main gun armament of 'short' MTBs.

20mm Oerlikon
This gun weighed 150lb, but with a ring mount and turret, this would be increased considerably.
The wartime Mk I version, with stand and shield weighed 1120lb and the lightweight Mk VIIIA version fitted to Coastal Forces craft from about 1943, weighed 616lb.
Rate of fire was around 475rpm.
Effective range was about 1200yds.
In 1940, the rights to manufacture the Oerlikon in Britain were obtained. Prior to production commencing, a few Swiss-made versions were imported, being introduced into the Royal Navy in 1939. The Oerlikon went on to become one of the outstanding weapons of the Second World War, and is still (1989) mounted in a few British warships, having seen further action during the Falklands campaign of April to June 1982.

Displacement and speed

An extract from the diary of the late Sir Stanley Goodall, Director of Naval Construction 1936–44, for 31 May 1937 reads 'At Portsmouth on Vosper MTB. Sea very smooth. Speed on about 17 tons displacement 43.9kts ...'. The low displacement figure of 17 tons recorded by Sir Stanley Goodall, may be accounted for by another reference by one present, which stated that Peter Du Cane was so enthusiastic that the boat did its first sea trial without a deck.

Later, on officially observed trials, the boat sustained a maximum of 47.8kts for half an hour. This was on a light displacement (without armament) of 28 tons. On further trials, on a displacement of 31.5 tons, with full fuel load and armament, she reached speeds of 43.7kts maximum and 35.5kts maximum continuous. These figures were before she was accepted and commissioned in May 1938. Later figures, relating to 1939–41, indicated an increase in weight and consequent decrease in performance: displacement 33 tons; maximum speed 41kts, maximum continuous 35kts.

Table 7. *PARTICULARS INCLUDED IN A MID-1942 LISTING OF MTBs*

11th MTB Flotilla, to go to 4th MTB Flotilla.
68ft
3 Isotta Fraschini engines of 1050bhp each. Silenced [Never actually fitted with silencers]
Fitted with auxiliary engines
1–0.5in Mark V (turret with twin Vickers)
2–SS guns (Shoulder Shooting 0.300in or 0.303in)
2–21in Mk VIII* E torpedoes
CSA (Chloro-sulphonic acid – smoke apparatus)

Not fitted with or for Asdic, depth charges, mines, echo sounder, RDF (Radar).
[Complement was 2 officers and 8 men]

▼ *August 1938: after refit at Vospers when bow door/flap removed, gunwale scallops installed and two deck tubes (dummies) fitted. Also centreline turret fitted, but no gun mounted. Aerials rigged bow to stern.* (Vosper Ltd)

August 1938, Portsmouth dockyard: a 20mm Oerlikon now mounted in centreline turret. (Wright & Logan) ▶

▲ *Around August 1938:* HMS Vernon, *Portsmouth: note recess in top of turret for slip ring on Oerlikon mount, cut-out in starboard side of turret enabling gunner to enter mounting and that turret is offset to starboard. Also steering whell on centreline on bridge, with additional steering position to port, inside wheelhouse.* (Vosper Ltd)

102

◀ *April 1938: following repairs by Vosper, when the extra sheer planks extending from frame 17 to the stern were fitted. Proper tubes are now fitted, (although the intermediate support bands appear less prominent in later photos) but the gun mounting and aerials have been removed. (*Wright & Logan*)*

▲ *In this photo, probably emerging from a mid-1939 Vosper refit,* MTB-102 *has the normal LC (light construction) tubes and probably the larger diameter gun turret. (*Vosper Ltd*)*

*Mid-1939, off Portsmouth: two 21in LC tubes, large diameter gun turret under canvas. Prototype CSA (smoke-making) gear can be seen aft. (*Author*)*

*August 1939, Weymouth Bay, Reserve Fleet Review: CSA now removed. Aerials replaced, bow to stern. Now has black painted hull. Note the 18in torpedo tube (fitted for firing trials of Mk XIII torpedo fitted with the Duplex pistol) and the base of the large diameter gun turret on the centreline. (*R Perkins*)*

▲ *Two views taken off Portsmouth in early 1940: Black painted*
▼ *hull with red numbers on bow, but white on transom. Gun turret removed.* (M V Gardener)

Cost

According to the 1938 Navy Estimates, the cost of *MTB-102* was £22,529. Peter Du Cane refers to Vosper selling the boat for about £16,500, whilst the ship filing card at the Naval Historical Branch gives an apparently unrealistic First Cost of £50,000. The variations between the first two amounts could well have been due to the various additions and alterations carried out between the date of purchase, 30 October 1937 and commissioning in May 1938. Based on the UK Index of Prices, the £22,529 cost in 1937 would amount to £480,000 in January 1986.

In January 1938 Vosper negotiated the purchase of United Kingdom and Empire manufacturing and selling rights for the Isotta Fraschini engine, for £15,000. No manufacturing facility was ever set up in Britain because the Admiralty believed that the Rolls-Royce Merlin aero engine could be used. However, Merlin production was reserved for the RAF, and so all Isotta engines were imported from Italy until 10 June 1940, when Italy declared war on Great Britain. Thornycroft and White, who installed Isotta engines in their MTBs in 1939–40, bought them from Vosper at a price of £4500 each. BPB, who were in 1938 planning to install Isotta engines in experimental 66ft and 75ft MTBs, refer to a price of £5250 each.

Fate

MTB-102 spent the early part of the war in trials and training based on *Vernon* and then *Hornet* at Gosport. She was involved in the Dunkirk evacuation, making eight round trips and, for a time, flying the flag of the Naval Force Commander, Rear-Admiral Wake-Walker; her distinguished evacuees included General Alexander and Captain William Tennant, the SNO Dunkirk. Therefore, her war service was not particularly distinguished and by late 1942 she was regarded as surplus to requirements, being transferred to the Army for target towing.

The boat was taken over by the Royal Army Service Corps on 21 January 1943 and on 5 May was named *Vimy*, being based at the Gunwharf, Portsmouth. Returned to the Navy at Poole on 14 March 1945, the craft was put up for disposal on 25 October and later sold into private hands. She survived as a motor cruiser up until 1973 when sold to the Blofield and Brundall Sea Scouts. Since then the boat has been restored to the characteristic appearance of a wartime MTB and, now owned by the Norwich Area Scout Council '102 Trust', makes appearances at Navy Days, Dunkirk Reunions and other naval occasions – the first and last of a long and distinguished line.

Table 8. *PRODUCTION OF VOSPER TYPE MTBs*

MTB-102 was the prototype for the highly successful Vosper 70ft and 73ft designs, of which 340 boats were ordered between 1938 and 1944.

In the UK for the Royal Navy			*MTB*	*Quantity*		
70ft	1938 class		*20–23*	4		
			29,30	2		
		– ex Greek	*69,70*	2		
					8	
	Experimental		*103*		1	
	1939 class		*31–40*	10		
		– ex Greek	*218–221*	4		
					14	
	1939 Extension class		*57–66*		10	
	1940 class		*73–98*	26		
		– by White	*201–212*	12		
					38	
	1941 class		*222–245*	24		
		– by White	*246–257*	12*		
					36	
	1942 class		*347–362*		16	
						123
73ft	Prototype		*379*		1	
	1943 class		*380–395*		16	
	1944 class		*523–538*		16	
						33
						156
In the USA for the Royal Navy						
70ft	1941 class		*275–306*		32	
	1942 class		*363–378*		16	
	1943 class		*396–411*		16	
						64
						220
In the USA for Russia						
70ft						120
						340

In addition to the above, a 68ft Mobile Torpedo Discharge Vessel, HMS *Bloodhound*, was ordered on 6 October 1937. In 1938 two 60ft MTBs for Sweden were ordered and in 1939 four 60ft MTBs for Norway. Two of the latter were taken over in May 1940, becoming *MTB-71* and *MTB-72*. These seven boats were also based on the design of *MTB-102*.

* The last six boats of this order from J Samuel White & Co Ltd of Cowes, were built to White's own design, and being delayed, known as the White 1942 class. (After *MTB-201-204*, in which Packard engines were fitted, all subsequent White-built MTBs were fitted with Sterling Admiral engines. These were considerably heavier than Packards. In *MTB-246-251*, this led the Admiralty to approve a change to the location of the fuel tanks, in an attempt to improve the trim of the Sterling-engined boats, and in *MTB-252-257* to a completely new hull design by White.)

*May 1985, off Dunkirk: ex-*MTB-102 *revisits Dunkirk 45 years on.* (Author)

THE SINKING OF THE YAMATO

The last moments of the world's largest battleship are here pieced together from surviving information by Tim Thornton.

Against the most realistic expectations, the battleship *Yamato* survived the innumerable hazards of Operation 'Sho-Go' (Victory) – known to the Americans as the Battle of Leyte Gulf – although she had not come through the battles of late October 1944 unscathed. Fuel and anti-aircraft ammunition could be obtained in the south of Japan's contracting empire and both were certainly necessary.[1] However, to replace the 173 rounds of 46cm (18.1in)[2] ammunition and to make structural repairs necessary for full operational effectiveness, Japan and her home port of Kure were essential.

Discounting splinter damage and one dud medium calibre shell, she had been hit by only four bombs and all of these had fallen forward of No 1 main turret. Two hit within an hour of each other on 24 October, and caused serious flooding. One hit the ship portside at frame 70 almost adjacent to No 1 turret and caused a 4m × 5m hole at the waterline, while the other fell outboard of the port anchor windlass and exploded below the waterline, having penetrated four decks. *Yamato*'s armour was concentrated almost exclusively over her centralized main armament and machinery and in consequence she swiftly shipped 3000 tons of water which lowered her trim by 3m (9.8ft)[3] and gave her a list of 5.5 degrees to port, although the latter was soon removed by counterflooding. On 26 October she received two more blows from large bombs which fell to starboard of the centreline at frames 63 and 72. The second detonated on impact blowing away the water-tight flange on No 1 main turret but the other went through the flying deck before exploding in a crew accommodation area[4] heavily damaging the 230mm (9in) thick forward main water-tight bulkhead. Happily these detonations were inboard and no flooding or fire ensued.

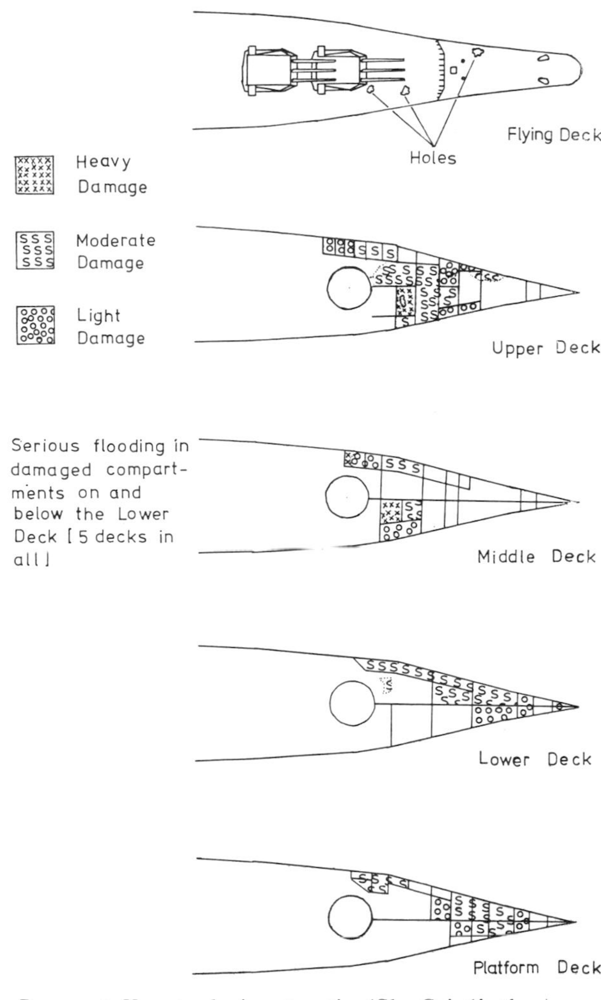

Damage to Yamato *during operation 'Sho-Go'. (*Author*)*

Return to Japan

Eventually after a month spent at Brunei Bay on the north coast of Borneo, *Yamato* and the residue of the surface fleet were ordered home, arriving unscathed in the first week of December. However, whether she should be repaired or not became a matter of hot debate in the ruling military clique, because the Japanese Army could see little point in wasting increasingly scarce resources on a project which they considered would be of minimal benefit to the defence of the Japanese home islands. For lack of fuel she promised to be little more than a moored anti-aircraft battery[5] and they suggested that she be stripped of her anti-aircraft guns which could be distributed more profitably ashore.

The Imperial Army and Navy had been in vigorous and acrimonious competition for power and resources since the early 1930s and these suggestions were simply symptomatic of a struggle which, as defeat loomed every closer, became increasingly bitter. In the end the Navy had its way and *Yamato* was repaired though she no doubt owed this privileged position to the fact that she was easily the most powerful warship Japan possessed, as was signified by her name which was an epithet for the whole nation.[6]

The wisdom of the decision to repair her, however,

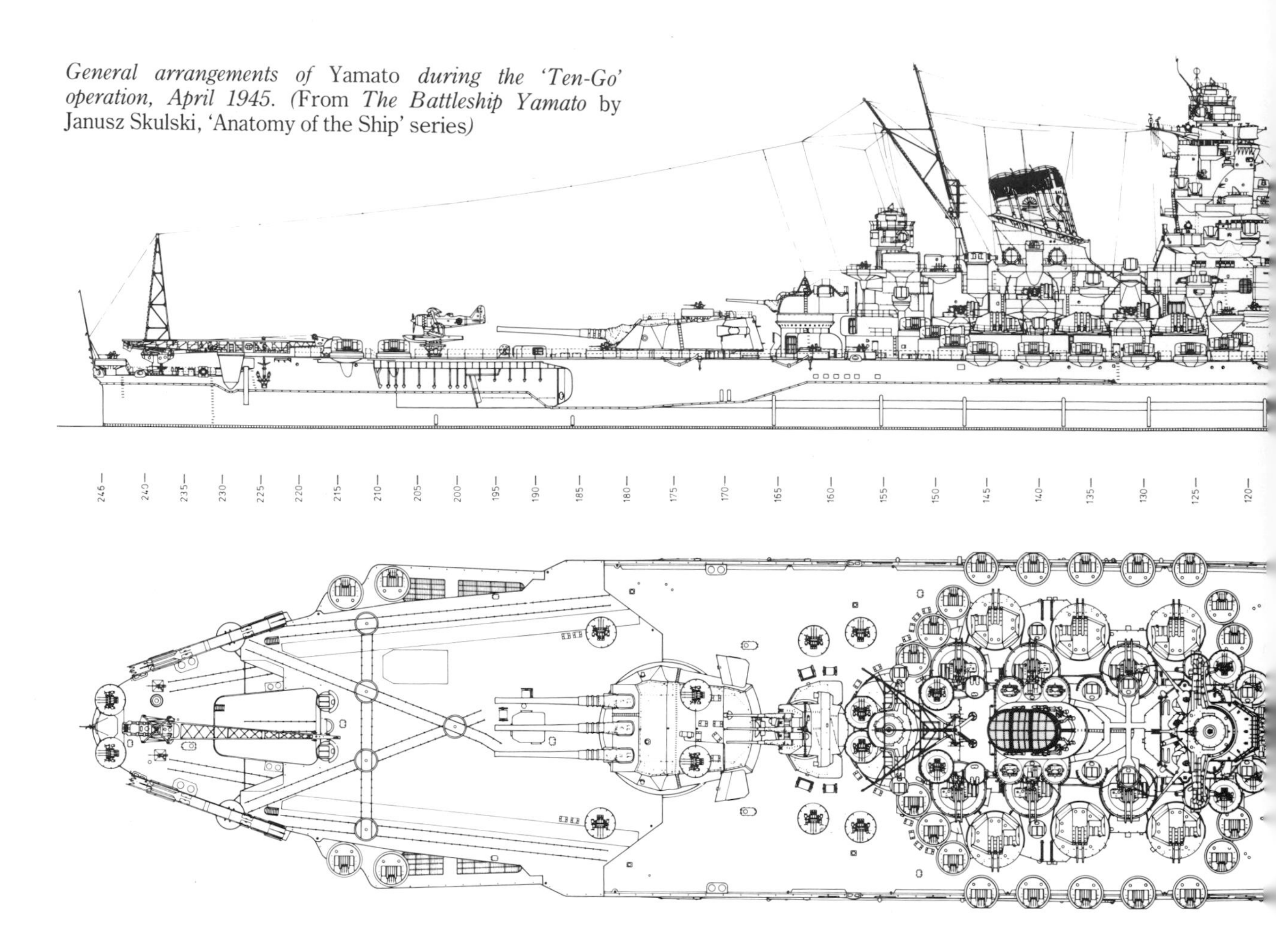

General arrangements of Yamato *during the 'Ten-Go' operation, April 1945.* (From *The Battleship Yamato* by Janusz Skulski, 'Anatomy of the Ship' series)

rapidly became open to question. Her repairs had not long been completed when American carrier aircraft began to attack the Japanese home islands for the first time, finding *Yamato* on 19 March in Hiroshima Bay. Her position was fortunate since most of the aircraft had dropped their bombs before she was sighted, and she survived a small attack unscathed.[7] Nonetheless if the Inland Sea was no longer safe the implications for *Yamato* were grim; the foggy Kuriles, north of Japan, offered a relatively safe refuge but she could contribute nothing to the defence of the homeland there, and the Army would make much capital from such a development. In practice such a move would have been repugnant to the people of a country whose only hope for salvation lay increasingly in the spirit of self-sacrifice which found ultimate expression in the Kamikaze, the Divine Wind.[8] Given this, the decision to use her as the biggest and most spectacular kamikaze of all does possess a certain logic.

The American carrier sweeps had been one of the initial stages of their plan to invade Okinawa, the largest of the Ryukyus, as a final stepping stone before assaulting the Japanese home islands. The Japanese had anticipated this development and kamikaze aircraft had been carefully husbanded to attack the invaders. The Americans landed on 1 April 1945 and 6 April was set for the main mass aerial attack designated Operation 'Ten-Go'.

The die is cast

Perhaps surprisingly the suggestion to use *Yamato* in a kamikaze operation in conjunction with 'Ten-Go' was only announced on 5 April. Such short notice might well seem extraordinary and would appear to be indicative of the increasing factionalism and dislocation of the Imperial Navy's High Command.[9] The germ of the idea may have started inadvertently with the Emperor on 29 March[10] but by 4 April Captain Kami on the staff of Admiral Toyoda, the Commander-in-Chief of the Combined Fleet, became convinced of its wisdom and persuaded his superior to endorse it. This may not have proved difficult since Toyoda believed the Navy should not survive defeat and his hatred of the Army[11] meant he wished to give them no excuse to criticize naval resolve.

While her future was discussed *Yamato* led a fugitive existence to avoid the frequent air attacks on Kure. Finally, in isolated Mitajiri Bay she was joined by the remainder of the active surface fleet, just one light cruiser *Yahagi*, and eight assorted destroyers, the whole being named the Second Fleet. It was here early in the afternoon of 5 April that the signal ordering a kamikaze attack on Okinawa was received.

Close-up of the superstructure with additional AA weapons, April 1945. (Janusz Skulski) ►

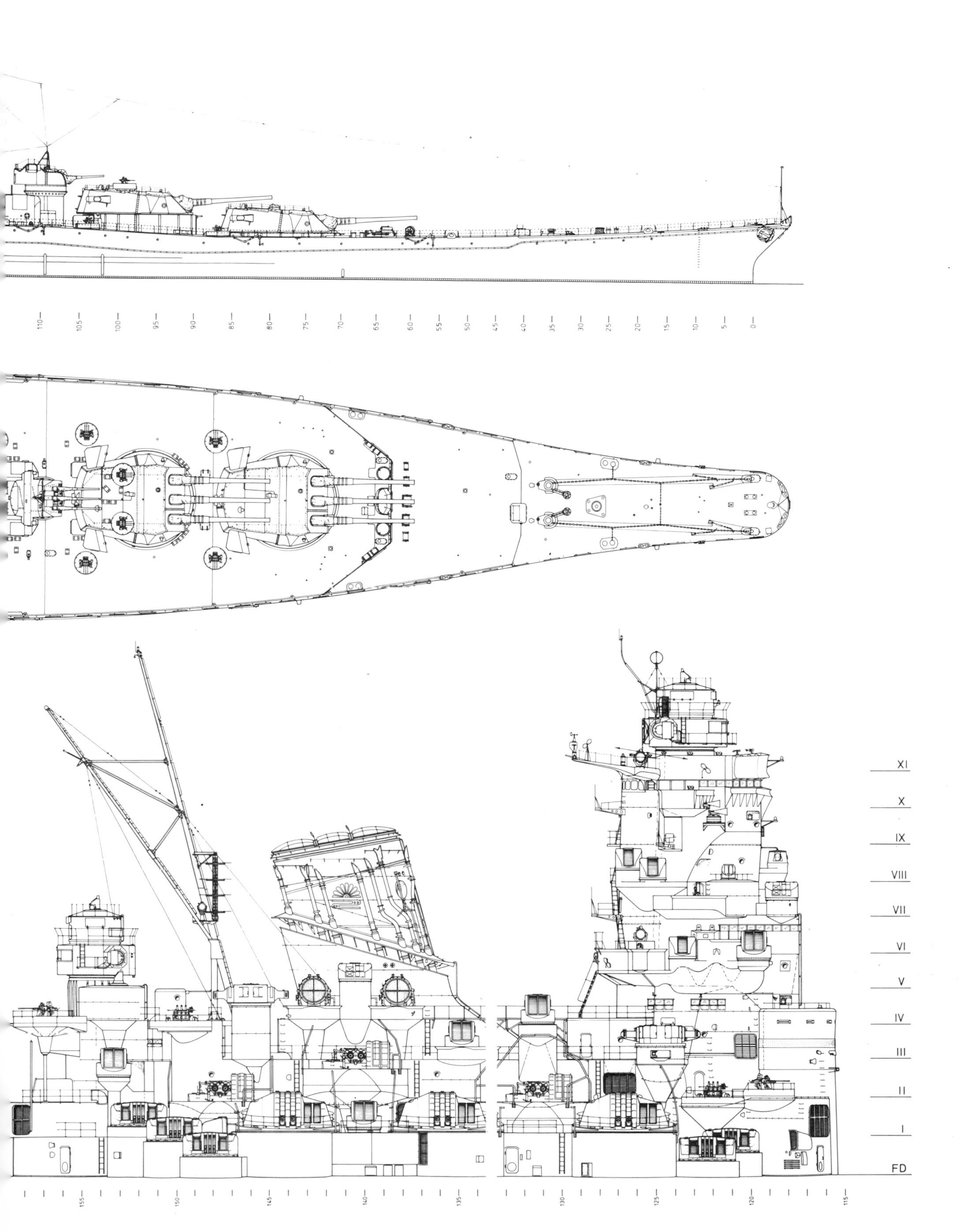
110
105
100
95
90
85
80
75
70
65
60
55
50
45
40
35
30
25
20
15
10
5
0
XI
X
IX
VIII
VII
VI
V
IV
III
II
I
FD
155
150
145
140
135
130
125
120
115

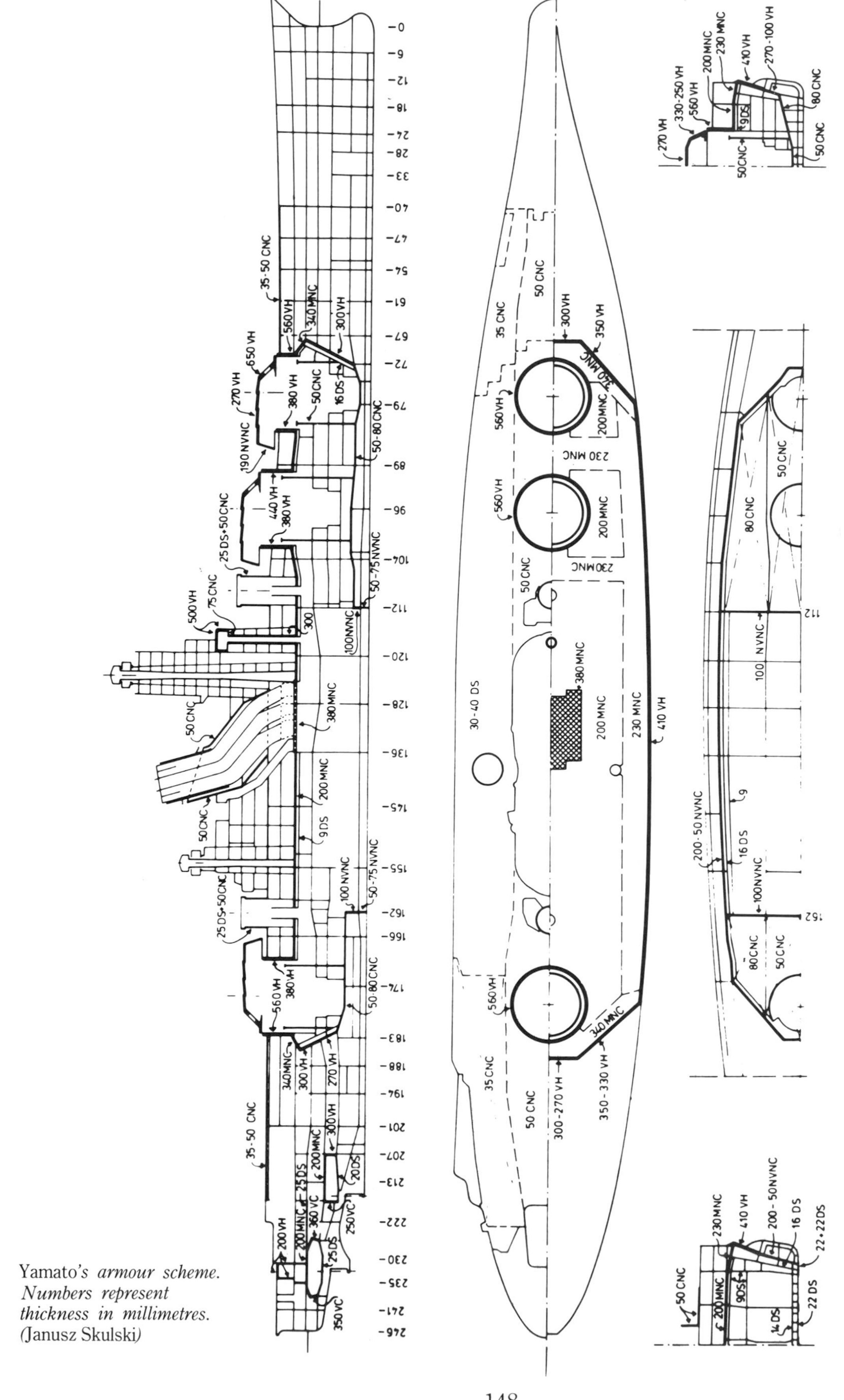

Yamato's *armour scheme. Numbers represent thickness in millimetres.* (Janusz Skulski)

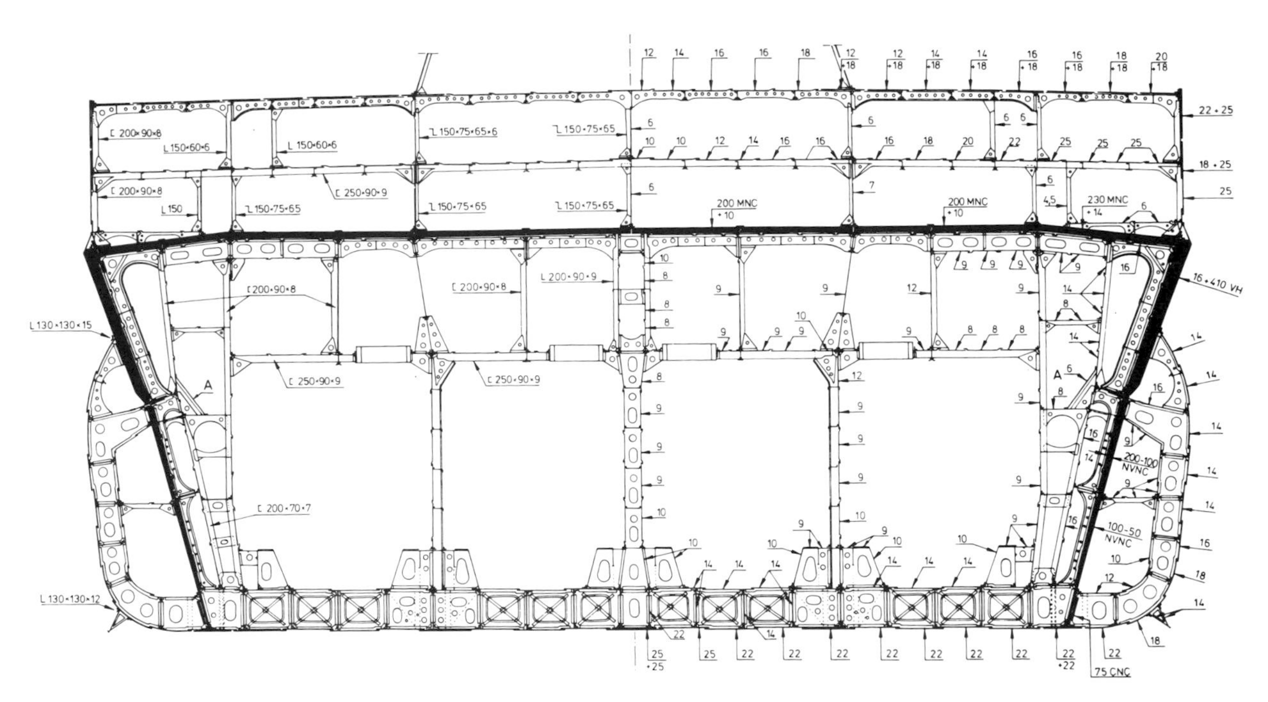

A structural cross-section of Yamato *showing the torpedo protection.* (Janusz Skulski)

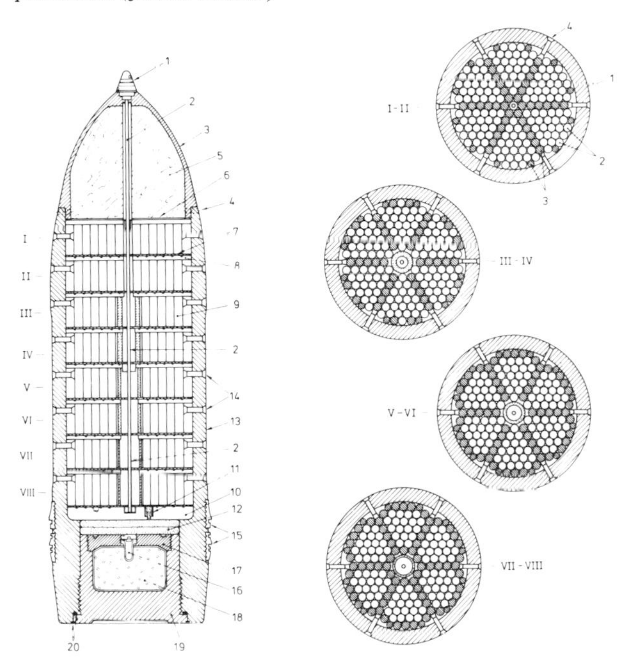

Details of the 'San Shiki' AA shell fired by Yamato's *main armament.* (Janusz Skulski)

1 Time fuze
2 Speed fuze rod
3 Projectile head
4 Projectile head set screw
5 Adaptor – wood
6 Filler lining
7 Quick match
8 Fuze plate
9 Incendiary fragments – rubber thermite
10 Base block
11 Delayed action charge
12 Ejecting charge and and black powder
13 Shell case
14 Rotating attachment rivet
15 Copper rotating bands
16 Detonating fuze
17 Fuze base
18 Bursting charge (picric acid)
19 Base
20 Copper gas-check rings

Such preparations as were possible in the time available were quickly put in hand and with the coming of darkness the fleet sailed for Tokuyama naval oil depot, although it now contained just 15,000 tons of heavy fuel oil, a third of all that was left in Japan. Against orders those in authority issued 4000 tons to *Yamato* and similarly generous amounts to her escorts. The extra fuel was enough for a return trip, and although such as eventuality was most unlikely it did permit continuous high speed steaming.

The final departure

Yamato weighed anchor at 15.18 on 6 April and preceded by four minesweepers she headed south across the Inland Sea toward Bungo Strait and Okinawa. Before night fell the only incident of note occurred when two B29s spotted the fleet and dropped a few bombs without result, the ships' guns remaining silent due to the bombers' great altitude. The Japanese knew Bungo Strait would be patrolled by US submarines and at 19.40 a destroyer found a suspicious contact, causing speed to be increased to 22kts, but due to the submarines' orders which stressed the importance of sighting reports rather than attack, and the vigilance of *Yamato*'s escorts, the Japanese passed through unscathed.

The Second Fleet commander, Admiral Ito, was well aware of the insurmountable difficulties which lay between his force and the invasion shipping off Okinawa. *Yamato* might well achieve something if she met enemy surface ships, though the large number of battleships available to the Americans ensured only one result was possible.

However, first she would have to survive huge carrier air attacks without any friendly air cover. A wealth of past experience showed survival was most unlikely and the only reassurance available was that the main kamikaze attack of 6 April would hopefully emasculate or at least reduce the carrier fleet's striking power beforehand.

Dawn revealed low grey clouds and with the light *Yamato*'s escorts formed a protective ring with *Yahagi* ahead of her and the two best anti-aircraft destroyers *Fuyutsuki* and *Suzutsuki*, to port and starboard in the best position to distract the aim of her most dangerous adversary, the torpedo bomber. Once this had been accomplished they could do no more than wait. As many pessimists in the Japanese ships feared, Task Force 58 had not suffered much damage during the kamikaze raids on 6 April, and on this day it could theoretically muster over 1200 aircraft. Forewarned of her sortie, scouts duly sighted *Yamato* at 08.23, 325 miles from the carriers. The main air strikes were, however, not launched until 10.00 since the range, as Ito intended, was too great and even then they could only hope to attack if the Japanese continued to steam south-west thereby narrowing the gap, which it was assumed rightly that they would.

Located and reported

At 10.00 two Martin Mariner flying-boats appeared and circled the fleet. *Yamato* immediately went to action stations and fired a total of three salvoes at intervals from the 46cm (18.1in) main armament of San Shiki anti-aircraft shells at the Mariners and a formation of six Hellcat fighters, but the huge detonations which scattered 20mm (0.8in) steel balls achieved nothing other than keeping the watchers circling at a respectful distance. At 12.20 *Yamato*'s air search radar detected a large formation to the south-east and twelve minutes later these broke through the overcast some 8 miles away.

Apart from her speed, escorts and manoeuvrability, *Yamato* would have only her guns to rely on. All were capable of firing in the anti-aircraft mode though neither the main armament nor the six 155mm (6.1in) main secondary armament had the training speed, rate of fire or elevation to engage aircraft effectively.[12] Indeed, two beam 155mm turrets had been removed for this very reason and the weight and space saved was used to install twelve additional 127mm (5in) dual purpose heavy anti-aircraft guns making twenty-four in all.[13] On this day the cloud base was often as low as 3000ft and this meant these guns often lacked the time to acquire a target effectively. For close defence she boasted four 13mm (0.5in) and 150 25mm (1in) machine-guns, 72 mounted in 24 triple turrets around the main superstructure, but despite a rate of fire of 250 rounds a minute these weapons lacked the weight of shot to destroy the robust carrier aircraft and there was also a shortage of directors to control them. In fact the low cloud made conditions so difficult that her barrage never achieved very good coordination and central control was soon abandoned in favour of the local battery commanders.

The Americans attack

The weather also hindered the attackers. Fifty-three aircraft from *Hancock* never did find *Yamato*, while for those that did the air attack coordinators were unable to see well enough to thoroughly control the attacks from the various carrier air groups. Nonetheless *Yamato* stood little chance since this first wave totalled no less than 280 aircraft – 132 fighters, 50 dive bombers and 98 torpedo bombers.

Naturally no definitive version of *Yamato*'s sinking can be given because any contemporary Japanese records did not survive the war[14] and even they would have had to rely on conjecture given the scale of damage and the relative rapidity with which she was lost. This account is based primarily on the recollections of survivors made at the end of 1945 and compiled by the US Naval Technical Mission to Japan. Their principal witnesses were Rear-Admiral Morishita, the Chief-of-Staff to Admiral Ito,[15] Captain Nomura, the Second-in-Command, and Lieutenant-Commander Shimizu, the Assistant Gunnery Officer.[16]

The first aircraft to attack (at 12.37) were four Helldivers which came in from astern to minimize the defensive fire. At this time *Yamato* was deliberately steaming into the westerly breeze so that when her Captain, Ariga, ordered an emergency turn to port to enable more batteries to engage, the wind on her starboard side served to push her round once the rudders initiated the turn. One aircraft was shot down but two bombs struck home close to frame 150 on the starboard side aft of the smokestack and level with the after fire control director. They were probably 500lb general purpose bombs since they exploded on impact blowing 20ft diameter holes in the deck, wrecking one 127mm (5in) dual mount and two 25mm (1in) triple mounts. Casualties were high[17] but no fires started and the damage was not serious.

Five minutes later two more bombs fell marginally to port of the centreline just forward of the aft 155mm (6.1in) turret. One passed through the after secondary battery control position, wrecking the director before detonating with its companion against the 200mm (7.9in) armoured deck two levels below. There was no damage below this but fires started which were never extinguished until the ship capsized, in part because the explosion wiped out the entire port after damage control party. Flames swiftly spread to the shell rooms below the 155mm turret where they ignited the ready-use cordite with dramatic consequences. The men in the turret were incinerated instantly, except for one lucky petty officer, and the roof of the turret was blown clean away. Fortunately the flash doors to the magazine below saved the ship from catastrophe although the after radar control room was lost along with more 25mm mounts.

Avenger torpedo bombers then made a coordinated attack and though one was downed, possibly as a result of the huge water geysers caused by a full salvo from the nine main guns fired at maximum depression, enough torpedoes were dropped to ensure *Yamato* could not avoid them all. Survivors consider that between two and four found their target, and two certainly hit in the middle of her armoured hull portside near frames 125 and 150. Containing 600lb of Torpex they were capable of rupturing her main defences which were centred on a heavy inclined armoured bulkhead 200mm (8in) thick and tapering down to 75mm (3in), protected outboard by an air filled anti-torpedo bulge which lacked the depth to dissipate the force of the explosion.[18] Inboard of the main defence there were two further thin water-tight bulkheads but they lacked the flexibility to deform without puncturing when the main bulkhead was displaced inwards by the explosion. In these two instances water leaked into No8 fireroom and the port outboard engine room although the amounts were small enough to be controlled by the pumps, at least initially.

In part because the outboard voids were air filled *Yamato* took on an immediate 5–6 degree list to port at which time

Yamato *under attack, 7 April 1945, taken by US carrier aircraft.* (CPL)

Nomura ordered immediate counterflooding of starboard outboard voids and this quickly brought it back to an acceptable 1 degree. One of the two possible hits may be questioned because it would have made her list far worse since it was thought to be to port aft near frame 190 outside the armoured section of her hull.[19] The other was said to be very far forward at frame 8 but as no reports of flooding were ever received it may also be questioned. Overall *Yamato*'s speed was scarcely reduced at all but in any battle of attrition her reserves of buoyancy were far from infinite.

At around 13.00 there was a lull while the aircraft of Task Group 58.1 retired to be replaced by those of TG 58.3. Surprisingly all agree that no dive bombers from this group managed to hit *Yamato* though she had less luck against torpedo bombers. Again they attacked her port side and three, possibly four, torpedoes found their mark. Ominously they hit near frames 124, 131, 143 and possibly 148 close to the sites of the damage caused in the first onslaught.[20] Fireroom No 8 had already been abandoned but flooding was now total and rapidly extended to No 12 fireroom aft. The port hydraulic machinery space between the firerooms and the outboard port engine room also filled and in the latter space flooding was equally massive and uncontrolled; only 20 ratings managed to escape in all.

Battered but unbowed

Most ships would have rolled over instantly after such a series of blows but even in *Yamato*[21] the consequences were very serious: her list swiftly climbed to 15–16 degrees to port and the loss of one shaft reduced her speed to 18kts. Although counterflooding of all starboard outboard compartments was ordered, this did little to remedy the difficulty in part because they were fitted with sea cocks, rather than pumps. Her list was such that they would not fill fully[22] and the transfer of fuel oil was also started which, in theory, could reduce a list of up to 4.5 degrees.

Temporary salvation was fortunately provided by the Americans; at 13.09 one torpedo hit her starboard side at frame 124 and caused immediate flooding of No 7 fireroom. That day US torpedoes were generally set to run at a depth of 18–24ft and given *Yamato*'s list to port, the outboard void should have been at its widest and fluid filled adding to this advantage, and yet still the defences failed badly. Either the torpedo struck the ship's less well defended bottom plates due to the list, or the strength of the rivetted hull, was fast being reduced by the shocks of repeated explosions. Whatever the cause her list swiftly reduced to a tolerable 5 degrees and by luck and skilful handling, the ship somehow avoided further serious damage, despite claims from the pilots of TG 58.3 that no less than 29 torpedoes hit the target.

Death of the ship

After this second attack *Yamato* could probably still have made it back to Japan, though, of course, that was not really an option. The futility of such speculation soon became clear, however, because after a lull of about thirty minutes, the third strike of the day comprising 115 aircraft from TG 58.4 broke through the thinning overcast. The US investiga-

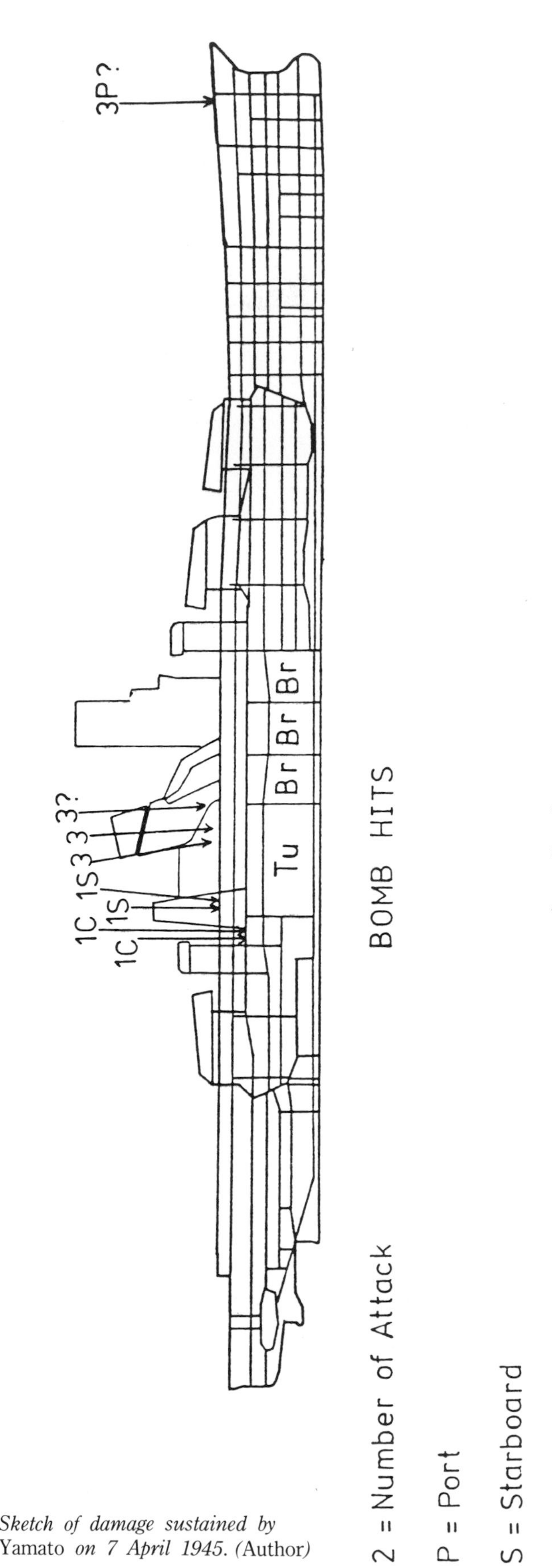

Sketch of damage sustained by Yamato *on 7 April 1945.* (Author)

The huge pall of smoke from Yamato *after the final explosion. (*CPL*)*

tors concluded that no bombs hit *Yamato* during this last fatal onslaught. Given her weakened defences, loss of manoeuvrability and reports from some eyewitnesses, this may be questioned. Possibly three bombs fell portside amidships exploding on impact and mowing down the anti-aircraft gunners in their vicinity. Another, though it may have been a large splinter from a near miss, hit the port capstan so that an anchor and part of its chain disappeared into the sea. There were also reports of a bomb in the senior wardroom which was being used as a casualty dressing station. Whatever the truth, in no case was her armoured deck pierced and it was torpedoes which completed her destruction.

Even before the attack, her port list was beginning to climb again and it was on this side that the attackers concentrated once more. Two torpedoes hit her badly ruptured central section, one near frame 135 on the junction between fireroom No 12 and the hydraulic machinery space. Both spaces were already flooded and the explosion extended this into fireroom No 10. The second struck close to frame 154 exploding in the flooded outboard engine room which led to flooding in the port inner engine room and the loss of power on that shaft. Another, according to Nomura also hit adjacent to the aft main turret but there was no record of flooding in the magazine which would have been certain.[23]

One torpedo also struck to starboard at frame 150 causing leakage into the starboard outboard engine room which was slow and controllable. Nonetheless, this good news was soon eclipsed because the collective damage from this attack gave her a list to port of 16–18 degrees, and such was the fear of capsizing that Nomura ordered the deliberate flooding of the remaining outboard starboard firerooms and the hydraulic machinery space leaving the ship with just one shaft turning. Even this drastic action only served to halt the list for a while and when it started to increase again the starboard outboard engine room was also deliberately flooded.[24]

This did stabilize the list at 22–23 degrees though with a speed of some 8kts on one shaft she was beginning to lose steerage way and the end was now inevitable.[25] Flooding was progressive and any decision about counterflooding the remaining firerooms was overtaken by events; shortly after 14.00 all power was lost and permission was given to abandon ship. By 14.20 she was on her beam ends and when her roll reached some 120 degrees there was a colossal explosion, the fireball and smoke rising so high that it was visible from Kyushu over 100 miles away.

Two explanations for this Wagnerian climax have been suggested. Nomura thought it was due to an explosion of the main battery anti-aircraft shells which had been stored vertically and could have slipped out of their fastenings.[26] US investigations after studying such shells considered this impossible and the most likely explanation lies in the fire which continued to burn in the aft 155mm turret. As the ship rolled over, the flames would have gone down the hoists and thus reached the magazine. This hypothesis is supported by eye-witnesses who noted that the seat of the explosion was in the after part of the ship.[27]

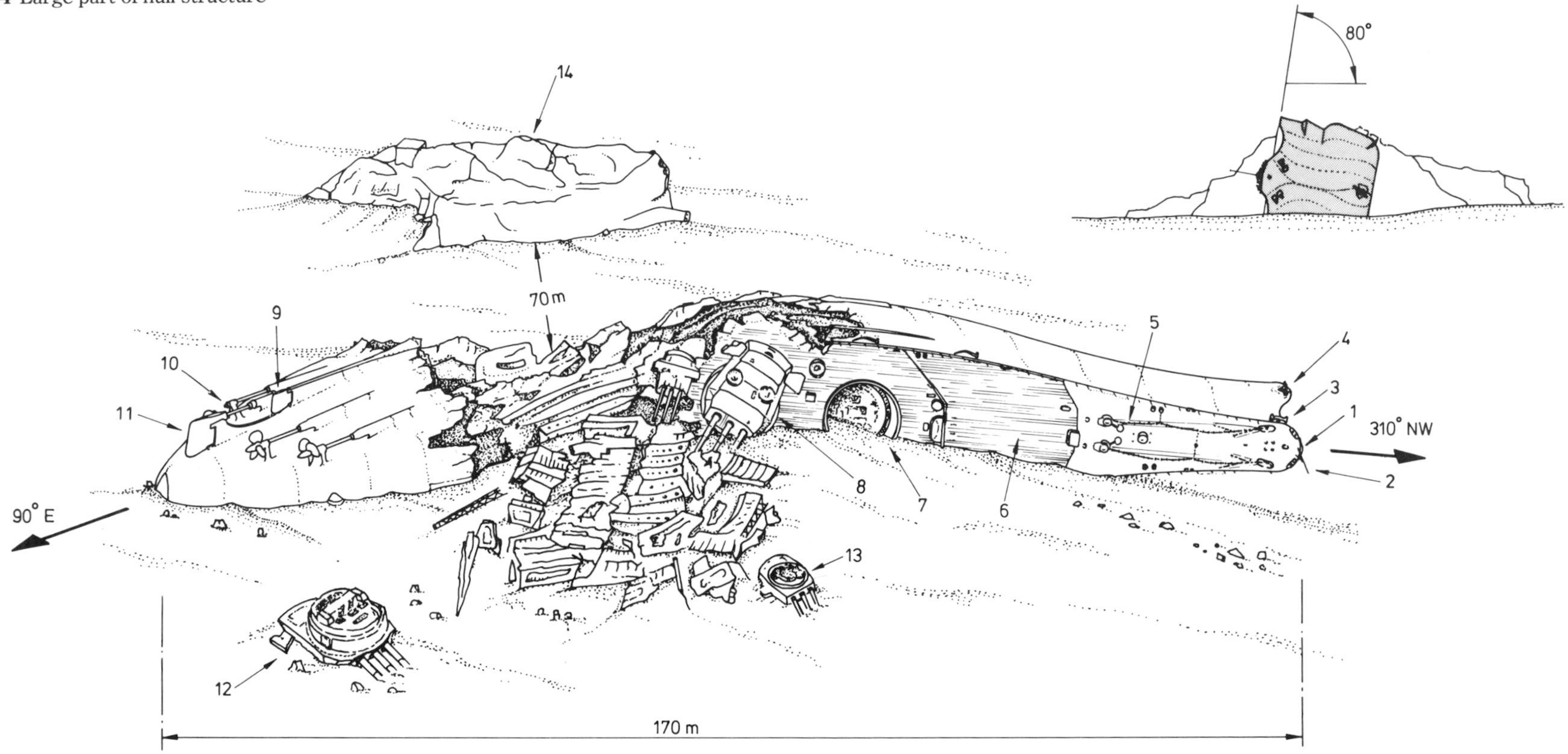

An artist's impression of the wreck based on the underwater examination of 1 August 1985. (Janusz Skulski)

1 Chrysanthemum crest
2 Jack staff
3 Anchor
4 Bulbous bow – damaged
5 Anchor chain
6 Wood deck
7 No1 main gun turret barbette
8 No2 main gun turret
9 Auxiliary rudder
10 Missing starboard side propeller
11 Main rudder
12 No1 (?) main gun turret
13 15.5cm gun turret
14 Large part of hull structure

Due to this explosion and American action there were only 280 survivors including 23 officers and warrant officers, out of a complement of at least 2400 men.[28] Only three destroyers were still relatively seaworthy and once the US aircraft departed, they collected the survivors and returned home, following orders from Combined Fleet Headquarters to abandon the sortie.

Once the decision to commit *Yamato* to the defence of Okinawa was taken, no other result was likely. Bombs from carrier-borne aircraft could not destroy such a powerful ship but Torpex-armed torpedoes were well able to sink any ship afloat. At most fourteen had found their mark against *Yamato* and while her main defences could tolerate some hits, repeated blows to one side inevitably led to her capsizing.

It was claimed that if nothing else her sortie would act as a decoy and allow the aerial kamikazes an easier run at the US carriers off Okinawa. Whilst plausible, even this ploy failed to bear fruit. The weather was so poor over Kyushu that only 54 Japanese aircraft were launched on 7 April and half of these returned having failed to find a target. Only the carrier *Hancock* was hit and she was operational again in a few hours. The aura of waste and mismanagement was complete. By comparison with Japanese losses, the American executioners lost just ten aircraft and twelve men.

Footnotes

1. Details of both can be found in *Action Summary of BB Yamato* US Microfilm AR-209-78, p41.
2. She carried 180 shells in each magazine, 60 per barrel, making 540 in all.
3. In deep condition her trim forward was 9.5m (25.9ft) at which stage her draught was 10.8m (35.3ft).
4. Casualties were slight since the ship was at action stations. Only 33 were killed throughout the whole operation and they were mostly manning the anti-aircraft guns.
5. This was precisely the fate of the remaining big ships. They were moored fully manned with just enough oil to provide electrical power for the gun turrets to traverse and elevate.
6. Yamato was the name of the province around Nara, the first permanent capital established by the Emperor's ancestors. The Japanese still call themselves the Yamato people.
7. Garzke and Dulin suggest that one bomb hit her main bridge tower but this cannot be corroborated. See *Axis and Neutral Battleships of World War II*, p59.
8. Kamikaze refers to a violent typhoon which destroyed a Sino-Mongul invasion fleet in the year 1281.
9. This had long been in some disarray. The Navy Chief-of-Staff was officially the operational head of the IJN but after the Pearl Harbor operation, masterminded by Yamamoto as head of the Combined Fleet, this latter post gained kudos and power and had become all powerful on matters of policy.
10. This has been suggested because on that day the Emperor on being briefed about 'Ten-Go' is said to have asked why no surface ships were involved. R Spurr, *A Glorious Way to Die*, p87.
11. His hatred for the Army is said to have stemmed from an incident at Tsingtao during the China Incident. A J Marder, *Old Friends and New Enemies*, pp180–181.
12. The main guns could train at 2° a second, fire 1.5 rounds a minute and elevate to 45°. The 155m turrets could train at 5° a second, fire only 5 rounds a minute and elevate to 55°.
13. The 127mm mounts could elevate to 90°, train at 16° a second and fire 14 rounds a minute, a performance much more suited to anti-aircraft work.
14. Many records were lost when the Navy Ministry was caught up in the great incendiary bombing raids of 1945. The remainder were mostly deliberately destroyed during the period 15–17 August 1945.
15. Rear Admiral Morishita had been Yamato's Commanding Officer before taking up the post of Chief-of-Staff and so was thoroughly familiar with the ship.
16. Senior Officers were used for such debriefs because it was found that Japanese enlisted men and junior officers were 'hopelessly ignorant'. Morishita was on the eighth level of the tower when the ship rolled over and he was carried under, losing consciousness before being picked up by a destroyer. Nomura and Shimizu were in the conning tower, the former suffering wounds from explosions which had still not healed by December 1945. The latter had climbed up to the sixth level before swimming off.
17. For example each triple 25mm mount required no less than nine men to man it.
18. For more detail see *Warship* 41, pp2–8.
19. Garzke and Dulin state that there was slow flooding into the auxiliary steering room as a result of this possible hit, p61.
20. It is reported that little water was thrown up by these explosions, a sure sign that detonation occurred deep within the ship.
21. At full load she displaced 71,110 metric tonnes (69,988 English tons).
22. When the flying deck on one side touched the sea, voids on the other would only fill to 55 per cent of capacity.
23. Garzke and Dulin. They report another hit at frame 211 to port which flooded the steering room and jammed her main rudder, p64.
24. Some have suggested that this caused the death of 300 men trapped in the compartment, though Nomura denied this. Whatever the truth, no officer survived from any of the machinery spaces.
25. Ariga ordered full port rudder to be applied in the hope that a tight turn to port would cause a heel to starboard and reduce the list, but she lacked the speed to make such a manoeuvre profitable.
26. All these shells had installed fuses set to safe, and a charge of 136lb of TNA (Trinitroanisde).
27. Garzke and Dulin reckon she sailed with a ship's company of 3332. Certainly the increased anti-aircraft armament swelled her original complement considerably, and she was a flagship, but this figure does seem on the high side.
28. In May 1982 her remains were found lying in a little under 1200ft of water, her broken hull half buried in sludge at an angle of 130° on its starboard side.

COMPLETING THE LAST BATTLESHIP

Robert Dumas, France's leading authority on capital ships, looks at the protracted fitting out of the *Jean Bart* after the war and reveals that the ship was never truly battle-worthy.

The decision to complete the *Jean Bart* was taken on 22 February 1945[1] but not without argument between those who believed that the war which was still in progress had proved the dominance of air power and those who believed that the big gun still had a role at sea. During two meetings of the *Conseil Supérieur de la Marine* (CSM) in July 1945, Admirals Barjot and Fenard emerged as fervent supporters of completing the *Jean Bart* as an aircraft carrier.

In the absence of any consensus among the admirals, the Navy Minister insisted on a definitive decision on one of three courses:

1 Stop work on the ship
2 Complete her as a battleship
3 Complete her as an aircraft carrier.

On 21 September 1945 the CSM reconvened, and its members were unanimous in rejecting the first alternative. However, Kahn, the *Ingénieur-Général* and head of DCCAN[2] (the equivalent of the British Director of Naval Construction) presented a scheme for the conversion of the ship into a carrier, at an estimated cost of 5000 million Francs and a delay of five years in completion. The design, drawn up in July 1945, included a 90mm thick armoured flight deck, which was a significant proportion of the cost. According to this scheme the *Jean Bart* would have carried 40 aircraft with 14 extra slung from the hangar deckhead, the defensive armament comprising sixteen 130mm AA guns in eight twin mountings.[3]

At the actual presentation, the CSM was decidedly unimpressed. Few aircraft could be embarked for such a large ship (half of the number operated by similar sized ships of other navies) and the arrangement of the boiler uptakes absorbed much of the available hangar space. The following passage from the report of the meeting demonstrates how little enthusiasm the carrier conversion engendered:

> The aircraft carrier design presented to the Board was described by one member as a 'caricature' of a project which was supposed to create an effective carrier. It is possible to conclude that the DCAN proposal was given only superficial attention, but one suspects that the real intention was to demonstrate *a priori* that the conversion of the *Jean Bart* into an aircraft carrier was a disadvantageous undertaking. The same impression is given by the estimated delay and cost: 5 milliard Francs and 5 years. Several members of the Board (Admirals Fenard, Sala and Barjot) expressed astonishment at these figures, whereupon Ingénieur-Général Kahn acknowledged

Leaving Brest for initial sea trials on 8 January 1949, Jean Bart *reveals a very bare profile, with AA armament, directors and electronics still to be shipped.* (Author)

In this aerial view, taken in 1950, the ship had acquired main armament directors and her initial suite of French-built radars. Note the temporary single 40mm Bofors on the quarterdeck. (Author)

> that they were exaggerated and gave his personal evaluation of 3.5 milliard and 3 years. This rapid climb-down only reinforced the impression of a design put forward by a Constructor Corps [*Services Techniques*] that did not want an aircraft carrier.[4]

Therefore, the CSM turned to plans for completion as a battleship. An exhaustive list of existing material was drawn up and from this a projected schedule of works was calculated, as follows:

1 completing the 380mm guns – 3 years
2 finishing Turret II (380mm) – 4 years
3 stockpiling ammunition – 5 years

Whatever course was taken the *Jean Bart* would not be available for some time, the alternatives being: 3½ years to 5 years if completed as an aircraft carrier; 4 years for a battleship without ammunition; or 5 years for a battleship with ammunition. The DCM finally decided to opt for a battleship (a second *Richelieu* but with much improved AA defence) on 21 September 1945, but the decision came in for a lot of criticism, particularly from the officers of the naval air arm:

> It is very surprising in 1945 to see the head of the navy dogmatically supporting the cause of the battleship against that of the aircraft carrier. This attitude, which dominated the discussions of 21 September 1945, clearly reveals that despite the experience of the war the mythology surrounding the big gun continues to rule our naval thinking.[5]

If the value of completing a battleship in 1945 is questionable, it is also worth remembering that no battleship converted into an aircraft carrier has ever been entirely satisfactory.

The work of completing *Jean Bart* began at Brest on 11 March 1946. The task involved repairing the damage done to the hull during the bombardment of Casablanca, finishing the main machinery, mounting the main and secondary armament, and modifying the superstructure to take the new radar and fire control equipment. The reconstruction aimed to provide a ship that could perform three roles: task force flagship, heavy AA vessel, and fire support ship for shore bombardment.

At the end of this initial fitting-out, the ship was not entirely complete; in particular she lacked the whole of her planned AA armament and the majority of her radars. Difficulties with budgets and technical problems conspired to delay the installation of this new equipment.

INITIAL CHARACTERISTICS

Displacement (tonnes)	*Draught fwd*	*Draught midships*	*Draught aft*
48,950 full load	10.09m (33ft 1in)	10.39m (34ft 1in)	10.69m (35ft 1in)
46,500 normal	9.86m (32ft 4in)	9.95m (32ft 8in)	10.04m (34ft 1in)
42,806 light	8.57m (28ft 1in)	9.27m (30ft 5in)	9.97m (32ft 9in)

Dimensions
247.855m (813ft 2in) length overall
35.542m (116ft 7in) breadth overall after fitting of bulges

PROTECTION

Hull

Armour belt 5.96m (19ft 7in) high inclined at 15°24′ angle	330m (13in)
Forward armoured bulkhead	335mm (14in)
After armoured bulkhead	233m (9.2in)
Lower armoured deck (first platform deck)	40mm (1.6in)
Second platform deck	40mm (1.6in)
Upper armoured deck (main deck)	
from frame 50,51 to 130	150mm (5.9in)
from frame 130 to 182,95	170mm (6.7in)
Protection for the propeller shaft and steering gear	
first platform deck from frame 19 to 51,50	100mm (3.9in)
from frame 8 to 19	150mm (5.9in)
after bulkhead at frame 8	150mm (5.9in)
bulkhead at frame 19	50mm (5.9in)

Protection against underwater explosion was provided by a water-tight longitudinal bulkhead, filled compartments and armoured decks.

Conning tower

Front and sides	340mm (13.4in)
Back	280mm (11in)
Roof of the admiral's bridge	170mm (6.7in)
Roof of the captain's bridge	170mm (6.7in)
Communication tube	160mm (6.3in)

An aerial close-up of the midship section, also taken in 1950, shows the empty gun positions and the makeshift AA armament of 40mm and 20mm guns. (Author)

General arrangement drawing of the ship in 1950. (Author)

Main armament turrets

Barbette above the upper armoured deck	405mm (15.9in)
below the upper armoured deck	80mm (3.1in)
Gunhouse face (inclined at 30°)	430mm (16.9in)
sides (vertical)	300mm (11.8in)
rear of Turret I	270mm (10.6in)
rear of Turret II	260mm (10.2in)
roof	195mm and 170mm (7.7in and 6.7in)

Secondary armament turrets

Barbette	100mm (3.9in)
Gunhouse face (inclined)	130mm
side (vertical)	70mm (2.8in)
rear	60mm (2.4in)
roof	70mm (2.8in)

A signficant percentage of the weight break-down was devoted to protection:
29.1 per cent for the hull
10.1 per cent for the armament
making a total of 39.2 per cent.

The ship was protected at the waterline by a main armour belt which extended from the after transverse bulkhead (frame 15,51) to its forward equivalent (frame 182,95). Individual plates were 5.96mm long and varied in width between 2.50m and 3,05m; the belt was inclined at 15°14′ to the vertical. It was mounted on a 60mm thick backing of teak or mahogany. The protection was the same as for *Richelieu*, except that anti-torpedo bulges were added, increasing the maximum beam from 33.08m (100ft 11in) to

Another 1950 view, at Brest. Judging by the staging around the masts, work is being carried out on the electronics. Note the 90mm sub-calibre gun on a platform at the side of 'B' turret. (Author)

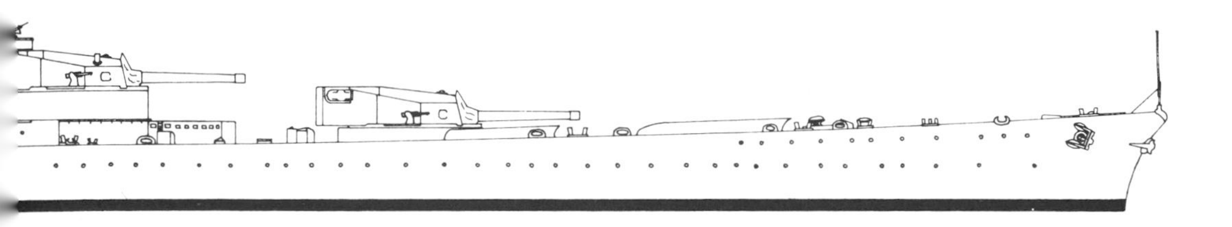

35.542m (116ft 7in). The bulge also offset the increase in displacement which would otherwise have meant modifying the hull form.

Machinery

Jean Bart was powered by four Parsons turbines driving four propellers, steam being supplied by six Sural type boilers. Performance was as follows:

Power
Normal maximum power, 155,000hp = 31kts
Full power trials (7 February 1949, 2 hours), 176,442hp = 32.06kts

Speed
Emergency full speed (combat) = 32kts
Normal maximum speed = 31.5kts
Economical cruising speed = 15kts

Endurance
8832nm at 15kts
7671nm at 20kts
3181nm at 30kts

Equipment

Guns

Eight 380mm	(15in), Modèle 1935, in two quadruple turrets, mounted forward.
Nine 152mm	(6in), Modèle 1936, in three triple turrets, mounted aft. The guns could be used against aircraft as well as surface targets.
Eight 40mm	Bofors AA guns in single mountings.
Twenty 20mm	Oerlikon AA guns in single mountings.

[Four 90mm, Modèle 1935, in single mountings, as sub-calibre weapons were installed on platforms either side of the 380mm turrets].

Searchlights
Two 75cm projectors (sided) were mounted on No6 Platform of the bridge.

Radar
All equipment was of French design and manufacture, and was among the first constructed after the war. The individual sets were as follows:

Surface search	–	one DRBV 10 (*Détection Radioélectrique par ondes hertzienne Bâtiment de surface Veille*) installed on a bracket above the conning tower in November 1948.
Air search	–	one DRBV 20 mounted on the lower mainmast platform in June 1949.
Navigation	–	one DRBV 30 fitted at the mainmast head in November 1948.
Main armament fire control	–	one ABM (*Artillerie But Marin*) carried on the front of the main armament director from the end of 1948.
Secondary armament fire control	–	the 152mm guns benefitted from the installation of the first AA fire control radar ACAE (*Artillerie Contre Avions Eloigné*) from the beginning of 1950. However, it was unstabilized; compensation for rolling and pitching was never perfected.

Boats
Five 11.00m (36ft) motor launches (3 old type and 2 new prototypes)
Two 8.05m (26ft) motor boats
Two 7.00m (23ft) whaleboats
One 5.00m (16ft) dinghy
Two punts
One 5.00m (16ft) Vosper motor boat

Also 104 liferafts (Brest type), 2273 lifejackets, and 8 enclosed lifebuoys.

Complement
The fitting out of *Jean Bart* was never completed during this period and the figures below represent the minimum necessary to take the ship to sea:

May 1950 – 911 men
1 August 1950 – 700 men

At the end of the first stage of the fitting-out *Jean Bart*'s

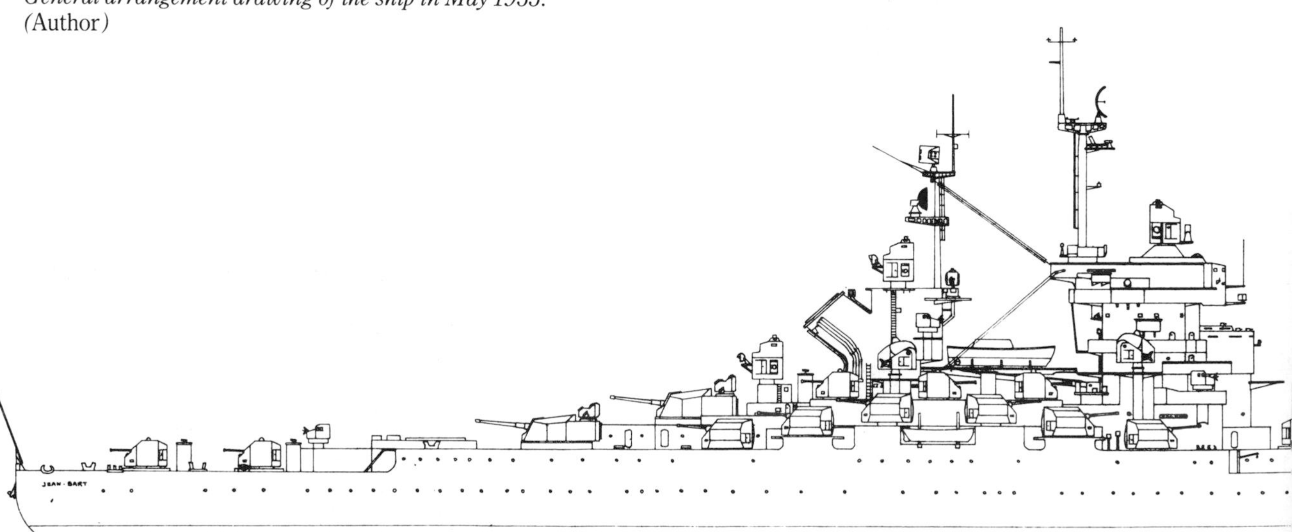

General arrangement drawing of the ship in May 1955. (Author)

machinery was complete and the main and secondary armament mounted. However, all the AA battery and the fire control equipment remained to be fitted. Early in November 1951 she was moved to the Ordnance quay in order to carry out the following programme of work:

1 Improvement to the main armament fire control
2 Modification to the 152mm mountings for AA fire, and recalibration of the fire control system.
3 Installation of twelve twin 100mm, Modèle 1945, AA guns, arranged in four identical groups each controlled by its own navy-designed director
4 Mounting of fourteen twin 57mm AA guns, arranged in five groups
5 Fitting a combat information centre
6 Installation of two master gyroscopes for fire control
7 Removal of the 40mm and 20mm guns.

The emphasis was principally on gunnery and electronics in this refit. Both of the superstructure towers and their masts were radically altered to allow the fitting of new radar and radio antennae and fire control equipment.

FINAL CHARACTERISTICS

Displacement (tonnes)	*Draught fwd*	*Draught midships*	*Draught aft*
49,196 full load	9.997m (32ft 10in)	10.346m (33ft 11in)	10.895m (35ft 9in)
46,809 normal	9.773m (32ft 1in)	10.003m (32ft 10in)	10.223m (33ft 6in)
43,053 light	8.45m (27ft 9in)	9.317m (30ft 7in)	10.184m (33ft 5in)

Dimensions were unchanged.

Armament
[Main and secondary amament were unchanged]
Twenty-four 100mm, Modèle 1945, AA guns in twelve twin enclosed gunhouses situated amidships on each side of the superstructure.
Twenty-eight 57mm Bofors, Modèle 1947, AA guns in fourteen twin mountings (two groups around the second 380mm turret, two groups abreast the boat deck, and one group on the quarterdeck).

Searchlights
Two 1.20m infra-red projectors for night search on the after superstructure.
Two 0.60m projectors for signalling on No6 platform of the bridge tower.

Radar
The masts were rebuilt to take the following equipment:

Surface search	–	one DRBV 30 (small radar on the foremast)
Combined air and surface search	–	one DRBV 11 (at the head of the mainmast). This set proved inadequate against jet aircraft; its replacement by DRBV 22 was planned for the second stage of modernisation
Air search	–	one DRBV 20 (ex GBVA). Satisfactory equipment
Height-finder	–	one SP (tested aboard the carrier *Bois-Belleau*). Of limited capacity
Fire control	–	one DRBC 10A (for the main armament) two ACAE (for 152mm guns) four ACAE (for 100mm guns) five DRBC 30B (for 57mm guns)

Boats
Five 11m (36ft) launches
Two 8m (26ft) motor boats
Two 7m (23ft) whaleboats
Two 5m (16ft) dinghies
One 3m (10ft) punt

Complement

As a training ship	– 757 total
For sea service	– 1149 total
During Suez operation	– 1280 total
Full war complement	– 70 officers and 2150 petty officers and men.

Completion of the main and secondary armament

380mm guns
From the end of 1951, Turret I was fully mothballed on a trial basis and Turret II partially so. This latter state enabled the guns to be reactivated in two weeks – from this condition at the beginning of August 1956, the first firings were able to take place on the 22nd. (When the ship operated with the French Naval Intervention Force during the Suez Campaign, only Turret II was reactivated.) Work on the main armament was confined to that necessary to get the ship into service. The main armament was controlled from a director tower on top of the bridge structure, and an earlier problem with vibration was remedied by increasing the height of the pedestal by 1.70m. The director utilized a fast reacting electric system similar to that used by the 100mm directors, and was regarded as very flexible in service. The DRBC 10A radar allowed surface targets to be engaged at 25,000m (27,000yds) and trials at the end of 1955 demonstrated that its performance was satisfactory.

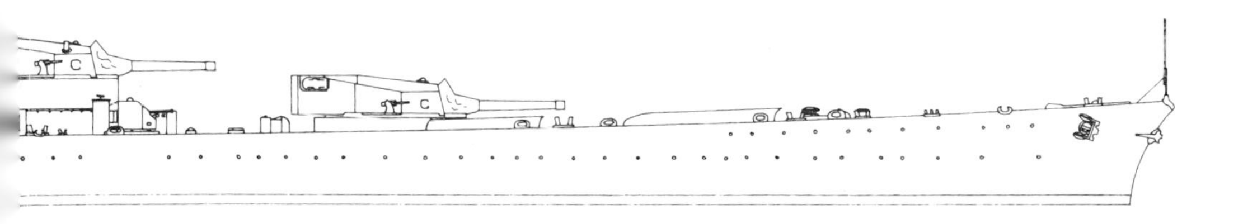

Jean Bart *entering Toulon for the first time (17 October 1955). She now has a full outfit of 100mm and 57mm guns.* (Marius Bar, by courtesy of the Author)

152mm guns
The Ward Leonard system was used for control. The main fuze-setters for each turret had been altered in anticipation of their conversion to AA fire, so surface fire was only possible by using the auxiliary fuze-setter. The firing circuits were electro-mechanical, with a split-second retard for the centre barrel. Both secondary directors were intended for surface firing, but the upper director was difficult to use in certain wind conditions since it was affected by funnel gases. For the same reason, fire control from both directors was always poor. In case of damage to the directors, the 152mm guns would be controlled from the centreline turret, or fired independently using the range-finders mounted on each turret top.

In June 1954 it was decided to install an anti-aircraft fire control system for the 152mm guns. In AA fire the secondary armament would be controlled by two after 100mm directors, via two 100mm Modèle 1947 fire control tables suitably adapted for the 152mm guns. Originally each 152mm director had an ACAE radar, but the upper one did not work and was removed. The one on the bridge tower was operational but could only be used for rangefinding, and was in any case obsolescent and not very robust.

Completion of the AA armament

100mm guns
The first magazines and turrets for the 100mm guns were fitted in July 1952; the twelve turrets were formally accepted after extensive trials of the rate and reliability of their firing during May to July 1953. The four directors were in place by May 1953, and the port forward group carried out the first firings against aircraft (a towed target) in July 1953. Important modifications followed, as a result of this early experience and by October 1954 the starboard forward group had completed calibration against surface targets.

The twelve turrets were controlled by four gyro-stabilized directors. Training angle and elevation could be transmitted via Remote Power Control using the Ward Leonard system (for more details of its operation see *Naval Weapons of World War Two* by John Campbell, pp280-1); there were also semi-automatic and emergency manual alternatives. Each director and corresponding fire control table could control three mountings of its usual group or the six mountings of the appropriate broadside. The changeover could be made instantly by automatic switches operated from the main AA fire control station or the target designating position.

The weak link in the system was the ACAE radar sets, whose capabilities were mediocre and although they could automatically generate height and bearing information, they could not provide range. They would have been better replaced by DRBC 11 or 30. The ACAE sets on the forward directors were never operational and were removed in April 1956, but those on the after directors did work after a fashion.

CHARACTERISTICS OF THE 100mm MODÈLE 1945 GUN

Gun	
Barrel:	Monobloc, autofretted, no jacket
Breech:	Vertical block, spring-loaded, semi-automatic, manual opening
Length:	55 calbres
Angle of rifling:	6°30′
Maximum pressure:	2800kg per cm^2 (18 tons per sq in)

A close-up of the midship superstructure, 17 October 1955. The 152mm directors and aft (above and below the funnel) while the sided 100mm directors can be seen abreast the bridge tower and the funnel. (Marius Bar, by courtesy of the Author)

Muzzle velocity:	875m per sec (2870ft per sec)
Maximum range:	Against surface targets, at 40° elevation – 17,000m (18,600yds) Against aircraft, at 70° elevation – ?
Weight of gun (including breech mechanism):	1840kg (4056lb)
Total weight (including mounting):	26,550kg (58,533lb)
Mounting	
Type:	Twin, armoured shield
Maximum elevation and depression:	+70° and −8°
Loading:	By hand, with hydraulic rammer
Firing mechanism:	Electro-mechanical, fixed on the cradle; or mechanical by hydraulic transmission, fired by the gun aimer after authorization of the breech operator
Sights:	In AA fire, a collimator telescope with illuminated screen and sight In surface fire, by B8 type binocular (with automatic cross-levelling)

57mm guns

The guns were manufactured under a licensing arrangement agreed with Bofors in 1947, but this did not include the mounting. The French Navy employed these guns only in a twin mounting, which was developed entirely by the Navy's Constructor Corps – including the loading arrangements, radar, mounting control and ammunition. However, the fire control gear was designed by the Swiss Contraves company to a French specification, and later the manufacturing rights were acquired by France.

The fourteen twin enclosed gunhouses, designated ACAD Modèle 1948, were controlled by five self-contained fire-control systems. Each of these comprised a stabilised (for roll, pitch and yaw) radar director and a Contraves fully automated fire control system. This allowed for:

1 Fire against targets outside visible range – range and aiming data provided by the DRBC 30 radar mounted on the director.
2 Fire against visible targets – optical aiming by director officer, range data from the radar.
3 Fire against visible targets (in case of radar failure) – range data from the director's rangefinder.

In all cases, the aiming data (bearing and elevation) was calculated and sent to the guns by the fire control system.

After acquisition, the DRBC 30 radar followed the target automatically; fire could then be opened and sustained until the ready-use ammunition on the mounting was expended (160 rounds) with no more human intervention than the pressing of a button in the central fire control station. The 57mm mountings could also use an auxiliary system of nine MkXIV gyroscopic optical fire control sights. In case of damage to the fire control system or communication, each mounting could fire under local control using a Bronzavia telescope sight.

Designated 'standard batteries' of two, three or four mountings could be controlled by single radar directors. Many different combinations of mountings and directors were possible: batteries could be reinforced by other superfiring groups under the same director, or control could be completely decentralized, giving each mounting its own control position (there were nine optical and five radar directors).

▲ Jean Bart *off Toulon in the autumn of 1955 – the world's last completed battleship.* (Marius Bar, by courtesy of the Author)

Firing trials were carried out in standard and reinforced batteries and were completed by September 1955. The optical positions were only fitted out in August 1956 and trials were carried out shortly afterwards.

CHARACTERISTICS OF THE 57mm MODÈLE 1947 GUN

Watercooled gun

Total weight of mounting:	18 tonnes, including 1cm thick armoured shield
Length of barrel:	60 calibres
Muzzle velocity:	865m per sec (2838ft per sec)
Maximum elevation and depression	+95° to −10°
Maximum theortical range:	10-second flight before explosion of projectile (*c*5500m or 6000yds)
Rate of fire:	120 rounds per gun (240 rounds per mounting) per minute. With full hoists (160 rounds) the mounting could fire for 40 seconds
Speed of aiming:	25° per second in training and elevation

The eight 40mm Bofors mountings were landed in 1952, and the twenty 20mm Oerlikons were removed at the beginning of 1954. *Jean Bart* was not to join the active fleet until 1 May 1955, but for the whole of her career she was to remain, in effect, uncompleted. A second and final programme of work was envisaged for the major refit of 1958, when new radar of improved performance and range, plus electronic countermeasures, would be added.

◀ *Another view taken on 17 October 1955 of the ship entering Toulon, where she was to become a gunnery training ship.* (Marius Bar, by courtesy of the Author)

new radar of improved performance and range, plus electronic countermeasures, would be added.

Conclusions

The *Jean Bart*'s unusual career was a unique case in the history of the French Navy. Many commentators have expressed surprise at the extended delays associated with the completion and modernization, and have given the impression that this magnificent ship was a victim of circumstance. Objectively speaking, however, it is necessary to remember the context:

firstly, the development of the French Navy had been almost brought to a stop during the period of German occupation, and it could only manage very limited research in the years immediately following the liberation;

secondly, during the postwar period, industrial capacity was equally limited (with a particular shortage of top-quality strategic materials) and oriented towards the needs of the army;

thirdly, personnel of all levels at every stage of construction (research, industry, the Constructor Corps and the dockyards) need to catch up with the latest technology; and

finally, funds allocated to *Jean Bart* were continually in question.

The ship never completed to the point where she might be regarded as a real warship, and under such a handicap, it is impossible to make a realistic judgement on the fighting qualities of the world's last battleship.

Footnotes

1. Ministerial Minute 10.683/STCAN of 21 February 1945.
2. D(C)CAN = Direction (Centrale) des Constructions et Armes Navales (the French equivalent of the British Royal Corps of Naval Constructors).
3. An improved version of the weapon fitted to the *Dunkerque*.
4. Report 858/EMG/DN of 24 September 1945 by Rear-Admiral Barjot.
5. Extract from above report.

PEGASUS CLASS HYDROFOILS

These missile-carrying hydrofoils are the US Navy's most sophisticated small combatants. Al Ross, an acknowledged authority on coastal forces, outlines the background to their construction and highlights their principal features.

The origin of the missile-armed hydrofoils (PHMs) of the *Pegasus* class can be traced to a 1969 CinCSouth operational requirement for a fast, missile-armed patrol boat to counter the threat of similar types in the Mediterranean. This requirement was soon expanded by NATO's Naval Armaments Group to include interdiction of Soviet major combatants in those areas for which NATO had responsibility. Consequently, Germany, Italy and the United States signed a memorandum of agreement in 1972, in which they agreed to share the initial design and development costs of such a craft. Since this was to be a standard design used by a variety of nations, the craft was to be built to metric standards and incorporate readily-accessible equipment from major international suppliers. Requirements for high speed, seaworthiness, and heavy weapons payload resulted in the selection of a hydrofoil configuration over that of a displacement hull.

The bulk of the design and development work was accomplished by the US, with Boeing as the primary contractor. However, NATO interest in the project quickly waned, primarily due to rising costs. By 1972, the project

Taurus *(PHM-3) on trials off Seattle. Note that only two dummy Harpoon launchers have been fitted and that the navigating radar is in its original location on the forward portion of the Mk 92 GFCS support.* (US Navy)

Aries *(PHM-5) in the summer of 1988, with the full Harpoon battery mounted. The original is a colour photo and shows* Aries *in overall Haze Grey with black boottopping, dark grey anti-skid decks, gloss black barrel on the 76mm gun, red fire fighting equipment (including hoses), and orange lifebelts. (*A Ross, via Tom Delrossi*)*

was abandoned by all original participants except the US. Funds for six PHMs were authorized in FY75 (Fiscal Year 1975) with others to follow, but cost overruns and major construction difficulties nearly resulted in complete cancellation of the entire project. Ultimately, funding was restored for the original group of six.

General description

The PHM is a hard-chined, canard configured hydrofoil, designed and built by Boeing for the US Navy. There are six craft in the class: *Pegasus* (PHM-1), *Hercules* (PHM-2), *Taurus* (PHM-3), *Aquila* (PHM-4), *Aries* (PHM-5) and *Gemini* (PHM-6). Assigned to PHMRON2, they currently operate out of Key West, Florida.

The all-welded hull, constructed of high-strength, corrosion-resistant 5456 aluminum alloy, is subdivided into nine water-tight compartments. Contained within the hull are the forward strut well, boatswain's stores, bow thruster room, crew messing and living quarters, fuel and water tanks, machinery control spaces, machinery spaces and magazine for the 76mm gun. Water-tight integrity is designed with sufficient reserve buoyancy to withstand flooding of any two adjacent compartments. In cross section, the hard-chine hull transitions from a deep-V forward to a high-deadrise planing surface aft, promoting good hull-borne performance and minimising high-speed drag during the transition from hull-borne to foil-borne configuration.

The rivetted aluminium superstructure contains the Combat Information Centre (CIC), communications room, electronic equipment room, turbine air intakes and auxiliary machine spaces. Surmounting the superstructure is the pilot house, within which are the controls for both hull-borne and foil-borne operations. The interior of the bridge is reminiscent of an aircraft cockpit, with seats for the helmsman and OOD, instrument panel and an aircraft-style helm.

The hydraulically-operated, retractable, stainless steel foils are arranged in canard configuration, the forward foil supporting one-third of the PHM's weight, the aft foil supporting the remaining two-thirds. Similar in concept to the control surfaces of an aircraft, the forward foil provides

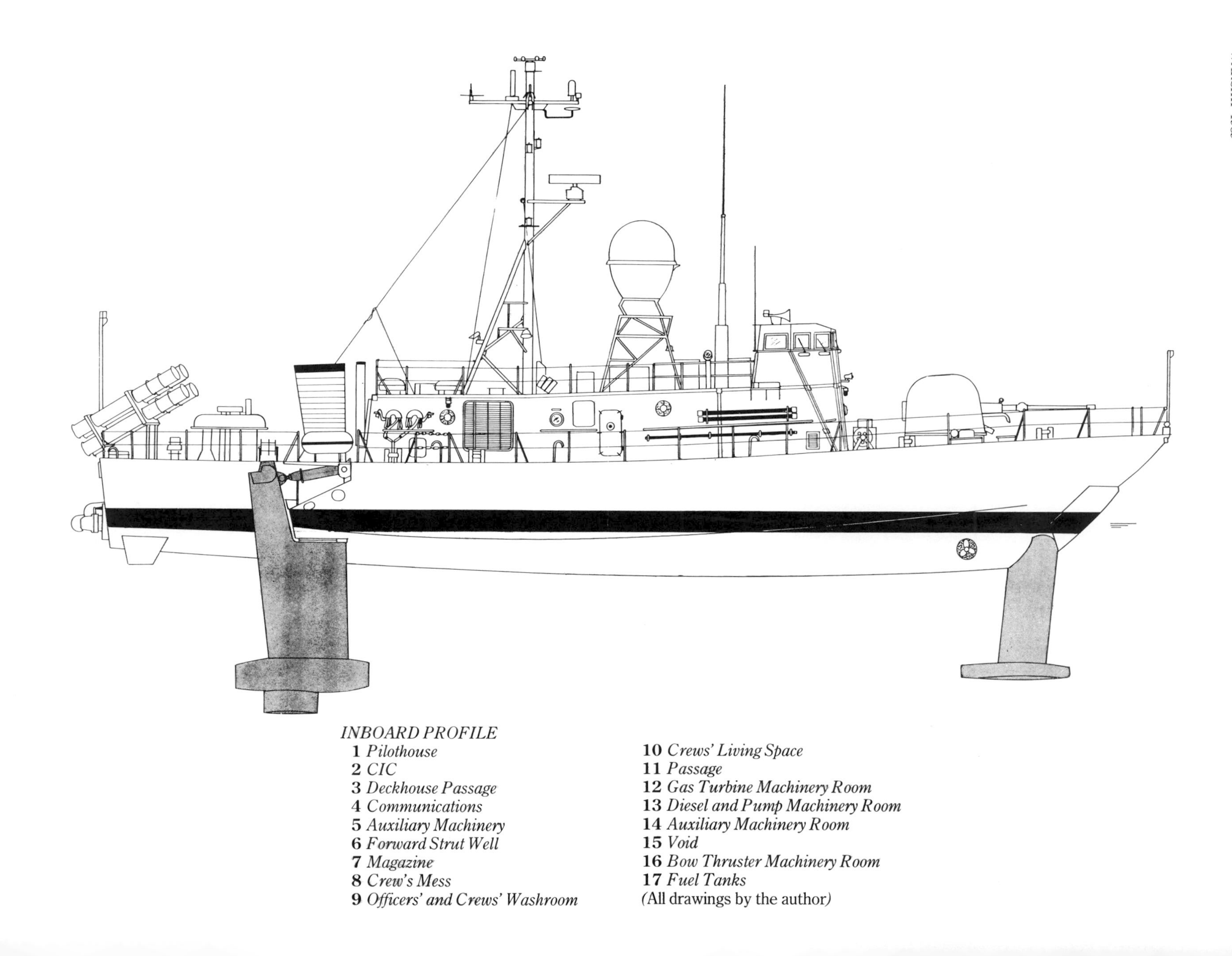
INBOARD PROFILE
1 Pilothouse
2 CIC
3 Deckhouse Passage
4 Communications
5 Auxiliary Machinery
6 Forward Strut Well
7 Magazine
8 Crew's Mess
9 Officers' and Crews' Washroom
10 Crews' Living Space
11 Passage
12 Gas Turbine Machinery Room
13 Diesel and Pump Machinery Room
14 Auxiliary Machinery Room
15 Void
16 Bow Thruster Machinery Room
17 Fuel Tanks
(All drawings by the author)

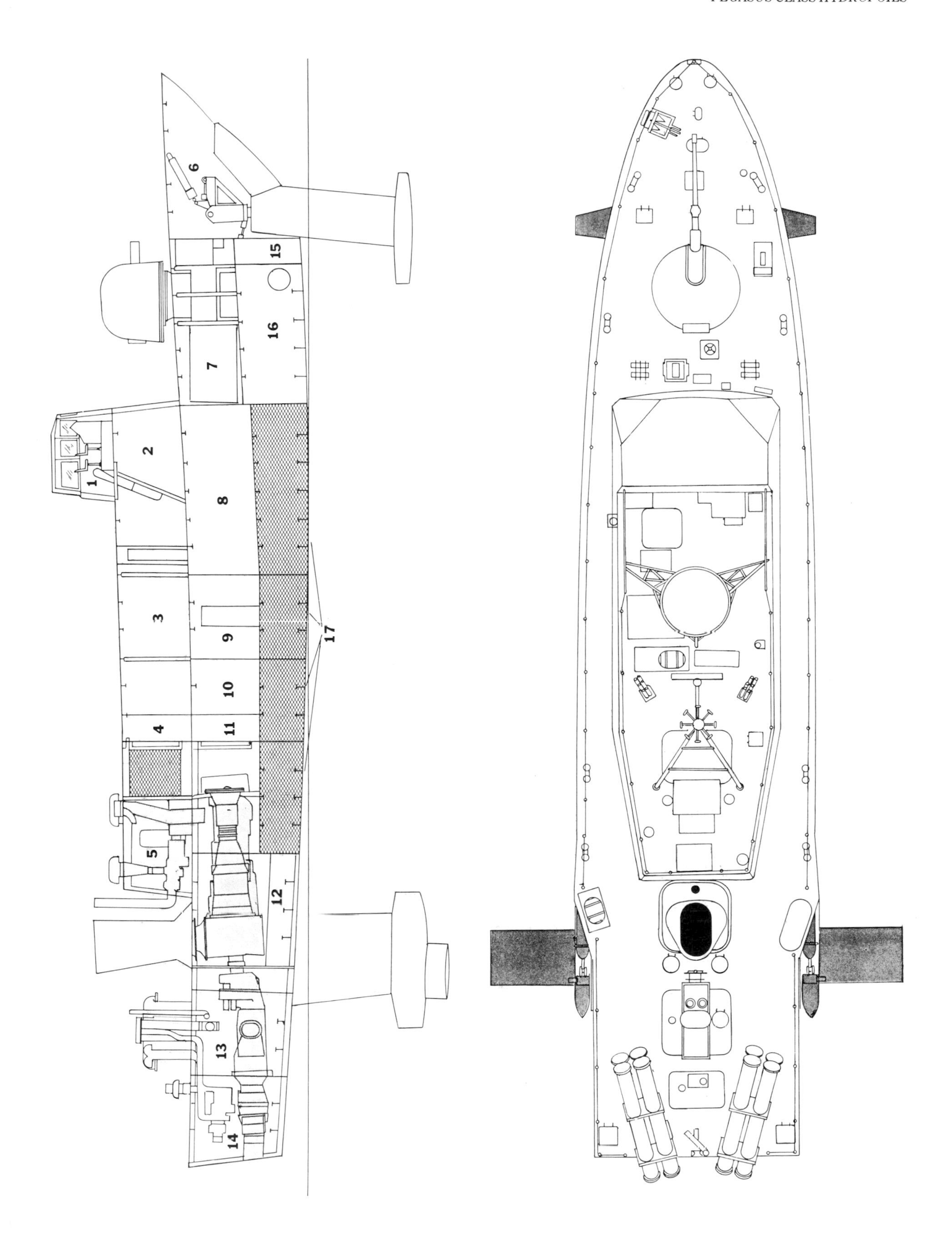
6
15
16
7
2
1
8
3
9
10
4
11
17
5
12
13
14

TAURUS
3
USS TAU
PHM-3

◀ *The upward and outward angles of the Harpoon mounts are evident in this stern view of* Taurus, *taken at Philadelphia in 1988.* (Tom Delrossi)

elevator (depth) control, while the aft foils provide aileron (roll) control. The strut for the forward foil acts as a rudder, rotating in response to the degree of banked turn.

Propulsion system

The PHM incorporates independent propulsion systems for hull-borne and foil-borne operation. Foil-borne propulsion is provided by a General Electric LM2500 gas turbine delivering 17,000 metric horsepower driving an Aerojet Liquid Rocket Company propulsor, a two-stage, axial-flow 90,000 gpm waterjet pump producing 85,176lbs of thrust. In operation, water is drawn up through the hollow aft struts, accelerated through the pump and expelled through the transom. For obvious reasons, no provisions are made for reverse thrust.

Hull-borne propulsion is provided by two 815 metric horsepower MTU 8V331TC81 diesels which drive two Aerojet propulsors, each capable of providing 7306lbs of thrust. Each nozzle is equipped with steering and reverser assemblies, much like those fitted to the riverine PBR boats. To steer, they vector 30 degrees right and left, ganged together on a rod, with one actuator electrically controlled and hydraulically powered. Each waterjet is independently reversed 135 degrees by moving the throttle in the reverse direction. Additional manoeuvring capability is provided by a hydraulically-powered bow thruster which develops 1200lbs of thrust at 3000psi, left or right.

The transition from hull-borne to foil-borne operation is controlled by the computer-operated Automatic Control System (ACS). In operation, a flying height is selected, the turbine is started and set at a specific power level, the PHM accelerates, and becomes foil-borne. Once foil-borne, craft attitude, control surface positions, response rates, accelerations, and operator inputs are sensed and automatically compared with desired values. Any deviations are compensated for by the computer.

Weapons systems

The mission of the PHM is to 'operate offensively against major surface combatants and other surface craft by utilizing surface-to-surface missile systems and secondary armament and to conduct surveillance, screening and special

Forward superstructure of Taurus *(PHM-3).* (Tom Delrossi)

▲*This excellent close-up of* Taurus' *Harpoon launchers shows the simple pivoting bolt arrangement used to mount the launchers to each other and the tubular frame.* (Tom Delrossi)

◀*Profile view of the Mk 75 mount on* Taurus. *The downward curved object beneath the barrel is the shell ejection guide.* (Tom Delrossi)

▲*The hydraulic cylinder controlling the aft foil is shown to good advantage in this view. The barrel-like object above the cylinder is a lifeboat canister.* (Tom Delrossi)

The two steering assemblies for the hull-borne propulsors can just be seen in this view of Taurus. *The cables between the transom and the assemblies move the 'buckets' on the ends of the propulsors, providing forward and/or reverse thrust.* (Tom Delrossi)

operations'. To accomplish this mission, the PHM mounts eight RGM-84 Harpoon missiles in canister launchers and a Mk 75 Mod 1 76mm/62 dual-purpose mount, both controlled by a Mk 92 Mod 0 GFCS (Gun Fire Control System). Close-in defence is provided by two Mk 135 Mod 0 RBOC (Rapid Blooming Offboard Chaff) launchers and electronic countermeasures equipment.

The main offensive armament of the PHM is the RGM-84 Harpoon missile, initially designed by McDonnell Douglas as an air-to-surface weapon. In its surface-to-surface configuration, Harpoon has a range in excess of 50nm. The PHM carries eight of these subsonic missiles in lightweight canister launchers mounted on simple tube frames at the transom. Both sets of launchers are angled upward and outboard at fixed angles to prevent damage to the PHM's structure and to aim the missile in the acceleration phase of the launch.

The Mk 75 76mm/62 mount is a licence-built, fully automatic weapon designed by the Italian firm of OTO-Melara. Above decks, the mount is unmanned and is enclosed in a lightweight shield designed to withstand temperature, erosion, green water and pressure inputs of missile blast. Below decks, the mount consists of the screw feeder hoist, revolving magazine, associated control panels, and ready-service racks. Intended as both an anti-air and anti-surface weapon, the Mk 75 is capable of firing up to 85rpm; magazine capacity is 80 rounds.

Readers wishing more detailed information on the PHM programme will find Norman Friedman's *US Small Combatants* (US Naval Institute Press, 1987) very useful.

PHM Particulars

Dimensions	
Length overall, foils down	40.5m
Beam, main deck	8.6m
Overall aft foil span	14.5m
Draft, foils up	1.9m
Draft, foils down	7.1m
Full load displacement	241.3 metric tons
Propulsion machinery	
Foil-borne	1 – GE LM2500 gas turbine 1 – Aerojet propulsor
Hull-borne	2 – MTU 8V331T81 diesels 2 – Aerojet propulsors with nozzle steering and reverser assemblies
Performance	
Foil-borne	40 kts+
Hull-borne	11 kts
Armament	
Missiles	8 – RGM-84 Harpoon
Guns	1 – 76mm/62 Mk 75 Mod 0
Chaff	2 – Mk 135 Mod 0 RBOC

Forward foil of Hercules *(PHM-2) in the raised position.*
*(*Author*)*

Port aft foil of Hercules, *also in the raised position. Note the control surfaces on the 'wing' at the bottom of the strut.*
*(*Author*)*

AIRSHIPS FOR EARLY WARNING

Robert Largess explains the thinking behind the US Navy's interest in the employment of airships for AEW, and looks at the capabilities of the ambitious new generation of lighter-than-air craft.

In 1962, after 45 years of continuous operations with lighter-than-air craft, the US Navy retired its last blimp. To many, who saw the airship as a relic from the pioneering days of aviation – man's first solution to the problem of powered flight – this seemed eminently sensible. What requirement is there for an aircraft which can not exceed 100kts, in an age of Mach 2 jets? However, in June 1987, the US Navy announced a contract for an Operational Development Model airship, to cost $118 million and fly before the end of 1990. This ship (and up to five more examples) was intended to prove the concept of an advanced Airborne Early Warning Airship, known variously as BSAS (Battle Surveillance Airship System) and OLEASS (Organic Long Endurance Airborne Area Surveillance Airship System). If successful, it was intended to lead to a fleet of perhaps 50 ships costing $2 billion.

Many will no doubt wonder at this ambitious plan for the revival of an obscure and peripheral vehicle, a slow and fragile competitor to the airplane. Many will also be surprised at the fact that the prototype ships, at least, will be of British design, the 'Sentinal 5000', proposed in recent years by Airship Industries Ltd [AI] for a wide range of applications, including Britain's Offshore Patrol Vessel, and under construction in the USA in association with the Westinghouse Co at Weeksville, North Carolina. (In spite of expectations, Goodyear Aerospace, long-time partner of the USN in airship development, and originator of the large modern non-rigid airship, failed to win the initial contract.)

'Intermediate' vehicles

Before describing the ship and the role it is intended to play in naval warfare, it is perhaps necessary to point out that the airship possesses unique capabilities as a vehicle, which provide cogent reasons for reviving it. (There are also very sound reasons for the choice of AI's design: it is cheaper and far closer to actual flight than the technically more advanced proposals put forward by Goodyear Aerospace and Boeing Military Aircraft.)

It is worth noting that in the decade that saw the abandonment of the airship, the US, Soviet, British, and other navies and numerous private developers spent huge sums on the perfection of a range of novel naval vehicles – the hydrofoil, the hovercraft or Air Cushion Vehicle, the Surface Effect Ship, and the Wing-In-Ground-Effect vehicle, whose performance fell into the 40kt to 100kt range – identical to that of the airship. All of them achieved speeds in excess of those possible for surface ships as well as gaining improved seakeeping ability by using some means to lift themselves free of the sea surface and its hydrodynamic drag effect due to friction and wavemaking. On the other hand, they used a range of physical effects which provide more efficient lift in terms of power consumption than the airplane and far more than that of the helicopter. Thus, these vehicles can achieve much greater endurance and payloads and can be built much larger and more cheaply than fixed or rotary-wing aircraft. The airship, which obtains its lift without necessarily *any* expenditure of motive power is potentially the most fuel-efficient and has the highest endurance of all these 'Intermediate Speed–Range–Endurance–Size–Payload Vehicles'. The USN airships of the 1950s performed 100-hour ASW patrols, AEW patrols with 50 hours on station, and a record unrefuelled endurance flight of 264 hours, including a round-trip Atlantic crossing.

Interestingly, several of these vehicles – hydrofoil, SES, and airship as well as very large airplanes – were repeatedly envisioned as replacements for surface ships in the 1970s. Such 'Sea Control' craft would have been much larger than any current examples and armed with the range of anti-surface, AA, and ASW weapons and sensors which typify surface vessels, the implication being that their advantage in speed would provide capabilities justifying the cost, in size, endurance, and development dollars. Such 'Sea Control' vehicles would have had a great speed advantage over the nuclear submarine, invulnerability to torpedoes, ability to screen a fleet dispersed over very large areas, and perhaps unique abilities to operate integral V/STOL aircraft from small decks or 'hook-on' apparatus.

In the event, neither the 'Sea Control' airship, the hydrofoil frigate, nor any other of these ambitious craft were built; although it is worth noting that airships of far larger size than any of the 'Intermediate' vehicles have been built, serving as aircraft carriers, and carrying 47ft radar antennae. However, the twin pillars of 'sea control' remain the surface ship and the airplane. Both possess the ability to carry a wide range of sensors and weapons, able to detect and attack enemies above, on, or below the surface of the sea. The speed and huge visual and radar surveillance horizon of the airplane give it the capacity to search a greater area in a shorter time than any other vehicle; whilst its speed also gives it the power to deliver devastating attacks which are difficult to intercept. Conversely, while the surface ship remains the slowest vehicle in the naval inventory, it remains the most efficient in terms of fuel

ZPG-2 commanded by Cdr J R Hunt, departing South Weymouth, Mass on 4 March 1957 for a non-stop double crossing of the Atlantic. Note external fuel tanks. The ship covered 9448 miles in 264.2 hours, flying eastward to Portugal, south to West Africa, then home to Key West, Florida. This flight held the record for unrefuelled endurance for two decades. (US Navy)

consumption and load carrying ability – relatively small surface ships can possess endurance and station-keeping ability beyond any other vehicle. And the advantage of economy of scale lies with the surface ship; they can be built large enough to perform a range of functions simultaneously for extended periods of time, far beyond the capacity of any other mobile vehicles.

Whether any of these novel 'Intermediate' vehicles will develop a similar range of capabilities and importance remains to be seen. To date, they have been produced only to fill very limited specific roles where they offer some truly unique ability. An excellent example is the Air Cushion Vehicle or hovercraft, whose speed and ability to transverse both land and sea surfaces has resulted in the development of ACV landing craft by the US, USSR, and Britain.

So also the airship. As mentioned in a previous article (*Warship* 44) the vast majority of all past airships were ASW convoy escorts. The USN's present project is based on the unique ability of the airship to provide high performance Airborne Early Warning to surface groups, particularly those lacking carrier decks and the E-2C Hawkeye.

The airship as radar picket

The number of USN carrier decks (and aircraft at sea) has drastically declined with the disappearance of the *Essex* class and smaller wartime carriers. At the same time, the threat of air attack has dramatically increased, with the appearance of the anti-ship cruise missile, which in effect renders any ship vulnerable to 'air attack' anywhere, even in the open ocean beyond the range of Soviet or Third World tactical air forces.

As the Battle of Britain proved, the efficient development of fighter interceptors made possible by radar detection of impending attacks was essential for effective air defence. No amount of undirected standing patrolling could have made up for the lack of radar early warning and tracking. The effectiveness of the Second World War carrier fighters also depended on, and steadily improved with, surface air warning radar, operating at ranges in excess of 100 miles. However, as Sir Arthur Hezlet points out in *The Electron and Sea Power*, low-flying aircraft could not be detected until much closer; since radar is generally blocked by the curvature of the earth, such aircraft could remain undetected outside a ship's surface radar horizon. In 1944, the USN began to use destroyer pickets thrown out as much as 50 miles in the direction of the enemy to provide timely detection of attacking aircraft. However, the picket destroyer's own radar horizon was restricted, so numbers were required for a complete screen. They themselves were very vulnerable to the same low-level attacks they were protecting the fleet against. The *Laffey*, for example, survived 22 attacks in one day including hits by six Kamikazes and four

GOODYEAR
AVIATION PRODUCTS

◀*ZPG-3W beside a smaller ASW ship in Goodyear's construction hangar in Akron, Ohio. Note dorsal height-finder radome. The largest non-rigids ever built, their basic design was retained in Goodyear's BSAS proposal. Chief visible difference would have been four props, including two ducted props for cruise and vectored thrust.* (Goodyear Aerospace)

bombers; nearly 20 destroyers were lost on this duty.

The USN experimented with radar picket submarines, but the true solution was the AEW aircraft, first introduced successfully postwar with the Douglas Skyraider carrying the AN/APS 20 radar. Just as an aircraft at altitude has a much larger visual horizon than an observer on the surface, so it has a vastly expanded radar horizon. As Admiral Hezlet says:

> This new radar set ... provided far better warning of the approach of low-flying aircraft, but it was an outstanding success in a number of other ways, too. It was also extremely useful for what was known as strike direction. The aircraft with AN/APS 20 could often take us to a position from which echoes of the aircraft carrier and the enemy were obtainable at the same time; it could therefore, direct attacking aircraft to their target. The AN/APS 20 aircraft was often able to pick up ships at distances of 200 miles or so and it proved a very effective general reconnaissance aircraft in its own right.

Since then, advances in radar and data processing have increased the effectiveness of AEW tremendously, giving the E-2C and E-3A AWACS vast detection ranges, the capacity to track hundreds of targets simultaneously, and the ability to receive display data from other aircraft, ships and ground radars. AEW is becoming so valuable in any air battle situation that numerous airframes are being adapted to deploy it. Some, like the Lockheed P-3C (to be purchased by Japan) or the C-130, are intended to provide high-endurance land-based AEW at less cost than the E-3A AWACS. The little Pilatus Defender with the Thorn-EMI Skymaster system is intended simply to provide a low-cost AEW solution for the poorer countries.

But what about sea-based AEW? Exocet attacks on the USS *Stark* and on the Royal Navy in the Falklands indicate the serious threat represented by the sea-skimming anti-ship missile, especially as the Soviet Navy possesses enormous numbers of the weapon, for launching from submarines, long range bombers, patrol boats and major warships.

The US Coast Guard is using ship-based 'aerostats' for maritime surveillance. These are, however, not truly mobile. Both the Royal Navy and the Spanish Navy are using Sea King helicopters with the Thorn-EMI Searchwater radar. These may perform well in service, yet the helicopter with its high fuel consumption, short range, low altitude, high maintenance requirements, vibration, and heavy demands on its crew in terms of skill and concentration, appears to be the least appropriate vehicle for AEW. (In addition, the Searchwater was not designed for AEW but rather as a powerful surface search radar. It is likely to be deficient in the ability to distinguish small moving targets in surface clutter.)

The airship, on the other hand, seems uniquely suited to AEW. The main requirements of AEW would seem to be the ability to, first, lift the heavy system and its bulky, oddly shaped antenna, and second, remain on station for as long as possible. Speed can reduce transit time to station, but once on station, it is irrelevant.

The high endurance requirement

The USN's ZPG-3Ws routinely made 75-hour patrols; however, the modern AEW blimp must be capable of far longer periods in the air to provide continuous coverage to USN Surface Action Groups – 60 days or longer. Indeed, the US Naval Institute has described the airship as a communications relay platform as 'in effect a low-level satellite'.

One of the most interesting features of both AI and Goodyear's design is the provision of dual-mode propulsion: highly fuel-efficient cruise engines for station-keeping and powerful turboprops for 'sprint' needs, an arrangement almost without precedent in previous aircraft. AI's ship will use two CRM diesels for cruise and vectored thrust with 1790hp and one PT6 1700 turboprop with 1200 to 1700hp for sprint. Goodyear's design is even more innovative, using two Allison C20B turboprops for maximum speed, and for cruise, two samarium-cobalt electric motors of 200 kilowatts each. They will be powered by an inboard turbogenerator which will also provide the electricity for the ship's radar.

However, for the AEW airship to be successful it must be able to escort a SAG for the length of its deployment. This can only be achieved by refuelling, replenishment, and crew relief at sea from surface craft. Throughout their history, since the First World War, airships have often been resupplied by winch from ship's decks, but this has never been a standard operating procedure. In the future this technique must become a matter of routine – and the airship become nearly as independent of its base as a surface ship to ensure the success of the AEW concept.

The experience gained by the Royal Navy in the Falklands, operating Sea Kings from *Hermes* at a distance of 180 miles, showed what could be accomplished. The helicopters changed crews by winch and refuelled repeatedly by hose from the frigates *Brilliant* and *Yarmouth*, establishing a world record for the longest airborne helicopter operational mission (10 hours 20 minutes), as reported by Ethell and Price in *Air War South Atlantic*.

The AI 'Sentinel 5000' has a normal endurance of 47 hours, (max 55+ hours), so time between refuelling would be measured in days not hours. And while the airship lacks the precise control in hover of the helicopter, its capabilities were thoroughly demonstrated in the French Navy trials of a small AI ship in 1984 for coast guard and shipping surveillance duties. This craft picked up passengers from a surface craft and swimmers by winch, as well as deploying a 5m Zodiac boat for boarding, a capability shared by few other aircraft.

In any case, crew endurance and rotation will be as significant as fuel; for an airship crew their several weeks aloft will more resemble a patrol aboard a submarine than an aircraft. The supply problem will be eased by the fact that these crews will be as small as 12 – roughly half that of the ZPG-3W craft while internal space will be roughly the same, and envelope size and thus lift will be considerably greater.

The ability to operate airborne continuously for weeks and refuel from tankers at sea as routinely as surface vessels, is the chief test the BSAS airship concept faces. Assuming it is solved, how will it operate?

▲◀ *Details of mooring equipment and hangar of ZPG-3Ws, showing their tremendous scale. Airships are always 'airborne' and thus vulnerable to the wind even when moored. Ground-handling was a source of problems in the past, requiring unique solutions. Most airship accidents have occurred on the ground; the ZPGs demonstrated their ability to operate in all weathers for long periods.* (Goodyear Aerospace)

SKYSHIP 600
MARINE
G-SKSC
MARINE
AIRSHIP INDUSTRIES

The airship in air defence

Air defence (including missile defence) as possessed by the USN today falls into three zones. The outer air defence zone is based upon the F-14 and E-2C; the inner zone is based upon the Aegis system and SM-2 missile; and finally there is the 'point defence' of individual ships, based on the Vulcan–Phalanx system. The picture is complicated by the presence of a number of other missile and gun systems and fighter types; but only these three embody the advanced electronics enabling them to react instantly and engage multiple targets at once (or in very rapid succession), the two essentials for dealing with a massed anti-ship missile attack of the sort which forms the Soviet Navy's main tactic against American surface groups. The function of the F-14s, with their ability to engage six targets at once with their 100-mile Phoenix missiles, is to reduce or eliminate the attack by intercepting enemy aircraft before they are within missile launching range. The F-14s are dependent on E-2Cs operating a hundred miles ahead and on the flanks of the surface group, to provide warning of approaching hostile forces beyond the fighter's maximum range.

The inner air defence zone must deal with aircraft and missiles which penetrate the fleet's fighter defences, or those which are launched from within it, as from 'Charlie', 'Oscar', or 'Echo' type nuclear submarines. Here the AEW airship will provide the same service (as well as using the same radar) as the E-2C. So why not simply station an E-2C directly over the fleet? Essentially because carrier decks are few; for SAG's based on battleships or smaller ships, the missile area-defence zone will be the first air-defence zone; neither F-14s or E-2Cs will be present. With carrier battle groups, perhaps a half dozen E-2Cs are necessary to keep two continually on station. However, two airships continuously on station will not burden the carrier or detract from the number of other aircraft types she can handle.

The missile inner defence zone depends on the SM-2 missile and the Aegis system with its phased array radar. The latter scans and directs its beam electronically without mechanically rotated antennae. Hence its beams can be switched nearly instantaneously, to track and illuminate dozens – even hundreds – of targets simultaneously. The SM-2 missile is designed to take advantage of this capacity and enable the Aegis ship to engage many targets at once, by using inertial guidance over the initial phase of its flight, thus requiring no direct control from the ship or continuous illumination of the target. Numerous missiles can be launched at the same time, each programmed to follow an intercept course out to the general area of its target. Actual radar illumination of the target is required only for a few seconds during the terminal, homing phase of the missile's flight, after which the illuminating radar beam is switched automatically without delay to the next target.

However, the range of the Aegis system is as limited as any surface-ship radar against low-flying targets, in other words, to the horizon, providing no more than the usual 60-second warning against sea-skimming ASMs. The AEW blimp's radar horizon, at 10,000ft, should be able to detect most ASMs from their point of launch, and certainly far beyond SM-2 maximum range. Hence, SM-2s can be launched in time to intercept ASMs at the limits of the Aegis ship's radar horizon; they can be hit as soon as they are illuminated. Future AEW airships may be able to provide illumination of targets themselves, permitting intercepts beyond the ship's radar horizon, out to the limits of missile range, thus controlling the Aegis system and the entire intercept, through automated data-link from the airship itself.

Thus, the AEW airship should dramatically extend the effectiveness of the Aegis system, providing a valuable supplement to the Carrier Battle Group's defences, and perhaps providing the SAG without a carrier sufficient self-defence capability to give it security against missile attack outside the range of Soviet tactical air and coastal craft. In the mid-Atlantic, the SAG faces missile threats from Soviet long range aircraft (Bear, Badger and Backfire bombers), cruise missile submarines, large surface ships, and Forger V/STOL jets – all potentially formidable weapons but strictly limited in numbers and generally vulnerable themselves to counterattack by the SAG's weapons.

◀ *The small Airship Industries 'Skyship 600' during 1984 French Navy trials off Cherbourg. The Zodiac boarding craft is handled by two winches; the crew enter the boat from a trap door in the floor of the car. This craft demonstrated passenger pick-up from a surface ship, swimmer pick-up from the sea, precision hovering, boarding by small boat, radar detection of surface ships at 50 miles from 2000ft, and also the use of infra-red and low-light TV sensor pods.* (Airship Industries Ltd)

Disadvantages of naval airships

Obviously, blimps might provide British and other groups built around V/STOL carriers with a better AEW solution than the Sea King/Searchwater combination – for Atlantic operations beyond the range of Soviet fighters. But what of European waters? The question of vulnerability to attack is the first of three objections which have been repeatedly raised against naval airships throughout their history; the others are fragility in the face of adverse weather conditions and the problem of ground handling.

The vulnerability of the airship to attack is, of course, relative, as is that of all naval vehicles. Airships in the First World War ultimately proved too vulnerable to operate safely within range of enemy aircraft. But almost all naval airship operations – ASW and fleet reconnaissance – took place beyond the range of enemy air support. Likewise, no USN airships were lost to air attack in the Second World War; they were not 'vulnerable' to fighters because there were no enemy fighters over the Atlantic or the Mediterranean where they operated. There is no doubt that a blimp could simply be shot down by cannon or air-to-air missiles, as could any other low-performance aircraft, such as helicopters, E-2Cs, or even E-3As. The vulnerability of such aircraft is limited by operating them either beyond the range of enemy fighters or behind air cover. Today, the Navy's SAGs will mostly operate beyond the range of Soviet tactical airforces in wartime. The USN's new 'Maritime Strategy' envisages penetration of Soviet-controlled Arctic Ocean 'bastions' with carrier battle groups (CVBGs), but in either case the projected AEW airship would be at the centre of the battle group's air defence.

Should the enemy penetrate both inner and outer air defence zones, the airship could and would be attacked if the opportunity occurred. But would it be rational to order numerous high performance aircraft to penetrate the fleet's air defence solely to attack the assorted low-performance AEW aircraft – blimp, helicopters and E-2Cs, in preference to the carrier and her escorts?

Of course in peacetime the USN operates carrier groups

SKYSHIP 600
G-SKSC

in the Mediterranean, within reach of concentrations of land-based tactical aircraft and fast short range missile boats. A blimp would be more vulnerable there, to a surprise mass attack opening a major war, or to a sneak attack such as that suffered by *Stark*. But obviously, if the AEW blimp can prevent a surprise attack and the loss of a valuable surface ship it has served its purpose.

The situation of the British Task Force attacking the Falkland Islands provides an excellent example of the question of relative vulnerability. The success of this operation was very largely tied up with the fact that the British were able to operate on the fringes of the Argentine Air Force's effective range. The V/STOL carriers, in particular, were able to avoid all but a single attack, and indeed were seldom located by the Argentines, who relied for reconnaissance on a few aged P2V Neptunes. Whether they could have survived if forced to operate closer to Argentine airfields is another story.

On the other hand, the British were unable to intercept a single Etendard (or Exocet). The warning provided by an AEW blimp could have cost the Argentines their Etendards and prevented their attacks. Operating over the V/STOL carriers, it would have been no more vulnerable than they were. It could have provided direct support to the British warships operating in San Carlos Water, and enabled the Harriers to intercept many more attacks. Without AEW, the Harriers were forced to provide wasteful 'pre-Battle of Britain' style standing patrols. However, the blimp would have shared the vulnerability of the British escorts to air attack.

One criticism is that the highly visible airship would reveal the position of the surface group. Against this is the fact that the AEW airship of the future will be operating at higher altitudes than in the past (up to 10,000ft). Furthermore AI has frequently advanced the argument that the airship will be far less detectable by radar than other craft. The airship naturally embodies 'stealth' characteristics, lacking radar-reflecting flat planes and metallic surfaces. Beyond her fabric envelope, the airship's car and fins will be constructed largely of modern lightweight composite materials, with little reflectivity. All metallic elements will be shielded with radar absorbent materials. Also, while operating on her cruise diesels, she will provide far less infra-red signature than gas-turbine engined aircraft.

One objection repeatedly raised against the airship is its vulnerability to weather, and indeed, many very large early rigids were lost to structural (or engine) failures under severe storm conditions. Many were over-ambitious in terms of the aerodynamic engineering of their day. However, very few fabric envelope pressure airships have been lost to this cause. They can deform under stress, or in collision with solid objects, without permanent damage, whereas similar accidents to a rigid will lead to the fracture of rigid members and ultimately destruction of the structure.

During the Second World War, the USN lost eight airships to weather, only one of which was due to aerodynamic stresses on the control surfaces. The others were lost on the ground, to shed door or mooring gear failures. In fact, few vehicles are less affected by weather conditions than the airship. Their endurance permits them to ride out storms that make operations by other aircraft impossible, and test surface ships severely. The ability to land and take off aerostatically, in slow-motion so to speak, permits operations in zero visibility. The USN's ZPG-3W ships routinely operated in gale force winds and heavy snow storms.

The real problem was caused by the airship's relatively low airspeed. In the First World War, surfaced submarines escaped blimps by heading into 30kt winds; gale force winds could render airships unable to attack, or reach base. This problem is effectively solved by dual-mode propulsion combining fuel-efficient cruising on diesels or electric motors with 100kt top speeds provided by lightweight turboprops.

The remaining problem is ground-handling. The airship will require special structures and equipment. Although the techniques involved have been tremendously refined and simplified, occasional accidents must be expected. As long as the airship is inflated it is, in effect, airborne, and because of its large surface area, the forces exerted on it by winds are very great. Because of their lightness of structure, contact with a solid object – ground or shed – can easily produce massive damage. But here again, the pressure airship enjoys a huge advantage, in that its flexible envelope is far less prone to contact damage than the rigid, and is easily and cheaply replaced.

Undoubtedly, airships cannot be operated without some losses, the same as any other aircraft. This fact argues against the revival of extremely large – if very capable – airships like the great rigids of the past. Instead, the relative cheapness and expendability of pressure airships will make for large fleets, and the inevitable occasional loss to weather and accident will then represent a minor percentage of the total investment.

The BSAS contenders

That said, it is appropriate here to examine the BSAS designs themselves. Perhaps the most interesting thing about both the Goodyear and AI designs is their extreme conservatism and simplicity. In general outline they conform to the basic pattern developed by Goodyear for the non-rigid airship in the 1920s: fabric envelope forming a single undivided gas space, flush-mounted car with propulsion units on lateral outriggers. All Goodyear-built USN airships from K-1 in 1931 to ZPG-3W in 1962 followed this pattern. AI added swivelling ducted props to provide vectored thrust in the 1970s. Less visible features of the BSAS ships will be their advanced electronics, modern avionics, 'fly-by-wire' fibre-optic controls, but most important of all, the use throughout of advanced composite materials based on graphite, resins, plastics, products of modern chemical engineering which have supplied tremendously lighter and stronger fabrics, cables, and hulls.

Thus these ships will be the largest non-rigids ever built (2.2 million cubic feet for the 'Sentinel 5000') and indeed approach the engineering limits for this type of airship. Goodyear's design essentially duplicates the ZPG-3W (described in an earlier article – see *Warship* 44) with its radar antenna suspended from the dorsal surface of the envelope, and crew accommodation contained within the envelope, above the external car. The chief difference will be its dual-mode turboprop and turbo-electric propulsion. Two turboprops will be mounted on lateral outriggers; outboard

◄ *'Skyship 600' handling boat by winch. Obviously, towed arrays, dipping sonars, and refuelling hoses could be similarly handled. Note sling being lowered to swimmer. (*Airship Industries Ltd*)*

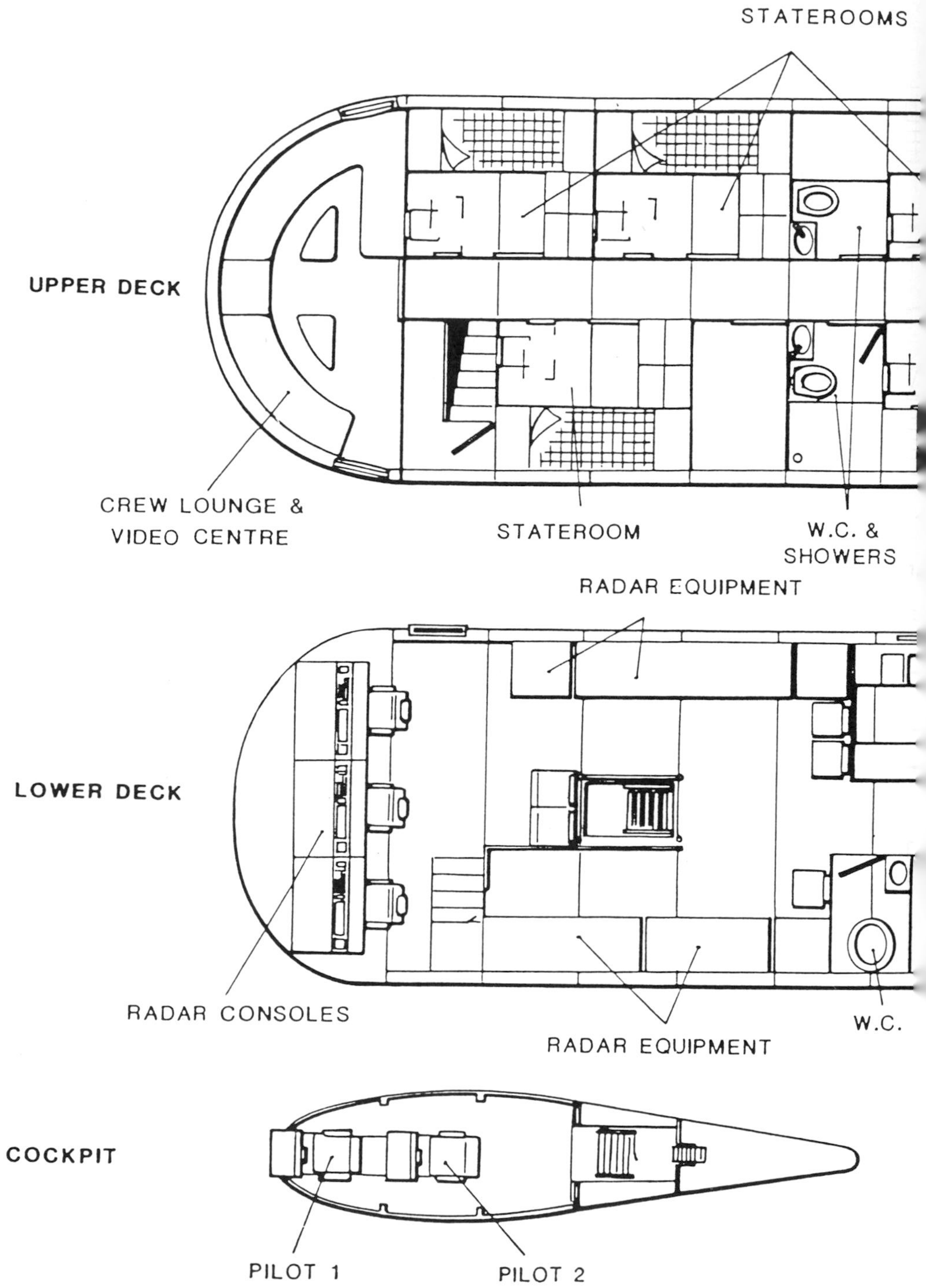

STATEROOMS

UPPER DECK

CREW LOUNGE &
VIDEO CENTRE

STATEROOM

W.C. &
SHOWERS

RADAR EQUIPMENT

LOWER DECK

RADAR CONSOLES

RADAR EQUIPMENT

W.C.

COCKPIT

PILOT 1

PILOT 2

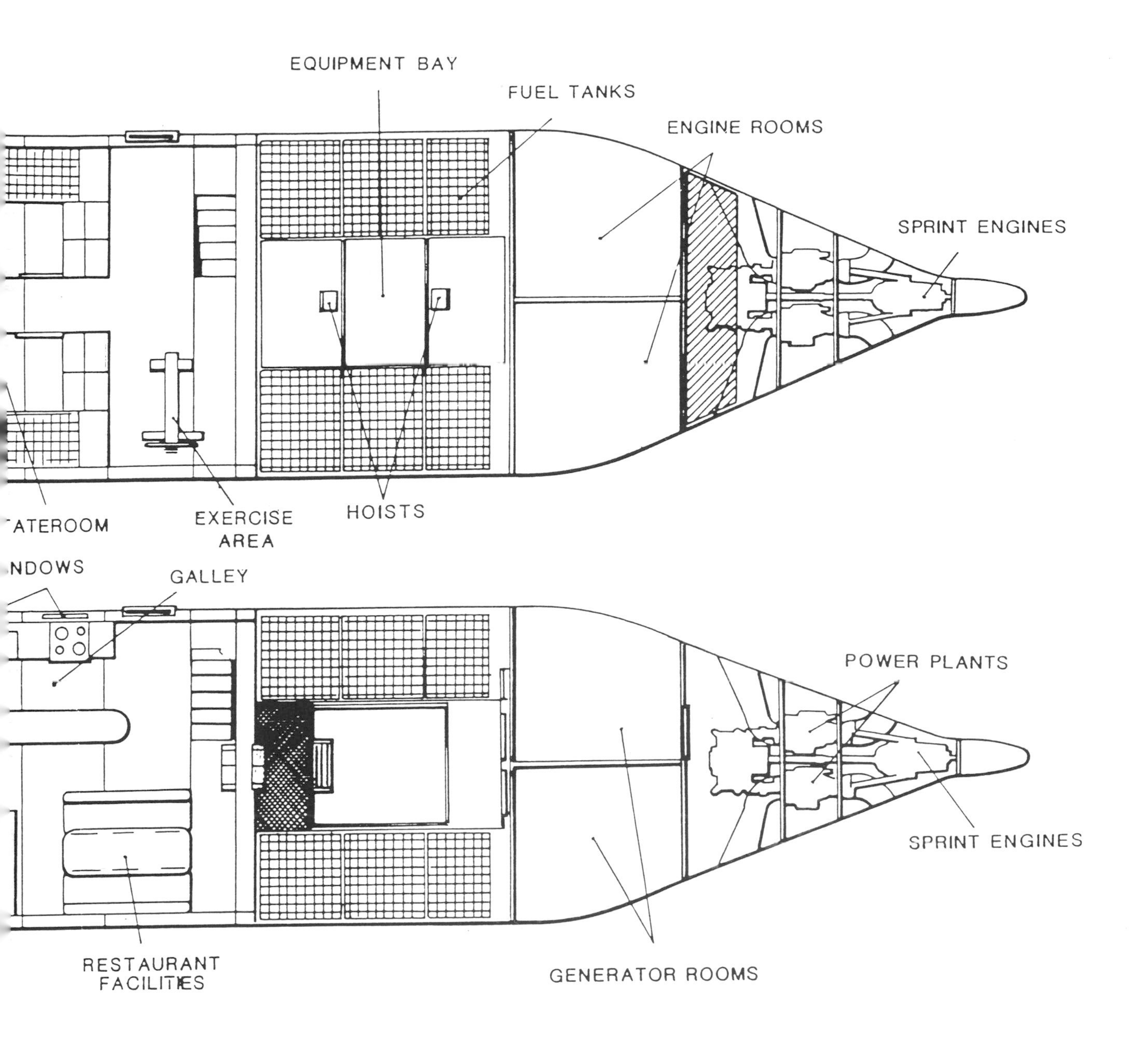

*Plans for the BSAS 'Sentinel 5000'. Note three decks, dual-mode engines, and swivelling ducted props, an Airship Industries contribution to modern airship design which has contributed greatly to ease of handling in hover, take-off and landing. (*Airship Industries Ltd*)*

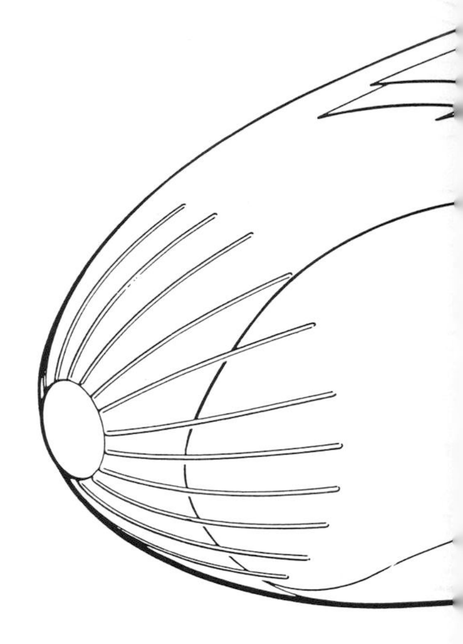

A perspective 'see-through' view of the Sentinal 5000 car or 'gondola'. (Airship Industries Ltd)

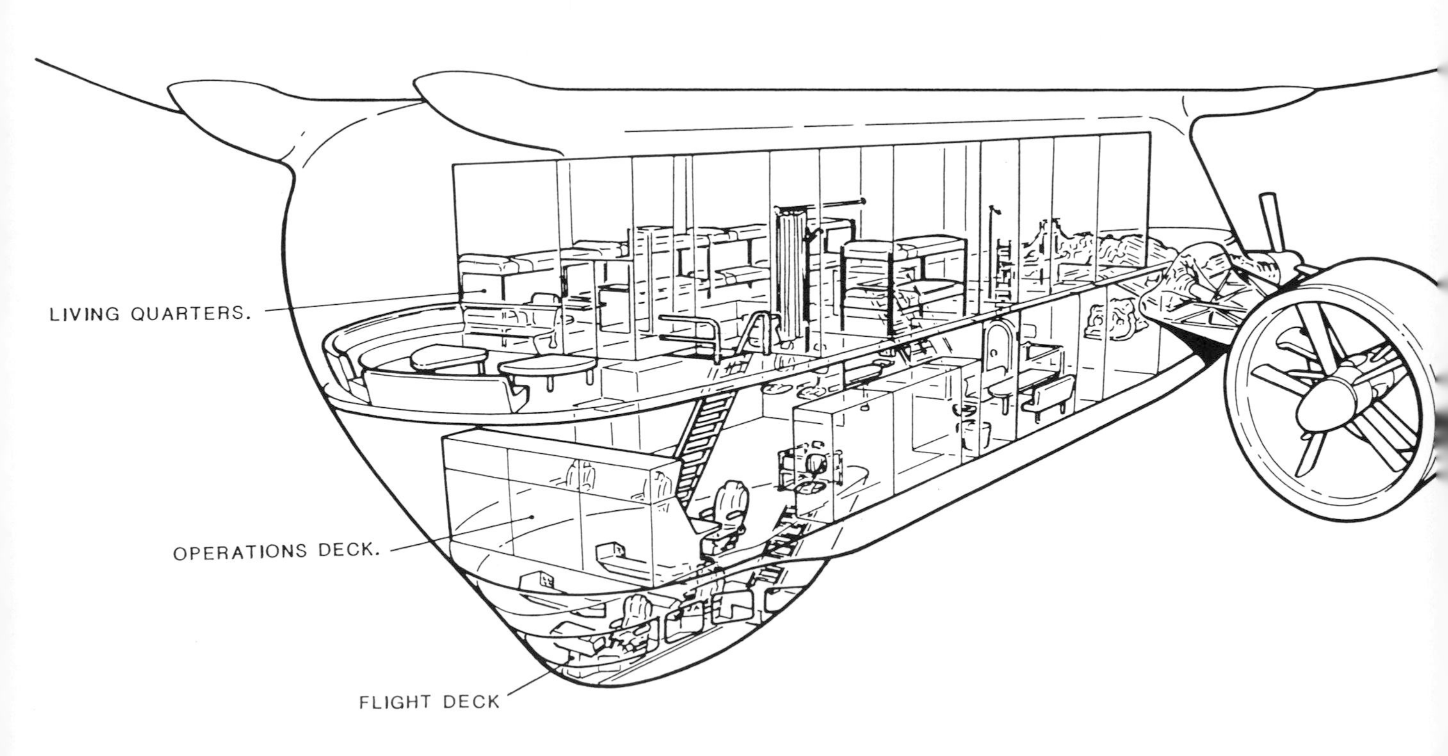

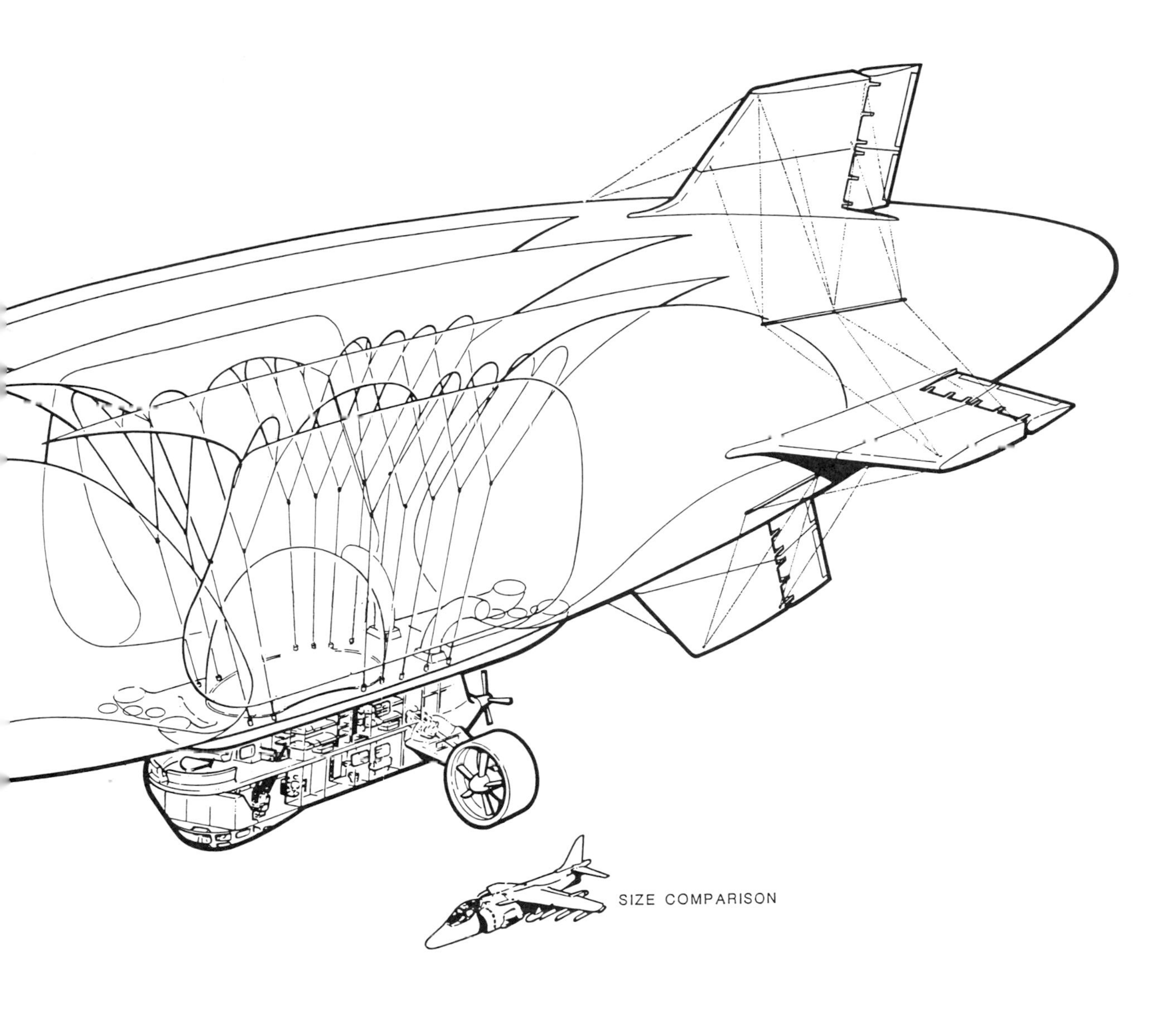

A general view of the Sentinal 5000 compared in size with a Harrier VSTOL aircraft. (Airship Industries Ltd)

will be two ducted swivelling electric-driven props for cruise and vectored thrust.

The 'Sentinel 5000' will be marked by its huge, three-decked external car with diesel-driven ducted props on lateral outriggers and single turboprop at the rear of the car. The internal antenna will apparently be mounted directly above the car, making it accessible in flight. Obviously, further size increases would produce much greater capabilities in the airship, in endurance, altitude, load-carrying capacity, and this lends interest to the extremely novel design offered by Boeing Military Aircraft in conjunction with Britain's Wren Skyships.

The Boeing–Wren design is highly individual and advanced, being neither strictly a rigid or non-rigid. Instead, it utilizes a hull of advanced composite material possessing rigidity of its own, but deriving additional structural rigidity from internal gas pressure and from internal structural elements – rings and stringers – which support engines, fuel tanks, crew spaces, radar, enabling these to be dispersed throughout the structure. It is similar in concept to no previous airship except the USN's metal-hulled ZMC-2 of 1929.

At 4.2 million cubic feet, this ship is considerably larger and has more potential (150 hours unrefuelled endurance) than its conventional non-rigid competitors. It has also, along with the pure rigid, great capacity for growth. Size in itself means greater individual expense and lessened expendability, plus greater demands on ground-handling and seaborne resupply facilities and techniques. The chief drawback of this concept is that much of the basic technology has yet to be developed.

If a 'Sea Control' airship armed with anti-air or anti-surface missiles ever becomes a reality, it will probably be based on a rigid or hybrid design like Boeing's. That some potential for such craft exists is shown by the Japanese Maritime Self-Defence Force's proposal for a long range high-endurance airborne air defence over its southern shipping routes.

Currently, Japan depends on land-based E-2Cs and Standard missile-armed DDGs for the air defence of shipping over its routes to Taiwan and ultimately to the Persian Gulf. But according to Mr Kensuke Ebata, writing in *US Naval Institute Proceedings*, the JMSDF has developed a plan for sustained wide-area defence in these distant ocean areas, which are accessible by fighter aircraft only with extensive in-flight refuelling support. This plan is based on the AEW version of the Lockheed P-3 already mentioned, but with the addition of the AWG-9/AIM-54 Phoenix missile system, and up to 12 missiles. This craft would have the potential to detect the approach of hostile forces at 200 miles, intercept them at 100 miles, and be capable of engaging 12 targets at once. Obviously, this craft could not challenge Soviet fighters for air superiority; it would operate beyond their range from Okinawa, against long-range Backfire bombers and anti-ship missiles. The answer to the problem of its vulnerability is similar to that of the BSAS airship: firstly operating beyond the reach of enemy fighters, and secondly the ability of the defence to outrange hostile air-to-air weapons.

If speed can and must be sacrificed for long range and endurance, why not the airship? Present designs – certainly the 4.2 million cubic feet Boeing – could lift the same air defence sensor and weapons fit as the P-3 plus numerous missile rounds. Yet instead of relays of craft limited to areas within range of land bases, a single air defence airship could provide coverage to a convoy over its entire route by refuelling at sea.

And this brings us back to the beginning of this article and the concept of the 'Sea Control' airship. A very large rigid, of *Macon* or *Hinderberg* size, could easily carry not only the AWACS and Phoenix systems, but also Harpoons (as do the USN P-3Cs) and ASW systems, towed arrays, sonobuoys and a long range Ikara- or Malafon-type missile; refuelling weekly, and providing all-around defence for a convoy. It would have the advantage over a surface ship, of far greater detection and missile ranges, greater tactical mobility, and invulnerability to submarine attacks except, in the unlikely event that a submerged submarine fitted a defensive missile.

However, the possibility of such advanced airships entering service depends very largely on the craft proving itself a practical proposition in more conservative roles. The 'Sentinel 5000' as BSAS signals possible rebirth of a significant airship production industry and the opportunity for the helium filled airship to prove itself as an accepted and commonplace solution to the military (and commercial) logistic problems for which its lifting and endurance capabilities make it uniquely suited.

At present, the airship seems about to be reborn as a pure AEW craft. To succeed in this role it must be as reliable, simple, and inexpensive as possible. It must be able to do the job of an E-2C Hawkeye while refuelling at sea and keeping station aloft as steadily as a 'low level satellite'. If it can be done, the 'Sentinel 5000' must prove it is the craft for the job.

Postscript

After seven years of uninterrupted growth in defence spending, the Reagan administration came under heavy political pressure to reduce the US Treasury deficit. In February 1988, when the coming year's defence budget was released, numerous long-term programmes had been cut, including the ASAT anti-satellite missile, the ASW variant of the VTOL V-22 Osprey – and the Naval Airship Programme. In many cases, the cuts represented hard choices between the most and the somewhat less essential. From all reports, there has been no positive criticism of the NASP or denial of its utility.

According to Airship Industries, the contract was never cancelled, however, only experiencing a slowdown and a loss of several months while the source of funding was undetermined. The contract, under the original terms, was transferred from the US Navy to the Defense Advanced Research Project Agency (DARPA) a separate branch of the US Department of Defense. Thus, the 'Preliminary Design Review' took place in January 1989, perhaps six months behind schedule. AI is 'still targeting' November 1990, the original contract date, for the ship's first flight, but admits a delay of perhaps as much as a year is possible.

Meanwhile, the ship has grown to 2.5 million cu ft, by far the largest non-rigid, and tenth largest airship ever built, exceeded only by nine rigids built between the wars, exceeding all First World War craft, except perhaps the

A company-funded demonstration of the car of the 'Sentinel 5000' under construction at the Westinghouse facility at Weeksville, North Carolina. AI has proposed this design for a variety of roles including employment as Britain's Offshore Patrol Vessel and a passenger carrier. (Airship Industries Ltd*)* ▶

REACH CO., INC.

NAVY
BOEING

German *L-59* and *L-57*, at 2,418,700cu ft. The limiting factor on the growth of the non-rigid has been fabric technology, but development in this field has been 'leaping ahead' while the ship is under construction. Mr Peter Buckley, General Manager for flight operations, states that AI believes the ultimate limit for the non-rigid has not been reached, and points out that while the volume of the 'Sentinel 5000' is less than half that of the half-dozen largest rigids like the *Hindenburg*, her weight of structure is also far less.

AI reports also that a 'major milestone' towards the flight of the 'Sentinel 5000' was reached in October 1988 with the flight of the first fibre-optic controlled airship, a 'technological hurdle we had to overcome' to complete the AEW ship.

Smaller AI ships will shortly begin tests of the techniques for in-flight refuelling from ships to be utilized by the USN craft. Extensive tests of winching, hovering, in-flight stabilization procedures have been made, refined from those demonstrated to the French Navy in 1984, which included deploying and recovering a boat from a small airship. AI reports that French Navy interest remains strong but the problem there too is budgetary. Ships of the size tested in the shipping surveillance role are not large enough to provide the required performance. Obviously, the success of AI's prototype of a truly large and efficient non-rigid will provide a developed and inexpensive vehicle for many applications including passenger 'cruises', support for offshore activities such as oil drilling and fisheries, and ASW escort.

A final footnote: the long involvement of Goodyear in the history and development of the airship, spanning eight decades, may be at an end. Although the Goodyear Tire and Rubber Corporation continues to operate its small fleet of advertising ships, Goodyear Aerospace was acquired in 1987 by the LORAL Corp. LORAL officials have expressed their disappointment at losing the NASP contract to AI, and their lack of interest in the future construction of airships. Should the 'Sentinel 5000' open up a widened market for the airship, however, perhaps this accumulated body of technical expertise may again become valuable.

Table 1. *ZPG-3W Characteristics and Demonstrated Performance*

Total Volume:	1,516,000cu ft
Length:	403ft
Engines:	2 Wright R-1820-88 Cyclones
Horsepower:	3050
Operating Altitude:	5000ft
Design Ceiling:	10,000ft
Maximum Speed:	76kts, EAS
Rate of Ascent:	2400ft/min
Rate of Descent:	1200ft/min
Endurance	75 hours with military equipment and 21-man crew
Gross Weight	93,485lb (10,500lb heavy at take off)
Empty Weight	67,566lb
Envelope	33,115lb
Car	30,750lb
Empennage	3701lb
Useful Load	25,919lb
Crew & Provisions	7204lb
Fuel	19,712lb
Mission Equipment	(Included in Empty Weight)

The four type ZPG-3Ws, operational from 1958 to 1962 were the largest non-rigid airships built. Goodyear's present proposal utilizes the same basic design. However, it could be expected to show improved peformance similar to its 'Sentinel 5000' competitor, derived from increased envelope size (and thus increased gas volume and lift) use of modern lighter materials, crew decreased to 12, and increased maximum speed and endurance, from its dual mode propulsion, combining twin turboprops for increased top speed and total power and two 200-kilowatt turbo-generator-driven electric motors for cruising.

◀ *Model of the Boeing–Wren Skyship proposal for a 4.2 million cu ft ship of advanced design.* (Boeing Military Aircraft Corporation)

Table 2. *Sentinel 5000 Specifications & Performance*

The USN contract awarded to Westinghouse-Airship Industries in June 1987, called for first flight in 41 months, with operational trials beginning six months later. Contract price is $118,196,431 for the airship and $50,733,143 for its AEW suite. Cost of a single additional airship will be $83.2 million or $294.2 for five. Obviously should the programme lead to production of the 50-ship fleet envisioned, individual unit costs would be much lower.

Specification

Envelope	
Length overall	410ft
Diameter	102.5ft
Gross volume	2.2 million cu ft
Nominal S/L Helium Volume	1.65 million cu ft
Gondola (car)	
Length overall	80.8ft
Width overall	16.0ft
Height overall	25.5ft
Height Main Body	21.0ft
Accommodation	
Length of Pressurised Section	42ft
Internal Width Parallel Section	15ft
Decks (two plus cockpit)	3
Deck Height	7.5ft
Power Plants	
Cruise – two CRM Diesels, each	1790hp
Sprint – one PT6 Turboprop	1200hp
or one T700 Turboprop	1700hp
Vectored Thrust	
Cruise Propulsors	21,000lb
Fuel	
Maximum Fuel Load (Ferry)	48,000lb
Rated Operational Load	24,500lb

RFP Performance requirements

W-AI's 'Sentinel 5000C' design for the Navy ODM airship exceeds all RFP requirements

	Sentinel 5000C Guaranteed Performance
Max level Flight Speed (Max Heaviness)	78kt +

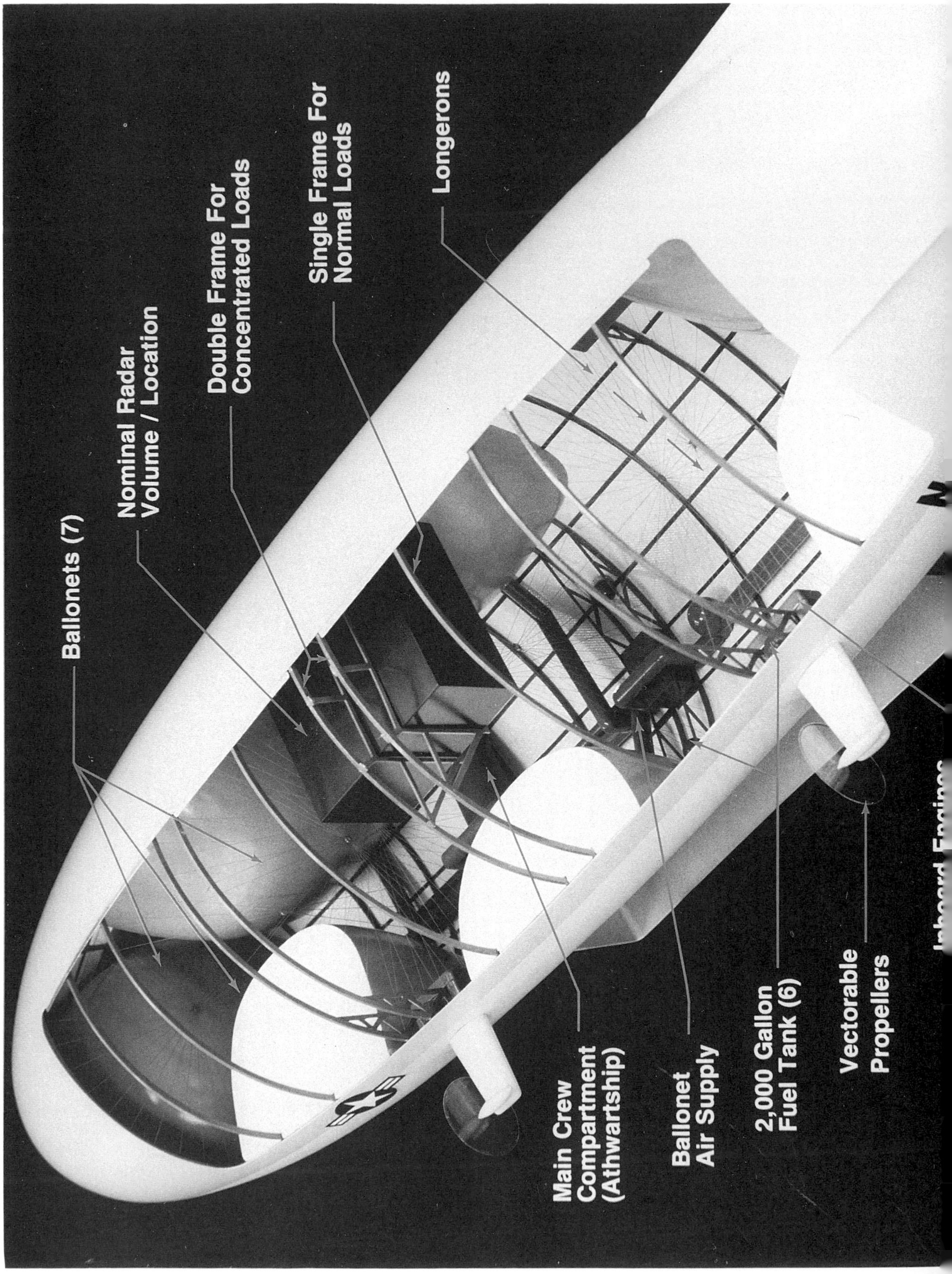

Ballonets (7)
Nominal Radar Volume / Location
Double Frame For Concentrated Loads
Single Frame For Normal Loads
Longerons
Main Crew Compartment (Athwartship)
Ballonet Air Supply
2,000 Gallon Fuel Tank (6)
Vectorable Propellers

Max level Flight Speed (Equilibrium)	82kt +
Max Pressure Altitude	14,000ft
Unrefuelled Endurance at 40kts, 5000ft	55 hours +
Unrefuelled Endurance at 70kts, 5000ft	20 hours +
Vertical Rate of Climb	630ft/min +[1]
Forward Rate of Climb at Max Heaviness	2500ft/min[2]

Other performance data

Max continuous speed (at 10,000ft)	87kts
Max continuous speed (2 cruise diesels only)	70-76kts[2]
Max continuous speed (1 cruise diesel only)	45kts
Endurance at 50kts 5000ft with full mission load	47 hours
Endurance at 40kts 5000ft with full mission load	55+ hours[3]
Max range at 5000ft, rated fuel load	2450 nautical miles
Max ferry range	3500 nautical miles (approx)
Vectored thrust to Max Take-off Weight Ratio	16 per cent

[1] vital for safe low level manoeuvrability (for T/O & landing/replenishment)
[2] dependent upon altitude
[3] depenent upon temperature

'Sentinel 5000' has performance margin beyond minimum threshold

Table 3. *Boeing-Wren Skyship Proposal*

Volume:	4.2 million cu ft
Crew:	17 (growth to 23)
Mission length:	30 days
Max speed:	90kts
Cruise speed:	70kts
Transit speed:	50kts
Speed on station:	30kts
Unrefuelled endurance:	150 hours
Design payload:	20,000lb
Useful lift to 10,000ft:	85,000lb

Wren Skyships Inc was reported in 1986 to be seeking financing for a similar ship described as 419ft long, powered by four R-R/Turbomeca RTM 322 turboprops, with a 27-ton payload, to fly in 1987.

◀ *Internal plan of the Boeing ship, reveals a wholly novel combination of rigid and pressure airship characteristics. Unique rigid hull of advanced composite material, supported by traditional rings and stringers prevents collapse of hull in the event of a loss of gas pressure, and enables concentrated loads to be dispersed throughout the hull, whilst single undifferentiated gas space and use of gas pressure to increase the rigidity of the hull recall the non-rigid. (*Boeing Military Aircraft Corporation*)*

WARSHIP NOTES

This section comprises a number of short articles and notes, generally highlighting little-known aspects of warship history.

AFTER THE YALU

The Fu Ch'ing, *and other Chinese-built steam warships of the 1890s*

By Richard N J Wright

China's first modern dockyards came into being in the 1860s at the Kiangnan Arsenal at Shanghai and at Foochow. The Kiangnan Arsenal had, in due course, reverted to the production of armaments, but the Foochow dockyards, over a span of two or three decades, produced a useful supply of ships for the four regional fleets (the Peiyang or Northern, Nanyang or Nanking, Fukien and Kwangtung), mostly in the shape of composite-built sloops or transports, the one being converted into the other as the situation demanded. Photographs of these early Chinese steam warships, loosely called 'cruisers', are usually lacking, as are many of the details, but the accompanying photo of the *Kwang Chia*, launched in 1887, provides an illustration common to most.

Of the four fleets the Peiyang had access to the most funds, and in the 1880s was modernised with warships purchased from Great Britain and Germany. When war broke out with Japan over Korea in 1894 the Peiyang Fleet was a formidable force on paper, comprising nine foreign-built battleships, armoured and protected cruisers; one Foochow-built armoured cruiser; two elderly training ships (*Wei Yuen* and *Kang Chi*), and some torpedo-boats and gunboats. In addition it had been reinforced by three ships from the Kwangtung Fleet, the *Kwang Chia*, and two new style 1000-ton torpedo cruisers built at Foochow, the *Kwang Yi* and *Kwang Ping*. (The Fukien Fleet, after the débâcle of the war with the French in 1884, had little to offer; the Nanyang Fleet, although it had exercised with the Peiyang Fleet, was noticeable by its absence from the war zone.)

The fate of the Peiyang Fleet is well recorded. The *Kwang Yi* was sunk in a preliminary skirmish with Japanese cruisers off Asan. Later, at the fleet action off the Yalu River, the *Kwang Chia*, virtually unprotected but included in the line of battle because of her speed, broke away and fled the action, only to be tracked down and destroyed off Talienwan. Four more of the Chinese cruisers were sunk and the remainder badly mauled, with the one exception of the Foochow-built armoured cruiser. She had been too slow to include in the battle line, and had formed a small separate group together with the *Kwang Ping* and some torpedo-boats. They survived the battle intact, but were eventually blockaded by the Japanese with the remainder of the Chinese fleet at Wei Hai Wei. By the time the Chinese Admiral had surrendered and subsequently committed suicide in February 1895, only one Chinese battleship, two cruisers, the *Kwang Ping*, the training ship *Kang Chi* and a handful of gun- and torpedo-boats were still afloat. The Japanese appropriated the lot as prizes of war except for the *Kang Chi*, which was allowed to proceed to Chefoo carrying the body of Admiral Ting. As the result she was the sole survivor of the Peiyang Fleet to remain in Chinese hands.

Contracts were immediately made abroad for replacement cruisers; but in February 1897 a newspaper[1] reported that the northern (Peiyang) squadron now consisted of only five ships: *Fei Ting, Fei Ying, Fu Ch'ing, Kang Chi* and *Tung Chi*. Of these, the *Fei Ting* and *Fei Ying*, despite both being torpedo cruisers and similarly named, were completely different in appearance; one had been purchased in Germany and the other in Great Britain, and neither had arrived in time to take part in the hostilities. But it is of the other ships of this motley squadron, the *Fu Ch'ing, Kang Chi* and *Tung Chi* that this article is mainly about, as the published information on them in the reference books is not entirely accurate. The following contemporary detail which has been sifted from the *Peking Gazette*, China Coast newspapers and British Consular reports, adds a little bit more to the history of the Chinese Fleet in the 1890s.

Fu Ch'ing. This vessel has never been properly identified. She is usually quoted as a steel-hulled, Foochow-built cruiser of about 2200 tons, armed with 8in and 4.7in guns, possibly a copy of two German-built cruisers of the Nanyang Fleet. Only in Brassey's *Naval Annual* from 1896 onward is the description changed slightly, arming her with three 5in; and Rawlinson[2] quotes '? tb'. Both are closer to the truth.

She is first mentioned in the press in December 1890: 'The Foochow Naval Yard has constructed a new cruiser of the best steel, named *Foo Ch'ing*, for the use of the Foochow Squadron.'[3] However, she was not actually completed at that stage as in March 1894 the British Consul at Foochow had the occasion to make a report[4] on the doings of the arsenal, and in the process he provided some first hand information about the ship.

> ... Towards the end of the year a cruiser called the *Fu-Ching* was launched. She is of the same style as the *Kwang-I* and the *Kwang-Ping* which were built here but are now engaged in the Viceroy of Canton's service. The designs for these vessels are supposed to have come from France about seven years ago, although it is claimed that they were originally made here. They are altogether different from the old model as left by the original French instructors, which was copied with variations until within the last few years, and are of a much newer type. The *Fu-Ching* is 1000 tons displacement, 2400 horsepower, 234ft long, 27ft 8in beam, with 14ft

draught [word illegible]. She carries 140 tons of coal, and at ordinary steam burns 1½ tons an hour. On her trial strip she steamed 16 knots an hour. Her armament consists of three 4½in and four 2½in guns of German manufacture, and her crew of 56 hands all told ...

The report goes on to mention another vessel, the *Chien-Ching*, intended for use as a transport and expected to be launched at the end of the year; displacement 1800 tons, cargo capacity 600 tons of rice, dimensions 253ft x 34ft x 15ft. The significance of this piece of information becomes apparent later on.

The *Fu Ch'ing* next comes into the news in April 1896:

> The *Fu Ch'ing* cruiser was sent up last year in September to Nanking at the request of Chang Chi-tung, then acting Imperial High Commissioner of the Nanyang administration, for the purpose of reinforcing the Nanyang Squadron ordered to rendezvous in Port Arthur etc at the retrocession of the Liaotung Peninsular ...[5]

Finally, in February 1897 it was reported[6] that *Fu Ch'ing*, completed and commissioned in 1895, had been taken over by the Peiyang administration. Her armament of quickfirers and new guns had been returned to the arsenal, and were intended to make up the armament of a new cruiser, the *Fu An*.

Fu Ch'ing's service with the Peiyang Squadron was short: she sank in a storm off Port Arthur in 1898[7] and has remained a bit of a mystery ever since.

From the British Consul's account, it is clear that she was in fact a torpedo cruiser (or torpedo gunboat) of the same type as the *Kwang Ping* (illustrated). What is not clear is why she took so long to build (from 1890 to 1895), and why Foochow yard constructed only one of her type for the Fukien Fleet. The answer is to take a closer look at the Kwangtung Fleet.

In the 1880s a large building order had been placed by the Canton-based Kwangtung government with the Foochow yard. In October 1887 this was reported[8] as comprising:

Kwang Chia	fast sloop
Kwang-Yi *Kwang-Ping* *Kwang-Ting*	armed scouts
Kwang Keng *Kwang Hsing* *Kwang Jen* *Kwang Kuei*	dimensions 144ft x 25ft
Kwang Wu *Kwang Chi*	river cruisers of 150ft x 20ft

The *Kwang Chia* was duly completed in 1888 and was subsquently sent north to 'drill' with the Peiyang Fleet. But in 1890 the Kwangtung government had money problems and second thoughts. A report in November[9] stated that the *Kwang Yi* and *Kwang Ping* were nearly 'ready' (presumably for launching), but the Kwangtung government had asked for the *Kwang Ting* to be deferred. As a considerable expenditure had already been incurred in assembling the materials for her, the intention was for the *Kwang Ting* to be taken over by the Fukien government and completed 'during the slack season'. A substitute could be built if so required by the Kwangtung government at a later stage.

The launch of the *Kwang Ping* was reported in June 1891.[10] Her details were given as: dimensions 226ft x 26ft x 11½ft; armament three 12cm QF, 8 Hotchkiss, 4 torpedo tubes; 3 boilers, 2 engines, 2400hp.

Further information about the new Kwangtung ships comes in July 1892.[11] The *Kwang Chia* had been sent north to be drilled. The *Kwang Ping* and *Kwang Yi* were completed in May, were at Canton in June, were fit for active service and were now to be drilled with the Peiyang Fleet. The *Kwang Keng* had been retained for service at Canton, 'not being adapted for going to sea' (Rawlinson lists her as a shallow draught gunboat).[12] Four other ships had been postponed. The names were not given, but would seem to have been *Kwang Ting, Kwang Hsing, Kwang Jen* and *Kwang Kuei*; the last three names do not appear again.

Thus the *Kwang Chia, Kwang Yi*

Kwang Chia, *as completed in 1888.* (NMM)

Fu Chi (ex-Kang Chi), sole survivor of the Peiyang Fleet remaining in Chinese hands. (US Navy)

and *Kwang Ping* joined the Peiyang Fleet, and never returned. As to the last ship of the trio of torpedo cruisers, and *Kwang Ting*, she was listed in Brassey's *Naval Annual* until 1912, and in *Jane's Fighting Ships* from 1900 to 1911, and then with a lesser degree of confidence until 1918. But despite a launch date of '1891' she was not mentioned by the British Consul at Foochow in his report of 1894, did not seem to have been used to bolster up the Peiyang Squadron in 1897, is not included in Rawlinson's detailed list of Chinese warships up until 1895,[13] and never suceeded in being photographed; all of which suggest that the listing in the naval annuals was due entirely to lack of precise information, *ie* she was laid down, was not destroyed, and so must exist. What actually happened to her? The most logical solution is that she was indeed incorporated into the Fukien Fleet on the stocks in November 1890, and was then renamed *Fu Ch'ing* (December 1890: 'The Foochow Naval Yard has constructed a new cruiser of the best steel, named *Foo Ch'ing* . . .'). This would explain why *Fu Ch'ing* was 'one off' and took so long to build, as she was completed 'during the slack season(s)' at the dockyard.

◀ *Kwang Ping under the Japanese flag in 1896. She was a sister ship of Kwang Ting. (US Navy)*

Kang Chi. She was Foochow built in 1879 for the Peiyang Fleet, and probably resembled the *Kwang Chia* in appearance. Later on she was modernised as a training ship,[14] and having survived at Wei Hai Wei was used to carry the body of Admiral Ting to Chefoo. She was the only ship of the Peiyang Fleet to be returned by the Japanese.

In September 1896 it was reported:

> Two Chinese gunboats have had their names changed, viz:
>
> *Kong Chi* to *Fu Chi*
>
> *Kian Ching* to *Tung Chi*
>
> The character 'Fu' means returned again and as the *Fu Chi* (late *Kong Chi*) is a boat that the Japanese seized at Wei Hai Wei and, when sending Admiral Ting's body over to Chefoo, handed this ship over as well, hence we suppose, the Chinese reason for giving her the character 'Fu', 'returned again'.[15]

The name *Fu Chi* is seldom mentioned and, oddly enough, she was still quoted as the *Kang Chi* in the report on the composition of the northern squadron in February 1897 – but confirmation of the name change comes from another source. The US Navy photograph NH 1596 (illustrated) is annotated:

> *Fu Chi* (Chinese Naval Vessel). Note: This name is almost certainly incorrect as it appears on no list of Chinese Naval Ships. The correct name is not known. The photo was received by the office of Naval Intelligence in 1900.

The *Fu Chi*'s appearance in the photograph, from the Foochow hull form to the long, left-over bowsprit, would seem to be entirely consistent with that of the *Kang Chi*, converted for use as a training ship.

Tung Chi and Fu An. The *Tung Chi* started life as the transport *Chien Ching*, whose details were supplied by the British Consul at Foochow in 1894. A memorial of April 1896 reported on the recent disposition of the Fukien Fleet:

> The new cruiser *Chien-Ching*, lately completed by the Naval Yard at Pagoda Anchorage, has been bes-

poken by Wang Wen-shao, Imperial High Commissioner of the Peiyang administration etc who wishes to make the new cruiser a training ship for naval cadets at Tientsin. [The former training ship, *Wei Yuen*, had been torpedoed and sunk at Wei Hai Wei.] Hence the Captain, officers and crew of the *Chien-Ching* will be sent down from the north to take over as soon as her armament shall have been mounted.[16]

The memorialist goes to point out that the *Fu Ch'ing* had been sent up north, and that three other ships of the Foochow squadron were employed on other duties, thus

leaving oft times the harbour of Foochow completely deserted by war vessels. Memorialist has therefore instructed the Tsao-tai Yang Chen-yi, Director of the Foochow dockyard, to commence the building of a steel cruiser at once, there being several sets of engines and boilers built by the said dockyard in reserve, available for the purpose. The new crusier will be named the *Fu An*. Her cost, apart from the armament, will be Taels 200,000.

In both September and November 1896[17] there were reports that the *Chien Ching* had been renamed *Tung Chi*.

A report on shipbuilding in the Foochow Arsenal and Dockyard in February 1897 adds the final touches, with a description of the official trial trip of the *Chien Ching*.[18] Her keel had been laid down in 1893, when she was destined to be a transport to carry grain for the government. Her dimensions were given as 252ft 7in pp, beam 34ft 1in, depth of hold 25ft 1in, draught loaded, 14ft forward and 16ft aft; burthen 1900 tons.

In April 1895 her machinery had been put in. This consisted of horizontal compound engines with four boilers (two large, two small); ihp was 1600. On trials in August 1896 at 100lbs pressure, giving 84 revs, she had made 11½kts, and demonstrated that with better fuel she could make 13kts.

It had been first intended to complete the vessel in 1897, but owing to the urgent need by Peiyang the work had been hastened. She was now the training ship *Tung Chi* and had been turned over to Captain Li Ho of the Peiyang Fleet on completion of trials, and was to be armed in the north. Taels 180,000 had been paid for her. Later on she was credited in the reference books with an armament of two 5.9in, five 4in (or two 6in, five 4.7in). The 5.9in were mounted in sponsons either side of the bridge. In appearance she was very similar to the *Kwang Chia*. *Tung Chi* served as a training ship for forty years and eventually succumbed, just like her predecessor, *Wei Yuen*, to Japanese attack.

Name	Laid Down	Launched	Completed	Notes
Kwang Yi	?1889–90		May 1892	
Kwang Ping	?1889–90	June 1891	May 1892	
Kwang Ting	?1889–90			Probably completed as *Fu Ch'ing*
Fu Ch'ing	By 1890	Late 1893	1895	Probably ex-*Kwang Ting*
Ting Chi	1893	Expected at end of 1894	1896	Ex-*Chien Ching*
Fu An	1896	?1897		

The same report of February 1897 gave a little more detail on the *Fu An*. Her engines and boilers were ready for fitting at that stage, and she only needed 'the steel protection for her battery'. Work was proceeding rapidly, and her armament was to include guns from the *Fu Ch'ing*.

While the *Kwang Chia* had been of composite construction, both the *Tung Chi* and *Fu An* were all steel. *Tung Chi* had started life as a grain transport and had then been converted to a training cruiser; on the other hand, *Fu An* had started life as a cruiser and was subsequently converted into a transport. *Jane's Fighting Ships* volumes from 1921 show her as such, with dimensions and tonnage which indicate that she had originally been a close copy or even a sister ship of the *Tung Chi*. Her reversion to transport duties was probably due to the purchase abroad of better, foreign-built cruisers.

References:

1. *Peking & Tientsin Times*, 20 February 1897.
2. *China's Struggle for Naval Development, 1839–1895*, John L Rawlinson, USA, 1967, p251.
3. *Chinese Times*, 20 December 1890.
4. Public Record Office, FO-17-1208, 5 March 1894.
5. *Peking Gazette*, 29 April 1896.
6. *Ibid*, 17 February 1897.
7. Rawlinson, p251.
8. *Chinese Times*, 22 October 1887.
9. *Peking Gazette*, 20 November 1890.
10. *Ibid*, 11 June 1891.
11. *Ibid*, 28 July 1892.
12. Rawlinson, p254.
13. *Ibid*. pp247–259.
14. FO-17-1249. Described by the British Consul at Chefoo as a wooden training ship, about 20 years old, with no guns.
15. *Peking & Tientsin Times*, 19 September 1896, two references.
16. *Peking Gazette*, 29 April 1896.
17. *Ibid*, 4 November 1896; see also P & TT, 19 September 1896.
18. *Ibid*, 17 February 1897.

CANOPUS QUERIES

Some oddities about these Victorian battleships unearthed by K D McBride

The *Canopus* class battleships of the British 1896–97 and 1897–98 Programmes have often been described. Everyone interested in warships knows that they were a smaller, faster edition of the *Majestic* class, designed to pass through the Suez Canal; that they were the first British battleships to use water-tube boilers and that their 6in Krupp armour was the equivalent of the 9in Harveyised armour of their predecessors. It is also well known that they were provided with an additional upper armoured deck to cope with the menace of howitzer fire, with which the French were experimenting.

While hunting for material on armoured cruisers in the Public Record Office, I came across items from the Admiralty papers of the time which rather altered the picture. The initial memoranda on the class refer throughout to Harveyised armour, and contain some fine arguments to prove that 6in of Harvey was as good – well, almost – as 9in of the same. On looking into the source of all battleship wisdom, Oscar Parkes' *British Battleships*, I found that the picture was hazy; he said that 'contemporary unofficial sources said that the first five ships had Harvey, only the sixth and last ship, *Vengeance* of the 1897–98 Programme, having Krupp; however, all official documents refer to Krupp'. This is borne out by

Albion *being towed down river from Thames Ironworks, her builder, to have her main armament fitted.* (CPL)

the 1913 'Brassey', while *Steam Ships of England*, the official publication definitely credits them with Krupp armour. It is also interesting that the design was regarded by DNC's staff as an improved *Renown*, to be capable of meeting the *Fuji*, which was being built at Blackwall with much help from Sir William White and his men! When first proposed, the *Canopus* was to carry only ten 6in, reduced outfits of ammunition, and to use the old cylindrical or Scotch boilers. The skill of Sir William and his staff permitted all these points to be improved before the design was submitted for Board of Admiralty approval.

There was another difference as well: not only was the *Canopus* able to resist the howitzers of the dreaded French, but also she could pay them back in their own coin as well. The memorandum states that she was to have enough space, stability and buoyancy to carry six or eight howitzers in addition to her normal armament; these would not interfere with the 12pdr tertiary guns.

What howitzers? Another file revealed that tests were carried out on a 6in howitzer in October and November 1898. On 19 January 1897, Sir William White wrote to his colleague Captain Kane, the Director of Naval Ordnance (DNO), suggesting action on previous discussions with their mutual superior, the Controller, about the addition of howitzers to the upper deck armament of the *Canopus* class and cruisers. The object was to fire large shells full of explosives. Captain Kane had already been in touch with the Inspector-General of Ordnance, his Army opposite number, on the subject, but Sir William understood that the Army had 5in and 8in howitzers, and nothing in between. He was anxious to use 6in, to share ammunition with the numerous Royal Navy 6in guns, if this proved possible.

On 30 January, Captain Kane reported that the Ordnance Committee, responsible ultimately for the provision and safety of all RN and Army weapons, had just 'sealed the patterns' for two different 6in howitzers made by Woolwich Arsenal for the Indian Army, and carried out trials with them. The Indian Army had chosen the 25cwt 12cal howitzer, but when forwarding details, which arrived at the end of February, the Inspector-General recommended the 30cwt 14cal weapon for naval use, because of its lower internal and external pressures. He also suggested that a maximum elevation of 40 degrees rather than 70 degrees would be ample for naval use.

(The optimum angle of elevation for range is 45 degrees; equivalent ranges are obtained for elevations paired about that angle, *eg* 40 = 50, 35 = 55. 'Upper Register' firing is much used by land gunners for shooting out of forests, onto reverse slopes, over mountain ranges etc, but not by their nautical colleagues. A lesser elevation of course permits a lighter and lower mounting.)

The approval of the First Sea Lord had been obtained to further studies; it was agreed that a test programme could be worked out when a naval mounting was available and costs had been estimated. The Army's advice on the model of gun and on elevation was accepted and approval to obtain a gun and mounting given on 15 March. The 30cwt howitzer had a muzzle velocity of 777ft per second and normally fired a 118lb shell using a charge of 1¾lbs of size 5 cordite; 40-degree elevation would give 5000yds range – beyond normal naval ranges in 1897. The 118lb shell could not be used in naval 6in guns, but the howitzer could use the 100lb naval shell. After various minor points concerning the shield and mechanism were settled, approval was given in September to design and make a mounting for £900. The howitzer itself was to be borrowed from the Army. Delivery was to be in 7 months, which would take it into the 1898-99 Financial Year.

In the meantime Elswick got to hear of what was going on and offered a 33½cwt howitzer of their own; they were invited to send in drawings and when these arrived at the end of November, they showed *two* howitzers; a 32cwt 14cal 6in and a 97cwt 16cal 8in. The DNO, who was by now Rear-Admiral Jeffreys, decided to await the results of the trials already arranged.

At that time, British war plans called for cruiser squadrons in the Channel to 'keep up a continual system of annoyance' off French bases, especially torpedo-boat bases. It had been noted that a 6in howitzer, shield and mounting weighed little more than a 4.7in gun installation, and there were a number of torpedo gunboats with 4.7in guns available, which had been done out of a job by the new torpedo-boat destroyers. Sir Frederick Richards, the First Naval Lord – the mastermind of the pre-dreadnought era – conceived the idea of fitting the torpedo gunboats with howitzers in place of one or both of their 4.7in, attaching them to cruiser squadrons, and using them to blast the French naval bases, and especially to destroy the pestiferous torpedo-boats at source. Study showed that the idea was technically practicable; some stiffening would be needed and ammunition outfit would be 150 rounds per gun, not 300.

Sir William White and Rear-Admiral Jeffrey were not keen on the idea: the former noted that in 1891 a sketch design had been produced for a slow twin-screw mortar vessel to carry an 18-ton rifled muzzle loader on a high angle mounting; the latter claimed that the extreme range of the 6in howitzer would be 5200yds, while its shell would be 'a very poor projectile for bombarding purposes'. More seriously, the French bases all had well-armed outlying forts which would disable the bombarding ships before they could do much damage. If bombardment vessels were needed, he suggested bringing some of the old gunboats out of reserve and giving more elevation to their rifled muzzle loading 10in.

As usual with R & D, the howitzer mounting was late, arriving in June 1898, and six rounds were fired for proof purposes in July. It was decided to put it and a 6in gun for comparison into the gunboat *Kite*, attached to HMS *Excellent*, and to fire a series of tests at 2000 and 5000yds, in smooth and in rough water, the targets being overlapping areas marked out by buoys to represent:

a) A battleship, with deck, sides and danger areas, 350ft x 75ft x 20ft.
b) A battleship's deck, broadside on, 350ft x 75ft.
c) A battleship's deck, end on, 75ft x 350ft.

Then the weather turned bad.

The tests were finally carried out on 25 October 1898, when there was a strong south-west wind, and 10 November, when it was calm, the targets being 3¾ miles south-east by east of the Horse Sand Fort. Ten rounds were fired with full charges to test the mounting at different elevations, followed by 20 rounds from each weapon at 1600yds and the same at 5000yds. The scores were:

		Ship	Deck broadside on	End on
25 October				
1600yds	Howitzer	12	7	11
	Gun	17	3	8
5000yds	Howitzer	8	8	3
	Gun	12	8	12
10 November				
1600yds	Howitzer	12	2	12
	Gun	15	3	10

Apparently no long-range shoot took place on the latter day; it was felt that the gun had shown itself decisively superior. The howitzer was returned to the Army, and the mounting put in store at Portsmouth.

This was not quite the end of the story: HMS *Hyacinth* was completed about this time and spent most of her life on the Cape Station. It is believed that she was fitted with 6in howitzers in lieu of two 6in guns, to facilitate bombarding land targets. Whether she used them in anger is not known. It seems likely that the *Kite* mounting was dug out of store in the First World War; did it grace the *Majestic*'s fore turret, or was it carried by *E-20?*

With regard to the *Canopus* class, one wonders how the six or eight 6in howitzers, if fitted, would have been manned and supplied with ammunition. They would have been no use at Coronel or the Falklands, but at the Dardanelles it might have been another story. And the Navy might have learnt something about defence against plunging fire and bombing before they found out the hard way.

PRINZ EUGEN'S RADAR

Werner F G Stehr identifies the cruiser's final electronics fit

The accompanying photograph shows the *Prinz Eugen* in Philadelphia Navy Yard on 31 March 1946. A barrel of A turret (20.3cm/8in) has just been dismounted. The following radar antennae are to be seen:

1. FuMO 26 resp. 34. The shadow behind its upper part is an enclosed observation position.
2. FuMO 81 'Berlin' ex-FuS 224. The set is in the Forces Communication Centre [3330MHz – 9cm –, 20kW].
3. Fittings for FuMB [radar interception device/wireless monitoring gear] Antenne [antenna] 7 'Timor'. The set is in the uppermost rotating stand behind the search antenna of FuMO 34.

Not on view – perhaps already dismantled – are the antennae for the following FuMB: Antenne 3 'Bali' and 'Bali I' for the sets FuMB 4 'Samos', FuMB 26 'Tunis', FuMB 9 'Cypern 2' and

(Breyer Collection)

FuMB 10 'Borkum' as well as the antenna for FuME 2 (IFF) 'Wespe g 2'.

4. Two of four FuMB Antennae 4 'Sumatra'.
5. FuMO 25 ex-FMG 40 G (gO) antenna.

a. Life rafts
b. 4cm Bofors AA. Already removed are the guns on the roof of B turret and the sponson above the Admiral's bridge in the fighting tower.
c. Winch for second pair of paravanes.
d. Shield of twin 10.5cm (4.1in) HA/LA.
e. 2cm quadruple AA mounted in the former searchlight sponson the funnel casing.
f. Searchlight stand.
g. Covered position for torpedo gunner's mate on the triple 53.3cm (21in) torpedo tubes.
h. Twin 10.5cm HA/LA, barrels dismantled.

Note the spherical HA directors. The forward one was to be dismantled within the next few days.

NONSUCH: British views of a German Destroyer

The German 1936A (Mob) type destroyer Z-38 was taken over by Britain after the end of the war. Formally acquired on 22 September 1945, the ship was commissioned as HMS Nonsuch *and subjected to trials by the Royal Navy, before being broken up in 1949. Below we reproduce the commanding officer's notes on the behaviour of the ship dated 27 October 1948. These notes were submitted by D K Brown.*

1. Although classed as a Destroyer by the Germans, the ship bears very few of the characteristics associated with our own destroyers and can best be described as a very fast gun and torpedo platform.

2. For the strategic use for which she was designed, namely for short operations in the English Channel and the North Sea, she has much to recommend her. Her five 5.9in guns are more than a match for any British destroyer and working in pairs this class of ship would have been a serious problem to many of our smaller cruisers.

3. Trials were carried out on 18 October in a Gale Force 8 and she showed no sign of bumping at 21kts steering right into the sea. It would probably take a great deal to make it necessary to ease down in a head sea owing mainly to the very fine bow sections but this design might be detrimental to the fitting of modern ASDICS owing to lack of space.

4. The wind deflecting arrangements consist of having the sides of the bridge bent over and are very effective. On either side of the bows about midway between the waterline and deck there are ledges fitted which form a bow wave suppressor. They are effective and definitely reduce the

spray on the bridge.

5. The anchors stow on the fo'c's'le horizontally and reach the stowage with no difficulty. By being high up they do not throw up any spray as they would if stowed in a hawsepipe. In addition, being horizontal on deck, most of the weight is taken off the coupling and in fact at times a little persuasion is needed to start them veering.

6. All the items in the ship's favour would not alter the fact that a similar class of ship would find no useful place in the British Navy. With a complement of 165 men and 9 officers the ship is very cramped. Her full war complement was 350 men and 14 officers and with these numbers it was necessary to live ashore or in a depot ship. These conditions, coupled with her very short radius of action, would limit her use to that for which she was designed, namely to fight over short periods of time in the Channel or North Sea.

Two views of HMS Nonsuch *(ex-*German Z-38*) lying in the Clyde in December 1945. The British R40 pendant number has been painted up.* (CPL)

NAVAL BOOKS OF THE YEAR

The reviews are divided into three main sections: firstly, the most important books given full reviews; then short notices of the less significant titles or those less relevant to the themes of this annual; and finally, a straightforward listing of books announced but not received. In all sections the order is alphabetical by author.

Ronald Bassett, HMS Sheffield, *published by Arms & Armour Press, 1988.*
253 x 198mm, 224 pages, illustrated.
ISBN 0 85368 911 3. £19.95

This is a most comprehensive single ship history based on the thorough ground-work prepared by the late Lieutenant-Commander Hubert Treseder, RN and amplified by the personal recollections of very many officers and men who served in *Sheffield* throughout her active career. By all accounts she was a consistently 'happy ship' and this is borne out in the narrative, which takes the reader in considerable detail from launching day in 1937 to the final demolition at Faslane 30 years later.

Her wide ranging war and subsequent services are thoroughly explored and there is a wealth of information in these pages which will repay close study. It has to be said that this is one of those books that picked up and opened at random holds the reader's attention. Indeed as an introduction to the Royal Navy in war and peace *Sheffield* can hardly be bettered, particularly as all ranks made their contribution.

Ian Grant

Paul Beaver, World Naval Aviation, *published by Jane's Defence Data, 1989.*
258 x 195mm, 192 pages, c200 photographs, c90 sketch maps.
£30.00

An unusual offering by Jane's Defence Data, this book consists of listings by country (88 of them) of those armed forces and Coastguards etc which operate aircraft, including helicopters, in over-water roles. The UK entry for example covers the RN, Royal Marines, 18 Group RAF, Coastguard and Scottish Agriculture and Fisheries Department. The structure of each major operating arm is briefly summarised, and skeleton listings are given of air-capable ships, shore bases (shown also on small outline maps), the numerical strength of each type of embarkable and shore-based aircraft, and designations of the squadron-level units which operate them. Where applicable short summaries cover recent operations, typical deployments, weapon systems and general background, with an indication of impending re-equipment programmes. Since several medium size powers only get three pages each the facts are condensed with little or no information about ship or aircraft characteristics. Hence it is unlikely to appeal to the general reader although as a ready reference for Service staffs, journalists and sales and marketing people it has attractions despite the price.

David Stanley

A Compton-Hall, Submarine versus Submarine, *published by David & Charles, 1988.*
250 x 225mm, 192 pages, illustrated. ISBN 0 7153 9178 X. £13.95.

Cmdr Compton-Hall has, as usual, written a provocative book with much of interest and plenty of ideas on which to ponder. The book is in two parts: the first is a review of contemporary technology of submarines and their weapon systems; the second consists of a series of 'factional' incidents – war games – demonstrating the power of modern submarines. The book is very well illustrated with many photographs and plenty of clear diagrams, together with a few specially created paintings in Part II. There is a considerable number of fascinating, inserted notes on specific topics – *eg* the dreadful performance of Soviet submarines in the Second World War, the Stirling cycle, etc.

Part I leads through the Soviet threat, submarine construction, propulsion and speed to weapons and sensors, including a brief note on non-acoustic detection. The special subject of operation under ice receives a chapter to itself as does the author's favourite subject of midgets. Though the author points out that Russian submariners are not 10 feet tall, he takes a more rosy view of their engineers and scientists. He frequently uses the world 'conjectured' with a strong implication that they have solved the technical problems of boundary layer control, shock attenuation by bubbles, magneto-hydrodynamics and computer based automation. A technical annex to this review discusses the current state of these technologies as revealed in published papers.

The Soviet Union devotes a very considerable effort to research and to educating a very large number of scientists and engineers, many of them, as individuals, of very high standard. However, their technical achievements are, more often than not, due to the large scale application of very conventional engineering – brute force. If they learn to manage their research effort more effectively, Soviet advances may well be rapid.

Part II begins with two incidents involving Russian SSK and SSN in a major war. The problems they face of over-rigid control, the obsession with security even affecting control room layout, the number of men who cannot speak Russian, and alcoholism are brought out. The next two chapters cover the use of submarines for blackmail or even piracy by maverick Third World countries, a very worrying theme. Surveillance, merging into espionage, both by big boats and by midgets follow, leading into other covert operations.

The book is not aimed at those who are serving in submarines or have recently completed a long anti-submarine course, but at the general public. The non-expert will learn much, the expert may find food for thought, but technical 'conjectures' should be taken with a large pinch of salt.

Technical Annex

It is always dangerous for an ageing engineer to say that something is impossible (Arthur Clarke's First Law). However the technology is well understood for the topics to be discussed and a breakthrough seems unlikely. The topics discussed are quite frequently mentioned by writers and entrepreneurs as likely to be areas in which the Soviets have, or about to have, a lead.

Boundary layer control. The flow over any normal surface will be turbulent at Reynolds Numbers greater than about 10^6. At ship speeds, the frictional drag over the main hull would be reduced to about a quarter of that in turbulent flow if laminar flow could be achieved. Other components of resistance would not be reduced to the same extent and, realistically, an all laminar flow submarine would have about half the resistance of one in turbulent flow, corresponding to some 17 per cent or 5kts increase in speed. Complete laminar flow is a dream but there are ways of achieving laminar flow over part of a body or of reducing the turbulence over the whole hull.

The best known and most successful method is to bleed long chain molecules into the boundary layer. Even at concentrations of the order of 10 parts per million (weight) reductions of the order of 30 per cent in frictional resistance have been demonstrated. A number of natural substances have this property and, following use in the oil industry, the US Navy tried guar gum on a minesweeper in 1963. Polyethylene oxide ('polyox'), with a molecular weight of about 10 x 10^6, is more effective and was used in a trial on HMS *Highburton* in September 1968 (reported in *Trans RINA* Vol 113, 1971). With about 10 per cent polyox in the boundary layer, reductions of about 17 per cent in shaft horsepower were achieved, despite the poor condition of the hull. Similar reductions were obtained on a large model of a frigate.

There were, and remain, two difficult problems. The very large molecules necessary are very slow to dissolve and easily settle out of solution. A large mixing plant is needed as is a sizeable ready use tank. The other problem is cost; the daily consumption of polyox as used in the *Highburton* trial would cost 1500 times as much as the fuel saved. It was thought that the large scale production of polyox would reduce the penalty to 500 times. It has been suggested that leaching the polymer into the laminar sub-layer or incorporating it into a paint would reduce consumption but no success has been reported. In military applications success might be indicated by a black-out on publication but this is not obvious either.

It is also claimed that turbulence can be damped out by a flexible skin, backed by a viscous liquid. Success was claimed by Kramer in about 1960 but has not been repeated elsewhere. It is certain (as Compton-Hall says) that such an approach is inconsistent with a tiled surface. Tiles will inevitably deform under pressure and the joints open up generating turbulence.

Many aircraft wings have been designed in which laminar flow is maintained for some distance from the leading edge by using section gradually increasing in depth so as to maintain a positive pressure gradient. This can be extended by applying suction at the point at which break away would occur. Success would demand a very smooth hull, unlikely to be maintained at sea (incompatible with tiles) and a fair amount of power for suction. In one study the power required to suck at 40kts was equal to the power to drive the submarine. The 'Victor III' form is not a laminar flow form despite the caption on page 150; and nor does polyox leave stains.

Air Lubrication. Before her polyox trial, *Highburton* had been used for trials of air lubrication which were totally unsuccessful as was every other reported trial. It is easy in the laboratory to lubricate a small plate, more difficult to deal with the same area on a rough and rolling ship and, so far, impossible to cover the whole ship. At the turn of the century, Sir John Thornycroft tried to use air lubrication to make his torpedo boats go faster and his experiments led him to the design of a large model of a plenum chamber hovercraft which worked well. He could not apply his ideas for lack of lightweight machinery. Many years later, Sir Christopher Cockerell followed a very similar route to his hovercraft.

Air bubbles, free or in a foam, do attenuate explosions but a foam rigid enough to withstand the pressure at depth will transmit shock quite well and it would not be easy to generate the large quantities of gas required in a submarine.

Magnetohydrodynamics. The principles are well known and have frequently been demonstrated in the laboratory and even on television. It is reported that Japan is thinking of a demonstration ship. However, all such devices are incredibly inefficient. The new breed of superconductors will help – when someone finds how to make a wire – but even so efficiency will be bad. The laws of momentum show that any propulsive device works on reaction by moving a mass of water backwards. For good efficiency, the mass should be large and its speed low, criteria even more important if silence is wanted. The properties of water do not encourage hopes of a large, slow jet.

Computers. The suggestion in this book that the Soviets are ahead in the use of computer-based automation and of sound signal analysis is contrary to all that is known of Soviet weakness in this area and their desperate efforts to acquire Western expertise.

D K Brown

A drawing of the seaplane carrier Nairana *by Roger Nailer, one of the many previously unpublished illustrations in Friedman's* British Carrier Aviation, *reviewed opposite.* ▶

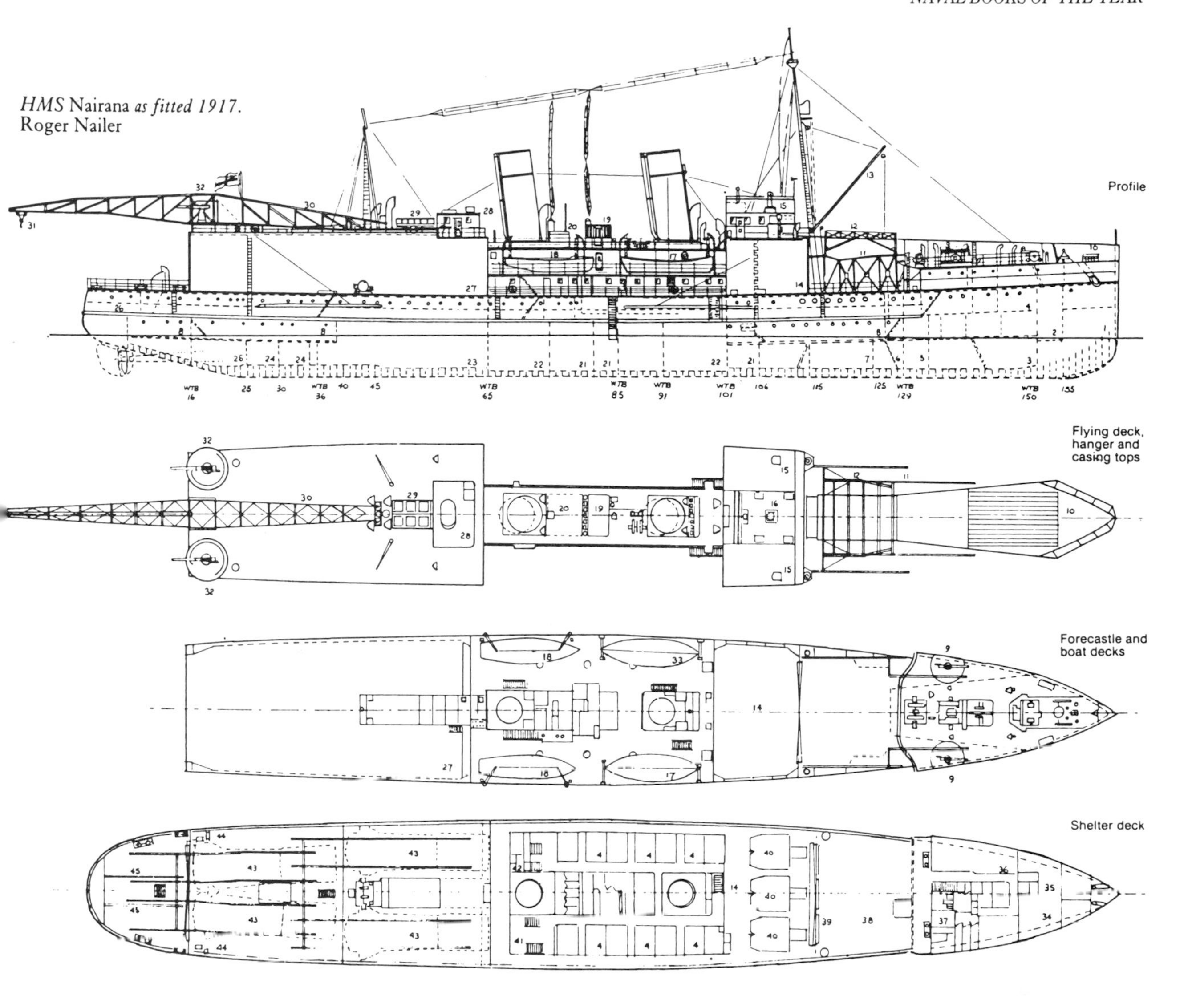

HMS Nairana *as fitted 1917.*
Roger Nailer

Norman Friedman, British Carrier Aviation: The Evolution of the Ships and their Aircraft, *published by Conway Maritime Press, 1988.*
295 x 248mm, 384 pages, 300 photographs, 100 line drawings. ISBN 0 85177 488 1. £35.00.

For his latest book Norman Friedman has culled from official records a vast mass of facts concerning the material side of British naval aviation and produced a unique fund of information on the evolution of naval aircraft and carriers from first beginnings to the *Ark Royal* of today. He covers the strategic and economic factors which governed successive staff proposals and naval programmes and links them with the resulting ship and aircraft developments. Carrier layouts and characteristics are treated in detail with appropriate plans, from initial sketch designs to fruition or rejection. Aircraft staff requirements are summarised and projects described. Much of all this will be new to readers. He shows the effects on carrier design of aircraft developments as these progressively called for upgraded catapults, arrester gear, lifts, flight deck and hangar size and stowage for fuel and weapons, until the helicopter and the Sea Harrier partially reversed the trend.

No previous author has offered more than a small fraction of this detailed coverage and inevitably there are mistakes, including some confusing passages about deck landing. Clarification may be helpful. In British terminology (and I believe in the USN) the term 'bolter' only applied when there was no crash barrier across the deck; then, if an aircraft failed to pick up an arrester wire (*eg* because the aircraft floated or bounced or the hook skipped), the pilot, realising there was no retardation, would bolt – *ie* would slam the throttles fully open as the aircraft rolled down the deck and would climb away, the process from the moment the wires were missed being called a bolter. Now consider the 'barriers up' case, which presupposes a pre-1954 straight deck carrier with a deck park forward protected by the barriers, into

Key

1 Fore peak fresh water tank	23 Engine room
2 Chain locker	24 Fresh water tank
3 Stores	25 12pdr magazine
4 Officers' cabin	26 Steering gear
5 Petrol store	27 After hangar
6 Magazine & spirit room	28 Captain's cabin
7 Shall & bomb room	29 Skylight to engine room
8 Mess deck	30 Cantilever gantry
9 12pdr LA gun	31 Traveller (carriage)
10 Flying-off deck	32 12pdr HA gun
11 Support rails for portable platform	33 28ft lifeboat & 18ft dinghy
12 Portable platform	34 RNAS ratings' mess
13 Twin-boom derrick	35 Bosun's store
14 Forward hangar	36 Lube oil store
15 24in searchlight	37 Paint room
16 Wheelhouse	38 Forecastle deck handling space
17 28ft lifeboat	39 Forward hangar shutter
18 30ft motor boat	40 Aircraft (wings folded)
19 Ship's W/T office	41 Dark room
20 RNAS W/T office	42 Signal office
21 Coal bunker	43 Seaplanes (wings folded)
22 Boiler room	44 Hoist controller
	45 Seaplane trolley rails

which the aircraft would run if it missed the wires; this would be called a barrier engagement not a bolter. Barrier prangs and bolters were both unsought whereas both the 'wave off' (ordered from the ship) and 'overshoot' (often pilot initiated) were deliberate aborts before reaching the deck.

Barrier prangs were highly expensive, although usually (like mine) injurious only to one's pride. To minimise their frequency the DLCO (batsman) was introduced at the same time as the barrier. He had a far better view of proceedings than the pilot (who could seldom see much over the engine cowling), and being an experienced specialist could accurately judge how much correction to signal to the pilot to achieve touchdown among the wires. From 1954 the mirror usurped his function in the vertical plane, and line-up could now be left to the pilot because, unlike most piston aircraft, jets afforded an adequate view of the angled centreline. However some years later the narrow operating margins of heavy jets made it prudent for the DLCO to be reinstalled, this time to monitor and if necessary to warn of major divergencies on radio. The angled deck made barriers redundant except for those rare aircraft emergencies which precluded a safe bolter (*eg* stuck wheels) or precluded arresting (stuck hook). Then, after the rest of the aircraft had landed on, the long pull-out nylon barrier would be rigged between stanchions abeam the last wire and the sick aircraft would be driven into it, seldom with much damage.

The author frequently discusses the vexed matter of the inferior performance of those British naval aircraft conceived in the 1930s. An important factor was RN insistence on carrying an Observer in fighters to navigate, as opposed to the USN practice of pilot navigation. (One wonders how Japanese Zero fighters with a potential radius of 500 miles coped?) The RN unwisely hoped that with bigger engines parity with single-seaters would soon be achieved. Another factor, he points out, was the authority of the RAF over aircraft operation, which influenced carrier characteristics and methods to suit slow-landing aircraft which operated from 1927 to 1933 without arrester gear; an evolutionary dead end.

Heavier faster-landing modern monoplanes were in fact better in many respects for deck operation, being fairly insensitive to turbulence (not bumping as the author calls it!) and usually less liable to float before touchdown or balloon from a bounce. Furthermore carriers operating them did not need to be streamlined with exaggerated round downs which wasted deck area and reduced the number of aircraft which could be operated simultaneously. The author feels that the USN may have been ruthless in maximising flight deck area, hence striking power, by ignoring streamlining; but perhaps the USN realised that a deck park would kick up turbulence anyway, and correctly judged that the aircraft of the 1940s would easily ride it. (Vortices, which generate the 'black hole' astern of angle-deck carriers, were a different problem.)

The author suggests that, over and above the space constraints suffered by armoured flight deck ships, the FAA embarked aircraft strength has always been limited by a long term doctrine favouring stowage of all aircraft in the hangar(s) with no permanent deck park. Doctrine *per se* is an un-British concept and the RN has I believe veered and hauled according to circumstance. In the period of divided control before 1937 permanent deck parking would have been blocked by the RAF on economy grounds because of the consequent need to repair barrier prangs and defects due to exposure on deck. Repairs and maintenance were RAF tasks and such potential additions would have been fiercely resisted; not least because as we know from Roskill the RAF leadership was dogmatically opposed to any expansion for *Ark Royal*. Their Lordships were sensible in concentrating first of all on the decisive battle, for control of the FAA, while concurrently fitting crash barriers, a prerequisite for deck parking, to new ships; but it is a pity that Avgas stowages were not made larger, anticipating the adoption of permanent deck parking once enough aircrew and aircraft had become available.

Once they were forthcoming full deck parks as well as hangars were, contrary to the author's impression, normal practice throughout the rest of the conventional carrier era. The flight deck: hangar stowage ratio was usually around 1:2, sometimes nearer 2:3; less than in US carriers because overall flight deck area was less, and after subtracting landing area, an irreducible commitment, disproportionately little remained; most of that was over the bow catapults which were always parked on. In order to carry viable air groups the smaller ships *Centaur* and *Hermes* were operated to very tight margins and seldom was there more than one spare deck park slot available for emergencies during final land-on.

The CAH (*Invincible*) requirement for 14 aircraft in the shed and none on deck appears a reversal; but only because at the time a forecast 14 per ship was as much as could be extracted from savagely slashed long-term costings. Aircraft and their manpower are just as difficult to finance as ships and crews (often forgotten by proponents of ingenious schemes for getting more to sea!). Sensibly, all 14 aircraft were given space below, allowing margin on top for contingencies; *Invincible* now carries 20.

As the author says, the underlying problem from the 1920s onwards was the inability of the British economy to sustain a fleet commensurate with national strategic commitments. Then as now maritime power was the prime source of strategic mobility. Although traditional elements in the RN viewed the rise of the aviators with misgivings the Admiralty was, as the author points out, quite air-minded by contemporary standards. Comparing the tonnage of carriers and battleships laid down during the 1930s the RN ratio was not inferior to the USN. The RN got less capability for its tonnage (until the Light Fleet carriers) for reasons which the author explains, although he underrates the handicap of 'dual control' from 1918 to 1937/9.

Notwithstanding caveats the book makes a fair and understanding assessment of the achievements of British naval aviation against daunting odds. The main meat is in the copious coverage of projects and designs and their rationale, and the sheer magnitude of interesting detail justifies its price. Those who know naval aviation will find things to question and correct, but like the general reader will be fascinated by the complex story of proposals and arguments and projects, some few of which eventually bore fruit in the ships and aircraft with which we were once familiar.

David Stanley

Admiral I J Galantin, USN (Ret), Take Her Deep! A Submarine Against Japan in World War II, *published by Unwin Hyman, 1988. 235 x 165mm, 262 pages, illustrated. ISBN 0 04 440258 9. £12.95.*

The author entered the US Navy in 1929 and was appointed to the command of USS *Halibut* in August 1943. He carried out five war patrols, harassing the Japanese where and whenever he found them. On her fifth and final patrol *Halibut* narrowly escaped destruction in Luzon Strait (one depth charge is thought to have exploded on the breech of the deck gun). In the main this is the story of *Halibut* during the period the author was her captain. It is a measured account of one submarine's part in the Pacific War, her successes and failures duly evaluated, whilst the routine of American submarine life is placed before us in context. In his narrative Admiral Galantin does his best to convey what it was like to fight in that war, its frustrations – the US Navy's torpedo problems are covered in some detail – and the moments of light relief.

In view of its comprehensive coverage, a valuable source, well written by one who served and led to the best of his ability. If one can find fault with the book it is that it lacks an index.

Ian Grant

Ahmet Güleryüz, Bernd Langenspiel, Die Osmanische Marine (The Ottoman Navy) 1839–1923: Volume I Torpedo Boats and Destroyers, *published by Kampmeier Druck & Verlag, Hamburg, 1988. 300 x 210mm, 176 pages, 62 halftones, 24 line drawings. ISBN 3 927330 13 2. DM68.50.*

Of all major maritime powers the navy of Ottoman Turkey is undoubtedly the most poorly represented in print, so the appearance of this book is very welcome. According to the authors, surprisingly good documentation survives from this period, including plans and photographs, and this is now becoming accessible to lay researchers for the first time. Consequently, they plan a series of volumes, each on a self-contained subject which will eventually cover all Ottoman warships of the steam era – an extremely valuable contribution to naval history.

This volume comprises a narrative account of the introduction and development of the torpedo-boat in the Ottoman Navy followed by a reasonably detailed survey of their activities in the pre-1914 Balkan wars and the First World War itself, concluding with tabular data on all the relevant Turkish torpedo craft. The history is self-confessedly pro-Turkish (which is an understandable counterweight to the usual unsympathetic treatment of their efforts in western histories), but the German influence on Ottoman efficiency is rather over-played. The parallel text is in German and English, which is a blessing since the subject is too specialised to ever justify commercial translation and so the work would not otherwise be available in English. However, the English is very crude, often ambiguous and occasionally meaningless, so the blessing is decidedly mixed.

There is an interesting collection of historic photographs, mostly reproduced very large, depicting all the types, but either the originals are very poor or the printing leaves a lot to be desired since the halftones are universally lacking in detail. The plans are better, and in one or two cases include internal arrangements. Among the less crucial, but nevertheless interesting, pieces of information is a list of translations of their names, which rival those of the Imperial Japanese Navy for poetry – they include 'Messenger of Glory' (*Şanaver*), 'Sword of the Ocean' (*Seyf-i Bahri*) and 'Gift of the Nation' (*Yadigar-i Millet*).

Despite the technical shortcomings of the book, the subject is treated in more depth than has been available previously, and both authors and publisher should be encouraged to press on with the follow-up titles in the series as quickly as possible.

Robert Gardiner

Arnold Hague, The Towns, *published by the World Ship Society, 1988. 245 x 190mm, 92 pages, 108 photographs, 1 gatefold drawing. ISBN 0 905617 48 7. £10.00 paperback.*

W J Harvey & K Turrell, Empire Tugs, *published by the World Ship Society, 1988. 245 x 190mm, 160 pages, 162 photographs, 11 plans. ISBN 0 905617 47 9. £10.00 paperback.*

Two follow-ups to John English's monograph on *The Hunts* (reviewed in *Warship* 46), taking the same basic approach, whereby a concise design history is followed by potted career histories of each vessel. *The Towns* covers the fifty US flush-decked destroyers transferred to the RN in 1940 and naturally concentrates on their wartime service, with a lot of new detail relating to their British modifications.

Empire Tugs deals with a far broader and more varied group of ships, the 147 war-built tugs that carried the *Empire-* prefix. Their important, if unsung, naval service qualifies the book for inclusion here; it is a significant move towards filling the great void in published work on British naval auxiliaries of the Second World War.

As is often the case with amateur scholarship, both books are very thoroughly compiled, and much effort has obviously been expended in searching out good photographs. Furthermore the standards of productions are far better than many society publications and so, on the whole, the photographic research has not been wasted by poorly reproduced halftones. The World Ship Society is performing a valuable role in publishing – at a reasonable compromise of cost and quality – this series of books, which are perhaps on too narrow and specialised a scale to interest a commercial publisher but are nevertheless on subjects that deserve to be publicly available.

Robert Gardiner

Paul G Halpern, The Naval War in the Mediterranean 1914–1918, *published by Allen & Unwin 1987.*
236 x 156mm, 656 pages, no illustrations.
ISBN 0 04 940088 6. £50.00.

For most people the First World War in the Mediterranean is a matter of the *Goeben* incident and the Gallipoli campaign. That it hardly seemed crucial to the participants at the time has led to its neglect by historians, but it was a far from insignificant theatre for all that. As with all authors setting sail on relatively uncharted waters, Professor Halpern is keen to prove that his voyage is really necessary, but in this case he seems entirely justified.

The great strength of the book is that it is essentially non-partisan. The author has utilised documentary sources from all the major participating nations (with the exception of Russia) and the result is a balanced review of the entire war. However, its perspective is that of governments, ministries and higher commands, so tends to concentrate on the strategic factors – traditional rivalries that bedevilled Allied co-operation, narrow national interests that dictated priorities, and so forth. Actual engagements are noted – particularly if they influenced strategic thought – but there are no detailed blow-by-blow accounts of battles. Nevertheless, a clearer picture emerges of a fascinating series of little known campaigns in the Adriatic, the Straits of Otranto and the Eastern Aegean. Naturally, much of the book is given over to the increasingly important submarine war, in which the British were forced to take a hand despite having ceded primary responsibility for the Mediterranean to the French in 1914.

Material factors are given less attention, but in passing the reader with a technical bent can pick up a lot of interesting background information on how the various navies, and even individual warships, performed – the great superiority of German over Austrian submarines is apparent, for example, while the efforts of both the French and Italian navies were hampered by the lack of fast light cruisers and seaworthy flotilla craft. Overall it is academic history at its best, with the bonus of being lucid and readable.

[**Note**: this book was published in 1987 but has not been mentioned previously in *Warship*; it is too important to be omitted entirely, so is noticed here.]

Robert Gardiner

D G Harris, F H Chapman: The First Naval Architect and his Work, *published by Conway Maritime Press, 1989.*
270 x 200m, 256 pages, 150 photographs, 35 drawings.
ISBN 0 851177 486 5. £20.00.

Chapman is best known today for his great treatise on shipbuilding, quickly translated into French, English and Russian as the text book for the new generation of naval architects. Harris' book tells us much more about Chapman as a man, as a successful designer of warships and as an innovator in modernising Dockyards.

He was born in 1721, the son of a British naval officer who had joined the Royal Swedish Navy in 1716 and an English mother, herself the daughter of a shipwright. He was able to spend many years educating and training

Although not widely appreciated outside Sweden, one of Chapman's principal achievements was his work for the Inshore Fleet, for which he created – in effect – the world's first purpose-designed amphibious warfare ships. These included vessels for the transportation of horses, and, illustrated below, boats for landing field artillery.

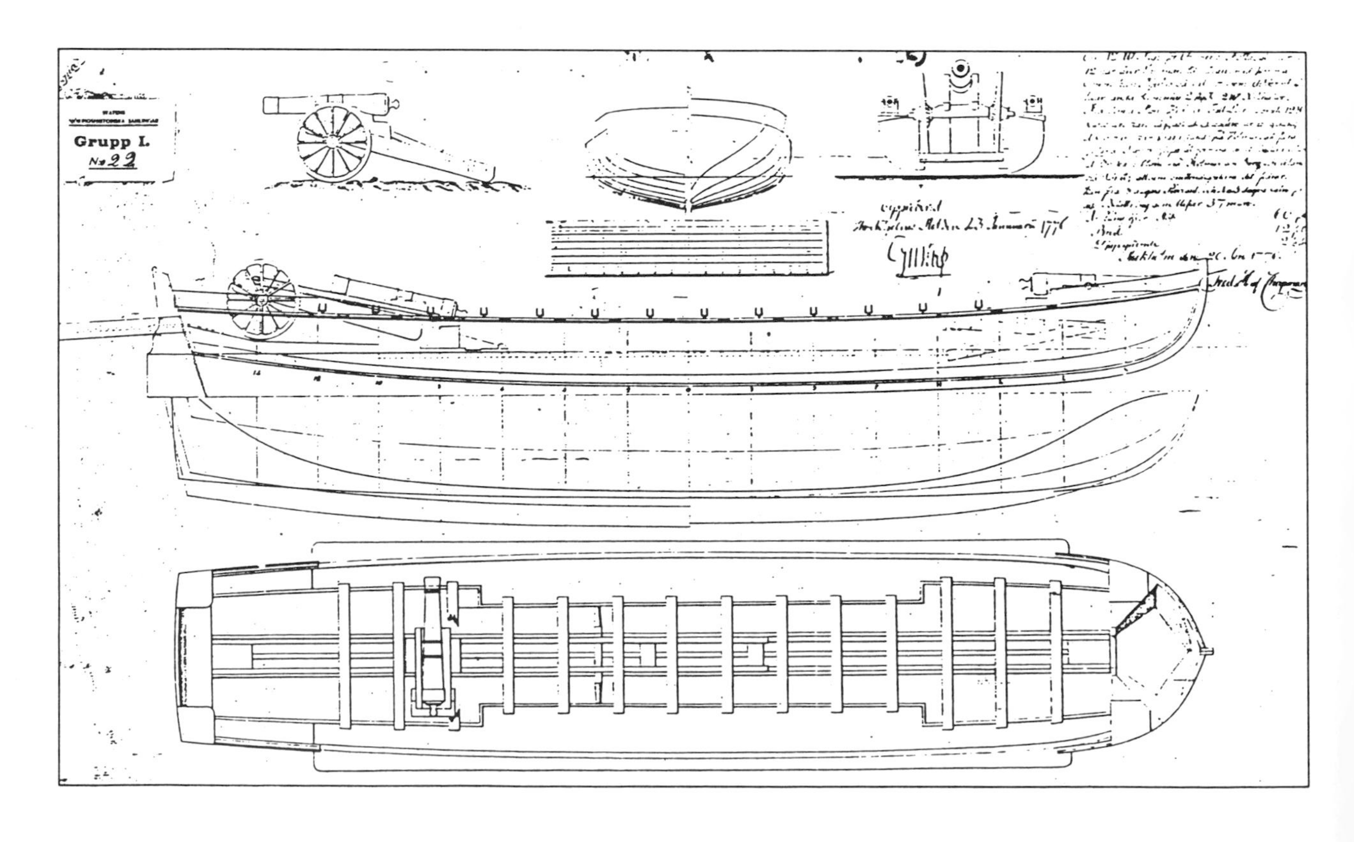

himself in different aspects of his chosen profession. At the age of fifteen he went to sea for three years and later worked in London as a ship's carpenter. From 1748 he was part owner of the Goteborg shipyard which he left to study mathematics for two years. He then came to England again where his study of the Royal Dockyards led to his being arrested as a foreign agent.

By 1757 he was Assistant Shipwright at the main dockyard, Karlskrona, and in 1760 he began his first major design task. He was to design a range of ships to operate in the shallow waters round the islands of Sweden. These included shallow draught frigates, galleys, gunboats and transports for guns and horses. They seem to have been very successful, though not surprisingly, the frigates were slow.

He rose rapidly in the naval service, finally winning a long battle with Sheldon, the leading traditional shipwright. There were a number of competitive trials between ships designed by Chapman and Sheldon and, like all such sailing trials, the results were inconclusive. He constructed many fine and useful buildings in the yard at Karlskrona – including a distinguished residence for himself. Mainly after 1780, he designed 16 ships-of-the-line and 12 frigates for his navy and these were generally seen as successful.

His fame properly rests in his books and scientific papers and I would suggest that the author is too clear cut in his judgement between the traditionalists and the scientists *at that time.* The future lay with science but at the end of the eighteenth century there was no understanding of the loads experienced by a ship or of structural design; that had to wait for Robert Seppings. The 'theory' of hydrodynamics was totally wrong and though the metacentric theory of stability was well understood, no one had thought how to calculate the position of the centre of gravity. (Chapman confuses the issue by using centre of gravity for what is now called the centre of bouyancy.) No wonder the experienced shipwrights were not over-keen on science. It is clear that British shipwrights were well aware of theoretical work as French books on the subject were translated and published in English quite quickly. The evidence for the low standard of British design is insubstantial and needs re-examination; certainly, the stories that British ships were slower than those of other countries are ill-founded.

The book is well written and well illustrated. It uses Swedish sources not readily available to most writers and covers some little known wars in the Baltic. It is recommended as a fine account of a little known but very influential man.

D K Brown

Richard Holmes, The World Atlas of Warfare: Military Innovation that Changed the Course of History, *published by Mitchell Beazley, 1988.*
300 x 235mm, 304 pages, profusely illustrated with photographs and drawings.
ISBN 0 85533 7184 4. £17.95.

A substantial compilation put together by Dr Richard Holmes, Senior Lecturer at the Royal Military Academy, Sandhurst with the assistance of eight other well known contributors. Within the constraints imposed by 293 pages of text, they have covered the art and technique of warfare from the earliest times to the Falklands Campaign and the Gulf War. The illustrations are excellent, the maps clear and the photographs judiciously selected. There are 20 chapters in all, each providing a general view, either of a particular period in history or, beginning with World War I, an individual theatre of operations. Each technological advance is discussed and its impact on the course of events assessed. Despite the vast scale of their canvas the contributors have succeeded in reducing it to manageable proportions, and there is much to stimulate the mind in the text. The contemporary material is especially valuable. As is inevitable with a work of this kind there are a small number of minor errors, but the overall impression is excellent. A selective bibliography is provided and a comprehensive index. At the price, value for money.

Ian Grant

John Keegan, The Price of Admiralty, *published by Hutchinson, 1988.*
235 x 150mm, 292 pages, 39 photos, 6 maps.
ISBN 0 09 173771 0. £14.95.

The author seeks to tell the story of 'how men fought at sea' by considering the Trafalgar campaign, Jutland, Midway and the battle of the Atlantic. As a former senior lecturer at Sandhurst and now defence correspondent of the *Daily Telegraph* one expects a new oulook on these well known events.

The Trafalgar section contradicts, rightly, the idea that the big gun at sea was a ship-killer. The sinking of a wooden warship was a rare event. He also makes a fascinating comparison between the power of Napoleon's artillery at Waterloo – 366 guns from 6 to 12pdrs – with that in Nelson's fleet – 2232 guns from 12 to 68pdrs. He does not mention the much greater rate of fire of the British fleet, about 5:2, due both to superior metallurgy and better drill.

The treatment of the later battles is conventional and fails to take account of more recent re-examination of the evidence. In consequence there are many errors which seriously weaken the value of the conclusions. For example, *Seydlitz* at Dogger Bank was not hit on the roof of an after turret but on the barbette and the Germans did not materially alter their anti-flash measures before Jutland. The conclusion that German naval technology was superior to British is an overstatement; they were superior in two vital aspects, shell design and propellant safety (see J Campbell's *Jutland*, referenced by the author).

In the build up to Midway there are the usual stories of British Admirals' opposition to aircraft carriers, largely refuted in Friedman's book, reviewed in this issue. The reconnaissance before the battle and the failure of *Tone*'s seaplane is given very sparse coverage. USS *Nautilus* did not sink *Soryu* with three hits; post-war research, readily available, shows that she fired 4 torpedoes at *Kaga* of which one hit but failed to explode. On page 238 there is mention of experiments with depth charge throwers; these had been in service since the First World War.

D K Brown

Paul Kemp, Malta Convoys 1940–43 *(Warships Illustrated No 14), published by Arms & Armour Press, 1988.*
245 x 185mm, 64 pages, 122 black and white photographs, Paperback.
ISBN 0 85368 922 9. £4.95

It must be said at once, that although of historical interest, very few of the photographs contained in this selection appear to be of good quality. Also one questions the use of views of Italian warships taken after the surrender, and of pre-war views of British units, particularly *Nelson*, taken in 1937 at Portsmouth. This shortcoming may be related to the extensive use of material from the Imperial War Museum in preference to casting the net somewhat wider. On balance, an opportunity missed.

Ian Grant

D W Knox (ed), The United States Naval Railway Batteries in France, *published by Naval Historical Center, Washington DC, 1988.*
230 x 146mm, 110 pages, illustrated. Paperback.
ISBN 0 945274 00 9. No price quoted.

This slim publication is a long overdue reprint of the sixth of the seven monographs dealing with the US Navy's participation in World War I, published by the Office of Naval Records between 1920 and 1923.

The need for these long range mobile weapons first became apparent to the Chief of the Bureau of Ordnance during the summer of 1917, when the German Armies began to threaten the Channel ports, the loss of which would have been catastrophic to the Allied cause. The defending British guns were far out-ranged by the German Navy's land batteries. Initially the weapons were offered to the British, but owing to the changing conditions in the threatened 'Dune' Sector in Belgium, they were unable to name a port of disembarkation with any degree of confidence.

They were then offered to General Pershing, and it was at his urgent request that five 14in/50 calibre Mark IV naval guns, manned by 525 officers and men, complete with their own locomotives and special trains, were prepared for service as railway batteries in the short time of less than ten months between concept and the first round fired at an enemy target in France.

The construction of five railway mountings and complete train equipments for each gun was approved on 26 November 1917 and the contracts were awarded in mid-February. The first naval railway mounting was completed on 25 April 1918 and proof fired with complete success. Construction and shipment overseas went forward without delay, and the complete equipments arrived at St Nazaire between 8 July and 15 August. Following assembly, despite the mislaying of the working drawings, the first two trains left the port on 18 and 19 August respectively. Battery No 1 went into action at Soissons on 11 September, and all five were in position by the 25th. From then on until the armistice they moved along the front pounding German railheads, ammunition dumps, stores assembly points and troop concentrations at long range.

The monograph is in two parts, the first tells the story of the batteries, whilst the second deals with the professional and technical aspects. An absorbing account and a salutary reminder that it was the intervention of the United States that brought the Allies victory in 1918.

Ian Grant

Derek G Law, The Royal Navy in World War Two: An Annotated Bibliography, *published by Greenhill Books, 1988.*
243 x 160mm, 306 pages.
ISBN 1 85367 002 2. £25.00

The compiler of this extremely handy reference source is the Librarian of King's College, London and an *ex officio* Trustee of the Liddell Hart Centre for Military Archives.

In scope the work covers the operational histories, campaign histories and biographies of the Royal Navy, the Dominion Navies and the Allied Navies, excluding the United States. It is conveniently broken down into four sections, *viz*: Campaign Histories, Allied Unit Histories, The Axis Forces, Technical Studies and Miscellanea. Each heading covers a number of sub-headings, some 30 in total, dealing with all aspects of the war at sea including small sections on anthologies, art and poetry, war correspondents and fiction. There are three indexes based on authors, book titles and ship names respectively. This reviewer who must have read well over half of all the naval books published in the UK during and since World War II, searched his memory at random for titles and authors, and was gratified to discover that all were listed with helpful annotations. A must for all those interested in the subject, but rather expensive at £25.00.

Ian Grant

Lloyds Register, Warship Hull Design Enquiry, *published by HMSO, 1988.*
298 x 210mm, 302 pages, illustrated with drawings and charts. Paperback.
ISBN 0 11 772600 1. £15.00

This most exhaustive study was commissioned to resolve the 'short fat v long thin' frigate controversy once and for all. That the members of the Inquiry left no stone unturned in their determination to be completely impartial is evident from the report. The basic premise that the hull forms favoured by many designers of small working craft could be scaled up to produce a warship with characteristics superior to those of the MoD Navy Type 23 design proved untenable in the light of the expert advice placed before the Inquiry.

The Inquiry found no reason to disagree with the MoD's preference for the Type 23. Indeed they went further, stating that they were firmly of the opinion that the construction of a prototype based on a 'Sirius' hull form for evaluation was unnecessary.

The report is well laid out, easy to follow and a model of conciseness. Including the introduction it consists of eight chapters supported by ten appendices covering procedural matters, the ship design process, assessment of the original S90 design proposal, development of an S90 Geosim design, the S102, assessment of the S102 design, consideration of Thornycroft, Giles and Associates Ltd response to the S102 design (S115 proposal), principal conclusions and recommendations.

Ian Grant

Peter Nailor, The Nassau Connection: The Organisation and Management of the British POLARIS Project, *published by HMSO, 1988.*
264 x 156mm, 150 pages.
ISBN 0 11 772526 9. £10.00

'The Polaris programme was, by any standard of comparison a significant undertaking. ... it was completed within the required timescale and within the forecast budget.' Peter Nailor was part of the team and tells the story of this successful project from the point of view of politics and high-level administration with only passing attention to technical and managerial matters.

It is a fascinating story, well told; beginning in the confusion when first the British Blue Streak rocket was cancelled and then its intended successor, the American Skybolt. The author criticises the Navy for not pressing the case for Polaris earlier but they were afraid of the future drain on resources, particularly of technicians.

Agreement in principle for the supply of the Polaris system to the UK was reached at the Nassau conference in December 1962 but this left many major points undecided. Should the RN use the A2 missile or the later A3? Should they be carried in dedicated missile boats or in hybrid attack boats with 8 missiles? There was even more uncertainty over what the agreement meant in financial terms. There were quite legitimate disagreements over the UK share of research costs and over the way in which costs were averaged over a long production run.

The high level organisation was planned by Admiral Le Fanu and put under Rear-Admiral Mackenzie as Chief Polaris Executive, reporting to the Board. The Director Polaris Technical (DPT) was Rowland Baker RCNC. Nailor brings out some of the character of this brilliant but unusual man but fails to point out that his unique command of language was learnt during his upbringing on a Thames barge!

The staffing arrangements were unusual, with some senior men entirely part of the Executive, some full time professional staff having dual responsibility to the DPT and to their 'Tribal Chief' and others designated to Polaris only part time. It all worked due to the dedication of all concerned and due to the feeling that the Executive got things done and that the DPT was on your side. This showed even in little things; DPT got the first Xerox machine, won authority to phone the USA without getting permission for each call and could even book its own flights.

Management control was clear and effective. Network scheduling had been brought in by Baker in the Dreadnought project and he introduced the more sophisticated PERT system for Polaris, backed by his own brand of 'management by terror'.

It worked. The first boat, *Resolution*, was accepted on 2 October 1967 and the last just over two years later on 4 December 1969 – and it is still working. Anyone involved in a large Government project should read this book and others will find the story of this great British achievement fascinating. One is tempted to ask for more; what, for example, was the effect on other projects of the priority given to Polaris in terms of resources, particularly skilled staff?

D K Brown

Kenneth Poolman, Allied Escort Carriers of World War Two in Action, *published by Blandford Press, 1988.*
275 x 210mm, 272 pages approx. 340 photographs, many maps and diagrams.
ISBN 0 7137 1221 X. £22.50

The only complaint one can make about this excellent book is the way that the title is printed on the cover. The last two words are in such small type that it seems to be a book about the ships rather then about the actions of their aircraft. It is a rather more serious work than some of the author's earlier works but is just as readable.

It follows the aircrews flying from British and USN escort carriers from the introduction of HMS *Audacity* in September 1941 through the Battle of the Atlantic to final victory, USS *Guadalcanal* even capturing *U-505*. The machinery and petrol supply problems of the early American-built escorts are covered as is the production of the Kaiser carriers which were much better ships and, understandably, kept by the USN for their own service. These small ships operated aircraft in support of the Russian convoys and in most of the invasions; North Africa, Salerno, South of France and in a successful and little known Aegean operation. They laid mines in Norwegian waters and attacked the *Tirpitz*. The USN carriers fought at all the main landings – Tarawa, Kwajalein, Iwo Jima, Okinawa etc. In the Philippines operation they even found themselves in a gun duel with Japanese battleships. They suffered from the suicide bomber but exacted a heavy price on their attackers.

The illustrations are particularly good. Most are original and many are dramatic action shots. The author has made good use of private collections and though, in a few cases there is some loss of quality, there is a great gain in realism. At first sight the number of photos of deck crashes may upset readers but the text makes it clear that these tragic events were an all too common feature of escort carrier life and hence must be covered.

There seem to be few errors: one notes the omission of *Pretoria Castle* from the list of British ships (she was listed as an escort carrier though serving as a deck landing training ship); on page 183 it is claimed that *Haguro* was 'designed by Hiraga to comply with the 10,000-ton limit'; in fact she was designed for 11,500 in breach of the Treaties (a constructor can do a lot with an extra 15 per cent); the B bomb was a very different weapon from the Mk 24 'mine' – *Fido*. Overall it is a very readable and well researched history of escort carrier operations, a short but glorious interlude in two navies.

D K Brown

J P M Showell, U-Boat Command and the Battle of the Atlantic, *published by Conway Maritime Press, 1989.*
240 x 184mm, 224 pages, 150 photographs, 14 maps.
ISBN 0 85177 487 3. £18.00

This is the first book in the English language to discuss the overall story of the Battle of the Atlantic from the viewpoint of the German Command. The author, son of a U-boat man, and a fluent German speaker has made good use of German documents including Doenitz' diaries.

It is clear that U-boat Command had many more difficulties than is generally realised. Doenitz as Commodore, U-boats had limited authority and none over design, training or policy. Until he became Commander-in-Chief in 1943, Doenitz was frequently at odds with the High Command.

German torpedo problems were serious and took a long while to cure. Conventional torpedoes ran deep and both the magnetic and percussion detonators were faulty. The acoustic homing torpedo (T5 or Gnat) brought new problems and at least two U-boats were sunk by their own weapons. The boats, too, had reliability problems, particularly in the early days. French workers were found to be quicker and more reliable than German. Severe losses of personnel led to reduction in training time and in realism. It is almost incredible that they failed to realise that their codes had been broken, particularly in the light of their own success in breaking RN codes.

In view of these and other problems it is remarkable that the U-boats were able to keep up such a heavy pressure and that, with a very few exceptions, morale remained so high.

The book is very readable and, despite its deliberately one-sided outlook, it is the best short account of the Battle yet published. The numerous photographs are mainly action shots and are enhanced by unusually clear and comprehensive captions. The author has clearly taken a great deal of trouble to identify the time, place and any unusual features in the photograph.

D K Brown

Claus Bergen's atmospheric painting of U-103, *the cover of Showell's latest book.*

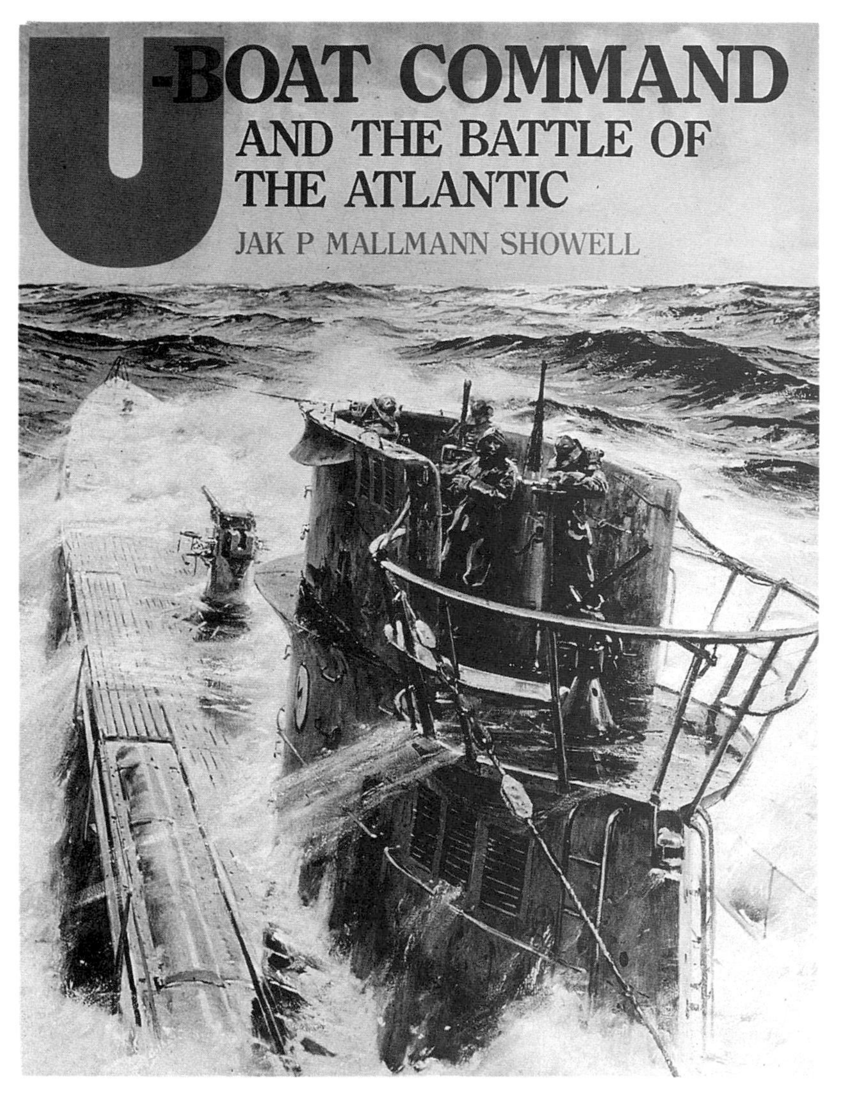

Jon Tetsuro Sumida, In Defence of Naval Supremacy: Finance, Technology and British Naval Policy 1889–1914, *published by Unwin Hyman, 1989.*

232 x 156mm, 400 pages, 8 photographs, 11 line drawings. ISBN 0 04 445104 0. £38.00.

By any standards this is a remarkable book. First of all, it is written by an academic historian who not only understands the technical details of warship design but actually delights in them; secondly, its argument suggests that apparently trivial technicalities – in this case, fire control – can have enormous impact on historical events (long understood by warship enthusiasts but rarely acknowledged at this level of scholarship); and finally, it offers a highly original version of that most significant of naval revolutions, the introduction of the *Dreadnought.*

In brief, the author's thesis is that financial restrictions in the face of growing overseas rivalry forced the Royal Navy to consider radical new technology. However, Fisher regarded the *Dreadnought* as only the first stage, most of his erratic genius being concentrated on another 'secret weapon' – the Battlecruiser. But if speed was to dominate an engagement, there had to be a method of hitting at very long range, which in turn implied a reliable fire control system. Sumida believes that one potentially existed in the arrangement proposed by Arthur Hungerford Pollen, but due to ignorance, professional jealousies and faction within the navy, it was never adopted – with dire consequences for the whole fleet in the ensuing war, particularly for the battlecruisers at Jutland.

Whether the whole argument holds water can be left to the individual reader's judgement, but the meat of the book is a detailed account of Pollen's battle with the Admiralty. This offers many insights into the workings of the RN at this period but also suggests that the reputations of various senior officers could do with reassessment: some, like Beatty, for the better; others, like Jellicoe, for the worse. In passing, it also gives an admirably clear explication of the subtleties of fire control, and is worth reading for this alone; all the constituent parts of both Pollen's and the competing Dreyer systems are described in detail, including the improvements from one mark number to the next.

Pollen's instruments were very advanced for their time and form an important step in the development of the analogue computer. Nevertheless, he was unable to persuade the Admiralty to adopt his approach to fire control, and significant parts of the system remained unbuilt, although examples of his rate and deflection machine (the Argo Clock) did go to sea. The book concludes with a brief look at the actual fighting up to and including Jutland and produces evidence indicating that, all other things being equal, the Argo-equipped vessels made marginally better shooting on the day.

The question remains as to whether the whole Pollen system would have worked as well as its inventor so strenuously maintained. Naturally, Sumida is convinced of the superiority of Pollen's theoretical approach and the greater sophistication of his company's equipment. If he is right then the Royal Navy missed a golden opportunity.

Robert Gardiner

Dan van der Vat, The Atlantic Campaign, *published by Hodder & Stoughton, 1988.*
424 pages, 55 illustrations, 4 maps.
ISBN 0 340 37751 8. £17.95.

In his preface the author says that the book is aimed at the general reader and claims that it differs from most of the previous surveys of the campaign in that it is written in the light of the disclosure of Ultra, that it brings out the major Canadian contribution more clearly than earlier books and that it shows how study of the First World War 'throws light on the successes – and mistakes – of the second'.

The book opens with a necessarily brief survey of the First World War submarine campaign and goes through the sorry story of the Admiralty's reluctance to adopt convoys. The value of aircraft is mentioned but rather briefly. In view of his declared aims it is surprising that the author does not attempt to use these lessons in forecasting the operations of the next war. It is not easy, as shown by Robert Grant in his classic *U-Boats Destroyed* (neither this, nor Grant's later, and important *U-Boat Intelligence*, are listed in the sources). There follows a lengthy and interesting discussion of pre-war plans and technology in Britain and Germany, with brief mention of parallel US work. The clandestine German submarine design programme is well covered.

The Battle of the Atlantic is dealt with in chronological order with a short review at the end of each phase of some 6–9 months. Most of the major actions are described, including slightly peripheral operations such as the St Nazaire raid and the Arctic convoys. These events are clearly set in context with mention of shortage of resources, food rationing etc. The Tizard mission is described, though strangely, without mentioning the priceless gift to the USA of the cavity magnetron.

It is interesting that the author puts the turning point of the battle as July 1942, when Allied (mainly American) shipbuilding began to exceed losses. There were terrible battles and disasters still to come but the issue was no longer in doubt. There is no discussion of how close the UK came to defeat in the Atlantic.

The author considers that the value of Ultra has been over-rated and, when the ability to read signals was lost for much of 1942 it made little difference. However, by 1942 as a result of earlier interceptions German planning was fairly well understood and informed guesses were often right. Most of Roskill's Official History remains valid as he had access to much Ultra material and, with hindsight, there are plenty of hints about 'information received'. The claim that earlier writers have not paid proper tribute to the Canadian contribution seems unfair: there have been two excellent academic works and at least one good book has been published as a paperback in the UK, suggesting fairly large sales (Lamb's *Corvette Navy*, not referenced). Roskill is a history of the RN but there is full and frequent mention of the RCN.

In general the author has achieved much of his three aims. In a moderate sized and priced book he has covered all the main operations and put them in context. The picture would have been clearer if more use had been made of maps to show how the battle area and sinkings moved, and of graphs, bar charts etc to show how sinkings and new building of U-boats and merchant ships compared.

The book is very weak on technical aspects: more than once Asdic (Sonar) is described as using a 'radio beam', the hedgehog projectile is described as a depth charge despite its contact fuse and, though the value of ship borne HF/DF is mentioned, the author does not say that the technical problems were so difficult that the Germans thought them insoluble.

There is a marked tendency to praise German technology and ignore Allied achievements: the 'pocket battleship was a triumph of the German shipbuilder's art, a demonstration of how to get a quart into a pint pot'. Since the Germans had cheated and the pint pot was about a litre, there was no technological magic there; the pocket battleships were not successful, vibration made gunnery control difficult, and *Graf Spee*'s armour was easily penetrated by *Exeter*'s 8in shells. *Bismarck* is said to have had 'the world's most effective armour' but postwar tests on plates from *Tirpitz* showed that its quality was almost as good as British armour but so badly arranged that *Bismarck* lost her fire control communications in the first quarter of an hour of her last battle. Most of the shells which hit *Prince of Wales* were duds. In view of this bias it is surprising that there is little or no mention of the two great German achievements, their superb passive sonars (Hackmann's *Seek and Strike* is not referenced) and the major German lead in pressure hull design theory.

Factual errors abound and are so numerous that only a few can be pointed out here.

The Liberty ship was not an old design dating from 1897 with equally 'venerable' engines, but was based on a very recent and successful design from Sunderland.

The Boards of Inquiry into the loss of the *Hood* did not find that a 15in shell penetrated the 15in magazine. She was not 48,000 tons unladen and nor did she carry 6in guns.

Audacity was not converted from a large and fast merchant ship; she was of 5537grt and 15kts and she did not operate Swordfish.

There are so many errors, some small, even trivial, but irritating and in total seriously degrading the value of the book and lowering the reader's confidence in the author. The list of sources is sparce and as well as those already noted one would expect to see Gretton's books mentioned. A real popular history of the Battle of the

Atlantic is still needed and, as a first step, it is hoped that RN Historical Branch will organise a conference in 1991.

D K Brown

Michael Wilson, Destination Dardanelles; The Story of HM Submarine E-7, *published by Leo Cooper, 1988.*
242 x 164mm, 191 pages, illustrated.
ISBN 0 85052 885 2. £13.95.

Based on the hitherto unpublished diaries of Lieutenant Oswald Hallifax, this account covers his thirteen months service in *E-7* until he was invalided home in early September 1915, as the result of severe burns received when setting fire to a small Turkish steamer with petrol in Rodosto Bay, Sea of Marmora. Himself a former submariner, the author has matched the contemporary flavour of the diaries with other research, and his narrative forms a well rounded account of life in a World War I British submarine, in the North Sea, the Mediterranean and up the Straits. Much of the ground has been covered before, but the diaries provide a fresh viewpoint and the end result is an enjoyable and informative read. Recommended.

Ian Grant

SHORT NOTICES

'Anatomy of the Ship Series': Sergio Bellabarba, The Royal Yacht Caroline 1749
John Mckay, The Armed Transport Bounty
Janusz Skulski, The Battleship Yamato
all published by Conway Maritime Press Ltd, 1989.
*Each: 240 x 254mm, 120 (*Yamato *192) pages, approx 20 photographs and 300 (*Yamato *600) line drawings.*
Caroline *ISBN 0 85177 496 2. £15.00*
Bounty *ISBN 0 85177 502 0. £15.00*
Yamato *ISBN 0 85177 490 3. £20.00*

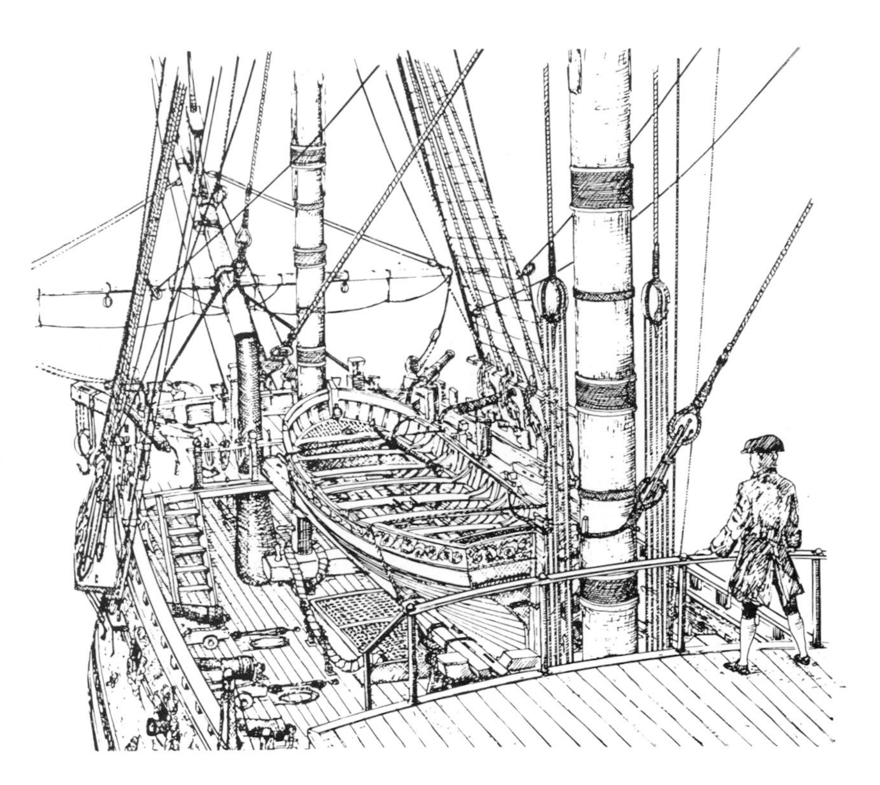

An illustration from The Royal Yacht Caroline.

The latest in this well established series cover the most sumptuously decorated of eighteenth century royal yachts, a small converted merchantman made eternally famous by a mutiny, and the largest battleship of all time. Assuming that the last will be of greatest interest to the readers of this review, it is only necessary to say that it is the most extensive yet, and the quality of the draughtmanship is second to none. Despite containing an astounding degree of detail on a ship whose documentation was supposedly destroyed in 1945, there are gaps – most noticeably the machinery and internal details for which no sources can be found – but the concentration on the external is unlikely to bother the modelmaker who is the prime market for these books.

Jean Boudriot, The Seventy-Four Gun Ship, *Volume 4, published by Jean Boudriot Publications, 1988.*
310 x 230mm, 394 pages, 17 colour plates, 167 line drawings.
ISBN 2 903178 17 8. £65.00

The fourth and final volume of this monumental work is devoted to matters of manning, life on board, navigation and shiphandling. The remarkable illustrations look as fresh as they did in the original French edition and the translation, by David Roberts, is highly competent. There is so much on so many topics relating to the sailing warship in this series that it seems churlish to complain, but they are decidedly over-produced and could have been published with little loss of effect for half the price.

Mike Critchley, British Warships and Auxiliaries, *published by Maritime Books, 1989.*
*210 x 148mm, 112 pages, c*120 illustrations.
ISBN 0 907771 41 6. £4.50

The latest edition of this useful 'spotter's' guide to the ships (and aircraft) of the RN. Well illustrated but the data is very basic and could be made far more detailed for little additional effort.

One of the author's exquisite line drawings – a sheer, or masting, hulk – from volume 4 of The Seventy-Four Gun Ship. ▶

René J Francillon, Tonkin Gulf Yacht Club: US Carrier Operations off Vietnam, *published by Conway Maritime Press Ltd, 1988.*
270 x 200mm, 224 pages, 160 illustrations.
ISBN 0 85177 484 9. £20.00

One of the finest aviation writers of his generation, Francillon has here turned his attention to the naval air war off Vietnam. The book contains some interesting narrative (particularly relating to *Coral Sea*'s part in the war) but the strength of the work lies in a superb feat of data-compilation, reproduced as appendices. These give details of every carrier combat cruise (dates, squadrons carried, their aircraft, victories and losses) and the aircraft of Task Force 77 (units, their carriers, tail codes and deployment dates), combined with tabular data on the planes themselves. The book is heavily illustrated but the photos are curiously devoid of drama – this may reflect an aviation historian's preference for good formal portraits of aircraft, or maybe for the US Navy the war did not seem quite so immediate.

John Franklin, Navy Board Ship Models 1650–1750, *published by Conway Maritime Press Ltd, 1989.*
295 x 248mm, 200 pages, 166 photographs (16 in colour), 220 line drawings.
ISBN 0 85177 454 7. £25.00

Since the official 'Admiralty', 'Dockyard' or 'Navy Board' model is primary source of information on seventeenth (and even early eighteenth) century warship design, the significance of this book is far wider than merely model-maker interest. The second half is a catalogue of some 25 models, analysed, sketched and photographed in depth, with some perceptive remarks, about their construction and relationship to the full size prototype. However, the lengthy introduction is even more valuable since it is the first book to pose – and answer – various highly pertinent questions about the *raison d'être* of these models, their role in the design process, and the reasons for the apparently stylised convention used for the framing.

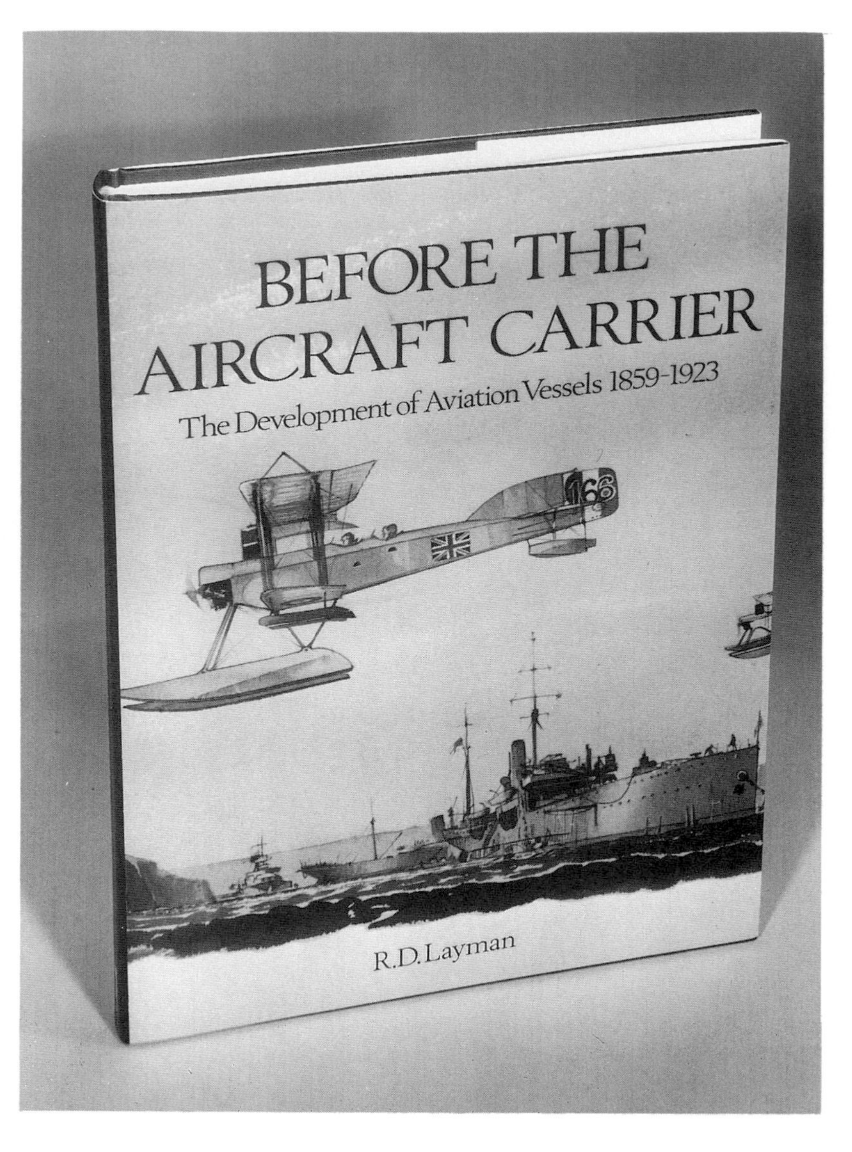

Dr D G Kiely, Naval Surface Weapons, *published by Brassey's, 1988.*

250 x 170mm, 136 pages, 46 illustrations.
ISBN 0 08 036689 9
(0 08 036688 0 paperback).
£19.95 (£9.95 paperback)

Volume 6 in the 'Sea Power' series, this title is a companion to *Naval Electronic Warfare* reviewed in *Warship* 48, and the same general favourable impression persists. However, the paucity of reference to the weapon systems of the superpowers must cast doubt on the balance of the survey. Nevertheless, for the non-technical reader seeking a brief overview of the intricate workings of modern weapons on surface ships, this is a good introduction.

R D Layman, Before the Aircraft Carrier: The Development of Aviation Vessels 1849–1922, *published by Conway Maritime Press, 1989.*

270 x 200mm, 128 pages, 125 illustrations,
ISBN 0 85177 516 0. £15.00

Apart from the better known seaplane carriers and early aircraft ships, this book chronicles some of the world's most obscure warships, including balloon transports, catapult trials ships, and a pair of paddle-drive Humber ferries converted for anti-Zeppelin duties in the North Sea. Surprisingly, virtually all these ships (and many of their aircraft) are illustrated, although many of the photos are of poor quality. The information is arranged like the *Conway's Fighting Ships* series, to which it forms a sort of appendix.

Michael A Palmer, Origins of the Maritime Strategy: American Naval Strategy in the First Postwar Decade, *published by the US Department of the Navy's Naval Historical Center, Washington 1988.*

240 x 168mm, 152 pages, 34 illustrations. $7.50 paperback

The first in what the Naval Historical Center plans to make a 'Contributions to Naval History' series, this volume sets out to show that the current Maritime Strategy is not new, but a restatement of postwar policy. The reader might well be suspicious of the independence of this kind of 'history', but on a purely descriptive level it is a revealing insight into a decade that formed international attitudes almost to the present day.

Gordon Smith, Battles of the Falklands War, *published by Ian Allan, 1989.*

235 x 170mm, 128 pages, 16 photographs, 40 maps.
ISBN 0 7110 1792 1. £13.95

Is there anything more to be said about the Falklands War? Not until a lot more original documentation is released; but this seems to be no bar to many writers and publishers. There is nothing new in this book, but it is a competent compilation of data, and the forty maps are a useful summary of the state of play at various stages, during the campaign.

Peter C Smith, Battleship Royal Sovereign (and her Sister Ships), *published by William Kimber, 1988.*
230 x 154mm, 208 pages, 16 plate pages.
ISBN 0 7183 0704 6. £12.95

Despite the after-thought of the subtitle, this is essentially a narrative of the *Royal Sovereign* and mostly her Second World War career at that. As with many of Peter C Smith's books it is quite readable, but patchy, depending heavily on the anecdotes he has been able to glean from surviving members of her crews. The high spot is probably the comic-opera transfer of the ship to the Soviet Navy, but the amused superiority of the British involved rings rather hollow in the light of subsequent Russian achievement at sea.

Robert F Sumrall (with drawings by Tom Walkowiak), Iowa Class Battleships: Their Design, Weapons and Equipment, *published by Conway Maritime Press, 1988.*
295 x 248mm, 200 pages, 250 photographs (30 in colour), 25 line drawings.
ISBN 0 85177 479 2. £25.00

A suitably large monograph for such impressive ships, this book concentrates on the technicalities of their design, armament and equipment. Sumrall has served aboard *Iowa* and is particularly good on the weapons and fire control; he also has a splendid photo library from which the very best has been selected, covering the whole career of the ships from the drawing board to the present.

Stefan Terzibaschitsch, Geleitschiffe der US Navy, *published by Koehlers, Herford, 1988.*
270 x 210mm, 248 pages, 250 photographs and line drawings.
ISBN 3 7822 0457 3. DM98.00

The latest volume in Terzibaschitsch's familiar series covers escorts from the Patrol Frigates to the Destroyer Escorts of the *Claud Jones* class. These books emphasise visual appearance changes which works well enough with larger ships, but tends to be less than comprehensive when applied to the myriad of small variations in lesser vessels. Most of the previous books of this series have been translated, so the reader can probably afford to wait for English language publication.

Stefan Terzibaschitsch, Aircraft Carriers of the US Navy, *published by Conway Maritime Press, 1989.*
297 x 212mm, 352 pages, 385 photographs, 40 line drawings.
ISBN 0 85177 515 2. £25.00

A revised second edition of the work first published in 1979. Although concentrating on new ships, there are changes relating to all ships in service during the last 10 years. The new photographs could be better.

M J Whitley, Destroyers of World War Two, *published by Arms & Armour Press, 1988.*
245 x 240mm, 320 pages, 400 illustrations.
ISBN 0 85368 910 5. £29.95

In the same almost square format employed by this publisher for most of their naval reference titles, this book is something of a departure for the author, who up to now has concentrated on German warships. However, it has not involved him in any original research, being essentially a compilation of data from published sources, although it is competently executed, in reasonable detail, and all-embracing – including all the close relations of the fleet destroyer, variously termed destroyer escorts, escort destroyers and torpedo-boats. For the reader with a good naval library – or even the relevant *Conway's Fighting Ships* volumes there will not be much that is new on the technical side, but the potted service biographies are useful,

banks of tubes were carried. This was a very successful design and it is believed that a further twelve units of a modified design were authorized under the third Five Year Plan as 'Projekt B1'. This differed in a number of ways, in particular, a lower displacement, two 3-inch replacing three 45mm AA and only two banks of tubes, either quadruple or quintuple. Only four had been laid down prior to the German invasion, all on the Black Sea.

Modifications The only completed unit, *Tashkent*, was fitted on an interim basis with three single 5.1-inch guns when she arrived in Russia until her twin gun-houses were ready in 1940–41. It is probable that her 45mm guns were replaced by 37mm. During the war, one bank of tubes was replaced by two 3-inch AA.

Service *Tashkent* was actively employed during the whole of her brief period of service, mainly on supply runs to Sevastopol. In total, she made forty round trips, but on the last was bombed off the Crimea by German aircraft on 28 June 1942. Taken in tow by *Bditelnyi*, she was successfully brought into Novorossisk although many compartments were flooded. On 2 June she foundered and was abandoned when the German Army took the port. Her twin gun-houses were salvaged and later installed in *Ognyevoi*. Of the improved units, about eight were cancelled prior to laying-down. *Ochakov* and *Perekop* were captured on the stocks at Nikolaiev by the German Army and later demolished. *Kiev* and *Yerevan* were towed out to Poti and Batum in August 1941 where they lay incomplete throughout the war. Neither was ever completed and both were broken up post-war.

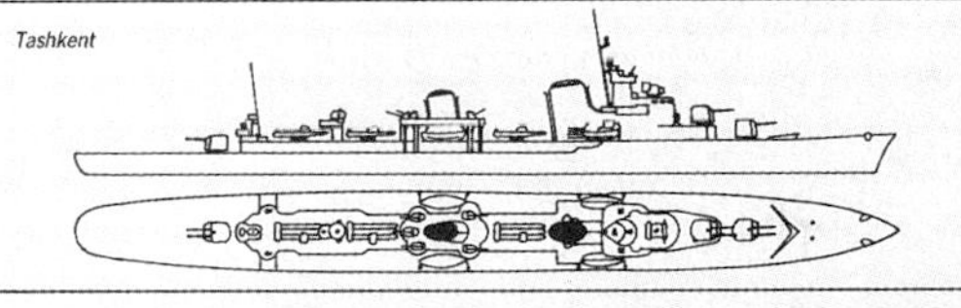

Below: *Tashkent* with extemporized armament. (A. D. Baker)

Below: *Tashkent* with designed armament. (Author's Collection)

NOVIK CLASS

Ship	Builder	Laid Down	Launched	Commissioned	Fate
Yakov Sverdlov	Putilov, St. Petersburg	19 July 10	26 June 11	22 Aug 13	Lost 28 Aug 41

Displacement: 1,271tons/1,291tonnes (standard); 1,801tons/1,829tonnes (full load).
Length: 336ft/102.43m (oa).
Beam: 31ft 3in/9.53m.
Draught: 11ft 6in/3.53m (mean).
Machinery: six Vulcan boilers; 3-shaft A.E.G. turbines.
Performance: 36,500shp; 36kts.
Bunkerage: 430tons/437tonnes.
Range: 1,800nm at 16kts.
Guns: five 4in (5×1); one 3in AA; one 37mm; two MG.
Torpedoes: nine 18in (3×3).
Mines: 60.
Complement: 168.

Design This ship, completed as *Novik* for the Imperial Russian Navy, was the prototype for a large series of powerful destroyers. The design was based upon German plans and much of the equipment was supplied from abroad with the Putilov yard assembling the ship rather than building it. The major advance as far as Russian destroyers were concerned, was the use of turbine propulsion for the first time and a three-shaft machinery layout. The main armament consisted of four 4-inch 60cal Obuchov guns in single, partially shielded mountings disposed in a rather peculiar fashion, with one forward and three on the quarterdeck. These after guns were very closely spaced and all axial. As a result, only one gun could bear directly astern and even that was later

Below: *Novik* later became *Yakov Sverdlov*. (W. B. Bilddienst)

and the book is well illustrated (the line drawings are crude but they do include deck views and while the majority of photos are familiar, there are a lot of them and mostly reproduced at a good size).

David Williams, Liners in Battledress: Maritime Camouflage and Colour Schemes for Passenger Ships, *published by Conway Maritime Press, 1989.*
270 x 200mm, 160 pages, 225 illustrations.
ISBN 0 85177 517 9. £18.00

Although this book is principally concerned with liners, there is enough general information on the development of camouflage techniques and theory to warrant the attention of warship enthusiasts. Furthermore, many passenger ships served as auxiliary warships, and this area of their activity is also covered, along with such subjects as peacetime troopship liveries, and hospital ship schemes.

PUBLICATIONS ANNOUNCED

D Brown, Warship Losses of World War II, *published by Arms & Armour Press, £19.95.*

Captain Eric Brown, Duels in the Sky: World War II Naval Aircraft in Combat, *published by Airlife, £14.95.*
A test pilot's evaluation of the relative merits of the many naval aircraft, Allied and Axis, that he has flown.

John D Byrne Jr, Crime and Punishment in the Royal Navy 1784–1812, *published by Scolar Press, £27.50.*

James Cable, Navies in Violent Peace, *published by Macmillan, £27.50.*
A new study of naval strategy and the function of navies.

Jonathan Coad, The Royal Naval Dockyards 1690–1850, *published by Scolar Press, c.£85.00.*
An extremely detailed academic study of the architecture and buildings.

A Crowhurst, The French War on Trade: Privateering 1793–1815, *published by Scolar Press, £30.00.*
An economic historian's appraisal of the effectiveness of France's privateering business.

Bradley A Fiske, The Navy as a Fighting Machine, *Naval Institute Press, £15.00.*
An influential work of 1916, reprinted as part of the 'Classics of Seapower' series.

Fotofax series: The German Naval Air Services *by Alex Imrie;* Japanese Battleship 1897–1945 *by Ray Burt;* Soviet Navy at War *by P Budzbon;* Escort Carriers of World War Two *by Kenneth Poolman; each published by Arms & Armour Press, £4.95.*

M Hattendorf, Maritime Strategy, *published by Macmillan, £35.00.*

N H Jones, Operation Catapult: Britain's Attack on the French Fleet, *published by John Murray, £14.95.*

S and Y Kaufman, Silent Chase: Submarines of the US Navy, *published by Airlife, £19.95.*
A collection of colour photos in large format.

Philip McDougall, The Royal Dockyards, *published by Shire, £16.50.*

K McPherson, River Class Destroyers *and* Frigates of the Royal Canadian Navy, *each published by Tri-Service, £12.95 and £14.95 respectively.*
Well illustrated handbooks on these RCN types.

Dwight R Messimer, The Merchant U-Boat: Adventures of the Deutschland, 1916–18, *published by Naval Institute Press, £17.95.*

Arthur Pearcy, A History of US Coast Guard Aviation, *published by Airlife, £16.95.*

Alan Raven, Essex Class Carriers, *published by Naval Institute Press, £15.00.*
Second in the series of 'Warship Design Histories' to follow the *Fletcher Class*, published last year.

James R Rechner, Teddy Roosevelt's Great White Fleet, *published by Naval Institute Press, £18.95.*

David Syrett, The Royal Navy in American Waters 1775–1783, *published by Scolar Press, £32.50.*
A scholarly history of America's leading authority on the Royal Navy at this time.

V E Tarrant, U-Boat Offensive 1916–1945, *published by Arms & Armour Press, £19.95*

John Terraine, Business in Great Waters: The U-Boat Wars 1916–1945, *published by Leo Cooper, £17.50.*

Geoffrey Till, The Sea and Soviet Strategy, *published by Macmillan, £35.00.*

U-Boat War in the Atlantic, *published by HMSO, £40.00.*
First publication of an official post-1945 classified report on the lessons of the submarine war.

Ray Willams, Fly Navy, *published by Airlife, £16.95.*
Covers the post-1945 Fleet Air Arm.

John Young, Britain's Sea War, *published by PSL, £14.95.*
A calendar of events affecting merchant shipping during the Second World War.

THE NAVAL YEAR IN REVIEW

The events covered by this review stretch from approximately April 1988 to April 1989, although there is some reference to earlier periods and, where possible, later updating has been incorporated. Compiled by Ian Sturton.

A. INTRODUCTION

The year in review was noteworthy for a ceasefire in the eight-year Gulf War, the Soviet withdrawal from Afghanistan (complete 15 February 1989), the Gorbachev disarmament speech at the UN in November, and a negotiated settlement in Namibia. Changes in Soviet policy were initiated by internal pressures on Moscow's defence spending; the huge US budget and trade deficits have resulted in parallel pressures on the Pentagon's spending powers. These trends were not limited to the superpowers; other governments found reasons to pass zero or negative growth defence budgets. As defence costs usually increase ahead of inflation, procurement programmes have been cut down, deferred or cancelled. The strengths of the major naval powers are listed in Table 1.

B. THE STRATEGIC BALANCE

In an East–West crisis, NATO's forward maritime strategy would place up to four US Carrier Battle Groups (CVBGs) in positions close to Soviet territory in the Norwegian Sea; the RN and NATO allies would supply ASW task forces, reinforce Norway and perhaps attempt to 'hold the ring' until the USN arrived. Soviet submarines and surface ships putting to sea would be intercepted and contained, while key land targets would be attacked. In the Mediterranean the forward strategy would similarly contain Soviet forces there and in the Black Sea, and restrict movement of reserves to the Central Front. In the Pacific, warships leaving Vladivostok and Petropavlovsk would be engaged by the US 7th Fleet. By Treaty with Japan (1981), America provides a nuclear umbrella for the defence of her airspace, coastal waters and territory, and vital sea lanes to 1000nm.

In the event of hostilities, the Central Front would require rapid and massive reinforcement from the continental United States. In 1986 the US and its European allies agreed each to provide 600 ships for this purpose; 800 ships crossing a month would be needed for two months, then reduced to 350 ships a month. Only certain high-value convoys would be sure of naval protection, as a general convoy system would take too long to organise and escorts are in short supply. Declining US and European merchant marines are leading to a shortfall in NATO's sealift capability.

Turning to the Warsaw Pact, the Soviet ballistic missile submarines (SSBN) are the core of the nuclear strategic forces. The long range of the SS-N-20 missiles in the 'Typhoon' class and the SS-N-23 in 'Delta IV' permit these boats to patrol in protected areas close to home or under the Arctic ice. In July 1988 the older 'Yankee' boats resumed patrols close to the US coast (withdrawn one year earlier), perhaps for covert short-range use against targets defended by ABM systems. Cruise missile submarines (SSGN and SSG) provide the major naval capability against surface ships: carrier battle groups, task forces and large convoys. Nuclear-powered hunter–killer submarines (SSN) have major ASW and ASUW roles. The surface fleet would have limited survivability in an East–West conflict.

Table 1 *MAJOR WARSHIP TYPES OF PRINCIPAL NAVIES, 1 APRIL 1989*

Type	*USA*	*USSR*	*UK*	*France*	*China*	*India*	*Japan*	*Italy*
CV (large)	15	–	–	–	–	–	–	–
CV (medium)	–	4	–	2	–	1	–	–
CV (small)	–	–	3	–	–	1	–	1
Battleship	4	–	–	–	–	–	–	–
Cruiser								
(helicopter)	–	2	–	1	–	–	–	1
(missile)	40	31	–	1	–	–	–	2
Destroyer	68	57	13	16	18	5	39	4
Frigate								
(fleet)	99	37	33	7	33	11	16	15
(escort)	–	153	–	17	–	9	–	4
SSBN	36	63	4	6	2	–	–	–
SSGN	} 97	52	–	–	–	–	–	–
SSN		85	16	4	2	1	–	–
SS (all types)	3	149	12	13	*c*50	16	14	10
MCMV (ocean and coastal)	20	311	38	21	*c*130	12	30	26

The Marshall Ustinov, *the second* Slava *class missile cruiser at a Northern Fleet base.* (TASS, by courtesy of Antony Preston)

Table 2 *THE EAST–WEST BALANCE: EFFECTIVE SHIPS*

Type	*USA*	*Other NATO*	*France*	*Spain*	*West, Total*	*USSR*
CV (large)	15	–	–	–	15	–
CV (medium)	–	–	2	–	2	4
CV (small)	–	4	–	1	5	–
Battleship	4	–	–	–	4	–
Cruiser						
(helicopter)	–	1	1	–	2	2
(missile)	40	2	1	–	43	31
Destroyer	68	50	16	5	140	50
Frigate						
(fleet)	99	111	7	14	231	37
(escort)	–	33	17	–	50	128
SSBN	36	4	6	–	46	63
SSGN	} 97	–	–	–	} 117	52
SSN		16	4	–		85
SS (all types)	3	90	13	8	114	*c*105

◀ *Soviet 'Typhoon' class submarine. Five of this type were in service by 1987, a sixth should join in 1989.* (MoD)

Table 2 provides a comparison of the naval forces in NATO and the Warsaw Pact. Where possible, obsolete or inactive types have been omitted, although categories are not always clearly defined. The very large US amphibious warfare forces and the numerous Soviet coastal attack and escort forces have not been included; neither has an equivalent in the other navy.

C. BUDGET PROPOSALS AND NEW PROGRAMMES

C (i). USA, NATO and Allies

NATO nations agreed in 1982 to an annual increase in military spending of at least 3 per cent in real terms. The tendency, particularly in the smaller countries, to move away from the 3 per cent commitment towards zero or negative growth defence budgets has been reinforced by Soviet disarmament initiatives.

MAJOR NATO NAVIES

(a) United States. The defence budget for FY89, beginning 1 October 1988, was agreed at $299.5b, of which $97.4b was for the US Navy and Marine Corps. In the FY90 and FY91 biennial budget presented by the out-

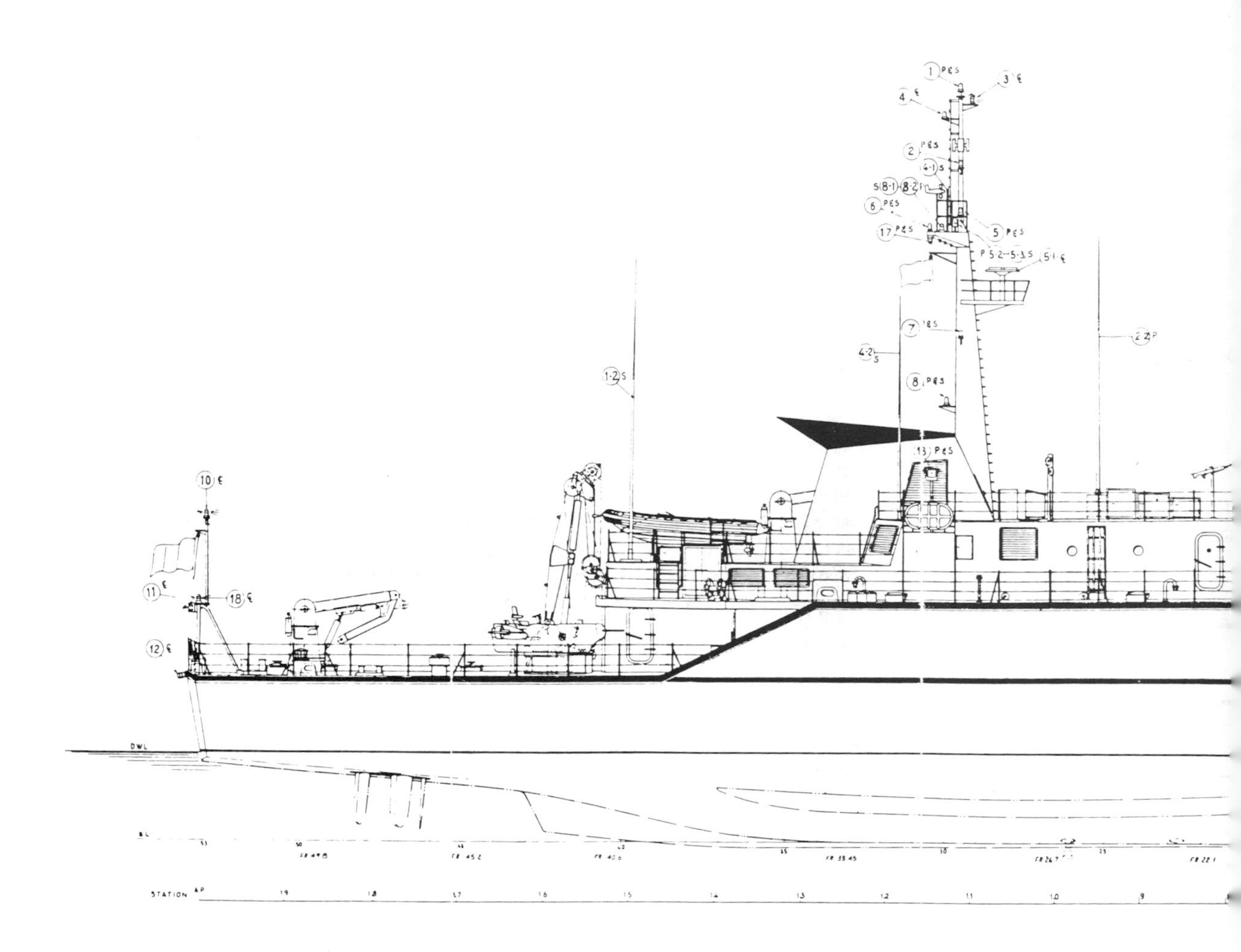

going administration on 9 January 1989, $107.1b was requested for FY90 and $105.6b for FY91, a real spending increase of 2 per cent in each year. Details of new construction shipbuilding proposals, up to and including this budget, are given in Table 3. It should be noted that it omitted several important items included in earlier Reagan programmes: CVN-76 (FY90) CG-74 (FY90) and SSN-775/777 (FY91 and FY92); these may be cancelled or deferred. The Bush budget for FY90 included a one-year freeze on military spending, with an real increase of only 1 per cent proposed for FY91 and FY92, increasing to 3 per cent in FY93. Proposals for attaining these goals have been published.

Because of budgetary constraints, the Reagan goal of a 600-ship navy will almost certainly not now be reached. The number of battle force ships, at a low of 460 in 1978–79, rose to 580 in 1988, but the withdrawal in 1988-89 of 16 elderly frigates will keep numbers below target. Plans approved in December 1988 for the US fleet in the year 2010 propose 120 'battle force combatants' (BFC, roughly present cruisers and destroyers), and 104 'protection of shipping ships' (POS, corresponding to frigates), not including carriers, submarines or amphibious warfare ships. These figures are slightly greater than present strengths, and are therefore distinctly unrealistic.

Table 3 *USN SHIPBUILDING PROGRAMMES 1987–92*

New Construction	*Approved (authorised and funded)*			*Proposed (subject to amendment)*		
	FY87	FY88	FY89	FY90	FY91	FY92
SSBN *Ohio*	1	1	1	1	1	1
SSN-688 *Los Angeles*	4	3	2	2	(2)	(1)
SSN-21 *Seawolf*	–	–	1	–	2	3
CVN	–	2	–	(1)	–	–
CG-47 *Ticonderoga*	3	5	–	(1)	–	–
DDG-51 *Arleigh Burke*	2	–	5(3)	5(3)	5(5)	5(6)
MCM *Avenger*	–	–	–	3	–	–
MHC *Osprey*	–	–	2	3	3	4
LHD *Wasp*	–	1	1	–	1	1
LSD	1	1	1	1	1	1

Figures in brackets are from earlier Reagan Programmes, now amended.

Procurement of existing aircraft types continues alongside development of replacement classes. Major surface combatants and fleet submarines are being fitted or retrofitted with Tomahawk cruise missiles. In mine warfare, new MCMV construction is replacing obsolescent types.

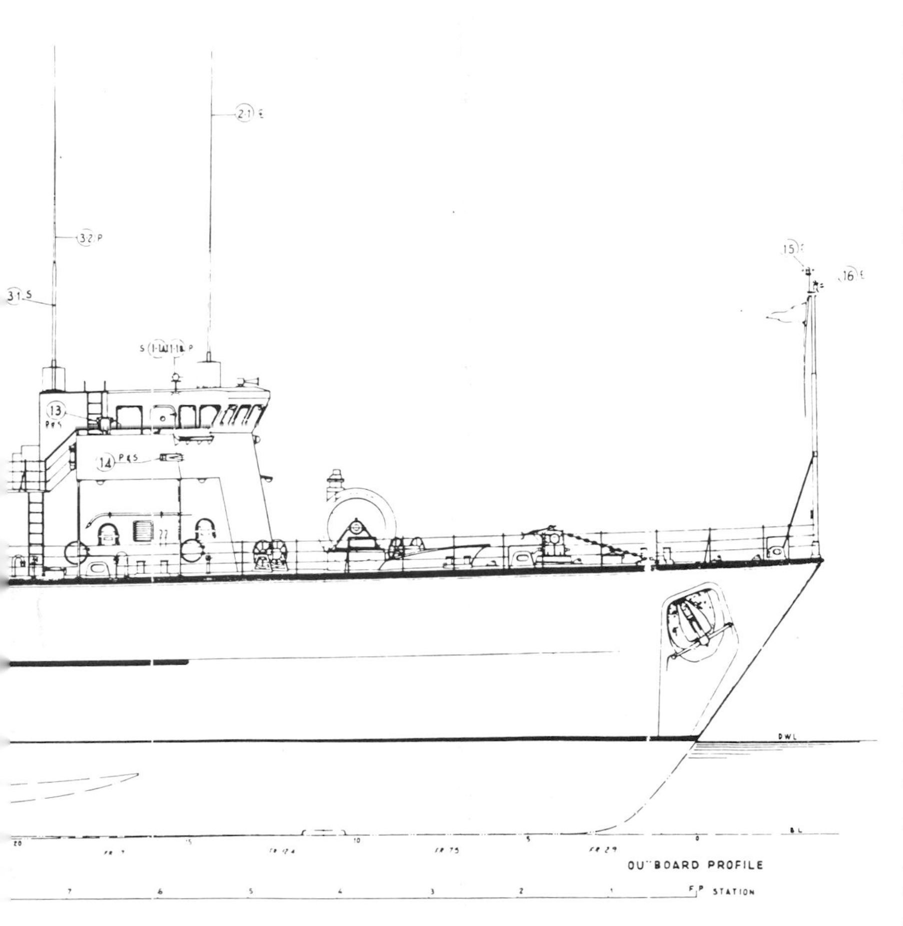

General arrangement drawings of the USN's Osprey *class coastal minehunters (MHC). Ordered with FY86 funds after the* Cardinal *surface effect type (MSH) was cancelled in 1986,* Osprey *(MHC-51) is due to commission in July 1991. Alleged cost overruns started a probe into Intermarine USA by the USN's Inspector General.* (Intermarine USA)

(b) United Kingdom. The 1988–89 Defence Estimates were for £19.2b ($34.2b), £2.58b ($4.59b) on maritime defence, a reduction in real terms of 2.6 per cent. No detailed programme of future ship construction is published, but the general outline is clear. Classes in hand include the Trident II SSBN, the *Trafalgar* class SSN, Types 22 and 23 frigates and the *Sandown* class single role minehunters, while design work for the next generation of SSN, the 'W' class (SSN-20), has begun. Britain's continued commitment (1986) to an amphibious warfare force led to tenders being invited for an Aviation Support Ship (ASS), and plans to replace *Fearless* and *Intrepid* are being compared with proposals for major extensions of their service lives (SLEP). For the third consecutive year, total estimated costs for the Trident II programme have fallen in real terms (the January 1989 figure

Upholder, *the first conventional submarine to be built for the RN in twenty years is due to commission at the end of 1989.* (VSEL, by courtesy of Antony Preston)

The British Type 22 Batch 3 frigate HMS Cumberland *on contractor's trials.* (Yarrow Shipbuilding Ltd)

M101

▲ Trenchant, *the latest* Trafalgar *class SSN for the Royal Navy. A modified version of this class was the British contender for the abortive Canadian SSN programme.* (VSEL)

was £9.09b ($16b), a fall of £104m ($185m) during 1988).

(c) Canada. Canada's defence requirements for the foreseeable future were detailed in the 1987 Department of Defence White Paper, which provided for major increases in funding, personnel and equipment. An annual increase in the defence budget of 2 per cent after inflation was proposed (the 1988 figure was 2.7 per cent), with extra funding as new equipment came on stream. The centrepiece of the proposed Three Ocean Navy was to be 10–12 nuclear-powered hunter–killer submarines, to be constructed over 27 years at an annual cost of $252m. Earlier programmes in hand include 12 large frigates of the *Halifax* and *Montreal* classes, an AAW update for the four 'Tribal' class DDH (TRUMP), a new MCM force, and the provision or updating of EH 101 helicopters, Orion maritime patrol aircraft and Trackers. On 27 April 1989, the SSN programme was cancelled, to help deal with Canada's budgetary deficit; a reversion to conventionally-powered boats is likely.

(d) Italy. The 1989 defence budget for $17.2b was the first in a 10-year plan to restructure and modernise the armed forces; expenditure would be $750m less than in 1988 and more cuts were forecast for 1990. The Italian Parliament approved (January 1989) the long-awaited constitutional amendment allowing the navy to operate fixed-wing aircraft. Work continues on new destroyers, corvettes and landing ships; other plans included two new submarines, re-equipping the air arm with the EH 101 helicopters, and a new stand-off ASW system.

(d) West Germany. The defence budget for 1989 was fixed at $28.8b, an increase of 2.4 per cent. Work continued on the last two Type 122 frigates and four Type 123 were ordered in November. The first of 12 Type 212 submarines will be ordered in 1990. Ten new Type 332 minehunters are to be ordered between 1992 and 1995, subject to Parliamentary approval. They will follow the Type 343 programme, and will replace the Type 340-341 minesweepers and some Type 331 vessels.

(f) Netherlands. The Dutch defence budget for 1989 was $6.6b, an increase of 0.6 per cent. Plans were modified by the 1989–98 Defence Ten-Year Plan, which shifted funds from the Navy and Air Force to the Army. In consequence, four of the *Kortenaer* class and the two *Tromp* class frigates will not be modernised and the last two *Van Speijks* will be withdrawn from service early. Plans for the fifth and sixth units of the *Walrus* class SS have been dropped and it is hoped instead to order two of the smaller *Moray* class in 1991. Also planned for the early 1990s are an amphibious lift ship for the Dutch Marines, new MCM vessels (in cooperation with Belgium) and new Fast Combat Support Ships. No Harpoon ASM missiles will be purchased for the 13 P-3C Orions of the Naval Air Service.

An artist's impression of the proposed Dutch amphibious warfare vessel. (Official)

◀ HMS Sandown, *the first single role minehunter (SRMH), on contractor's trials. Following* HMS Wilton *and the 'Hunt' class, she is the first third-generation GRP mine countermeasures vessel.* (Vosper Thornycroft)

PORTE-AVIONS NUCLEAIRE
Charles de Gaulle

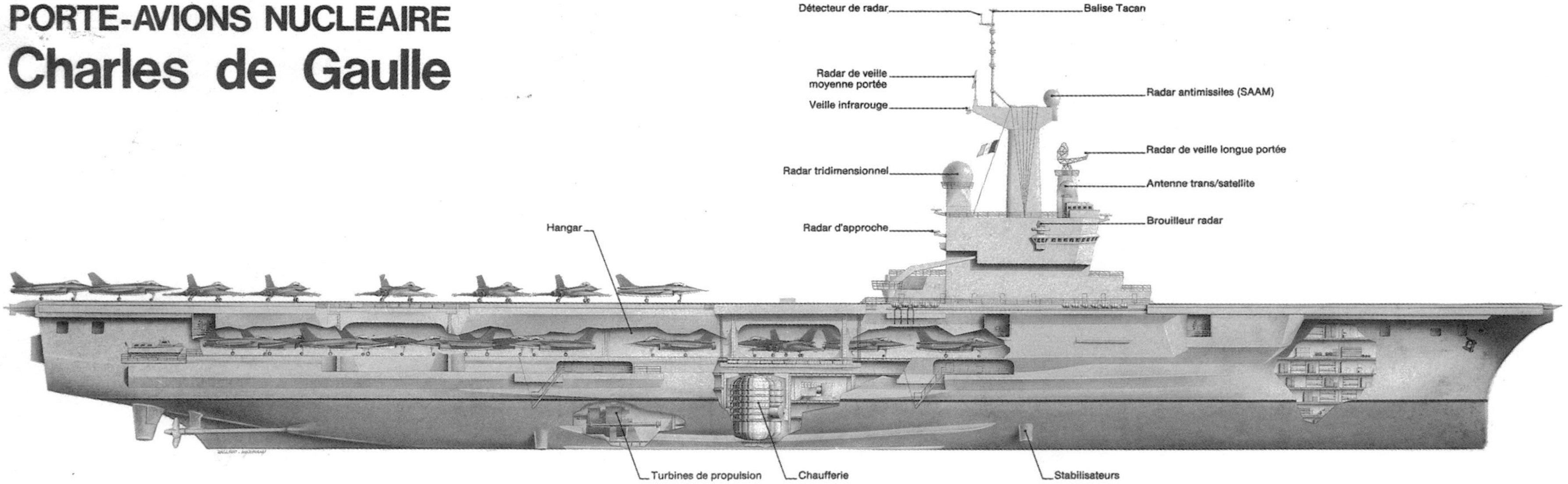

Détecteur de radar
Balise Tacan
Radar de veille moyenne portée
Veille infrarouge
Radar antimissiles (SAAM)
Radar de veille longue portée
Radar tridimensionnel
Antenne trans/satellite
Brouilleur radar
Radar d'approche
Hangar
Turbines de propulsion
Chaufferie
Stabilisateurs

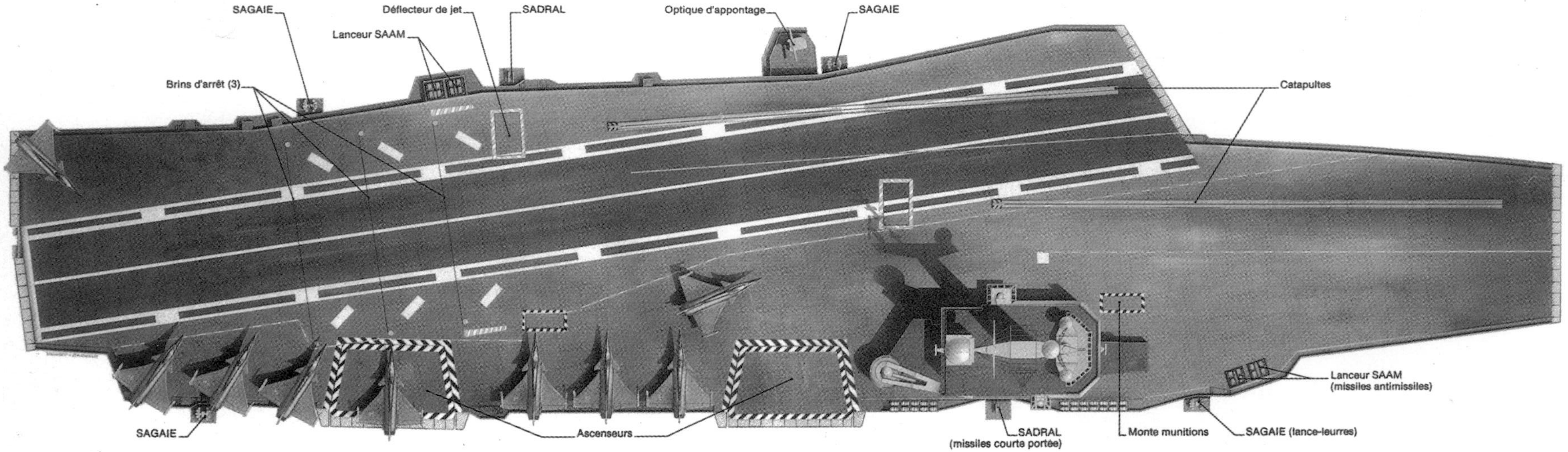

SAGAIE
Déflecteur de jet
SADRAL
Optique d'appontage
SAGAIE
Lanceur SAAM
Brins d'arrêt (3)
Catapultes
Lanceur SAAM (missiles antimissiles)
SAGAIE
Ascenseurs
SADRAL (missiles courte portée)
Monte munitions
SAGAIE (lance-leurres)

CARACTERISTIQUES

Pont envol

Longueur:	261,5 m
Largeur:	64,36 m
Hauteur au-dessus flottaison:	16,20 m
Surface pont d'envol:	12 000 m²

Déplacement pleine charge: 36 000 tonnes

Propulsion

Puissance:	83 000 ch
Vitesse maxi:	27 nœuds
Puissance électrique installée:	20 000 kW

Aviation

2 catapultes course:	75 m
2 ascenseurs charge:	36 tonnes
Capacité d'emport:	35 à 40 avions
Munitions embarquées:	> 500 t

Vie à bord

Capacité logement:	1 950 personnes + 800 commandos
Autonomie en vivres:	45 j

DCN

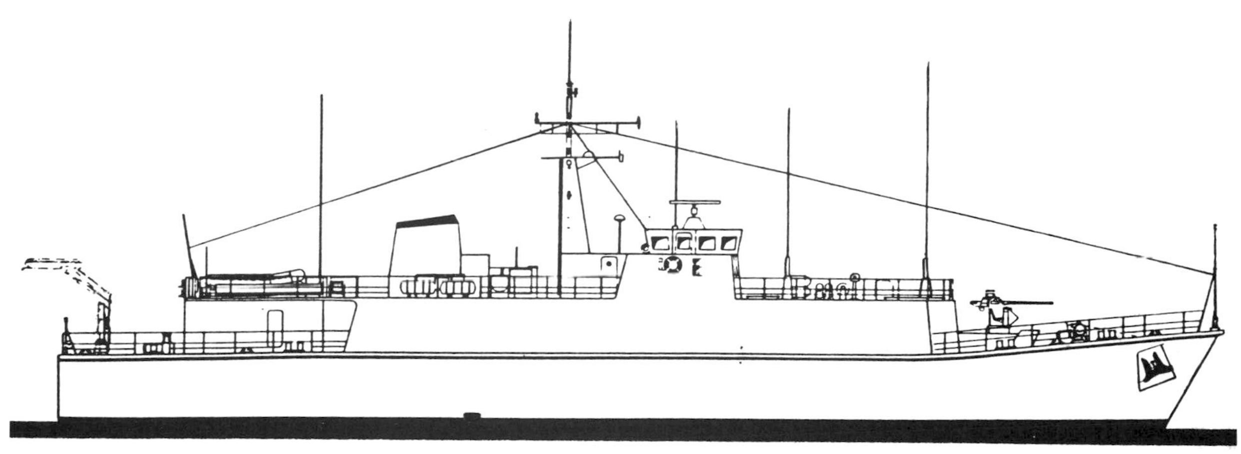

▲ *Vosper Thornycroft's successful* Sandown *class single role minehunters (SRMH). Five of a possible twenty for the Royal Navy are in service or building; six are on order for Saudi Arabia, and technology transfer to Bazan will allow four of modified type to be built for the Spanish Navy.* (Vosper Thornycroft)

(g) THE SOUTH-EASTERN FLANK. In spite of the Davos understanding, Greece and Turkey continue to eye one another jealously. **Greece's** 1989 military budget is up by 11.7 per cent to $4.2b, the highest as a percentage of GNP in NATO. The Meko 200 frigate type has been chosen in preference to the Dutch M (Multipurpose) type, and four were ordered in February 1989. New corvettes are to be acquired, and the four *Glafkos* class submarines modernised. **Turkey** decided (January 1989) to take up the option of two more Meko 200 frigates, for a total of six. The Type 209/1200 submarines are to be followed by up to twelve 1400-tonne boats, six to be built locally. With the completion of the frigate and fast attack craft programmes, Ankara's priorities includes new corvettes. The proposed transfer of frigates from the United States aroused Greek protests.

(h) LESSER NATO NAVIES. **Norway's** 1989 naval budget was $1.02b; the increase of 2.5 per cent from 1988 will largely be swallowed by wage and price increases. Most funding was for existing programmes, the *Ula* class submarines, 10 MCM vessels and 4 P-3C Orion Maritime Patrol aircraft; the fast attack craft modernisation or replacement programme is to be reassessed. **Denmark's** 1989 defence budget of $1.8b provided for inflation-proof zero growth; new orders, including four more 'Standard Flex' patrol craft, would be financed in part by withdrawing the two large frigates, although their Harpoon SSM will be retained ashore as coastal batteries. Work in hand includes seven 'Standard Flex' craft and the modernisation of 3 ex-Norwegian *Kobben* class submarines. The **Portuguese** programme of three Meko 200 frigates is partly financed by NATO, and the **Belgian** defence austerity plan will reduce frigate modernisation to a minimum.

◀ *Official drawings of the French nuclear-powered aircraft carrier* Charles de Gaulle, *laid down at Brest in April 1989 as eventual replacement for* Clemenceau. *Financial stringency may cause the launch and in-service dates of 1992 and 1996 to slip.* (DCN)

(j) FRANCE AND SPAIN cooperate with NATO but are not full military members.

France. The 1989 Defence Budget, for $29b, was up by 4.7 per cent from 1988 and represented 3.7 per cent of GNP. Military and civilian personnel would be reduced by around 8000; the navy would be the main beneficiary of a 5.6 per cent increase in procurement. The French programme includes a new generation of ballistic-missile submarines (SSBN), re-equipping the existing SSBN with the M4 missiles, an eighth SSN, the nuclear-powered strike carrier *Charles de Gaulle*, 12 new frigates, 6 MCM vessels and Breguet Atlantique 2 Maritime Patrol aircraft.

Spain. The 1989 defence budget is for $6.3, about 1.9 per cent of GNP and 25 per cent of public expenditure. To modernise naval forces, naval spending has been increased from 20 per cent to 30 per cent of the total defence budget. The FFG-7 frigate programme will be followed by a smaller type for surveillance duties, and 4 modified *Sandown* class SRMH are to be built in Spain.

(k) US ALLIES

Japan. Reflecting the nation's continuing economic growth, the FY89 budget for the MSDF will be $7.6b (out of $30.3b FY89 total for defence), 3.9 per cent over the planned FY88 figure, and a 3 per cent real annual increase is proposed for the next 10 years. Although the numerical strength of the MSDF stays roughly constant, older units are steadily retired and replaced by larger, more capable types. Japan is to buy AEGIS systems for four DDG, generally of US *Arleigh Burke* type but designed and built in Japan. Likely new construction in 1992–97 includes extra AEGIS destroyers, and possibly one or two ships able to deploy aircraft, if the opposition of surrounding countries – which would be infuriated by any attempt to substitute Japanese forces for the US 7th Fleet – can be overcome.

Australia. A mid-1988 mini-budget cut the defence estimates of $7.4b by 1 per cent. Australia is considering expanding its purchase of ANZAC frigates from 8 to 12. In **New Zealand,** interested in 2 frigates initially with an option on 2 more, the joint venture is opposed by much of the ruling Labour Party; the possibility of a lease arrangement instead of outright purchase has been discussed with Australia. The winners of the competitions for the frigates and their sensor systems should be announced in August 1989. Construction work on the first of the new submarines will begin in 1989.

C (ii). Neutral European Nations

(a) **Finland.** The defence budget for 1989 is $1.68b, an increase of 10 per cent. Apart from light craft the programme includes a new minelayer.

108

▲ *Soviet* Udaloy, *photographed before the Cross Sword fire control radars for SA-N-9 missiles were fitted. The ninth and tenth of the class,* Admiral Levchenko *and* Admiral Vinograd, *were completed in 1988.* (USN, official)

(b) Sweden. The 1987–88 defence budget was $4.4b, but public concern at the neglect of defence in recent decades may lead to extra spending. At present, submarines, fast attack craft ('missile corvettes') and minecraft are being built. These three types, with smaller local surveillance craft, are intended to form the backbone of the fleet in the next 20 years.

C (iii). Warsaw Pact and Associated Nations

USSR. In spite of *glasnost*, full details of Soviet naval budgets and future construction programmes are not forthcoming. In outline, defence personnel is to be cut by 500,000 in 1989–90, the defence budget by 14.2 per cent and defence procurement spending by 19.5 per cent. The Navy's primary missions are to keep a survivable fleet of SSBN and SSN and attempt to neutralise opposing SSBN forces, so the most likely victim of future economies would be the expensive new carrier building programme and not the subsurface fleet. The latest nuclear submarine types are faster, deeper-diving and much more silent than hitherto; the building programme includes 'Typhoon' and 'Delta IV' class SSBN, 'Oscar II' class SSGN and 'Akula', 'Sierra' and 'Victor III' class SSN. 'Kilo' class diesel–electric submarines are also being built, mostly for export. The main surface warship types under construction are aircraft carriers (the first of which has been variously reported as *Leonid Brezhnev* and later *Tbilisi*), *Kirov* and *Slava* class cruisers, *Sovremenniy* and *Udaloy* class destroyers, and 'Krivak' class frigates. A 'Krivak' frigate replacement is running trials. Fuel and other operating costs continue to be cut by reducing overseas deployments and fleet exercises. The Gorbachev UN speech in November gave no details of unilateral naval reductions, mainly because Warsaw Pact figures put NATO far ahead in surface ship numbers, and about equal in submarines. However, reductions in the strength of the Pacific Fleet have since been announced.

There is little to report on Moscow's allies: the transfer of submarines from the USSR continues, as does spasmodic construction of surface units from frigates downwards.

◀ *A fine view of the Soviet* Slava *in the Black Sea. The third of the class,* Chervona Ukraina, *will complete in 1989.* (TASS, by courtesy of Antony Preston)

East German 'Koni' class frigate Berlin, *a type still being built for export.* (USN, official)

The single role minehunter Sandown*; her sister* Inverness *is to be completed for Saudi Arabia as the first of six ordered in July 1988.* (Vosper Thornycroft, by courtesy of Antony Preston)

C (iv). Middle East

Major construction programmes are limited to Israel and Saudi Arabia. **Israel's** new construction programme has been reduced to three 'Sa'ar 5' missile corvettes and two 'Dolphin' class submarines. Although equipment and offset finance deals are in hand, contracts for both types had not been signed by April 1989. The 'Al Yamanah 2' arms deal between Britain and **Saudi Arabia**, announced in July 1988, included the construction of six *Sandown* class SRMH at a cost of about £250m ($445m). The ships were ordered from Vosper Thornycroft in November; the second of the British SRMH, *Inverness*, was to be completed for Saudi Arabia. The submarine programme has been deferred or dropped.

C (v). Pacific Rim ('PACRIM' and Indian Ocean

(a) China. China's defence budget is about 1 per cent of GNP, against about 2 per cent ten years ago. The existing construction programme continues, with efforts concentrated on enlarging the blue water navy, improving the submarine nuclear deterrent and modernising the amphibious warfare units. Progress is limited by lack of funds and restrictions on the transfer of technology from the West. A very long-term interest in carriers is seen as a possible consequence of the problems of geography: for example, Chinese land-based planes can barely reach the disputed Spratly Islands, in the South China Sea.

(b) India, aspiring to domination of the Indian Ocean, continues to build submarines, frigates and smaller craft, and to acquire warships from the Soviet Union: modified 'Kashin' class destroyers, 'Kilo' class submarines and 'Natya' class minesweepers. ASW and transport Sea King helicopters are being acquired from Britain, and there is a requirement for the AEW version. France has signed a contract to co-design a new carrier.

(c) Lesser Navies

South Korea ordered 12 Sea Lynx, with Seaspray Mk 3 radars and Sea Skua missiles; a submarine programme is in hand, to be followed by destroyers and maritime patrol aircraft. **Taiwan**, after deciding not to go ahead with the proposed 12 South Korean *Ulsan* class frigates, will build eight FFG-7 frigates locally. The second phase of **Thailand's** arms deal with China included orders for four Type 053 (Western 'Jianghu') frigates, but nothing has been heard recently about the submarine purchase, while the 8 minesweepers reported are thought to be small boats, for river and estuary use. A major expansion of the **Malaysian** armed forces includes submarine procurement (the deal for two ex-RN submarines has fallen through, but negotiations for the Vickers Type 1400 are progressing), helicopters and maritime strike aircraft. **Pakistan's** negotiations for British modified Type 21 and Type 23 frigates having lapsed, two UK *Leander* class frigates have been purchased and 8 ex-USA *Brooke* and *Garcia* class frigates leased for five years.

C (vi). *Latin America*

Latin American countries have been particularly hard hit by enormous foreign debts, very high inflation rates, and near empty treasuries. The 1988 **Argentine** defence budget was $2.0b, 75 per cent for the three services, but allowing for inflation the effective figure was only $1.5b. The Argentine's problem is not building but getting rid of surplus modern tonnage; Type 42 destroyers, Meko 140 frigates and submarines are variously reported to be for sale. **Brazil's** 1988 defence budget was reduced (July 1988) by 20 per cent to $1.6b, as part of across-the-board cuts. The 20 per cent reduction meant the freezing or cancellation of indigenous weapon programmes, and cuts in surface ship construction, although the submarine programme seems intact. The US has offered four surplus frigates. **Chile's** defence budget is $600–700m annually, 4 per cent of GNP, limiting the navy to secondhand foreign tonnage or reconstruction of the existing fleet. Two ex-RN 'Counties' are being converted to fleet command ships. Economic problems caused the **Peruvian** cruiser *Almirante Grau* to return from renovation without her missile systems.

C (vii). *Africa*

Nigeria is modernising her less unserviceable surface units and is investigating a submarine force. **South African** defence spending in 1988 increased by 1.1 per cent after inflation to $2.0b, of which the maritime share was 6.9 per cent. The new submarine programme has been shelved, and the existing class will be modernised.

D. WARSHIP BUILDING

D (i). *New Designs Announced and Principal Orders*

NATO Frigate. The eight-nation NATO frigate (NFR 90) continues to undergo the prolonged gestation predictable for a multinational project. The contract for the project definition phase was signed on 25 January 1989, with a baseline review scheduled for later in 1989; displacement is *c*5000 tons and current NATO requirements suggest an eventual 59 hulls (USA 18, UK 12, Italy 8, Canada 6, Spain 5, France and West Germany 4 each, Netherlands 2).

Table 4 *FRIGATE TYPES*

Country	*W Germany*	*Greece*	*France*	*France*
Class	Type 123	Meko 200 HN	FL 3000	Surveill
No in class	4	4	6	6
Builder(s)	Blohm & Voss	1 Blohm & Voss 3 Skaramanga	Lorient	St Nazaire
To be built	1989–94	1989–98	1989–2000	1989–94
Displacement (t)	*c*4300	*c*3200	3200	2850
L x b x d (m)		11.5.9 x 14.8 x 4.1	119 x 13.8 x 4	93.5 x 14 x 4.3
Missiles	4 MM38 VLS for MR-SM1 2 x RAM	8 Harpoon	8 MM40	4 MM40
Gun(s)	1–3in	1–3.9in or 5in 1 CIWS	1–3.9in 2–20mm	1–3.9in 2–20mm
ASW	6–12.75in TT	6–12.75in TT	–	–
Helicopter	2 Lynx	2 Lynx/AB 212	1 Dauphin	1 Super Puma
Machinery	CODOG	CODOG	CODAD	CODAD
HP	–	–	20,000	8000
Speed (kts)	*c*30	30	25	20

Table 5 *SUBMARINE TYPES*

Country	*USA*	*France*	*Australia*
Class	SSN-21	*Le Triomphante*	Type 471
No in class	29	6	6 + (2)
Subm disp (t)	9150	14,200	2700
L x b x d (m)	99.4 x 12.9 x 10.9	138 x 12.5 x –	75 x 7.8 x 6.8
VLS tubes	12	16	–
T Tubes	8–762mm	?4–533mm	6–533mm
HP	60,000	41,000	??
Subm speed (kts)	35	25	20+

Table 6 *MCMV TYPES*

Country	*Canada*	*W Germany*	*Norway*	*France*
Class	–	Type 332	–	BAMO
No in class	12 + (6)	10 + (10)	10	6 + (4)
Builder(s)	–	–	–	–
To be built	1991–96	1989–95	1990–96	*c*1990–95
MCMV type	Hunter/ Sweeper	Hunter	4 Hunters 6 Sweepers	Hunter/ Sweeper
Hull	–	Steel	?/catamaran	GRP/catamaran
Displacement (t)	900–1000	635	360	870
L x b x d (m)	*c*60 x – x –	54.5 x 9.2 x 2.5	54.5 x 13 x 2.3	52 x 14.8 x 3.6
Gun(s)	1–40mm 2 MG	1–40mm, SAM	1–40mm	1–40mm 2 MG
Machinery	Diesel	Diesel	Diesel	Diesel
HP	–	6140	1860	8000
Speed (kts)	15–18	24.5	30	15

(*Note:* Tables 4, 5 and 6 summarise data on new frigate, submarine and MCMV designs discussed below.)

(a) United States. New designs have not been reported, although work goes ahead on existing types and modifications thereof. General Dynamics is to build the first *Seawolf* SSN (SSN-21 Class); the first of a planned class of 29 will be laid down in 1989, for estimated delivery in 1995 at a cost of $726m. CVN-74 and CVN-75 were ordered from Newport News Shipbuilding in July 1988, to maintain the 15 carrier battle groups and one carrier in SLEP approved by Congress.

(b) United Kingdom. Preliminary studies for the next generation of nuclear hunter–killer submarines, the 'W' class (SSN-20), suggest a boat similar in size to *Trafalgar* but having a greater beam-to-length ratio and with the fin much further forward. It would have the new PWR-2 reactor, as in *Vanguard*, and Type 2074 sonar. According to unconfirmed reports, the 1988 construction schedule – first order placed 1990 for commissioning in 1997 – will slip by three years, for financial reasons.

Only three out of the four Type 23 frigates for which tenders had been invited in October 1987 were ordered in 1988 (*Iron Duke, Monmouth, Montrose*); tenders for a further four will be invited in 1989. The design includes several stealth features to reduce radar, infra-red and acoustic signatures, while the class's hull structure is being strengthened to allow for prolonged streaming of towed arrays. The main command system (replacing the CACS 4, cancelled in 1986) is to be chosen in May 1989 from two competitors, but will only be ready in 1993, in time for *Monmouth*, the sixth of the class; it will be retrofitted to earlier units. Unconfirmed reports suggest that the second batch will be lengthened for a CIWS, perhaps omitting the 4.5in gun. The frigate *Naiad*, with-

The first Type 23 frigate, HMS Norfolk *fitting out at Yarrow's shipyard, Scotstoun, Glasgow. The VLS Seawolf system is immediately behind the 4.5in gun; the Harpoon racks are between the VLS and the superstructure. (*Yarrow Shipbuilding Ltd*)*

Saphir, *the second unit of the French* Rubis *class SSN; later ships of this type are being built to an enlarged design (*Amethyste*). Changes to* Amethyste *proposed for the Canadian SSN programme included a heavier weapon payload (6 tubes, 22 torpedoes/SSM), bringing overall length to 79.65m and submerged displacement to 2890 tonnes. (*Marine Nationale*)*

drawn in 1987, is being converted to test various Type 23 innovations.

Plans for the first Trident II submarine, *Vanguard*, to be operational by 1994 and on patrol in the mid-1990s remain on schedule. A fourth refit for the first Polaris submarine, *Resolution*, will not be required.

Five consortia are submitting tenders for an Aviation Support Ship (ASS), to provide a helicopter lift and assault capabiility for a RM commando, including vehicles and equipment. Tenders are to be returned in 1989, an order hopefully following in 1990. The ship, operating Sea King HC4 and Lynx helicopters, would replace *Hermes* and *Bulwark*.

Design studies have been invited from three consortia for LPD to replace *Fearless* and *Intrepid*, while Swan Hunter have been asked to study an alternative, a service life extension programme (SLEP) for the existing ships. The new type would maintain, transport and supply RM Commandos in amphibious operations, landing by landing craft and helicopter.

(c) Canada. No decision was announced on the type of nuclear submarine to be acquired before cancellation of the project; 10 modified UK *Trafalgars* could have been built for the price of 12 modified French *Amethystes*. The UK reactor is based on technology transferred from USA to UK in the 1950s; US executive approval was given for transfer of this technology from UK to Canada, but Congressional amendment of two treaties (1958, with UK, and 1959, with Canada) would still have been required. Selection by Canada of the UK 'W' class, a possibility discussed but not seriously contemplated, would have required further US permission for technology transfer. In contrast, France owns its own technology, so the French reactor is not 'encumbered'; France offered to co-develop the successor to the *Amethyste* class with Canada, up to twenty being needed for both navies.

The delivery of *Halifax* is now expected in 1990. Plans to lengthen the second batch of six for extra accommodation and more VLS missiles may have been dropped.

The projected MCM vessels (Table 6) will be manned by reservists and used in peacetime for coastal surveillance and training. Two offshore supply vessels are being acquired as interim MCM vessels.

(d) West Germany. The Type 123 frigate (Table 4), replacing the *Hamburg* class, is generally an advanced Type 122 with modular construction, a VLS missile system forward and the same radar fit as the Dutch M type. The Type 332 MCM class (Table 6) will have many features in common with Type 343.

(e) Italy. Two further units of the Improved *Sauro* class were ordered in mid-1988; the follow-on 'S 90' Type may be delayed for evaluation and possible incorporation of GST submarine features.

(f) Netherlands. The design of the amphibious lift ship has not been finalised; the replacement for *Poolster* will be of *Zuiderkruis* type, with a CIWS armament.

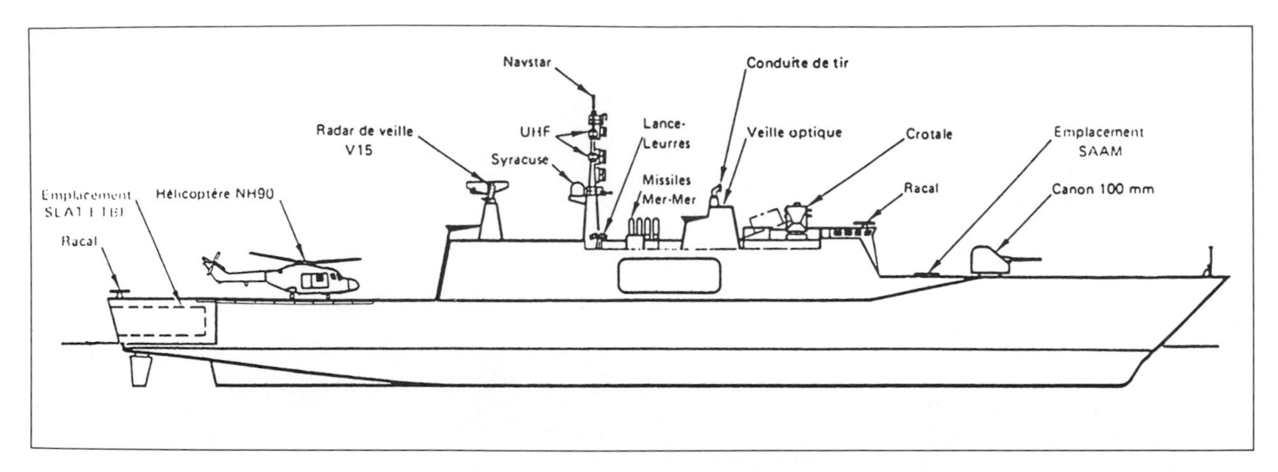

Lafayette, *the first French 'FL 3000' type light frigate, is scheduled to commission in 1994. The type is derived from the 'FL 2500' design; the Dauphin helicopter will be replaced by the NFH 90.*

(g) France. The first of the new SSBN class, *Le Triomphante*, was laid down in 1988 (Table 5), the carrier *Charles de Gaulle* in April 1989. Of the two frigate types (Table 4), the patrol frigates will replace the *Commandant Rivière* class on overseas deployments, while the surveillance frigates' duties will include low-risk fishery patrols and EEZ monitoring; there is no longer to be a common hull. The first two of the latter type, *Floreal* and *Prairial*, were ordered in January 1989. The first of the new ocean-going MCMV (Table 6) should be ready in 1992.

(h) Thailand. The four Chinese-built frigates will comprise two of the II variant and two of the V (helicopter) variant, and will be delivered between February 1991 and February 1992. They will have Chinese weapons and sensors, but MTU diesels will replace Chinese equivalents.

(j) USSR. Details of Soviet naval construction depend very largely on declassified Western intelligence reports. *'Tbilisi'* is not now believed to be nuclear powered, but probably has steam turbines, as in *Kiev*, with the possibility of CONAS, as in *Kirov*. Aircraft handling will probably be as in *Kiev* and *Baku*, with traditional catapults and arrestor wires excluded. The third carrier, laid down at Nikolayev South after the second *'Tbilisi'*s launch in November 1988, is estimated to displace 75,000 tons, some 10,000 tons more than the lead ship. The frigate 'Balcom 4', the replacement for the 'Krivak' class. is expected to run trials later this year. Brief data esti-

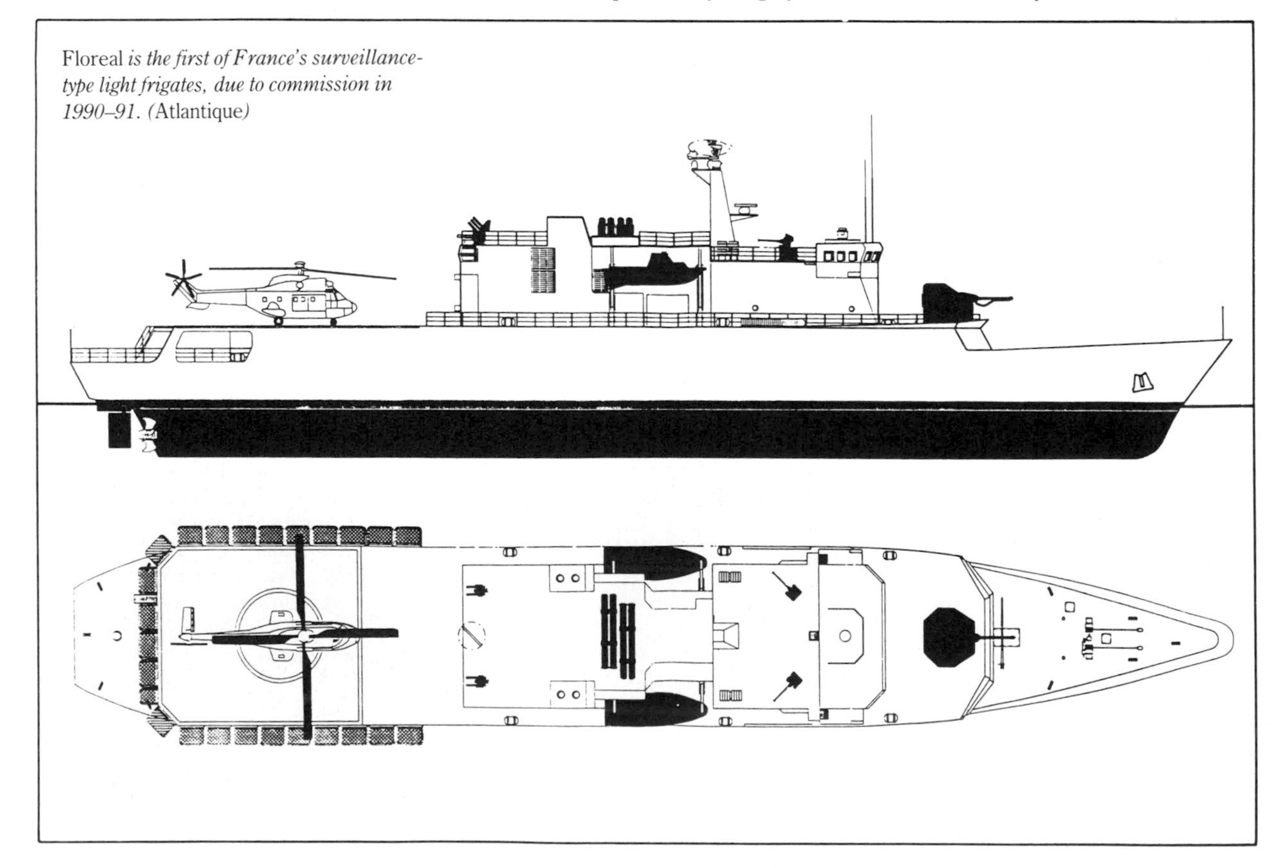
Floreal *is the first of France's surveillance-type light frigates, due to commission in 1990–91.* (Atlantique)

mate: 4000 tons, ASW helicopter, ASW system, VLS SAM system (probably SA-N-9), one or two guns, no surface-to-surface missiles.

(k) Iraq. Only 3 of the 11 ships ordered from Italy in 1981 have been delivered, because of the Gulf war, although over 80 per cent of the total cost has been paid. Four *Lupo* class frigates and four corvettes remain in Italian ports, and an Iraqi delegation visited Rome in January 1989 for discussions.

(l) Brazil. Only 4 *Inhauma* class frigates may now be built, and 4 IKL 209/1400 submarines. It is planned to follow these by 2 Type S-NAC 1 boats, the first to be ready in 1995–97. The indigenous nuclear S-NAC 2 is next in line; work on the reactor is progressing slowly.

PROGRESS IN SUBMARINE DESIGN

This section is concluded with a brief account of non-classified items of particular interest. Most attention has been focused on the GST submarine, unveiled by Maritalia in August 1988. GST stands for Gaseous Storage in a Toroidal hull; the submarine's hull is constructed from a series of circular pipes containing gaseous oxygen at about 350 atmospheres. The hull is stronger, weight for weight, than the usual steel pressure hull, and easier to fabricate, while the oxygen is used with fuel oil in a closed-circuit diesel engine. The concept has been tested in a 29-ton, 9.65m midget submarine, and a larger version (of 136 tons submerged displacement and 23–27m length) is reported building at Milan. Maritalia predict that a 2800-ton GST submarine would have a submerged endurance of 3000nm at 30kts, or 50,000nm at 5kts, comparable with the endurance of a far more costly nuclear-powered hunter–killer.

Two other important ways of increasing submerged endurance are being tested at sea. The West German submarine *U-1* is testing a hydrogen/oxygen fuel cell, producing electricity directly and driving the submarine at moderate speeds for several days. In late 1988 the Swedish submarine *Nacken* started trials of the Stirling anaerobic (air-independent) propulsion system. The pressure hull has been lengthened by 6m amidships for the storage of liquid oxygen in tanks. Using a close-circuit diesel system, the liquid oxygen supply determines underwater endurance, reported as two–three weeks at slow or moderate speeds. The Stirling system may be fitted in later Australian Type 471 boats (Table 5).

US and UK companies are jointly developing communications and sensor aerials that do not penetrate the pressure hull, electro-optics replacing (for example) line-of-sight optical periscopes. The submarine's command centre can be integrated with the sonar room, and vulnerability to damage through the fin is reduced.

Table 7 *NEW SHIPS ENTERING SERVICE 1 APRIL 1988 TO 31 MARCH 1989 (USSR, CHINA IN 1988)*

Type	*USA*	*USSR*	*UK*	*France*	*China*	*India*	*Japan*	*Italy*
CV (large)	–	–	–	–	–	–	–	–
CV (medium)	–	–	–	–	–	–	–	–
CV (small)	–	–	–	–	–	1	–	1
BB (refit)	BB-64	–	–	–	–	–	–	–
CAH	–	–	–	–	–	–	–	–
CG	CG-57 CG-58 CG-59	*Kalinin*	–	–	–	–	–	–
DD	– –	2 *Sovremenniy* 2 *Udaloy*	–	*Cassard*	–	–	3	–
FF (fleet)	–	1 'Krivak III'	3 Type 22	–	2	1	–	
(escort)	–	2 'Grisha V' 3 'Parchim II'	–	–	–	1	–	–
SSBN	SSBN-734	1–2	–	–	–	–	–	–
SSGN	SSN-723 SSN-750	1–2	–	–	–	–	–	–
SSN	SSN-751 SSN-752	2–3	1	1	–	–	–	–
SS (all)	–	1	–	–	–	3	1	1

Note: USSR nuclear submarine construction is estimated at 5–6 per year. Further SS are constructed for export.

The French Cassard *photographed on trials, without MM 40 and decoy launchers. The DRBV 15 on the mack will be replaced by a DRBJ 11B, covered by a large protective dome. The second of the class,* Jean Bart, *completes in 1991, but the third and fourth,* Courbet *and* Chevalier Paul, *have been suspended until the Aster VLS system is ready and may never be built. (*Marine Nationale*)*

D (ii). Ships Entering Service During the Year

These are listed in Table 7 (the figures for the Soviet Union and China are approximate).

The most important new ship, the Soviet carrier *Baku*, was completed in 1987 but did not encounter the world's

The 'Kara' class cruiser Kerch *at Sevastopol in February 1989, displaying her new 3D radar. (*Eric Grove*)*

The new Spanish CVL Principe de Asturias *entered service in 1988. (*Bazan, by courtesy of Antony Preston*)*

photographers until mid-1988. Differences from *Kiev* are most visible in the bridge structure, where a phased array radar system is fitted, one array in each quadrant. Vertical launch SA-N-9 in silos replace the SA-N-4 in the earlier trio, there are twelve SS-N-12 in place of eight, but no area defence missile system such as SA-N-6. The *Kalinin*, the third *Kirov* class missile cruiser, has a new point defence system, comprising a combined fire control radar systems with associated cannon, possibly 30mm gatlings, and a short-range SAM.

D (iii). Reconstruction

(a) United States. Here the main interest centred on the reconstruction of the *Knox* class frigates, imposed by Congress. Navy plans submitted in September 1988 would increase the nominal life of the class from 30 to 40 years; specific improvements include increasing the power of the AN/SQS 26 CX sonar, upgrading the towed array sonar and improving the CIWS.

USS *Stark* (FFG-37) returned to service after completing repairs costing $90m. *Stark* was hit by two AM-39 Exocet missiles (only one exploded) from an Iraqi Mirage F-1 on 17 May 1987, and devastated by fire with the loss of 37 lives. Post-repair trials were on 29/30 August 1988.

USS *Memphis* (SSN-691), an early *Los Angeles* class boat, will be withdrawn from active service later in 1989 to become the USN's interim platform for testing submarine R&D concepts. The submarine would be able to rejoin operational forces at 24 hours' notice.

(b) United Kingdom. The *Invincible* completed a 2½ year modernisation, to an improved *Ark Royal* standard. The air group now consists of 9 Sea Harriers and 12 Sea King helicopters (9 ASW, 3 AEW), but the EH 101 Merlin helicopter cannot be operated until after a further refit. The two Phalanx CIWS have been replaced by three Goalkeepers; sufficient fuel is

USS Gray *(FF-1054). Plans to modernise the* Knox *class (see text) may be modified, for financial reasons. (*Todd*)* ▼

Four views of HMS Invincible *after refit; points to note include deep sponson on port quarter for Goalkeeper CIWS, Type 996 3D radar, ski ramp extended further forward than in* Ark Royal. *(*(MoD and DML*)*

now carried for 48 hours' flight operations instead of 24 (the ship's radius being slightly reduced), the ramp is extended forward and angled to 12 degrees, and accommodation provided for the extra complement. The new Type 996 3D radar is fitted.

D96

◀ *HMS* Gloucester, *with Phalanx CIWS replacing GCM-AO3 30mm and showing longitudinal strengthening.* (MoD)

HMS *Gloucester* was the first Batch 3 Type 42 destroyer to be strengthened by external steel hull strakes, increasing overall beam by about 2ft and displacement by *c* 150 tons; *Cardiff* is the first Type 42 to be fitted with the Type 996 radar. A £40m ($72m) order for lightweight Sea Wolf systems for all three *Invincibles* and the Batch 3 Type 42s was placed early in 1988.

The flight decks of *Brave, London* and *Cornwall* have been enlarged to take the EH 101 helicopter; the Sea King Mk 5 ASW will be operated *ad interim*.

(c) Other reconstructions may be summarised more briefly. **Canada's** TRUMP update programme is to be completed in 1992. *Iroquois* has joined *Algonquin* in the shipyard. In **France**, *Foch*, refitted on the same lines as *Clemenceau*, is additionally able to operate Super Etendards equipped with the new French tactical nuclear weapon, the ASMP. The **Australian** *Perth* class DDG is being refitted at a cost of A$500m, including chaff decoy

▲ *The Type 22 Batch 3 frigate HMS* Cornwall
▼ *has an enlarged flight deck to allow the operation of Sea King helicopters.* (By courtesy of Antony Preston)

Canadian 'Tribal' class destroyers (DDH 280) after TRUMP modernisation. The VLS system for Standard MR-SM2 missiles will greatly increase the AAW capability of this formidable ASW class. (Litton Canada)

TRUMP: SPECIFIC PERFORMANCE BENEFITS

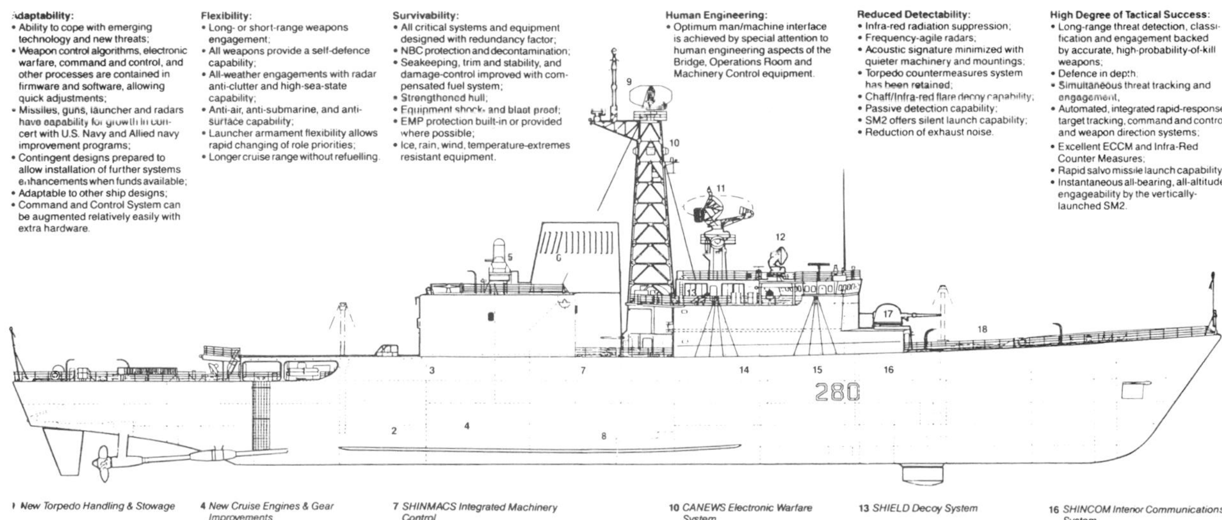

systems. In the Middle East, the US Tacoma company has been awarded a contract to modernise four **Egyptian** 'Romeo' class submarines, between 1988 and 1993. New sensors and interfaces fitted locally will enable them to launch sub-Harpoons and Mk 37 torpedoes. The first **Chinese** modified 'Luda' has been photographed: the after gun and superstructure have been replaced by a hangar and helicopter deck. **Pakistan** is to modernise the DDG *Babur*, probably on the general lines of the Chilean *Blanco Encalada*. **Argentine.** The carrier *25 de Mayo* is being re-engined with diesels to facilitate operation of Super Etendards, which are presently often unable to fly off because of the unreliable steam turbine machinery and low speed. **Chile** is converting two of the four ex-RN 'County' class DDG to fleet command ships, with Sea Slug missile magazine turned over to helicopter support, and enlarged hangar and flight deck to operate two AS 332F Super Puma helicopters. *Blanco Encalada* completed conversion late in 1988.

RFA Argus, *converted 1984–88 by Harland and Wolff as Britain's first Aviation Training Ship, relieved* Engadine *early in 1989. (*Harland and Wolff*)*

D (iv). Fleet Depletions (Decommissionings, Transfers etc)

Noteworthy items in this category are summarised below.

(a) USA. The frigates withdrawn in 1988–89 were transferred as follows in 1989: *Garcia* and *Julius A Furer* (*Brooke* class) to Pakistan on 31 January as *Badr, Saif; Brooke* and *O'Callaghan* (*Garcia* class) on 8 February as *Khyber, Aslat; Richard L Page* (*Brooke*) and *Brumby* (*Garcia*) to follow on 31 March, with *Talbot* (*Brooke*) and *Koelsch* (*Garcia*) on 31 May. Four *Garcia* class (*Bradley, Davidson, Sample, Albert David*) were offered to Brazil, and two *Brooke* and two *Garcia* to Turkey. USS *Alamo*, a *Thomaston* class LSD, has also been offered to Brazil.

(b) United Kingdom. Of the frigates deleted and on the Disposal List, *Ashanti* and *Galatea* were sunk as targets in 1988 and *Leander* in 1989; *Ajax* and *Rothesay* were sold in 1988 for breaking up; *Diomede* and *Apollo* went to Pakistan as *Shamser* and *Zulfiquar* respectively, while *Plymouth* was to have become a museum (her future is now in doubt). *Euryalus* and *Arethusa* paid off to the Disposal List (Commercial) at the end of March 1989. RFA *Engadine* paid off in 1989, a few months after the last Wasp and Wessex helicopters left naval service.

(c) Netherlands. The last two *Van Speijks* are being offered to Indonesia without their towed-array sonar (TACTAS, US SQR-18), which will be fitted in two *Kortenaers* pending completion of the M class.

(d) France. The last Type 47 (ASW) has been paid off, and only one Type 47 (DDG) remains. The frigate *Victor*

HMS Quorn, *the last 'Hunt' class MCMV, and the eleventh built by Vosper Thornycroft. The Oerlikon/DES 30mm/75 gun forward is the RN's replacement for vintage Bofors 40mm/60 and 40mm/70 guns.* (Vosper Thornycroft)

Schoelcher, sold to Uruguay as *General Artigas*, may be followed by two more of the class.

(e) Chile. An interest in four RN or ex-RN *Leanders*, including *Achilles*, and possibly two *Oberon* class submarines is reported, although two Type 209s might be built locally instead. Two FAC have been bought from Israel.

E. NAVAL WEAPON SYSTEMS

Salient developments in naval weapon systems are listed below.

E (i). Missiles, Including Ballistic Missiles

(a) United States. The first submarine test firing of Trident II D5 missile, from USS *Tennessee* in March 1989, failed, although following fifteen successful ground-launch firings. An air-launched Harpoon-derived SLAM for carrier launch against sea and land targets is being developed (range around 50nm). In early 1988, 30 SSN were launch platforms for Tomahawk cruise missiles; by the end of the year, 41 were so fitted and the 1995 target is 75; 26 surface ships were also fitted with Tomahawk at end 1988.

(b) France's ASMP (medium range air-to-ground missile) has a range of 80–300km, depending on aircraft height at missile launch, and a yield of 300 kilo tons.

(c) USSR. SS-N-X, the new missile seen on the small combatant designated 'Balcom 10', is carried in tubes like the Harpoon or MM40.

(d) China. In December 1988 the one fully operational 'Xia' class SSBN made the first successful underwater test firing of a JL-1 (Western CSS-N-3) ballistic missile; the missile had previously been launched from a submerged pontoon, and in 1982 from a 'Golf' class submarine. A new type of SLBM is being developed.

E (ii). Maritime Aircraft

(a) United Kingdom. The contract for upgrading 29 of the RN's 42 FRS1 Sea Harriers to FSR2 standard was finally signed. The main improvements are the Blue Vixen radar and the AIM-120 missile (AMRAAM). The RN's order for 50 EH 101 helicopters will not be placed until at least September; the decision on the engine has also been delayed.

NFR

◀ *An artist's impression of the latest configuration of the NATO Frigate.* (By courtesy of Antony Preston)

(b) Italy. The aircraft types being considered for *Giuseppe Garibaldi* are the RN's Sea Harrier or the Anglo-US Harrier II, with the radar-equipped Harrier III, presently under development, a remoter possibility.
(c) France. *Foch* has conducted trials with two F/A-18 Hornets as possible replacements for the F-8 Crusader, due for withdrawal in 1993. A naval development of the Rafale has been approved, but will not be ready until 1996 or even 1998. To avoid Hornet purchases, an interim electronics upgrade for the F-8 has been proposed.
(d) USSR. The air wing for the carrier *'Tbilisi'* and later, larger, types is likely to consist of the Yak-38, the Su-27 'Flanker' and the Su-24 'Fencer', with launch by ski-jump initially. Catapults are being tried, and a VSTOL derivative of the Yak-38, the Yak-41, is being developed.

E (iii). Anti-Aircraft and Anti-Missile Warfare (AAW)

(a) NATO Frigate. Two consortia are designing missile systems in competition; SAM, SSM and A/S weapons will be launched from a common VLS launcher. There will be a phased array radar, and the missiles will have active-passive radar seekers, with infra-red seekers for high ECM environments. The contract would be worth $45b over a 20–30 year period.
(b) France. The Sadral PDMS, to be fitted in *Cassard* and *Charles de Gaulle*, is being installed in UAE fast attack craft.

E (iv). Anti-Submarine Warfare (ASW)

USA–NATO. Major efforts are in hand for developing new methods of detecting submerged submarines. The emphasis is on refining acoustic and developing non-acoustic methods. The new generations of Soviet submarines will push passive sonar to its limits; Plessey announced a very high performance integrated chip (VHPIC) capable of 200 million calculations per second, for processing passive radar signals, including very faint sounds from the quietest submarines, which will be detectable without using active sonar. Nevertheless, interest is returning to active sonar, although it reveals the presence of the hunter; France is purchasing VLF active sonar transmitting from a towed array. A new US non-acoustic submarine detection device is being tested on Loch Linnhe, reportedly using synthetic aperture radar to detect and enhance slight surface disturbances ('surface scarring') produced by submerged submarines. The existing US Sound Surveillance System (SOSUS) of hydrophone arrays on the ocean bed is being supplemented by the Fixed Distributed System (FDS) at specific locations. The Towed Array Ocean Surveillance Ships (T-AGOS) cruise at low speeds deploying passive towed array sonar (SURTASS) for long-range detection of submarines; the sixteenth unit was launched during the year. The Mk 50 Advanced Capability torpedo will help keep US superiority in ASW, while two other systems will be introduced to the SSN-688 in mid-term: the AN/BSY-1 combat system and the Sea Lance stand-off missile, the latter to combat submarines well beyond torpedo range.

E (v). Guns, Including CIWS

CIWS continue to be fitted to FAC and above, when and where possible. Vickers announced a longer-range round (HE/ER = High Effect/Extended Range) for the 4.5in Mk 8, increasing range from 22km to 28km. The RN's new standard small calibre gun, the Oerlikon/BMARC DES 30mm/75 was introduced, in HMS *Cornwall.*

E (vi). Mine Warfare

The success of very ancient models of contact mines in the Gulf, and earlier in the Red Sea, has spurred MCMV programmes and the introduction of new mine types. Following the withdrawal of HMS *Abdiel* (5 May 1988), British MCMV are to be supported by shore-based containerised units, placed at UK ports with good communications and berthing facilities.

F (i). NAVAL ACTIONS

(a) Gulf War

On 14 April 1988, USS *Samuel B Roberts* (FFG-58) was badly damaged by a newly-laid Iranian contact mine; this incident and Iranian involvement in the hijack of a Kuwaiti Airways plane on 5 April led on 18 April to US retaliatory action against Iranian oil rigs. The Iranian Navy offered unexpected opposition, and, in scattered actions, heavy losses were inflicted by US warships and A-6 aircraft from the carrier *Enterprise.* The frigate *Sahand* was hit by two Harpoon missiles and sunk, and the *Sabalan*, left dead in the

The Iranian frigate Sabalan, *shown here in earlier days as the* Rostam, *was hit by at least one laser-guided bomb from A-6 aircraft on 18 April 1988 and immobilised, with back broken.* (Vosper Thornycroft) ▼

water, was under repair for over a year. The missile attack craft *Joshan* and two Boghammar type armed speedboats were also sunk, and a third speedboat sunk or badly damaged; Iranian casualties numbered at least 200, including 40 dead. American allegations that Iran used Silkworm or other anti-ship missiles were later withdrawn. The *Samuel B Roberts*, with a 3m x 3m hole in the hull, was dry-docked at Dubai with difficulty and returned to the United States aboard a Norwegian heavy-lift ship for repairs.

In mid-June the US Rules of Engagement were changed to allow assistance of non-US flagged ships under attack if requested, provided they were not in certain defined exclusion zones and that they were not carrying war-related cargoes. On 3 July, USS *Vincennes* (CG-49), while in surface action against two Iranian gunboats, detected the approach of an apparent hostile strike aircraft; two SM-2 missiles were fired and destroyed the aircraft, actually an Iranian airliner flying from Bandar Abbas to Dubai, with the loss of all 290 passengers and crew. The airliner had failed to reply to the cruiser's challenges, and in a hostile and stressful environment was adjudged hostile because of misinterpretation of AEGIS data by crew members. The AEGIS system did not provide technical justification for the misinterpretation, nor did it malfunction. Data interpreted incorrectly included items apparently showing that the plane was emitting a military call sign, was outside the civil air corridor, and was diving on the ship.

Nearly seventy NATO ships, from USA, UK, Belgium, Netherlands, Italy and France, were present at the height of the war, the only joint force being the UK–Belgian–Dutch minesweeping force Calendar II, set up shortly before the end. After the ceasefire on 20 August 1988, the various forces were rapidly run down, to about 50 ships (26 American) by the end of October. Warships in the Gulf, including Britain's Armilla Patrol, no longer escorted convoys, but patrolled particular areas. The flotilla of 20–25 Boghammar speedboats was withdrawn from Abu Musa in late October; no ships had been intercepted since the ceasefire, and interrogation by radio of suspects greatly reduced. By October, American P-3 Orion patrols in the Gulf and the tracking of aircraft by E-3 AWACS from Saudi Arabia had been discontinued.

USS Yorktown *(CG-48) firing a Standard MR-SM2 missile; such missiles from* Vincennes *(CG-49) claimed 290 lives in the Gulf.* (Ingalls)

Around 11 million tons of shipping were sunk or irreparably damaged during the war, mainly because of Iraqi air strikes. The three RN minehunters left the Gulf at the end of February 1989, ending minesweeping operations that had accounted for 10 mines since first deployment in September 1987. The last Dutch, Belgian and Italian MCM craft had already gone, leaving only the US and French ships; however, an estimated 200 mines remained, mainly in the northern part of the Gulf.

(b) Indian Ocean: Maldives Coup and Sri Lanka Emergency

On 3 November 1988, Tamil mercenaries from Sri Lanka staged a coup in the Maldive Islands; however, it was rapidly suppressed by Indian paratroops and the surviving mercenaries fled with hostages in the cargo ship *Progress Light.* Shadowed by the Indian training ships *Tir* and *Betya*, she was intercepted by the frigate *Godivari* early on 6 November, crippled by gunfire and then stormed by Marine Commandos from helicopters. Four of the 27 hostages died in the fighting and 3 were unaccounted for. The damaged *Progress Light* capsized and sank while under tow next day.

The Indian Navy's main function in the Sri Lanka intervention is preventing the entry of reinforcements and supplies for the insurgents; there is also a limited transport role.

(c) South China Sea

On 22 November, a Chinese warship fired on a Vietnamese naval vessel off the Spratly Islands, claimed by both countries. This was the second clash in 1988: on 14 March China had sunk or badly damaged a Vietnamese amphibious ship and a coaster, with 3 crew members dead and 74 missing. Tension was also evident further north; on 23 August, the Lynx helicopter from HMS *Sirius* was hit by Chinese small arms fire while searching for a sinking Taiwanese trawler near the Paracel Islands.

(d) Mediterranean

In another round of US–Libyan hostilities, on 4 January 1989 two F-14s from USS *John F Kennedy* shot down two Libyan Mig-23 'Floggers' off the North African Coast. The Libyans stated their planes were unarmed; the Pentagon produced videos to show the contrary.

(e) Latin America

In September, Nicaragua claimed to have sunk one Honduran 'Piranha' class river patrol boat in a border clash.

F (ii). MAJOR CASUALTIES AT SEA FROM 1 APRIL 1988 TO 30 APRIL 1989

(a) USS *Bonefish* (SS-582) was temporarily abandoned on 24 April 1988 after a battery fire that injured 22 crew members. Although recovered, she was not repaired and was retired from the active fleet on 28 September.

(b) On 23 July the Japanese submarine *Nadashio* collided with and sank a fishing boat with the loss of 30 lives. The accident led to the resignation of the Director-General of the Japanese Defence Agency.

(c) The Peruvian submarine *Pacocha* sank off Callao on 2 September after colliding with a Japanese trawler; 5 lives were lost, but 45 were saved, 21 by free ascent escapes.

(d) HMS *Southampton* was badly damaged in a night collision with the container ship *Tor Bay* in the Gulf 70km north of the UAE on 4 September, three crew members being slightly injured. With a 10m hole in the hull above and below the waterline, the Sea Dart magazine penetrated and mess decks wrecked, the *Southampton* was patched up to remain afloat and returned to Britain aboard the semi-submersible heavy lift ship *Mighty Servant.* After lengthy consultations, it was decided to combine repairs with the major refit planned for August 1989. The cost of repairs was estimated at £60m ($107m).

(e) HMS *Penelope* was damaged in collision with the Canadian support ship *Preserveur*, 12 September, requiring 8-10 weeks' repairs.

(f) USS *Hayler* (DD-997), badly damaged aft in collision with the German support ship *Rhon* during North Sea exercises on 23 October, was under repair at Rosyth until 20 November.

(g) The Soviet DDG *Boykiy* broke tow while being taken to Spain for scrapping and grounded on Skoysoya in the

Westeralen Islands, northern Norway, on 14 November. Salvage of *Boykiy* would not be possible until after April 1989, when the weather improved.
(h) The crew of the Peruvian (civilian) oceanographic ship *Humboldt* was rescued by HMS *Endurance* and MV *Stena Seaspread* after she grounded at the entrance to Marion Cove, Antarctic, on the night of 27/28 February 1989.
(i) The Soviet submarine *Komsomolets*, sole unit of its class (NATO 'Mike'), sank in 1800m off the Norwegian coast on 7 April 1989 after an explosion and fire on board; 27 crew members were rescued, but 42 died. The Soviet Navy intends to raise and examine the wreckage, reported to include two torpedoes with nuclear warheads.
(j) 47 crew members died and 10–12 were injured in a turret explosion in USS *Iowa* (BB-61) on 19 April 1989, while the battleship was on training exercises NE of Puerto Rico. Up to six charges, each containing 110lb HE, are believed to have exploded in 'B' turret as the centre gun was being loaded.

G OTHER ITEMS

(i) The death of Admiral Sergei Georgiyevitch Gorshkov, founder of the modern Soviet Navy and its Commander-in-Chief for almost thirty years, was announced on 15 May 1988.
(ii) In Rome, an Italian pilot was belatedly decorated for sinking the British destroyer *Bedouin* in June 1942. The Italians had previously credited the Admiral commanding Italian surface forces with the sinking.

USS Iowa *(BB-61). The disastrous turret explosion on 19 April 1989 claimed 47 lives, and cast a shadow over the Navy's 16in guns. The* Wisconsin *(BB-64), the last of the class to return to service, recommissioned on 22 October 1988 after modernisation by Ingalls at Pascagoula.* (Ingalls)

INDEX